SAINTS AND SOLDIERS

COLUMBIA STUDIES IN TERRORISM AND
IRREGULAR WARFARE

COLUMBIA STUDIES IN TERRORISM AND IRREGULAR WARFARE

Bruce Hoffman, Series Editor

This series seeks to fill a conspicuous gap in the burgeoning literature on terrorism, guerrilla warfare, and insurgency. The series adheres to the highest standards of scholarship and discourse and publishes books that elucidate the strategy, operations, means, motivations, and effects posed by terrorist, guerrilla, and insurgent organizations and movements. It thereby provides a solid and increasingly expanding foundation of knowledge on these subjects for students, established scholars, and informed reading audiences alike.

For a complete list of titles see page 353

SAINTS AND SOLDIERS

INSIDE INTERNET-AGE TERRORISM,

from SYRIA *to the* CAPITOL SIEGE

RITA KATZ

Columbia University Press

New York

Columbia University Press
Publishers Since 1893
New York   Chichester, West Sussex
cup.columbia.edu

Library of Congress Cataloging-in-Publication Data
Names: Katz, Rita, author.
Title: Saints and soldiers : inside internet-age terrorism,
from Syria to the Capitol siege / Rita Katz.
Description: New York : Columbia University Press, [2022] |
Series: Columbia studies in terrorism and irregular warfare |
Includes bibliographical references and index.
Identifiers: LCCN 2022011323 (print) | LCCN 2022011324 (ebook) |
ISBN 9780231203500 (hardback) | ISBN 9780231555081 (ebook)
Subjects: LCSH: Terrorism. | Right-wing extremists. | Online social networks. |
Online hate speech. | Radicalization.
Classification: LCC HV6431 .K3168 2022 (print) | LCC HV6431 (ebook) |
DDC 363.325/11—dc23/eng/20220315
LC record available at https://lccn.loc.gov/2022011323
LC ebook record available at https://lccn.loc.gov/2022011324

Columbia University Press books are printed on permanent
and durable acid-free paper.
Printed in the United States of America

Cover design: Milenda Nan Ok Lee
Cover photo: Reuters/Leah Millis

This book is dedicated to victims of terrorism, their families and friends, and all those whose lives were negatively impacted by violence driven and inspired by hate. Their stories, some of which are laid out on these pages, motivate us in the counterterrorism world to work diligently to try to prevent such attacks.

I also dedicate this book to my personal heroes, my mother and father. My father died to protect us; my mother devoted her life to my three siblings and me, working day and night to support us and provide for all our needs. Everything I do is inspired by their courage and relentless dedication.

Finally, my heartfelt thanks to my husband and four children. My life's work has pulled us in many unexpected directions and continues to pose numerous challenges, yet they have always been there by my side.
I am forever grateful for your support.

CONTENTS

ACKNOWLEDGMENTS

First, I am extremely grateful to my staff at Search for International Terrorist Entities (SITE), whose research, investigations, and hard work have not only enriched this book, but also made the world a safer place.

Bruce Hoffman was kind enough to provide a 24/7 helpline, always available for gems of advice based on his wealth of knowledge regarding terrorism and violent extremism.

I would also like to thank my publisher, Caelyn Cobb, for her belief and perseverance, and fighting tooth and nail to make sure these words were turned into print.

Last but certainly not least, I owe an enormous debt of gratitude to Philip Cole, without whom this book would not exist. Phil's countless hours of incredible patience and dedication, along with his true talent for words, helped me weave and shape this narrative into a finished product that went beyond my expectations.

NOTE TO THE READER

Warning: many sections of this book delve into extremist-related events, chatter, and media regarding deadly terrorist attacks, sexual assault, and virulent hate speech.

Some names, locations, and dates recollected in this book have been changed to protect individuals' privacy and safety.

SAINTS AND SOLDIERS

PROLOGUE

A Different Kind of Beast

I t was once true to say that terrorists *used* the internet.

Groups and movements that existed outside of the internet, "in real life," exploited it as an asset. The Klan had websites. Hezbollah had websites. These groups used the internet to announce events, showcase achievements, and even fundraise.

But the internet is more than just an asset for today's new breed of terrorists. It is a necessity. These terrorists cannot be traced to a specific location, organization, or command structure like those of longer-standing entities. All the same, their existence cannot be explained solely by political, social, and economic shifts, as in decades past. They are products of movements created *by* the internet and exist almost entirely on it. But as mass shootings and events like the January 6, 2021, Capitol siege show, their real-life consequences are no less severe.

They are internet entities. And, as such, they are global entities, with virtually unlimited audiences to reach.

While this internet-reliant element is more visible than ever in the far right, it is a feature of contemporary terrorism in a larger sense. It cannot be overstated how foundational certain websites, social media environments, and subcultures have been in shaping recent extremist movements. The results are extremist hives devoid of physical bases, coherent ideologies, and organizational structures. Take away the internet, and there's barely anything left.

The online nature of these new terrorist movements has not translated to a lesser threat. Rather, the two most significant terrorist threats to the West in the last decade, the Islamic State (ISIS) and the new far right, are products of this very terrorist landscape.

I wrote this book to provide an anatomy of this new kind of terrorism through the story of the new far right and its many intersections with ISIS. I've tracked both threats at the organization I head, the Search for International Terrorist Entities (SITE) Intelligence Group—the former for over a decade and the latter (including its parent group, al-Qaeda) for over two decades. ISIS not only shares a grimly similar trajectory as the far right; it is far more intertwined with its neo-Nazi and white supremacist counterparts than is commonly acknowledged. Describing these paths side by side not only gives way to a better understanding of the far right and ISIS, but also of internet-age terrorism itself.

This story includes all the internet-based components that comprise this new far right—the niche cultural forces that unite them, the conspiracy theories that fuel them, the online havens they fester in—and how these items have played into horrific events, from a mass shooting in Pittsburgh to the January 6 storming of the U.S. Capitol.

As I see it, the story of this new kind of terrorism is best told through the interlocked series of smaller stories within it: the young attackers describing their radicalization in their manifestos (often in more ways than they intend); the game-changing influence of events like the 2004 beheading of American telecommunications contractor Nick Berg in Iraq and the 2019 Christchurch massacre; the establishment-bucking rise of this younger generation of far-right extremists and the complementary story of ISIS establishing the Caliphate to the outrage of the Global Jihad's leading organization, al-Qaeda.

This book also includes many personal experiences that shaped my understanding of terrorism and my fight against it: being forced to flee Iraq for Israel as a little girl; the sobering experience of beginning my work tracking the far right a decade ago; my demanding and often life-threatening career in counterterrorism. These experiences have given me distinct vantage points. I've watched terrorism transform over more than two decades. My work in the days before 9/11 demanded physically *being* somewhere, including going undercover within crowds of hardline Islamist radicals and U.S.-based terrorist fronts with a tape recorder strapped to me. Now, as the majority of my counterterrorism work is spent in front of a computer screen watching right-wing memes of cartoon frogs radicalize toxic communities, I can feel in my bones what a profoundly different age of terrorism we're experiencing.

Together, all of these different events and developments paint a picture of a new kind of far-right extremism that requires everyone—governments, the tech sector, the media, and the general public—to completely redefine terms like "lone wolf" and "terrorist network." We are not dealing with the progeny of the skinheads, Klansmen, and neo-Nazis of previous decades, but rather with a completely different organism. This problem is not limited to the far right, right-wing conspiracy theorists, or ISIS. The online conditions that helped create these terrorist threats are wired to do the same for virtually any extremist movement in the future.

Throughout this book, I include recommendations for countering this new threat, but my foremost aim is to shed light on the sources and nature of the problem. A major obstacle in fighting these online extremist movements has been the slew of hasty and misguided actions taken before it was acknowledged just how new these crises were. Haste is of course predictable in a society inundated with mass shootings and violent unrest—not so different from a family demanding doctors do something, *anything* to save their loved one from a mystery illness. However, the effort invested in an accurate diagnosis is often what ends up improving treatment and saving lives. I look at this current extremist landscape the same way: by reshaping the way we look at internet-age terrorism at the most direct and fundamental levels—and yes, abandoning some of the conventional wisdom that no longer helps us—we can better fight the problem.

1

FROM JIHAD TO WHITE JIHAD

t was 2009. I was sitting in a restaurant booth in Washington, DC, catching up with two agents from the Department of Homeland Security (DHS). The conversation naturally went where it always did those days: how al-Qaeda was evolving, trends in its online activities, and so on. There were also plenty of recent developments to dive into. Bin Laden had just released a new message for the eighth anniversary of 9/11. A Yemeni American citizen named Anwar al-Awlaki was rapidly becoming a prominent figure in the Global Jihad, inspiring so-called lone wolf terrorists. Al-Qaeda affiliates were gaining momentum, whether it was al-Qaeda in the Arabian Peninsula (AQAP) in Yemen or the newly rebranded "Islamic State of Iraq," which would eventually veer off to become the Islamic State (ISIS). This affiliate in Iraq was proving particularly lethal, with three coordinated car bombings that August and a number of mortar strikes in Baghdad.

But by the end of our meet-up, one of them changed the conversation's course.

"Have you ever considered tracking right-wing extremists?" he asked.

I leaned back and sighed. He was far from the only one to ask me this question that year, and not without reason. The U.S. government (and frankly, the world) had noticed an uptick in far-right activity since Barack Obama's election and inauguration, the latter event happening just months before our meeting. Anyone old enough to read a newspaper can recall the stories: racist vandalism, death threats, and right-wing militias preparing for what they saw as a pending revolution. Across the country, crosses burned in front yards of Obama supporters, recalling the apogee of Ku Klux Klan (KKK) terror. Black effigies hung from nooses in trees. At the University of Alabama, an unknown person ripped off a poster of the Obama family that a professor placed on her office door. When she replaced it with another, a death threat and a racial slur defaced it soon after.[1]

The problem was bigger than sporadic hate crimes. Extremists and their organizations, from right-wing militias to neo-Nazi groups, were energized. In April of 2009, the Department of Homeland Security (DHS) even released a report titled "Rightwing Extremism: Current Economic and Political Climate Fueling Resurgence in Radicalization and Recruitment." Among the key findings of the report was that far-right extremists, incensed by the U.S. election of an African American president, were "focusing their efforts to recruit new members, mobilize existing supporters, and broaden their scope and appeal through propaganda, but they have not yet turned to attack planning."[2]

You didn't need an intelligence department to see it, though. David Duke, a former Louisiana state representative and past national leader of the KKK, said as much in an interview he posted on his website: "[Obama's victory] is good in one sense, that it is making white people clear [sic] of the fact that that government in Washington, D.C., is not our government . . . we have got to stand up and fight now."[3] Although Duke was part of the political wing of the far right seeking to advance his cause through politics as opposed to violence, that statement would have far-reaching implications on what was then a largely quiescent movement.[4]

Many often assume that an intelligence apparatus as massive as the U.S. government knows everything going on in every dangerous corner of the country, but that's not always the case. I'd been working with agencies like the FBI, the Department of Justice, the Department of Defense, and the Department of Homeland Security for a decade by that point, and I had seen the cracks bad actors fell through. Sometimes it was agencies' rigid bureaucratic procedures. Other times it was constant staff rearrangement and lack of institutional memory. I always saw my organization, the SITE Intelligence Group, as the institution to bridge these gaps. We were free to direct our research wherever we wanted. Jihadi terrorists constantly switched the names of their groups or the online platforms they inhabited, and we didn't need to submit any requests or wait for approvals to follow them. This allowed us to be just as quick and adaptable as they were, which my associates sitting across from me understood.

Yet as sensible as it would be to apply SITE's jihadist-focused counterterrorism methods to the far right, I couldn't dismiss the sobering weight of my circumstances. SITE's growth was steady but slow, and we were barely covering overhead costs and salaries. Every dollar earned went toward new hires and resources to match the pace of the growing, shifting terrorist networks we tracked online. My staff had enough work on their plate, so a new far right–focused operation would mean new employees, more salaries, and for me, more stresses that come with running a business.

It wasn't just the work that worried me. Over the years, I'd made a lot of personal sacrifices for my work, at times with immense regret. In 2004, my youngest son was twelve. Already an accomplished musician, he was selected to play a major role in a musical production at the famous Kennedy Center in Washington, DC. He was to be the young star of the show—truly a once in a lifetime event. For months, my husband and I couldn't stop gushing about this virtuoso we'd raised.

A couple of hours before his performance, my husband called me at work. He was all too familiar with the way I'd engulf myself in projects and end up late for engagements. It was 4:30 p.m. He stressed that I had to leave the office in no more than a half-hour. Otherwise, I'd be late. I promised I would.

At the time, I was assisting with a major federal terrorism investigation.[5] I needed to finish my report that day, but it didn't matter; there was no way I'd miss my son's performance. I just had a few more details to polish. Just a few minutes. Then a few more.

I was only five minutes late to the performance hall at the Kennedy Center, but the event had started and the doors were closed. I pleaded with the security guards and told them I had to see my son play, but they wouldn't budge. They offered me a spot to watch the recital from a TV in the foyer outside of the hall. Looking at the screen as my son performed, I saw the determined little boy who used to sit at the piano for hours at a time, diligently developing his ear and musical fluency. Now here he was, suddenly on the verge of being a teenager, showcasing his years of hard work to the audience. And here I was, watching it on a TV in the foyer like a stranger—or worse, a mother who once more couldn't keep her promise, nowhere to be seen when her son would look for her face in the auditorium. I broke down and cried like a little girl.

This was a recurring feature of my family life. Only a couple of years after the Kennedy Center event, at an open house night for parents at my daughter's second grade class, parents wrote letters for their children to find the next morning in their desks. My daughter found a letter signed by me in her desk the next day, telling her how proud I was of her. In truth, though, our friends whose child was also in that class really wrote the note.

These absences only increased as SITE grew. If it wasn't some major report, then it was a speaking engagement or a highly sensitive meeting with "I can't say who" regarding some project "I really can't get into detail about." I missed parent-teacher meetings, open houses, college graduations, you name it.

Eventually, my children realized that I would miss field trips, performances, and other school events. They just assumed I wouldn't be able to make it. Years later, now as doctors, educators, and college students, my kids tell me they aren't angry about these absences anymore. Their forgiveness means the world to me, because to this day, I have yet to forgive myself.

My lost time over the years begged a fair question: Why wrap myself up in this type of work? Was this the kind of parent I wanted to be?

But I wasn't sacrificing merely for the sake of work. I believed, just as I do now, in what SITE does, and I knew that the information we provided helped prevent terrorist attacks and saved lives. I was in DC in the aftermath of 9/11 when the U.S. government and its global allies were scrambling to initiate the War on Terror. The U.S. government was pulling personnel out of different agencies and throwing them onto counterterrorism projects, even though many of them lacked the proper training and expertise. I saw firsthand how many of them didn't understand how groups like al-Qaeda operated. Just a few months after 9/11, I got a call from a U.S. Customs and Border Protection agent who, after a career investigating drug trafficking, was assigned to work on al-Qaeda and affiliated entities. He had so many questions. *What does this phrase mean? How does this online forum work? Is this person important?* How could anyone blame him? Like so many others in the government, he was thrown into a subject that takes years to grasp. I gave everything I could during those days: training, actionable intelligence, assistance in investigations, and advice on formulating new terrorist designations. The stakes were high and the work was very important.

Still, I was intrigued by the agents' question that day at the restaurant in 2009. I decided I'd wade through some of the far right's online hangouts once I got back to the office. I wanted to see if whatever was happening on these websites would be worth the trouble.

I began with Stormfront, a white supremacist forum launched in 1995 that had become the movement's most popular site.[6] Its founder was Don Black, a David Duke acolyte who sought to create a virtual community of supporters of Duke's electoral activities.[7] He later transformed it to become a communal space for all white nationalists.[8]

I wasn't delving into these communities completely cold. My name, as I saw over the years, had long been a favorite among conspiracy theorists who believed that I, not al-Qaeda, created Osama bin Laden's videos to perpetuate the War on Terror.[9] It wasn't surprising. A common trait of conspiracy theorists in right-leaning circles is that they consume lots of news, but distrust elite explanations for world events, making them receptive to wild claims.[10] Apparently, al-Qaeda media was produced in my basement, which was why SITE was always getting the group's media before everyone else, even before the government.

It didn't take long into scrolling through Stormfront discussions before the first threat surfaced.

"I am hoping someone will pull a 'M.L.K.' on this Barack Obama," wrote one user by the name "Wayfarer."[11]

I read it a couple of times to make sure I wasn't misinterpreting, but it was exactly what it seemed: someone openly musing, if not outright proposing, the assassination of the president. Where was the Secret Service? U.S. political rhetoric was plenty vitriolic in those days, but this was on a completely different level. And this was just one post in a larger discussion thread filled with people who shared that same mind for violence. User "alexfp08" wrote in the same Stormfront thread:

> The revolution has to happen it is the only one way of liberating us of the oppression of the Jews and blacks . . . the only one solution is a war against them.[12]

While I am no stranger to anti-Semitism, I was still surprised that this conversation could be posted in a public forum with no apparent consequence. I wondered: What would I be able to see once I got an account on the forum to see the members-only content?

I needed more: profiles, post archives, any indication of if and how these users were interacting offline. Maybe I could even find out their true identities. Jihadi forums operated in full lockdown mode. If you wanted to join a primary source al-Qaeda site like Ansar al-Mujahideen or Shumukh al-Islam, you had to be trusted enough for a known member to give *tazakiya* (to vouch for) to an administrator on your behalf. Even during their occasional open registration periods, an applicant would still be at the mercy of these sites' distrusting administrators, who might interrogate you and ask several questions to verify your (supposed) ideology. But to my surprise, joining a white supremacist forum was easier than getting a library card. No interrogation, no white supremacist version of *tazakiya*. I just created a username, clicked, and I was a member.

Stormfront had just over 177,000 members when I joined in September of 2009,[13] far more than the 7,224 members on Shumukh and approximately 1,200 on a popular English-language one called Ansar al-Mujahideen English Forum (AMEF) at that time. Stormfront's member count doubled in the years to come. It is a massive site tailored to an entire global movement and its submovements, containing various sections for different languages and regions: Stormfront Italia, Stormfront en Español y Portugues, Stormfront Britain, Canada, Croatia, France, South Africa, Hungry, Greece, Scandinavia, and so forth.

Now free to browse all sections of the site, I spent the next weeks crawling deeper and deeper into white supremacist chatter. My jaw dropped when I came across a post reading: "i will wait and plot my war . . . and if dont get anything more than a casket i can promise a few will go with me, but i will die a proud southern white man."[14]

I was shaken when I read this one. I brought my staff in to look at the post.

"These people literally sound like al-Qaeda," I said. "How is this any different than what we see on those forums?"

Similar to the jihadist sites, Stormfront and other white supremacist forums used a forum template known as vBulletin. With this format, each user had an "About Me" section to their profile. The jihadis were highly guarded in the ways they would use this feature, usually entering Quranic verses, popular jihadi slogans, or excerpts from al-Qaeda media or leadership. Nothing too revealing. It was in fact a key rule of the jihadi forums that members weren't allowed to mention their locations or ask for such information from others.

Stormfront users, on the other hand, treated their About sections like everyday social media profiles. The very same type of information I would have to deduce from clues on jihadi forums—regional slang and spellings of words, corresponding usernames on other platforms—was willingly shared by these users. On discussion thread after discussion thread, it seemed that few of them even considered (or cared) that somebody from outside of their community could be watching.

The same Stormfront user who astonished me with his "wait and plot my war" post had no reservations in providing a thorough biography on his profile. A self-described electrician, the user was "southern born" and lived at the time in a small city in Florida, according to what he wrote on Stormfront. He even gave a link to his Myspace account, which showed him posing with Confederate flags and echoing the neo-Confederate slogan that the South "will rise again."

So many on the site shared this lust for violence. In one thread, another user called for whites to "take the steps necessary to take our country back and make it a safe place for our white children," writing, "just drive through Chinatown with a gas tanker, open the valve allowing the fuel to spill into the streets and once you get through there."[15]

I was losing my cool often in those early days on Stormfront—to my husband, my staff, whoever was in earshot. How was a post calling for people to set fire to a city's Chinatown so boldly placed onto a forum? And how was it not taken down immediately? And how did the person who posted it not get their account removed or, better yet, a knock on the door from the police?

It wasn't just the incitements that were scary, but the urgency with which they were put forth. Violent action was the only and ultimate avenue for so many of these users. A poll posted to the now-defunct website nazispace.net asked, "Do You Think Violence Is Acceptable to Achieve the Common Goals of the White Movement?" Ninety-six percent seemed to think so in some way or another, underscoring a critical factor by which an extremist community becomes a terrorist community: violence as necessity.[16]

I remember venting to my staff every other day how insane it was that people like those were allowed—yes, *allowed*—to incite terrorist attacks against Jews and Muslims, Blacks and "race-traitor" whites, and even the president himself. Meanwhile, jihadi terrorists were getting arrested for far less. Ansar Mujahideen English Forum (AMEF), its first two words meaning "Supporters of the Holy Warriors," was an important online hangout for English-speaking al-Qaeda supporters in those days. It was a place we monitored constantly at SITE for threats against Western entities, and given how hard it was to access, it was a good source of intel. The forum was closed for registration and had a few hundred registered members from Europe, the United States, Pakistan, Australia, and South Africa. Only less than a hundred of these users were active, though, making it an extremely contained venue. On April 15, 2010, a member by the name of "Abu Talha al-Amriki" alerted forum readers that the animated show *South Park* was planning to depict the Prophet Muhammad in its upcoming 200th episode, which hardliner Islamists consider a major act of blasphemy punishable by death. Abu Talha followed up with a post on his blog warning *South Park* creators Trey Parker and Matt Stone of the fate of people like Theo Van Gogh, a Dutch film director assassinated in 2004 after he produced a movie criticizing the treatment of women under Islam. Abu Talha's post read like a thinly veiled threat from a mob boss:

> We have to warn Matt and Trey that what they are doing is stupid and they will probably wind up like Theo Van Gogh for airing this show. This is not a threat, but a warning of the reality of what will likely happen to them.[17]

The post also posed the question "Where do they live?" followed by an article on *South Park* creators Parker and Stone's retreat in Steamboat Springs, Colorado.

We were very familiar with Abu Talha. It was Zachary Chesser, an American who had converted to Islam, embraced its most radical interpretations, and grew to become a recognized figure in the English-speaking jihadi community online. The media frenzied over his letter, and our office was flooded with phone calls from reporters, government officials, and other subscribers asking for more information about this persona behind the message: Was there an imminent attack at hand? Where did we think this Abu Talha person was located?

Chesser's letter triggered the authorities to watch him, and eventually indict him for attempting to migrate to Somalia to join the al-Shabaab Movement, al-Qaeda's branch in the country.[18]

Now compare Chesser's post to what I saw in my very first days of scanning white supremacist chatter: users instructing how to use gas trucks to destroy a whole neighborhood, others proposing to kill the president. A burning cauldron of hate and calls for an uprising against the U.S. government. Forum members were even creating guides for carrying out assassinations of politicians and government officials. One post from 2011, titled "Advice for 'Lone Wolves,'" identified people like

Federal Reserve chair Ben Bernanke and Anti-Defamation League national director Abraham Foxman as targets. It instructed in part:

> What we need is 1000s of lone wolves acting independently, striking separate targets, lots of the big name Jews will start finding themselves eliminated . . . We would be looking, every day, 5 or 6 separate hits, one day its the federal reserve chairman, next day someone gets Abe Foxman, next day someone gets Jew banker A, B and C . . . There isn't a race on this planet that fights as hard and as dirty as we do when we are backed in a corner.[19]

Don't get me wrong: Chesser undeniably deserved to be imprisoned, but it was mind-boggling to see him go to jail while so many white supremacist versions of him wrote far worse messages for an audience not of a few hundred like AMEF, but of nearly 200,000 from around the world. With this massive audience, when a Stormfront user writes a call to carry out an attack, they are not merely speaking to a few people; they are dispatching that incitement to a global network of tens of thousands of people.

The very fact that this community existed at all, let alone in such breathtaking enormity, is remarkable. In the year 2009, a prevalent narrative was that Nazism died with the end of World War II and that the United States, which had just elected its first Black president, had left its days of racism behind. But every bigoted user on these forums was yet another proof that you can't kill an idea. After all, did al-Qaeda die after the destruction of its training camps and Osama bin Laden's death? Not in the least. Nazism likewise endured after the fall of Hitler's Germany, despite efforts by the United States and other major powers to de-Nazify Europe with tribunals, the seizure of newspapers and other media outlets, and laws deeming the possession of Nazi literature illegal.[20] After the war, the United States itself even saw the formation of the National Renaissance Party (NRP) in 1949, the American Nazi Party (ANP) in 1967, and National Socialist Movement (NSM) in 1974.[21]

And of course, it didn't end there. Intersecting with these Nazi organizations were others pushing the same bigotry and violence, only by different names, themes, and slogans. During the height of the civil rights movement, KKK members carried out scores of bombings against African American churches, homes, and businesses.[22] Birmingham, Alabama—a city not in the Middle East, but in the United States—gained the nickname "Bombingham."[23] One street in the city was likewise named "Dynamite Hill" for the frequent bombings against Black residents who moved into the predominantly white neighborhood. On Sunday, September 15, 1963, three Klan members bombed the 16th Street Baptist Church in the city, killing four young girls and injuring twenty-two others.[24] The bombings eventually died down, but the ideas never did.

So here we were in the early 2010s, staring into our computer screens at these undead movements. The United States, the decisive force that helped take down Nazi Germany, would ironically house the servers helping keep Nazism alive alongside other racist and bigoted extremist movements. It was enough to make any sane American angry, but I'd be lying if I said there wasn't a personal element at hand for me.

———— ✺ ————

I was born into a Jewish family in the Iraqi city of Basra. Fueled by the recent foundation of the State of Israel, violent anti-Semitism was spreading across the Middle East. The Iraqi Ba'ath party, with Saddam Hussein then leading its Revolutionary Command Council, made no bones about its feelings toward the country's Jews when seizing power in 1968. That year, my father was arrested under the charge of spying for Israel. During his imprisonment, he convinced another prisoner who was soon to be released to smuggle a letter to my mother.

My father's letter told my mother that there was no doubt: he was going to be killed. He asked her to be strong for their children. He ended the letter with one last request: "Take our children to Israel—the only safe country for Jews." Not long after he had the letter smuggled, my father was hanged in a public execution along with eight others, seven of whom were Jews.

My mother was eventually imprisoned and abused at length in an Iraqi jail cell. She did manage to escape, though, and fled with my siblings and me to Israel, the land where our father assured her we would be safe. Still, it would take a while before things reached a state of normalcy—whatever that was.

Just a few years after we escaped from Iraq, the Yom Kippur War of 1973 broke out. It was an early lesson that the hell we'd escaped in Iraq was just across the border from Israel, dead set on destroying us and the entire country in which we had taken refuge. This menace was just as present in our classrooms, where we learned in painful detail what had happened to our people in the Holocaust. We'd stare into photos and footage of concentration camps and families with yellow stars on their jackets, unable to understand why people wanted to do this to us.

As the years went on, the same hate that killed my father was increasingly taking the form of terrorism. The fact that we Jews existed, living where we lived, inspired overseas horrors like the 1972 Munich Olympics massacre, in which the terrorist group Black September took the Israeli Olympic team hostage and killed them. We saw just as much within our own borders as groups like Hamas and Palestinian Islamic Jihad carried out attacks with improvised explosive devices (IEDs) and suicide bombers on buses and in markets, movie theaters, and hotels. Every single day, every walk we took to school or the local store, we were on alert. In the eyes of many we weren't even human—just walking vessels for gruesome political statements.

This was the upbringing that shaped me and those around me. Constant reminders that in every corner of the world, you are hated. Hunted. During these earlier years of my life I even came to resent being Jewish. It felt like a burden, like some mark I was born with and couldn't get rid of. I eventually grew out of this sentiment, but these continual fears were formative for me and every other kid I knew.

By 1997, I was married with three children. My husband got a job at the National Institutes of Health and proposed we move the family to the United States. I couldn't agree to it. Living in Israel was my father's will. Plus, we were happy there. My family, my mother, and my siblings' families all lived in a complex in which each of our homes were connected by paths. We were always together, and I couldn't imagine it any other way.

But as much as we loved Israel, our hopes for any sort of peace and reconciliation between Israelis and Palestinians were waning. In 1995, Israeli prime minister Yitzhak Rabin, a leader we deeply admired, was assassinated by a right-wing Israeli who opposed the 1993 Oslo Accords, a set of historic agreements Rabin signed with Palestinian leadership toward forging peace. Any optimism held in the Oslo Accords steadily diminished in the region. A vicious cycle of terrorist attacks by Hamas and Palestinian Islamic Jihad, met with retaliation from Israel Defense Forces, seemed to become a daily routine. My kids couldn't celebrate holidays or go out of the house. School days were canceled. They were missing out on their childhood, just as I had. At the same time, many of my family's Palestinian friends, with whom we kept in close contact, also felt agony as Israel Defense Forces' retaliations to terrorist attacks at times placed innocent families in the middle of it all.

Both sides were right and both sides were wrong, and the vicious cycle of violence would persist with no end in sight. So in 1997, we moved our family to the United States.

Our lives in the United States did give us a break from the threats of terrorism and extremism, at least in the beginning. I was amazed every time I turned on the radio or TV to hear "breaking news" about weather, not barrages of missiles or warnings to stay in the bomb shelter that day. Just thunderstorms, rain, and heat waves. It was such a far cry from our life in Israel. I found myself having to learn new categories of news: weather, game show winners, sports.

We slowly grew comfortable in our new country. My husband and I were becoming Americans, raising American children. Here, Jews, Muslims, Christians, Buddhists, Hindus, and others lived together in apparent harmony. It is perhaps a tired observation to many Americans, but to us it was something new and truly beautiful. The bad guys—those that preached hate and embraced violence—were the exception. When the time came to decide whether we'd stay in the United States or return to Israel, it was clear that we'd found a new home here. This was where we wanted to be.

But something changed in 2009 when I saw what was happening on sites like Stormfront. I wasn't naïve enough to think that racism and anti-Semitism were dead, and I was plenty aware of the neo-Nazi and white supremacist movements scattered throughout the West. Yet when I saw a movement so massive, threatening, and unconstrained as I did on places like Stormfront, I felt that same fear I did when I was young: that no matter where I ran to, I would forever have a target on my back simply for being Jewish. For the first time since I moved to the United States, I wondered if I'd made a mistake by staying here. Back in Israel, so many on all sides of our borders wanted us dead, but at least you knew what those dangers were. You knew that your neighbor—regardless of their former nationality, ethnicity, or politics—didn't secretly want to kill you. But in the United States, the idea that someone like these Stormfront users might live next door to me seemed like an increasingly possible scenario.

Did I really want to immerse myself into tracking the far right? Those first months of research brought me to a lot of dark places and old fears, and everyone around me could tell I was impacted by it. I'd sit on my laptop for long bouts of time, calling the closest person to me to come look at each post, asking if they could believe it was real.

Even if I were to hold my breath, clench my fists, and jump in, there was another issue at hand. For almost a decade prior to my introduction to monitoring the far right it was the activist side of me—the part that reads through terrorist forums at the dinner table and listens to extremist audio messages while driving—that powered the business side of me. My obsession was, in many ways, what made me good at my job. But for the first time, my activist side seemed at odds with the objective businessperson side. The evident lack of attention paid to white supremacists suggested that there wasn't going to be a sustainable income generated from tracking them. So how would I pay my staff? How would I get people to care? In those days, the image of the Twin Towers collapsing was imprinted into the American psyche and everyone understood that the Global Jihad movement posed a threat. The far right, on the other hand, made for a harder case. Would Americans push back if I were to warn them about a person who could be their next-door neighbor? Would I be ignored? Written off as a fear-monger? After the DHS released its aforementioned 2009 report on rising right-wing extremism, many in Congress and the conservative media lashed out against the findings, calling the report a "piece of crap" and "propaganda" against conservatives.[25]

A mountain of doubts started building in my head. I kept returning to 2004, when SITE had first started our subscription service for government agencies and private sector security departments. I met with a high-ranking official at the Pentagon at that time and showed him what kind of intel we collected, the extent of the access we had into jihadi forums, and the quality of our analysis. He dismissed my presentation without a second thought, asking, "You want to sell us something that's on the internet? Why would we need you if we can get it ourselves?"

It took years for that Pentagon official and individuals from other agencies to change their tune on the value of our work. So if it was that hard for people to understand the value of a service based on that time period's number one threat—one in which we translated and analyzed communications in Arabic, Urdu, and other languages on closed-registration forums—how long would it take to get funding for a service based on English communications on easily accessible forums? I could already hear the declines coming in.

But I knew beyond any doubt that I wouldn't be able to forget about all I'd seen, and what I continued to see every day. This was important.

The answer to whether I'd track the far right or not wasn't something I had to say out loud. Everything just started moving into place. Gradually, I built up a team of analysts who were savvy in all the venues, ideologies, and trends of these far-right groups and communities. We spent over a year developing protocols, monitoring rotations, and creating new research methodologies. We waded through all the noise to identify key individuals and networks, just like we had done with the jihadis.

Of course, it took a lot of studying. My earlier days reading these online conversations and viewing white supremacist media felt like learning a new language, and in many ways it was. But eventually we built up our vocabularies until we were fluent in the many niche phrases and codes of the far right. For example:

ZOG: an acronym for Zionist Occupied Government

1488: the 14 refers to the fourteen-word mantra *We must secure the existence of our people and a future for white children*, while 88 refers to the two H's in *Heil Hitler* (H being the eighth letter of the alphabet)

The Day of the Rope: a reference to the neo-Nazi novel *The Turner Diaries*, in which white race traitors are killed in mass via hangings[26]

We had always trained SITE's analysts with our own in-house "dictionaries" of what jihadists meant when they wrote something, and we began doing the same for the far right.

Yet language is just one of many elements necessary to understand an extremist movement. In tracking white supremacists, we took the time to understand how these subjects thought. Far-right ideologies are constructed from all sorts of pseudoscience, warped historical interpretations, conspiracy theories, and extremist political models.[27] But if one were looking for a simple, functional understanding of what the far right and far-right extremism is, the narratives such extremists put forth are very telling of their thinking: "white genocide" perpetuated by Jews; "replacement" of one's people by "invaders" of different races or cultures; poisoning of Christian values by the Jews and "cultural Marxists"; sedation of the masses by the media and "elites." Existential threats and enemies everywhere.

To track it all, we widened the scope of websites and forums we monitored, placing special emphasis on those like Vanguard News Network (VNN), a major neo-Nazi forum with roughly 6,000 members at that time.[28] VNN was a darker counterpart to Stormfront. While the latter would at least see some removal of vile content (threats, incitements, etc.), VNN did not. After the January 2011 shooting of Arizona Congresswoman Gabrielle Giffords by a man with a history of mental health problems, VNN users frenzied around the event. One user wrote, "Let the son of the bitches start feeling real fear. The kike may have the bribes, but we always had something more powerful all along."[29]

They didn't even seem to care that Giffords's attacker wasn't one of their own. They just kept on celebrating and posting calls for violence against Jews, politicians, and others.

I've learned in my counterterrorism work that where there is enough rhetorical upheaval, there will eventually be real-life action.[30] Think of it as a snowball effect: members of an extremist community rally around incitements to attack someone (or even just to attack in general) and the snowball grows, gradually picking up new viewers and participants. The groupthink grows and grows until it pulls in someone angry enough, indoctrinated enough, and groomed enough to take up the call. I had seen this words-to-action dynamic play out time and time again in the Global Jihad community, and it would soon prove no different with the far right.

On January 17, 2011, a VNN and Stormfront member placed a backpack at an intersection in Spokane, Washington, right on the scheduled route of the Martin Luther King Jr. Day Unity March.[31] Inside the bag was a pipe bomb filled with rat poison and over a hundred fishing weights as shrapnel. An FBI statement would later describe the device as "diabolically constructed using shrapnel coated with a substance meant to keep blood from clotting in wounds."[32] Police defused the bomb and began a thorough investigation, leading to the arrest of a forum user, a thirty-seven-year-old man named Kevin Harpham, two months later.[33]

Harpham was well known to us. He was a Stormfront user who later became a prominent member of VNN, where he went by the username "Joe Snuffy." His time on both VNN and Stormfront was a telling case study of how much these forums facilitated both radicalization and networking. Harpham even attested to this in a November 2004 VNN post, in which he credited Stormfront as his entry point into the same warfare mentality that consumed his fellow forum members:

I can remember sitting on my bunk with a buddy watching news of a "Nazi" rally in DC around 98' and saying "I know why these guys don't like niggers and mexicans but why do they hate Jews?" It wasn't till around 2002/2003 when I stumbled onto Stormfront . . . that I realized

I was at war and didn't even know it. The next year was the most edu-
cational time of my life.[34]

He wrote eerily on VNN that same year, "I can't wait until the day I snap."[35]

For white supremacists, Harpham's attempted attack was yet another
log in the fire: proof that the war they spoke of was real, and another push
to inspire others to do the same. As we'd soon learn, the more extreme
that violence was, the more it could unite even the most seemingly
incompatible corners of the far right.

———— ✠ ————

In October of 2008, a user by the name "year2183" joined Stormfront and
introduced himself: "I'm 29 years living in Sweden. I'm working full time
(And will spend the next 12 months) on writing a book about the Islamisation of Europe and how to cope with these upcoming problems. I
started this project 10 months ago." His post closed with a plea for the
far right to unify around this issue: "My hope is that the various frac-
tured right wing movements in Europe and the US can try to reach a
consensus regarding the issue 'Islamisation of Europe/US' and unite in
this cause."[36]

His message was met with support. "Welcome, friend!" wrote one user.
"Good to see a supporter from Sweden, from what I've read . . . that part
of the world is getting a really hard time these days. My sympathies."[37]

Another wrote, "Islam is certainly a virulent religion and Muslims
are a huge threat to Europe, especially in nations whose populations have
little experience in dealing with an enemy in their midst. Glad to
have you here."[38]

Year2183 did eventually finish his book. Three years later, on July 22,
2011, he delivered it via mass email to 1,003 email addresses, including
those of European far-right figures.[39] The book was a 1,500-page
Microsoft Word document that would soon be criticized not just for its
toxic ideas, but also for what appeared to be its blatant plagiarism.[40] It
was accompanied by a short video. Both were titled "2083—A European
Declaration of Independence."

As the world would soon learn, Year2183 was not a Swede, but a thirty-two-year-old Norwegian named Anders Breivik.

Less than two hours after emailing his document, Breivik parked a van on a busy street in Oslo, surrounded by several government buildings including the Office of the Prime Minister, the Ministry of Justice and the Police, and the Supreme Court of Norway. He exited the vehicle, outfitted as a police officer with a pistol and helmet, and quickly walked away to a nearby car. Shortly after Breivik drove off, the 2,090-pound bomb he planted in the van detonated in a massive explosion, shattering windows of surrounding buildings and killing six people instantly. Another two died shortly thereafter from their injuries.[41]

He wasn't finished. It was a twenty-mile drive to Lake Tyri, where Breivik boarded a ferry to the island of Utøya. On the island, hundreds of teenagers were attending a youth summer camp run by the Norwegian Labour Party. He entered the camp still dressed in his police officer disguise, armed with a semiautomatic rifle and a semiautomatic 9mm pistol. Breivik told the camp leader who greeted him that he was a police officer and that he was required to inspect the grounds after the bombing in Oslo. Suspicious, she brought the camp's security officer to help verify his credentials. Breivik killed them both.[42]

Breivik walked into the campgrounds. Using what effect was left of his policeman disguise, he ordered the teens to gather around him before firing into them. The full force of his attack started.[43]

The teenagers and camp workers fled across the island, some hiding and others attempting to swim away. Breivik fired into them indiscriminately. He walked past bodies on the ground, checking for pulses and killing those pretending to be dead. Others pleaded for him not to shoot from their hiding places; he shot them anyway.[44]

"You're going to die today, Marxists," he shouted numerous times.[45]

The shooting went on for an hour and a half until Breivik surrendered to police. He killed 69 people at the camp—67 died from gunshot wounds, and two others as a result of their attempts to flee. In the aftermath, the rocky edges of Utøya Island were strewn with white sheets covering the bodies of those who hid or tried to swim away. It was pure horror.[46]

On Stormfront, VNN, and other forums, users were embroiled in an impassioned debate about the event. To one faction of the community, his targeting of whites (white children, at that) was a horribly conceived attempt to advance their cause. Some anticipated getting "torn apart by the zog media" while others distanced themselves from Breivik, demanding that no one embrace him.[47]

But to others, his attack was justice served. Stormfront users devoted a massive thread to the Norway attack, cheering about how Breivik was a member of the forum.[48]

"I don't advocate targeting innocent children, but keep in mind his victims were the children of active Communist/Multicultist activists," one user wrote.[49]

Another defended Breivik against those claiming his attack would further marginalize the far right. The user countered, "I cant think of any successful revolution that did not use an insane amount of violence. In what sense are we not already marginalized?" In the same spirit, another characterized Breivik's attack as an inevitable act of getting one's "hands dirty" to advance the cause:

> People of the west have to realise that sooner or later you have to get your hands dirty. Do not be afraid of confrontation, this shooter . . . just prooves it that if white people set their minds to something they can not only achieve it but do it 100000x better then any other race on this planet.[50]

Other responses placed the same blame on either the Norwegian government or Jews. "Brutal attack. But what do they expect would happen when you flood Europe with browns, blacks and yellows? Stop the madness Jew man!!" wrote one.[51]

For such users, Breivik's killing of fellow whites was an essential component of the race war they were awaiting. Those white children were, to them, children of race traitors—or race traitors themselves, even if only in training. As one Stormfront user wrote, "What do you think a civil war is?? It is a war between your own people. He promoted civil war between the traitors of our race, did you read [Breivik's] book?"[52]

Up to that point, my team and I had worked through plenty of horrific material from terrorist events. We've seen gruesome footage of suicide bombings, beheadings, lone wolf stabbings, civilian bodies lying in streets. But these users' cruel responses hit a much deeper nerve, especially as new pictures of the victims emerged, some as young as fourteen: some with buzz cuts or long shaggy hair, some with lip rings or playing guitars, others clean-cut with serious facial expressions—glimpses of kids blossoming into their own personalities. One of our interns sifting through these responses and news updates told us it was all too much. She said she needed to take off early. I didn't blame her. I told her to go home. We never saw her again.

It was sickening to see fellow humans praise Breivik and uphold his manifesto as some sort of priceless artifact. It was also peculiar. Sure, the document's focus on the "invasion" of Muslims into the West spoke to a major component of the far right's "white genocide" narrative. But apart from that premise, Breivik contradicted so many core viewpoints of neo-Nazis and white supremacists.[53] His manifesto described neo-Nazism as something "pointless to try to resurrect . . . in any way or form."[54] He even denied the existence of a Zionist Operated Government (ZOG), one of the bedrock foundations of far-right anti-Semitism, and rejected anti-Semitism itself:

> The [National Socialist] claim that all European governments and the EU parliament are ZOG is completely ridiculous something which the EU's and European anti-Israeli policies prove. Many Jews do support multiculturalism (perhaps disproportionally), but that doesn't mean that all Jews are our enemies.[55]

If that wasn't enough, Breivik veered even further by repeatedly characterizing Jews and Christians as suffering the same historical and present-day threat by Muslims, and urged his readers to "embrace"

Europe's population of conservative Jews "as brothers." He characterized Jewish stereotypes as traits for whites to aspire to:

> I agree with most of these [perceived Jewish] principles/ethics and I fully support this mentality (Save/invest instead of spend+ focus on long term goals). Does that make me a Jew?[56]

But despite all the ideological differences, Breivik saw the racist, anti-Semitic far right as an ally. As he stated in his 2008 Stormfront post urging for far-right unity, "We agree on so many things, lets try to work on that and reach a common consensus if it is possible at all." All the same, a massive portion of them loved him back, including the neo-Nazis whose ideas he railed against. VNN's founder himself, a Missouri neo-Nazi named Alex Linder, defended Breivik's actions while using the very "ZOG" terminology Breivik found so foolish. Linder wrote admiringly:

> In the US, for example, the shitskins let in by ZOG kill about 4300 people a year. And now we have someone killing some ZOGgies. So it is an active war, just mostly one sided. What's new about Breivik is we have someone daring to shoot back.[57]

As strange as it seemed to say, the global far right didn't discriminate. *Why* you attacked didn't seem to matter as much as the simple fact that you *did*. All an attacker like Breivik needed at the end of the day was to spout some bigoted talking points and carry out any type of violence—even on white children—and swathes of the far right would embrace him with open arms. All his points against anti-Semitism and racism? Who cares? He got off the keyboard and did something, and action was what the movement needed more than anything.

From here comes the greater danger of an attack like Breivik's and his accompanying document. It's very often in the days after a terrorist attack that many of the true red flags of an extremist community start to show themselves. As more attention swirled around the topic, users started projecting their own grisly ideas and aspirations onto

Breivik's: Why not take what Breivik did but apply it to Black people? Muslims? Jews?

Perhaps the most shocking response was that of Frazier Glenn Miller. Miller's decades-long resume included membership in the National Socialist Party of America and founding of the Carolina Knights of the KKK, along with a saga of terrorist exploits: assassination plots, attempts to acquire stolen military explosives, ties to a murderous organization called The Order, and multiple jail sentences.[58] After serving time, Miller became a staple of the online far-right community, forming online connections with other white supremacists across the country. Among them was Harpham, who Miller thanked on multiple occasions for his "generous financial contributions" to his far-right newsletter projects.[59] By the time Breivik's attack took place, Miller was in his early seventies with thinning hair and worn, pale skin. He still had plenty of venom left, though. He wrote in the aftermath of the Norway massacre that he'd love to see something similar in the United States:

> I mean, if some enterprising American fellow, went to a youth camp in the Catskills, Camp David, or Martha's Vineyard, and "sprayed" some young'uns belonging to our immigrant-loving JOG [Jewish Owned Governments], I dare say I might not lose a whole lot of sleep on account of it. In fact, as much as it "pains" me to say it, I just might sleep even better than my norm, possibly with a wide grin on my face.[60]

"Breivik fired up Aryan blood, and inspired young Aryan men to action," he ranted in another post. "Mark my words."[61]

We dispatched many of Miller's statements to subscribers, including his post-Norway musings about killing children. But every time, whether our alert was about Miller or some other human time bomb, no one seemed to respond or follow up. This was especially unfortunate because it turned out that Miller was willing to act.

On April 13, 2014, Miller opened fire on the Overland Park Jewish Community Center in Kansas City, where children were rehearsing a production of *To Kill a Mockingbird*. Others were trying out for a singing competition. He then continued his attack at a Jewish retirement community nearby. He killed three people that day.[62] Miller would state at his trial that he wished he had killed more.[63]

Miller had been eyeing the community center for the six days leading up to his attack, driving back and forth between there and his home. He was convinced the police had been tracing him, but never at any point did they know he was there.[64]

"I parked right in front of it and drove around," he stated in an interview not long after his attack, seemingly amazed he was able to pull it off. "If the feds had been monitoring me, they'd have stopped me right then because they were afraid I was going to kill somebody."[65]

That line—"if the feds had been monitoring me"—was infuriatingly accurate. For all the widespread reporting and DHS warnings about far-right extremism in the Obama era, it seemed that most of U.S. law enforcement still saw these terrorist attacks as random and unforeseeable, as if these individuals weren't openly musing about shooting children online.

The same disconnect occured after the shooting at a Sikh temple in Oak Creek, Wisconsin, which killed six people and wounded four on August 5, 2012.[66] The attacker was Wade Michael Page, a buzz-cut forty-year-old Army veteran covered in white supremacist tattoos. He was a prominent member of the Hammerskins skinhead group and its Crew38 forum, and he had a clear history of posting explicit intentions to commit racial violence on VNN and Stormfront.[67] Yet when asked about his motive, the Oak Creek Police Chief stated of Page, "I don't know why and I don't know that we'll ever know, because when he died, that died with him what his motive was or what he was thinking."[68]

These types of "who could have seen it coming" statements were standard to hear from law enforcement in those days. Just one year earlier, after Harpham's attempted bombing in Spokane, a special agent with the city's FBI office said, "Kevin Harpham was the lone wolf that all of us in law enforcement dread . . . He lived alone, he worked alone, and he didn't foreshadow the bombing plot in any meaningful way."[69]

These stories of far-right forum users carrying out terrorist attacks would continue. It seemed that neo-Nazi and white supremacist terrorists had everything they'd ever wanted: rules-free online venues, and no attention paid by investigators. I'd think to myself when scrolling through these forums, *What else would these guys need?* But as technology and global events were intersecting, a different terrorist movement was revolutionizing recruitment and outreach, blazing a new path for the far right to follow.

∞∞∞

I can't fully blame the United States and other governments for not adequately acting on the threat this far-right online community posed, especially as a new attention-grabbing threat was coming out of the Middle East. By the mid-2010s, the effects of the Syrian civil war were spilling out around the globe. Men, women, and children across the West were leaving everything behind to join the fight in Syria, and they were increasingly doing so on behalf of a rising force in the region: ISIS.

ISIS completely revolutionized the way terrorist recruitment works. The very same social media platforms a teenager scrolled through between classes was often where they were groomed by predatory recruiters stationed in ISIS territories. My staff and I often refer to the time between 2013 and 2015 as "the Wild West days" of ISIS on social media platforms like Facebook and, more prevalently, Twitter. The same types of activity once reserved for password-protected jihadi forums were now effectively broadcasted to the entire planet via American servers, and little was being done to stop it. Twitter alone was filled with thousands of ISIS accounts in various languages, from group officials and recruiters to media workers and supporters. They openly tweeted advice on making bombs and migrating to its territories. They posted links to their blogs and their Messenger usernames, where users could converse with them out of the public's eye.

With its recruitment machine pushing ISIS forward, terrorist attacks flooded the world: Paris, Brussels, San Bernardino, Berlin, Orlando, London, Manchester, Nice, Amsterdam, and elsewhere. Attackers were setting off bombs, opening fire, and driving vehicles into crowds of people. Meanwhile, news outlets were streaming ghastly footage of beheadings and threats to enemy nations. There was little nuance to ISIS's message:

You are all our targets. We are coming for you. In a year's time, ISIS seized all popular understanding of the word "terrorism."

The U.S. government panicked as it tried to keep up with the waves of citizens either traveling to the Middle East or carrying out terrorist attacks domestically. Many counterterrorism government officials had never even used social media, and the ones who did were overwhelmed by the magnitude and persistence of ISIS online. As FBI Director James Comey said in 2015, "The haystack is the entire country now and here's the really hard part—increasingly the needles are invisible to us."[70]

Most of my staff and I were consumed with all the group was throwing at the world: a prolific propaganda machine, game-changing social media presence, and attacks taking place around the globe. Every day at the office was a mountain of urgent developments: a British fighter offered bomb-making advice. Pledges of allegiance to ISIS by another faction abroad. A massive suicide bombing in Baghdad. Another city in northern Iraq taken over by ISIS forces on the ground—and then another, this time in Syria. Then in Libya, then in Yemen. Every time we thought the group couldn't get any stronger, any more emboldened, it did just that. ISIS was growing by the day, whether it was a new territory or a new internet platform to inhabit. My team and I worked around the clock to keep up with these new developments, but we needed to drastically increase our staff.

"It wasn't always like this here," I exhaustedly told a new staff member in the summer of 2014 after yet another hectic day at the office. Not long after taking over Iraqi cities like Mosul and large swathes of Syria, ISIS had just declared its own so-called caliphate, making what was sure to be another steroid injection into its recruitment game. The new staffer nodded, unable to fully grasp the strange new normal he was now engaged in. The worsening threat posed by ISIS added more weight to longer-standing issues in its orbit, particularly immigration. Western citizens' sense of security was rattled, feeding a new mood of discontent and, with it, a surge of tribalism. June 2015 saw Donald Trump capitalize on these sentiments by calling Mexican immigrants "rapists and murderers" upon the launch of his campaign. After the ISIS-inspired attack in San Bernardino that December, Trump, then the presumptive Republican presidential candidate, even called for a "total and complete shutdown" of U.S. borders to Muslim countries.[71]

The same forces were in play in Europe, where mounting attacks by ISIS and ISIS-inspired operatives, many of whom were migrants from regions like North Africa, were driving the rise of far-right political candidates and monumental events like the 2016 Brexit referendum. News of rampant sexual assaults during New Year's Eve celebrations in Cologne, Germany, reportedly carried out by men of "Arab or North African appearance," were used as justifications for attacks against refugees and immigrants in Germany, not to mention nativist outcries across the continent.[72]

Something deep within Western societies was changing. The once-unquestionable values our children were taught in school—tolerance, religious freedom, diversity—were becoming fair game for scrutiny. Concurrently, the fear-based, hateful forces once reserved to the fringes of political thought were carving their way into the mainstream. Media had to acknowledge a new political force called the "alt-right," a far-right movement lacking any clear-cut definition that nevertheless boldly embraced misogyny, xenophobia, racism, and other hateful themes.

During these years of the mid-2010s, it was hard not to worry how these political and societal changes would affect the far right. How could they not? The very narratives of civilizational clashes and immigrant invasions were perceivably coming true. Every ISIS attack and crime by an immigrant worked in the far right's favor, whether it be by hardening their own member base or pulling in new minds looking for answers to the ills of the world. Neo-Nazis themselves were even taken aback by how everything was unfolding and how powerful it would all be if they could weaponize it. In the aftermath of the Cologne assaults and retaliatory attacks against refugees that followed, "Zorost," a VNN member, wrote:

We are living in interesting times. I never thought I'd live to see the day when revolutions and civil wars would break out in civilized countries. That sort of thing only happens in history books. But once the bonds of civilized behavior are loosed, it is hard to tie them down again.[73]

Commenting on one of the Cologne sexual assault victims' stories, Stormfront user "daen1488" wrote, "It doesn't shock me and maybe it's a good thing. I find it very unlikely that she and the hundreds like her will be supporting the refugee project. With luck, we'll find her here one day."

Daen1488, Zorost, and other far-right extremists knew that if there was ever a chance for them to be heard, this was the time. People were angry, scared, and vulnerable—exactly as the far right wanted them. But however fitting these circumstances were, it was never circumstance alone that far-right extremist movements needed to become a global terrorist threat.

Many on far-right forums wouldn't say it outright, but they had long been envious of ISIS's recruitment and terrorism successes. It wasn't lost on them that the group's successes worked in the far right's favor. But if they were indeed counterparts, why was all the victory so lopsided? What was ISIS doing to pull in so many zealots willing to die for its cause? Where were the white warriors? If the world was so clearly doused in gasoline, as they believed, where was the spark to set it all off? Exasperated by politicians' pro-diversity stances, one Stormfront user wrote in July 2014, "The more stories like this I read the more I hope to see a WN [white nationalist] version of ISIS."[74] Or, as they would increasingly come to put it, wage their own "White Jihad."

2

SCREW YOUR OPTICS

On the Saturday of October 27, 2018, my husband and I went on a nature hike. We were in the U.S. South for a weekend visit to the college where our daughter, the youngest of our four children, had just started as a freshman. I silenced my phone and tucked it away, hoping no urgent work-related matters would emerge during our walk through this beautiful trail in the Appalachians. The last week had been nerve-racking at the office. Dangerous rhetoric from President Trump—not to mention what was then an ongoing investigation into pipe bombs mailed to Democrats and Trump critics by a pro-Trump extremist named Cesar Sayoc—was creating a palpably tense environment.[1] As I tweeted in part the day before our hike:

> The threat of #WhiteSupremacists movements—and stress the word *threat*—continues to fester, especially under @realDonaldTrump.[2]

Even as my phone began buzzing in my pocket, I ignored it, which was an exercise in restraint. After the fifth buzz, though, I realized that something was up. I looked at my phone. My staff was feverishly posting into our work group chat reports about a Pittsburgh synagogue.

Emergency situation at US synagogue

Gunman opens fire at US synagogue

Pittsburgh police confirms active shooter at synagogue; multiple victims reported

"We've got to go back right now," I told my husband.

The evening before, our daughter sat across from us at a nearby restaurant with a grim facial expression. She told us how she and her friends from the college's theater club were putting on a play with LGBTQ characters, and how the local KKK caught wind and held a demonstration outside of the building. The professor running the production tried to calm the cast and crew before the opening, but their fear couldn't be dissolved. It was the year 2018, and right outside of the halls of the music theater was an organization, notorious for lynching and bombings, laser-focused on our daughter and her friends' performance.

"How is the Klan not illegal?" she asked me and my husband. "Aren't they a terrorist organization?"

"Yes and no," we told her.

My husband and I had managed to keep our daughter sheltered from many of the harsh realities that plagued our own childhoods. She grew up in an area on the East Coast where people worship whatever they want and love whomever they want without much, if any, objection from the community. She went to a diverse school where religion and race-related events were subjects of discussion, but never before had she experienced such blatant hatred herself.

I thought about what my daughter said as I scrolled through updates about Pittsburgh on the car ride back home. Encountering a group like the KKK face to face is more than just scary; it adds a disheartening tint to the way you look at the world. I've spent many years digging through the details of terrorist attacks and gory executions, and my friends and colleagues often ask me how I handle it all on an emotional level. I'm never completely sure how to answer. Even after all these years,

I've never grown able to stomach much of the content I work with day to day. I sat in the passenger seat scrolling through the details of the attack on my laptop as my husband drove, and that same wave of hopelessness was creeping up as strong as ever.

Even so, information is the best tool we have against terrorist radicalization and violence.[3] Every attack and every detail pertaining to it matters. These fragments of information, and the ways they all interconnect, are lessons. They teach us how to see the threats that hide in plain sight, how they fester, who is vulnerable, and how to better prevent future violence.[4] Knowing this helps to push the sorrow of a terrorist attack to the side, at least enough to answer the essential questions at hand.

First and foremost, we need to establish the basics of the attack: Is it a jihadist? A far-right terrorist? Did the attacker act alone? If not, who are the others? An attacker's online presence is a critical source of answers, but in the frantic haze of an attack, this type of information disappears very quickly, often a few minutes after the attack. Therefore, accessing this information immediately is of critical importance. Major platforms like Facebook and Twitter remove attackers' social media profiles upon being notified. At the same time, accomplices, associates, and even family members of the attackers sometimes begin bleaching their digital footprints.[5] There's also the problem of *too much* information.[6] When a terrorist attack takes place the internet is a frenzy of speculation, conspiracy theories, and trolling. To navigate through the weeds, my staff and I use a range of tools, depending on the attack and its timing: person-search databases, police scanners, social media, and police records, among others. We also use far more exclusive resources: access to password-protected deep-web forums, chat groups and channels on encrypted messenger applications, and our decades-spanning data archives.

We divide work between different teams. One monitors for updates via real-time briefings and news sources across relevant languages, while another monitors incoming responses from the extremist communities themselves. Is the ISIS community saying anything about the event? If so, are any ISIS accounts indicating prior knowledge of the attack? The same goes for the far right and other extremist communities. We also check archived chatter and terrorist propaganda in our database and archives: Has anyone incited for an attack against this target before? If so, how recently? These questions are particularly important because most terrorist attacks don't happen in a void; they are, more often than not, results of some sort of nudge, whether it be a swell of outrage against a certain group or community or a direct incitement or threat against a specified target.[7]

Upon first evaluation, there were several plausible scenarios for this attack in Pittsburgh. Synagogues—and, by extension, Jews—are targets of both the far right and jihadists. ISIS, al-Qaeda, and their supporters constantly call for attacks on Jews.[8] At the time, President Trump's formal recognition of Jerusalem as Israel's capital the year before was still regularly being cited as justification of attacks.[9]

For the far right, news of refugee and immigrant "invaders" across the United States and Europe was a significant theme of chatter at that time.[10] In the weeks leading to the Pittsburgh attack, white supremacists were united in outrage over stories like Immigration and Customs Enforcement (ICE) officials being forced to release immigrants and asylum-seekers in Arizona, sparking vicious condemnation of a "third-world invasion" happening across the West.[11] To far-right extremists, U.S. acceptance of refugees was part of a Jewish conspiracy to dilute the country of its white majority. The Jews, as they saw it, were funneling populations from war-torn countries into the United States while Israel, to their ire, took none.[12]

Our search for a possible motive would end more quickly than we thought, though. As the Pittsburgh attack was still under way, some of my researchers were monitoring streams of police scanners. It put them into chilling earshot of officers' updates on the attack and the attacker's proclaimed motive:

Alright . . . be advised, we have suspect giving us hands in view. We're negotiating his surrender at this time. All units, hold what you've got.

. . . Be advised, suspect says his name is Robert Bowers. Rob Bowers.

. . . Suspect is talking about, "All these Jews need to die."

Now having what appeared to be a suspect name and motive, he wasn't hard to find: Robert Bowers, forty-six years old, multiple living relatives, lived in the Pittsburgh area. All useful information, but it was his account on Gab, one of the first places we searched, that put the picture together.

Gab is a social media platform created in 2016 in response to what some perceived as Silicon Valley's "discrimination" against conservative speech.[13] We'd been monitoring the platform since it was announced, constantly reporting on incitements and other activity taking place on it. White supremacists were migrating to the platform from longer-standing discussion forums like Stormfront, hailing it as the perfect place to set up shop.[14]

"I am a member [on Gab], like to spout my mouth off there, all my anti jew stuff," a user on Stormfront wrote in February 2018, roughly eight months before Bowers's attack. Another user in that same discussion thread stated, "I think [Gab is] a net positive because it connects Jew-wise people."[15]

Indeed it does.

Gab's growing popularity among the far right was a problem to which its creator, a former tech entrepreneur named Andrew Torba, seemed indifferent. According to Torba, Gab was a platform where people could say whatever they wanted, however they wanted.[16] If white supremacists and neo-Nazis were setting up shop on it, then so be it.

"Free speech means you can offend, criticize, and make memes about any race, religion, ethnicity, or sexual orientation," Torba wrote in an August 2018 Gab post.[17] "Sick and tired of the double standards for 'acceptable speech' and 'protected classes' on both the left and the right."[18]

On Gab, Bowers was immersed in the same type of toxic bubble we so commonly find terrorist attackers in, whether they be ISIS-pledged "mujahideen" or far-right race warriors. In the two months leading to his attack, his posts and shares shed light on the toxic thinking behind his actions: conspiracy theories about "filthy" Jews and their "propaganda war," Holocaust denial, fear of whites' pending "extinction," and an existential imperative for whites to "stand up." From posted photos of his guns all the way to his threats against the target of his massacre, you could see the time bomb rapidly ticking toward detonation.

On September 29, a month before the shooting, Bowers posted a picture of three pistols, which he called his "glock family," to a Gab group called "Guns of Gab." It was a shocking flash of the near future: pistols of a count and make consistent with those that police would describe Bowers as using in tandem with an AR-15 during the attack.

In the United States, it's not uncommon for people to post pictures of their guns to social media. But those guns become a lot scarier when their owner obsesses about throwing Jews into ovens. On September 28, the day before he posted about his "family" of guns, Bowers posted a threat to "oven dodgers," referencing one of the many ways

Robert Bowers @onedingo ▶ Guns of Gab
a month ago · edited

my glock family.

with a plastic training and kkm 40s&w barrels for each. truglo tfx on the 31 and xs big dots on the 32&33.

and grip tape on the gen 3 on the right so it's not so greasy when wet.

edit: in this pic 33 still had tfx sights

︿ 12 ● Comments 3 ↻ Repost 1 ❝❝ Quote

FIGURE 2.1 Gab post by Robert Bowers showing three handguns

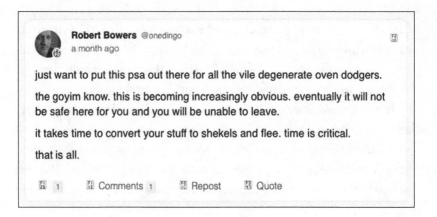

Robert Bowers @onedingo
a month ago

just want to put this psa out there for all the vile degenerate oven dodgers.

the goyim know. this is becoming increasingly obvious. eventually it will not be safe here for you and you will be unable to leave.

it takes time to convert your stuff to shekels and flee. time is critical.

that is all.

1   Comments 1   Repost   Quote

FIGURE 2.2 Gab post by Robert Bowers

Jews were killed in concentration camps during the Holocaust. As a Jew, his post made my stomach turn:

> just want to put this psa out there for all the vile degenerate oven dodgers.
>
> the goyim [non-Jews] know. this is becoming increasingly obvious. eventually it will not be safe here for you and you will be unable to leave.
>
> it takes time to convert your stuff to shekels [Israeli currency] and flee. time is critical.[19]

With every post about burning and gassing Jews, you could see Bowers's hate boiling over. Less than a week after his "oven dodgers" post, he weighed in on fellow white supremacists' complaints of Jews using Gab. "That's ok," he wrote in reply. "The ovens run 24/7."[20]

One day later, he commented on a news report of a rabbi accused of sexual assault. In his response, he posted a picture of a furnace and stated, "Make Ovens 1488F Again"—1488 being a reference to the white supremacist "14 Words" ("We must secure the existence of our people and a future for white children"), and "88" standing for the two H's in "Heil Hitler."

In the few days leading to his attack, Bowers's attention zeroed in on something more specific. Between October 24 and 27, he made eighteen

FIGURE 2.3 Gab post by Robert Bowers

posts and reposts. Among them, five consecutive reposts pertained to refugees, a topic we'd been seeing swell among others in the far right. He reposted an October 4 post by one user exclaiming, "It's the filthy EVIL jews Bringing the Filthy EVIL Muslims into the Country!! Stop the kikes then Worry About the Muslims!" Another one of the messages he reposted sounded the alarm of white "extinction" at the hands of the Jews:

> Jews are waging a propaganda war against Western civilization and it is so effective that we are headed towards certain extinction within the next 200 years and we're not even aware of it
>
> You are living in a critical time in history where the internet has given us a small window of opportunity to snap our people out of their brainwash[21]

FIGURE 2.4 Gab post by Robert Bowers

Seeing this echo chamber of Jewish-orchestrated invasions of Muslim migrants, Bowers's attack target, the Hebrew International Aid Society (HIAS), was tragically fitting. The organization was founded in 1881 to help Jews fleeing persecution in Russia and Eastern Europe, and has since expanded to provide "welcome, safety, and freedom to refugees of all faiths and ethnicities from all over the world," as it states on its website.[22] And it's lived up to its word, having assisted and resettled refugees from Vietnam and Cambodia in the 1970s, and others from war-torn regions like Afghanistan in more recent years.[23] Whether by petitions, demonstrations, or other forms of activism, HIAS wore its advocacy on its sleeve, and was particularly active in protesting efforts by the Trump administration to cut the flow of asylum-seekers into the United States.[24] I can only imagine the rage neo-Nazis must have felt when seeing pictures of HIAS members standing before the U.S. Capitol holding up signs reading "Refugees Welcome" and "My People Were Refugees Too."[25]

In those last few days before his attack, Bowers reposted threats against the HIAS by "Farmer General," a popular neo-Nazi Gab account with Nazi swastikas and SS bolts in its very name. Farmer General posted them to a Gab group called "Gabstapo," referring to the Nazis' secret police, the Gestapo. Farmer General's posts showed pictures of HIAS refugee advocates while exclaiming "How about GTFO [get the fuck out] jews!"[26]

FIGURE 2.5 Gab post by user "Farmer General," reposted by Robert Bowers

FIGURE 2.6 Gab post by user "Farmer General, reposted by Robert Bowers (person's face in photo censored)

Bowers's focus on HIAS became even more foreboding when he reposted his own message from seventeen days earlier. His post referenced HIAS's upcoming National Refugee Shabbat, which would use Judaism's holy rest day (also known as the Sabbath) to reflect on refugee crises and how to better resolve them. The event would span different locations across the United States between October 19 and 20.

"Why hello there HIAS! You like to bring in hostile invaders to dwell among us?" Bowers wrote of the event. He posted HIAS' list of participating congregations, threatening, "We appreciate the list of friends you have provided."[27]

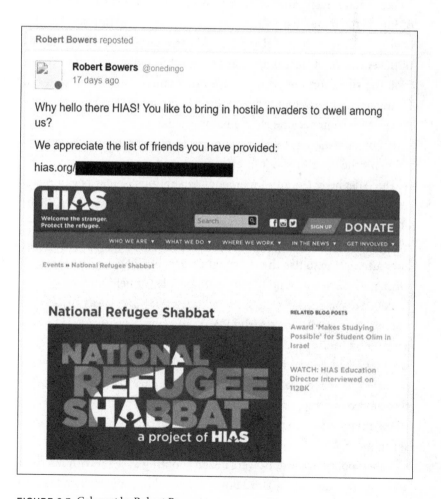

FIGURE 2.7 Gab post by Robert Bowers

Bowers's next post, made at 9:49 a.m. on October 27, 2018, would also be his last. His blunt explanation of his attack echoed the existential alarms he had been posting about in the weeks prior, as well as the railing against "invaders" we'd been noticing in the weeks leading to his attack. Bowers's post read:

> HIAS likes to bring invaders in that kill our people.
> I can't sit by and watch my people get slaughtered.
> Screw your optics, I'm going in.[28]

Less than fifteen minutes after posting this, Bowers entered the Tree of Life Synagogue, just five minutes after three separate services had begun. Armed with an AR-15 rifle and three handguns, he opened fire in the entrance of the synagogue. Some at the synagogue initially mistook the shots for something more innocuous—perhaps "a coat rack falling over" or "a senior citizen falling [who] might have needed help." However, it soon became clear what was going on.[29]

Rabbi Jeffrey Myers told his congregants in the property's Pervin Chapel to hit the floor. "Do not utter a sound, and don't move," he said.[30]

The Allegheny County Emergency Operations Center began receiving multiple calls from those inside the building at 9:54 a.m. Barry Werber of the New Light congregation was hiding in a closet in the basement when he dialed 911 to report the attack. Rabbi Myers likewise called it in after attempting to flee the synagogue's Pervin Chapel with others, but ultimately turned around for the eight people left behind.[31]

Police dispatched two cars immediately, but Bowers was already well into his rampage. He shot Melvin Wax, an eighty-seven-year-old retired accountant leading the New Light service, as he exited the storage closet where he had been hiding. Bowers checked the closet, but by some miracle didn't see the others hiding in the dark there.[32] Bowers shot three more worshippers in the basement and then proceeded upstairs to where members of the Tree of Life congregation were hiding, killing seven more.[33]

When police arrived, Bowers began shooting at them with his AR-15 and then retreated to the third floor of the building and barricaded himself in. SWAT personnel entered the building around 10:30 and started evacuating injured victims and those in hiding. The team gradually secured parts of the building for the next fifteen minutes before locating Bowers. He fired on them, critically wounding one officer.[34]

"Shots fired," declared one officer in the radio feed. "Give me additional resources. Additional resources, third floor." Seconds later, the officer followed up with "Come on, we've got a guy barricaded, activity shooting at SWAT operators." A fuzz of inaudible yelling and motion followed.

When the gunfire stopped, police began negotiating with Bowers, giving him orders to crawl out of his barricade. Bowers soon after put his hands in view and gave his name and age. Finally, at 11:08, Bowers crawled out of his barricade and gave himself up to police.[35]

Eleven people were killed in the attack, and six injured. Those killed ranged in age from their mid-fifties to late nineties. The oldest was ninety-seven-year-old Rose Mallinger, who was as sharp and energetic as ever, according to those who knew her. The youngest was fifty-four-year-old David Rosenthal, who was killed along with his fifty-nine-year-old brother Cecil.

Bowers's attack, albeit deadlier than most, was seen by many as another hate crime in the United States: something to mourn, but not investigate any further. But the more the reactions to Bowers's attack came in from all different corners of the far right, it became clear that he had tapped into something horrifying. Something that terrorists of recent years, like Frazier Glenn Miller and Dylann Roof, didn't. In all the years I'd been watching the far right I'd seen nothing like it. October 27, 2018, made way for a fervent departure from the old ways of the white supremacist movement. A harsher, uninhibited contingent of the far right—the same one to cheer on Anders Breivik's killing of children and other brutal events—was finally having its day. A militant drumbeat was pounding across the far right, centered around those six words: "Screw your optics, I'm going in."

In the decade before Bowers's attack, violence was a controversial topic among white supremacist and neo-Nazi communities. For every white supremacist that cheered on Charleston church attacker Dylann Roof or Norway attacker Anders Breivik, there was another that saw their violence as harmful to the public's perception of their cause—or, as it was more commonly put, their "optics."[36] In the aftermath of Roof's 2015 attack, one white supremacist on Stormfront compared him directly to Breivik:

> I don't consider either one of them heroes, I consider them individuals who cracked and then lashed out in a very counterproductive way for the rest of us. They are also beyond a doubt, patsies. Fall guys, people who are useful idiots, or were useful idiots the Jews are so fond of creating, and using for their nefarious agenda.[37]

This followed in line with the thinking of older-generation white supremacist leaders like David Duke. These stalwarts of the American far right had seen how violence begat scrutiny from law enforcement in the 1980s and 1990s, stigmatizing the movement.[38] Starting in the early 2000s, David Duke and others argued that white nationalists needed to ditch the white hooded robes and the shaved heads to appeal to Americans sympathetic to their messaging but who were reluctant to join.[39] Indeed, Don Black, the founder of Stormfront, claimed to have left the KKK because of its ties to violence, explaining the relatively moderate appeal of his forum compared to other online platforms.[40]

White nationalists were having this exact optics argument even just one year prior to the Pittsburgh synagogue shooting. It was during the aftermath of the August 12, 2017 "Unite the Right" rally in Charlottesville which was, as most recall, a disaster: fights between protesters and counterprotesters, a woman killed in a vehicular attack, and authorities unable to control it all. As white nationalists planned another rally, many within the community had a lot to say.

"Make sure you do what worked so well in Charlottesville," a user on Stormfront wrote with vicious sarcasm. "Announce that you will hold a huge rally in Washington DC months in advance, so the Deep State has plenty of time to roll out the welcome wagon for you. Whites brawling with each other in the streets was such good optics."[41]

This was where Bowers's final post, "Screw your optics, I'm going in," came from. It was a statement of rejection of the optics concerns and of appeals to nonviolence. And in declaring this rejection upon carrying out his massacre, he triggered a paradigm shift, chillingly similar to another international extremist movement: ISIS.

It is often said that white supremacists and jihadists are different sides of the same coin: that a terrorist attack is a terrorist attack, regardless of what ideology one ascribes to. This is all true, but the extent to which these two seemingly unconnected movements mirror each other remains understated. Bowers's "screw your optics" declaration, to that point, was stunningly similar to the sentiments expressed by ISIS and its support- ers upon its rise to power in the early 2010s.

While the "jihad" of groups like al-Qaeda was primarily framed as struggles against oppressors, the promise of a caliphate—a funda- mentalist form of Islamic statehood and governance—was the light at the end of the tunnel.[42] This promise of returning to the noble past of the Umayyad Caliphate, Ottoman Caliphate, and others moti- vates the Global Jihad movement, much the same way promises of white ethno-states motivate neo-Nazis and white supremacists. And, like the pragmatism-versus-violence debates among the far right, the topic of pursuing a caliphate had long been a point of disagree- ment in the Global Jihad movement. Al-Qaeda and its spiritual lead- ers had long led the jihadist community by a grand vision of gradual steps toward establishing a caliphate.[43] However, decades of *not* get- ting a caliphate made room for ISIS, once al-Qaeda's affiliate in Iraq, to become a loudspeaker of dissent against its perceived incremental and pragmatic approaches.[44]

"The al-Qaeda of today is no longer the al-Qaeda of jihad," ISIS declared to the Global Jihad community in April 2014, three years after Navy SEALs killed Osama bin Laden in Pakistan.[45]

ISIS was of course paving the way to declare its own so-called caliph- ate just a couple of months later in June 2014, something that drove jihadi scholars, spokespeople, militants, and others to cry bloody foul.[46] Al- Qaeda chided that "the announcement of such a serious step" as declar- ing a caliphate required far more scholarly consensus.[47] Al-Qaeda's affiliate in Yemen called the declaration "unjust," warning it would lead to "breaking of relationships" across different factions.[48]

None of the condemnation mattered, though, because ISIS's bold move worked. In its signature our-way-or-the-highway fashion, ISIS would go on to be far more violent and brutal than al-Qaeda had ever aimed to be. Factions around the globe pledged allegiance to ISIS's self-proclaimed caliph, Abu Bakr al-Baghdadi, and jihadists from all over the world flocked to its territories.[49] Meanwhile, the group rapidly published high-quality videos of executions and other exploits, much to its followers' warped enjoyment. ISIS's movement was energized.[50] It was no longer waiting around for the old generation to take things further.

And, just like ISIS supporters, a very loud and dangerous portion of the far right was now ready to challenge the status quo of their own movement. For decades, leaders like former KKK Grand Wizard David Duke, white supremacist writer Jared Taylor, and others had played the political game, but the United States and other Western countries were no closer to ethno-statehood.[51] In many ways, they were more racially diverse. The United States, which elected its first Black president in 2008, was seeing growing racial and ethnic diversity while strictly white populations were, to the far right's dismay, lacking growth.[52]

With these changes came a growing sense of cultural anxiety. According to a 2017 study by the Public Religion Research Institute (PRRI), more than two-thirds of white working-class Americans "believe the American way of life needs to be protected from foreign influence" and that "the growing number of newcomers from other countries threatens American culture."[53] Other research was also finding over a third of non-Hispanic white Americans expressing "strong feelings of white solidarity."[54]

The same sentiments were creeping across Europe. Violence, poverty, and increasingly inhospitable climate conditions across the Middle East and Africa were bringing growing waves of refugees, changes that striking numbers of Europeans believed were making their countries "worse place[s] to live."[55]

The West's new changes and the anger they were causing served as proof to many in the far right that their longstanding movement establishments, and all of their concerns with optics, were failures. Weak. Useless. It only took a disturbingly zealous extremist like Robert Bowers to come along and say "screw your optics" to ignite a flame to this percolating anger.

That, and the immeasurable power of social media.

—— ∞ ——

"Screw your optics, I'm going in" became an instant mantra in far-right social media spaces. These words were echoed everywhere, from propaganda by groups like the so-called Feuerkrieg Division, a now-disbanded

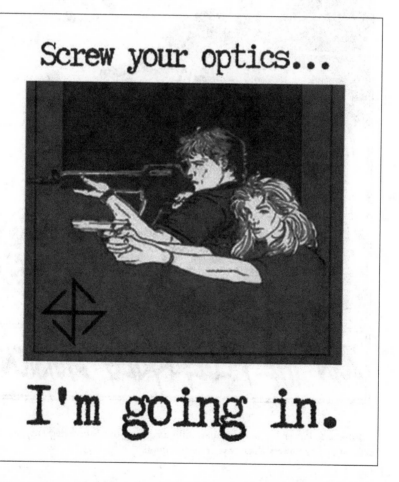

FIGURE 2.8 Image disseminated on social media applying Robert Bowers's "screw your optics" quote to the cover of *The Turner Diaries*, a book written by Andrew Macdonald (the pen name of longtime neo-Nazi William Pierce)

FIGURE 2.9 Poster by neo-Nazi paramilitary group the Feuerkrieg Division (now defunct), using Bowers's "screw your optics" quote

neo-Nazi paramilitary organization with branches across North America and Europe, to unbranded posters and memes spread by far-right accounts on Gab. They placed Bowers into meme templates like "thinking face," quoting his words, "All Jews must die." Some users placed the words at the top of their own profiles.

Bowers's act was to many in the far right the only way to "fight back" against the changing world they saw as an existential threat to their race, something the old guard of the movement didn't have the stomach to take on. "Fight or Die," said a user on Stormfront in the immediate aftermath of Bowers's attack. "No other choice . . . They have imported so many 3rd World scum they can not keep pushing White people and not expect people to push back." Another user in the same thread wrote, "Whoever the shooter was probably just got fed up with all the crooked scams and dishonest activities of the jews and just decided to take matters into his own hands."[56]

The optics camp was still chiming in, but they were suddenly on the defensive against a much louder and seemingly larger population of terrorism advocates. To those in the far right still trying to characterize Bowers as a stain on the white supremacist movement, one Stormfront user wrote:

> Here is a thought.
> Maybe a non medicated, healthy minded, normal, average White man finally said enough is enough.
> Where would he go to seek vengence?
> A synagogue.
> Just maybe it is not a false flag, slobbering lunatic that hates his mommy, but a man that sees the writing on the wall.
> A man that knows how and what the jews truly are.[57]

With the rejection of optics also came rejections of much larger ways of thinking. While many neo-Nazis had long fantasized about infiltrating the levers of political power,[58] users on the VNN forum were now characterizing Bowers's attack as proof that political engagement doesn't work, pushing the same type of anti-democratic sentiments you hear from jihadists who proclaim voting to be an act of apostasy. VNN owner Alex Linder, a widely recognized neo-Nazi, exclaimed bluntly, "Violence works."

"The right move now is to create a White Liberation Army," he stated. "Voting etc won't do anything—not unless there's a White Racial Loyalist armed force."[59]

"The voting booth is the cuck shed of democracy," one user agreed.[60]

As these memes and posts celebrating Bowers kept coming in, it brought me back to the sentiments I experienced when I first started exploring Stormfront years ago. Here was again brazen promotion of terrorism, years later, only worse this time: no longer confined to forums, but instead flowing out onto a social media platform that clearly didn't seem to care. The U.S. white supremacist movement "is a growing problem that demands far more attention than it's gotten," I wrote on Twitter, explaining that "while major platforms like Twitter and Facebook receive brunt of criticisms, smaller ones like Gab often evade such demands for accountability."[61]

Hours after tweeting my critiques about Gab, *Politico* approached me to write an article on the topic. I've written enough articles across different media outlets to know that they rarely bring about sweeping change, but this seemed like an opportunity to join others in guiding the conversation somewhere productively. After all, this wasn't about some bad apple hanging out on a platform; Bowers was the product of a movement and its online terrorist-generating machine.

I accepted the offer. People needed to see the cesspool that housed Bowers, and not in some watered-down way. All the ugliness of Gab needed to be shown, regardless of how uncomfortable it made us.

And indeed, there was plenty of ugliness to choose from.

A poll posted to Gab used the "#treeoflifeshooting" hashtag while posing the question, "What should the future of Jewish people in the West be?" Forty-seven percent voted for "repatriation," and 35 percent voted for genocide.[62]

One user replied, "Repeating the acts of Repatriation, Segregation, and Assimilation does nothing to alter their inborn hostility and

Brett Stevens @alternative_right
3 hours ago

What should the future of Jewish people in the West be?

#treeoflifeshooting

35% Genocide

47% Repatriation

5% Segregation

9% Assimilation

5% "Chinatowns"

43 votes

FIGURE 2.10 Poll posted to Gab after Robert Bowers's attack

arrogance against everyone else. Only that it repeats the same old same old. Just end them."

"Mass graves. Period," another user wrote. "What you tolerate is what will continue."

"Remember, these jews murdered sixty million whites just like you and me," Linder posted to his Gab account along with a "#DeathToThe-Jews" hashtag. "And they're priming the pump to do it again—if we let them."[63]

Linder was referencing the Holodomor, the Soviet Union's imposed famine on Ukrainians that killed millions in 1932 and 1933. White supremacists and neo-Nazis believe the atrocity to be a Jew-orchestrated genocide of whites, claiming the Soviet Union was controlled by Jews (despite Stalin's documented persecution of them).

A Gab user by the name "Angry Goy" commented on Linder's post, "If every jew currently alive was exterminated it still wouldn't even come close to paying for the evil they have inflicted on us."[64]

And then there was the artwork: offensive drawings of Jews and other minorities, described as "trash," calling the Holocaust the "Holohoax," and calling to "kill all the kikes." It was too much to fit into one article.

After hours of wading through this filth, I had to stop. It was the year 2018, and I'd just spent two days on a virtual nonstop tour of Nazi Germany. Even for all my cynicism, I sometimes forget how much I hold

FIGURE 2.11 Image distributed on Gab

FIGURE 2.12 Gab post by neo-Nazi Robert Sterkeson

onto notions of social progress and of human decency, until it all vaporizes right in front of me.

Aside from the horror of the content itself, people needed to understand how a place like Gab breeds terrorists—how powerful social media can be in someone's path to a terrorist attack, regardless of their ideology. The more I studied Bowers's Gab activity via the file we archived, the more I was reminded of an ISIS-pledged young man named Elton Simpson.

Just like Bowers, Simpson's radicalization appeared to be less the result of some lone, self-made journey into extremism but rather of a steady stream of messaging and propaganda on social media by recruiters. This was a tactic that ISIS exploited to great effect. Even as the United States and its allies ramped up efforts to cripple ISIS's physical caliphate and shut off its pipeline of foreign fighters, the group turned to its sophisticated online propaganda apparatus to recruit individuals in Western countries to commit acts of violence.[65]

On Twitter, Simpson had regular conversations with "Mujahid Miski," the online alias of an American man named Muhammed Abdullahi, who joined the Shabaab al-Mujahideen movement, al-Qaeda's branch in Somalia, in 2008. After ISIS's announcement of its so-called caliphate, Abdullahi used his remote position on the other side of the world to recruit on its behalf via social media.[66] He even cautioned against joining the Shabaab, the very group he was living under, in favor of ISIS in Syria, writing in 2014:

> If I was still in Minnesota and I had the choice between Somalia and Sham [Syria] . . . I would choose Sham without any hesitation. Unfortunately I can not go to sham right now because If I'm caught I will face 45 years in prison.[67]

The following year, Simpson sent Abdullahi news of a prophet-drawing competition in Texas, the type of stunt jihadists consider punishable by death. Abdullahi shortly after tweeted an incitement for his followers in the United States to attack the event.

"The brothers from the Charlie hebdo attack did their part," he wrote in reference to the attack against the shock-humor newspaper in Paris earlier that year. "It's time for brothers in the #US to do their part."[68]

Simpson, a devoted follower of Abdullahi, remained in contact with him after his incitement, talking about ISIS and sharing jokes until he attacked that very prophet-drawing contest less than two weeks later. With his accomplice, Simpson drove from Arizona to where the event was being held at the Curtis Culwell Center in Garland, Texas. They arrived at the event at about 7:00 p.m. and fired dozens of rounds into a police car parked next to a barricade. Both attackers were swiftly shot dead by SWAT officers. One officer was injured.[69]

Simpson and Abdullahi's relationship mirrors that between Bowers and the aforementioned Farmer General account on Gab. Farmer General was a major source of content for Bowers, who reposted from the account at least seventeen times in the month leading to his attack. Posts by Farmer General exclaimed, "Kick the jews OUT . . . No One Wants the Whiny kikes," and "We know the true enemy of White People, jews and their sycophants!"[70]

And, just as Abdullahi reinforced Simpson's fixation on the prophet-drawing contest he would attack, so too did Farmer General for Bowers's fixation on the HIAS. This was the same account from which Bowers, within a few days prior to his attack, reposted an image of a woman holding an HIAS-labeled paper with the handwritten message, "I support refugees because I am Jewish, period." Farmer General's image contained the comment: "What a shock ((((she)))) supports refugees, I wonder if she supports them going to Israel."[71]

Even Bowers's and Simpson's final posts were eerily similar in their tersely stated motives. "HIAS likes to bring invaders in that kill our people . . . I can't sit by and watch my people get slaughtered . . . Screw your optics, I'm going in," Bowers wrote. Simpson wrote with similar brevity, "The bro with me and myself have given bay'ah [allegiance] to Amirul Mu'mineen [Abu Bakr al-Baghdadi]. May Allah accept us as mujahideen . . . #texasattack."[72]

So here are two terrorists who, despite their completely different ideologies, show nearly identical stories of poisonous online content bubbles, agitating associates in those venues, and their final falls into violence. The only difference is that one pledged to a movement that the entire world didn't hesitate to mobilize against, while the other belonged to a movement able to hide behind "freedom of speech."

The day of Bowers's attack there were 465,000 members on Gab, many of whom, even if not yet radicalized, would be exposed to users like Farmer General and the scores of other accounts posting the same type of content. For it to remain online would be a recipe for more violence, whether it be against Jews or other minorities threatened on the platform. But these far-right breeding grounds online aren't just threats to minorities; they are threats to entire societies. This emboldened far-right extremist movement has made it clear that anyone not with them is their enemy, from Pope Francis and the LGBTQ community to Muslims and God-forsaken "race traitors."

Were we supposed to accept these horrid exchanges of hate and incitements as a new normal of the internet age? Does a fringe community's evasive outcries about "free speech" take more priority than another community's right to peacefully worship? Perhaps the most pressing question was in the United States' blatant double standard at that time: when an ISIS supporter posted a message about attacking America, it resulted in an investigation. But when a neo-Nazi like Bowers—and thousands like him—posted messages urging for the death of Jews and other groups, they received no attention from law enforcement or the companies providing them online venues.

The day after the Pittsburgh attack, just after I handed off my article to *Politico*'s editors, my husband and I joined some family friends at their synagogue for a meeting on the event. It felt like a funeral, and in more ways than one. Beyond the somberness, there was a spirit of acceptance.

"We want to assure everyone that we will make our establishment safer," the head of the congregation said. He promised increased security around the synagogue, describing in detail the new fences and gates that would be installed and how the place would now be fully guarded.

Gates. Security guards. Like a prison, or a war zone.

The rabbi then consoled us. He talked about our history as Jews, about how suffering and perseverance were part of who we are. He told us that the solution to what threatened us lied not in anger and sorrow, but in forgiveness and unity.

It sure is sad how in the United States, a country founded on principles of freedom, a religious group can so easily be left high and dry to fend for its own safety. Indeed, Jews and other religious and ethnic groups have endured unthinkable treatment throughout history, but at no point should anyone accept hatred and persecution as some sort of default way of life.

So yes, we were all sad, but was that all? As we all sat in that room, there were thousands of people elsewhere cheering on what Bowers did and calling for more. How could we address this problem if so few even knew it existed? I wanted to see Jews—alongside Muslims, Sikhs, Christians, Hindus, and Buddhists—protesting this unwritten contract that some peoples' freedom of religion or safety takes the back seat to others' distorted notions of "free speech." Whatever amount of demonstrations and petitions were already in the works, I wanted a hundred more.

You don't have to be a religious or ethnic minority to see the injustice I describe. Ask yourself: What really happened after August of 2017, when James Fields mowed down a group of people in Charlottesville, killing a young woman named Heather Heyer? She and the other individuals were counterprotestors, rejecting hate at the white nationalist "Unite the Right" rally. The commander in chief of the United States, Donald Trump, said there were "some very fine people on both sides," while the media gave a fleeting wave of coverage, paying plenty of attention to the president's horrid apologies for white nationalist groups but not nearly as much to the white nationalist groups themselves. Shortly thereafter, everyone just moved on.

And what of white supremacist Dylann Roof's June 2015 killing of nine Black worshippers at Emanuel African Methodist Episcopal Church in Charleston? There was national sorrow for a while, but did anything change? Should we have expected Pittsburgh to be the same? Did we have any reason to be hopeful? Or would our short attention spans and the indifference of our government policies, mixed with the far right's new mantra of "screw your optics," indeed lay the groundwork for a scary and violent new normal?

⚙

I hoped that my *Politico* piece would help in some small way to start a conversation on this far-right threat. Perhaps it would contribute to a new demand for change too large and too loud to be ignored.

Things did seem to be promising for a brief moment. Within a day of Bowers's attack, Gab was dropped by payment processors PayPal and Stripe as well as hosting services GoDaddy and Joyent. By October 29, that following Monday, Gab's web address led to an angry and jaw-droppingly un-introspective statement from the platform:

> Gab.com is under attack. We have been systematically no-platformed by App Stores, multiple hosting providers, and several payment processors. We have been smeared by the mainstream media for defending free expression and individual liberty for all people and for working

with law enforcement to ensure that justice is served for the horrible atrocity committed in Pittsburgh. Gab will continue to fight for the fundamental human right to speak freely.

As we transition to a new hosting provider Gab will be inaccessible for a period of time. We are working around the clock to get Gab.com back online. Thank you and remember to speak freely.[73]

As it often goes after an event like the Pittsburgh attack, though, positive initial steps are often confused with problems solved. A week after Bowers's attack, Gab found another webhosting client, the Seattle-based Epik.com, willing to give it venue. Gab's Twitter account commented on its return in a November 4, 2018, message beginning with "Here is our press release to the media." In a fashion completely fitting to Torba's tone-deafness, the message exclaimed to all who had raised issue with the neo-Nazi playground that is Gab:

You failed. We are back online. We grow stronger by the hour. Free speech lives at http://Gab.com. This is only the beginning. May God have mercy on you for what you people have done this past week. Peace, love, and prayers.[74]

Gab's comeback was celebrated, even by some soon-to-be new users. "I was never very interested in joining [Gab] but I think I'll try now," said a Stormfront forum member. "I didn't know they talked a lot about jews there . . . The more Americans that know about jews, the more we can fight them and defeat them."[75]

"It is great to now be a part of Gab," another said. "I am an Australian, white male . . . I look forward to sharing and discussing on Gab. Long live free speech !"[76]

Just like that, it was as if Pittsburgh had never happened. Even Farmer General, that horrifying staple of Bowers's account, continued business as usual on Gab, posting pictures of Jews with devil horns and Hitler quotes—nothing less than what you would have seen a couple of weeks earlier.

"The Existence of jews anywhere on Earth is a Threat to Every non-jew on this Planet. Especially Aryans and Christians!" the account wrote in a November 8 post. "Don't be Surprised when Aryans teach your Satanic Tribe a Violent, but needed Lesson." The same day, Farmer General posted to another group on Gab that "the holocaust never Happened, but it Should have!"[77]

So here was Gab, fighting. Here was Farmer General and an entire hate-based movement, fighting. And there were we, the civilized world, after only a few weeks, taking every single punch thrown at us. Refusing to hit back. Waiting for the next strike, wherever and whenever it would come. I thought about the words I'd read by Rabbi Jeffrey Myers, a survivor of the Pittsburgh synagogue shooting, and how wonderfully he described the pursuit of future peace and tolerance as a duty—as something not given by any default, but rather as something that was up to us to pursue if we did indeed want it.

"This can be a watershed moment in our country if people choose to because we have a choice every minute of the day what comes out of our mouths," he said to the *Pittsburgh Post-Gazette* in a piece published in mid-November, roughly two weeks after he'd phoned Bowers's attack into the police.

I wondered, as Gab resurfaced, and as Farmer General and others continued to carry on as they had prior to Bowers's attack, if Rabbi Myers felt let down by his country.

"As easily as we spew hate, we also can spew love," Myers said. "To me, if that can begin to happen, then the deaths of these 11 people will not be in vain. If there's no change whatever, then it confirms our worst fears about the path we're heading down, and it's the wrong path."[78]

To *spew hate*. Sites like Gab gave this concept such new weight. Just a couple of weeks ago, I had been telling my daughter not to worry herself after her run-in with the Klan. But what could I possibly tell her about this massive hive of people shouting "screw your optics" across the internet? Did a group like the Klan even apply anymore when staring into these digital swarms? And indeed, to Rabbi Myers's point, what path was it taking us down?

3

THE TERROR SYMBIOSIS

The trajectory of extremist movements is often determined by game-changing moments of shock. These events might seem insignificant compared to the 9/11 attacks that forever changed our world, but they nonetheless create tsunami waves through such movements. In 2004, I witnessed one of the first of such events from the end of a conference table in an Idaho courthouse. I still have nightmares about it.

I was alone in a room, two rows of empty chairs in front of me, scrolling through an al-Qaeda forum. Two federal agents guarded the room on the other side of the door. Further down the hall was the thirty-four-year-old man I was waiting to testify against, Sami Omar al-Hussayen. I had been assisting with the Department of Justice's prosecution since al-Hussayen was indicted two years earlier for running websites promoting violent jihad.[1] His trial had just started and already my roles as a mother, wife, and employer were completely curbed by the process. As a government witness, you don't know when you're going to testify, so for three weeks I made layover-packed flights from DC to Idaho on Sunday evenings, only to fly back on Friday nights. My husband was on an extended work trip at the time, so for the days I was away, my mother watched the kids at home and my brother-in-law drove them between after-school activities. All so I could sit in that room, day after day, waiting for someone to tell me it was my time to testify.

I spent much of my time in this fluorescent-lit purgatory reading through a forum called Ansar al-Mujahideen Network. In those days, it was one of our more valuable intelligence sources: a closed-off forum with only a few hundred members, among whom were top-level al-Qaeda operatives and hardliner militants in Iraq. As I scrolled through the posts that day, one caught my eye. "A message from Abu Musab al-Zarqawi," it read, accompanied by a link to download a video. I clicked.

Zarqawi. The man was a staple of the Bush administration's justification to invade Iraq in 2003—a mysterious al-Qaeda associate from Jordan who was using the war to establish a massive jihadi militant movement across Iraq, Jordan, and Syria.[2] Even those in counterterrorism knew very little of him beyond his role as the leader of a hardcore jihadi faction called Tawhid wal-Jihad ("Monotheism and Jihad") and snippets of his background in a Jordanian prison and al-Qaeda training camps.[3] His was a name surrounded by clouds of rumor.

The video finished downloading and I opened the file.

It began with the title "Abu Musa'b al-Zarqawi slaughters an American." Next, a man in an orange jumpsuit stated to the camera, "My name is Nick Berg, my father's name is Michael, my mother's name is Suzanne. I have a brother and sister, David and Sarah. I live in West Chester . . . near Philadelphia." It then cuts to a shot of Berg sitting in front of five masked militants, with the one in the middle, Zarqawi, calling Muslims to revolt against the United States. A moment later, Zarqawi begins cutting off Berg's head as the others hold him down.

In the dead silence of the witness room, I shrieked.

The federal agents on the other side of the door, whom I knew well by that point, ran in, perhaps thinking an attacker had gotten to one of the prosecution's witnesses. After I explained, they asked to see the video. Judging by their faces moments later, they regretted asking. I had seen plenty of violent combat and execution footage by that point in my career, and I learned how to look at it all without fully taking it in. It's a sort of self-numbing skill that I wouldn't make it through many days without. Still, every so often, something gets around the wall. Or, in the case of this video, breaks through the wall altogether.

The noise of the dull knife, the screaming—it reverberated in my head and haunted me for weeks, in conversations, while I was preparing my testimony, as I was eating. It was there when I closed my eyes too, the visual of this innocent young man forced onto the floor by faceless monsters. I kept bringing myself to near-panic attacks imagining his fear and the sorrow his family must have felt.

But as this spectacle instilled paralyzing horror in people like me, it generated enormous elation in the Global Jihad movement. The reactions were like salt on an open wound. "I swear, you have made us extremely proud," they exclaimed to Zarqawi, praising him for what he accomplished with "his two noble hands."[4] The community started requesting more beheadings. "We propose that you hang the heads of the American infidels on the bridges and roads," wrote one. Others suggested that British hostages be made to watch beheadings of American coprisoners.[5] Jihadists even sought religious advice from a jihadi sheikh on the matter, asking, "Is it permissible to use a saw in slaughtering hostages in order to terrify the Blasphemers?" The cleric responded that a saw might be too dull and thus lack the "compassion" of a religiously permissible beheading. He instead suggested chainsaws. "It can, in one strike, separate the head from the body, which makes it more relieving."[6]

Basking in the hype, Tawhid wal-Jihad released more beheading videos of American, South Korean, Turkish, Egyptian, and British prisoners.[7] Zarqawi eventually picked up the nickname "Emir [Leader] of the Slaughterers."[8] This style of execution even gave way to its own twisted genre, with other factions releasing their own beheading videos to get in on the trend.[9]

The ripple effects of Berg's beheading went far beyond excitement. During the mid-2000s, jihadists called Zarqawi the "Reviver Imam" who brought the fight to the Americans and enemies of Islam. Zarqawi framed his rise in grandiose apocalyptic language: "Behold, the spark has been lit in Iraq and its flames will blaze, Allah willing, until they consume the Armies of the Cross."[10] Osama bin Laden himself, once reluctant to embrace the brutish Zarqawi, saw how popular he had become around the world and eventually brought Tawhid wal-Jihad under the al-Qaeda umbrella, rebranding it as its newest affiliate, al-Qaeda in Iraq (AQI).[11] This branch quickly became what many considered to be the most dangerous terrorist force in those years and eventually evolved into what we now know as ISIS.[12]

The beheading of Berg, just one man among a rising sea of terrorist victims, had become something so much larger than *just* an execution. Rather, it had become a critical chapter in the history of the Global Jihad—the catalyst of a much larger domino effect. Why?

For years, while training different government task forces across the United States, I stressed that Zarqawi could have just shot Berg, but he didn't. He chose the grislier route because the execution was more than simply punishment of an enemy; it was theater. It was a message of intimidation to the American public that was sending its military to fight in Iraq, and an invitation to jihadists around the globe: *Don't wait to act. America might have a powerful military, but we have a fearlessness that they don't.* There was also the element of practicality. Not anyone could put together a plot as complex as the 9/11 attacks, but seeing Zarqawi cut a man's head off? Anyone could do that. All you need is the callous will to do it, and that's exactly what Zarqawi was calling for.

It was consistent with a key lesson Zarqawi preached to his followers: it doesn't matter how many people you killed in an attack, or whether you won a battle; what mattered was how you leveraged it via propaganda. If you lost a battle but inspired many via corresponding propaganda, it was a net positive.

This concept had not escaped terrorists since the term itself came into existence.[13] Anarchists in the nineteenth century exploited newspapers to great effect to exaggerate their power and generate fear in the masses, setting off bombs in areas meant to draw attention to their cause.[14] Anarchist terrorists abided by the philosophy of *propagande par le fait*, meaning *propaganda of the deed*.[15] Like the 2000s jihadi militants of Iraq, they believed that attacks had more value than just the attacks themselves. Assassinations, bombings, and stabbings against political and "ruling class" leaders were leveraged as rhetorical demonstrations, advancing their cause far more than any manifesto or speech could. German American anarchist Johann Most summed up the spirit of this philosophy in an 1885 article, stressing the need for "not only action in and for itself, but also action as propaganda. . . . In order to achieve the desired success in the fullest measure, immediately after the action has been carried out, especially in the town where it took place, posters should be put up setting out the reasons for the action in such a way as to draw from them the best possible benefit."[16]

Zarqawi brought "action as propaganda" into the twenty-first century while giving the jihadi world a brutal terrorist hero, someone to take terrorist violence out of the abstractness of news reports and communiques and throw it right onto the world's computer screens to watch again and again. In the following years, Iraq overflowed with migrant fighters from around the world signing up for suicide operations, in no small part because of the spark Zarqawi lit.[17] ISIS, the descendent of AQI, was only following in his footsteps when it created its notorious movie studio-quality propaganda machine of beheadings, multiangle battle footage, and high-production documentaries.[18] A decade and a half later, in 2019, far-right extremists got their own Zarqawi to come along and light a spark for the movement.

A few short months after Robert Bowers's attack at the Tree of Life Synagogue in Pittsburgh, the world had moved on. Celebrities were entwined in the most massive college admission scam ever taken on by the United States Department of Justice, and Congress was already weeks into a fight with President Trump over his attempt to declare a national emergency to build a wall at the U.S.–Mexico border. The United States joined other nations in grounding the Boeing 737 after two deadly crashes, and HBO had just dropped a new trailer for the final season of *Game of Thrones*. With every news story that emerged, the once-urgent question of how to address the conditions that led to the Pittsburgh massacre got further and further buried—as if it had happened years ago, or never at all.

Pittsburgh fell even further through the cracks as ISIS tore its way back to the top of news headlines. Amid losing the last shred of its territorial caliphate in the Syrian town of Baghuz, the international community was forced into the uncomfortable question of what to do with many of their own citizens, now battle-hardened foreign fighters, sitting in rickety prisons in northern Syria.[19] These individuals became all the less appealing after major ISIS attacks like the December 2018 Strasbourg Christmas Market shooting and stabbing in France and the January 2019 Sulu Church Bombing in the Philippines.[20] The massacres felt like warnings of what such militants might bring back home.

One particularly disturbing terrorist attack in Morocco caught the world's attention. On December 20, 2018, a video emerged of ISIS-pledged men murdering two female hikers from Denmark and Norway, twenty-four-year-old Louisa Vesterager Jespersen and twenty-eight-year-old Maren Ueland, in the Atlas Mountains three days before. The men, armed with knives, sneaked into the girls' tent in the middle of the night and stabbed them as they slept, decapitating them after.[21]

A few weeks before the brutal murder, I had been hiking those very same mountains after providing a training workshop to counterterrorism units in Rabat. "Greetings from the Atlas Mountains," I wrote to my staff with a picture of myself standing before snow-covered mountain peaks and stone houses built into the terrain.

"Wow! Very pretty," my staff replied. "Hell of a view."

I haven't looked at this photo the same way since.

By this point there was no chance of keeping a national conversation centered around Pittsburgh, which was worrisome to me because it wasn't like anything had died down in the far right. To the contrary, the far right's "screw your optics" energy pushed on well into these months. Far-right extremists, often prompted by news of such attacks, espoused adoration for Bowers and called for more attacks like his. Pittsburgh had "awakened the consciousness of the people," the very purpose behind so many terror attacks.[22]

"Bowers did nothing wrong," they wrote. Profile avatars were set to Bowers's picture. His six-word declaration was now a movement-wide mantra slapped on posters and other types of propaganda. A neo-Nazi music creator by the name "Terrorschism" created an electronic track called "I'm Going In" in honor of Bowers. The lyrics read:

> Fuck your optics
> I'm going in
> What do you want?
> What do you need?
> Total Aryan Victory[23]

This energy was spreading across Stormfront, VNN, and Gab, but more so on alternative venues like Discord, a messenger platform for video gamers, and Minds, a social media platform with a similar free-speech stance as Gab. Gaining the most noteworthy traction was 8chan, a free speech-oriented image board that was quickly becoming the new go-to for the "screw your optics" camp of the far right.

Like other chan boards ("chan" being short for "channel"), 8chan facilitated toxicity through the anonymity it granted. On Stormfront, VNN, or Gab users had to register to participate, and could thus be removed or even investigated for problematic posts. An 8chan user, on the other hand, was nothing more than an anonymous ID, with each new thread generating a new ID to start over with. No usernames, no actual identities—just a sea of so-called anons with no sense of accountability or inhibition.

Hitler quotes, Nazi memes, and death threats were nothing new on chan boards, where users often convey such activity as free speech activism (or just plain trolling). Yet it was looking less and less like a joke on 8chan's Politically Incorrect board, commonly referred to as "/pol/." This humor was its own kind of radicalizing element, cloaking extremism in irony and making something as vile as neo-Nazism seem more palatable. These conversations on /pol/ were steered by—and thus tailored to—younger white supremacists and neo-Nazis who were creating a more transgressive, more violence-embracing environment than the old heads on Stormfront.

Throughout that fall and winter and into the early months of 2019, attention on 8chan and the community it housed grew, but it wasn't until mid-March that an act of mass violence brought new demands for accountability.

⸎

By Friday, March 15, 2019, debates over ISIS and what to do with its foreign members were still at the top of the headlines. "France Repatriates Several Orphan Children Who Were Stranded in Syria," read one headline that day.[24] Another read, "Australia Will Not Risk Bringing ISIS Families Back from Syria, Scott Morrison Says."[25]

On the same day, a message was posted to 8chan's /pol/ board, accompanied by an amateurishly drawn cartoon of a man wearing an Australian bush hat. The cartoon face was based on "Australian Shitposter" memes from chan boards, which later came to be associated with an online community of far-right Australian podcasters and social media users known as "The Dingoes."[26] The picture's file name nodded to Bowers: "Screw your optics.jpg." The message read:

> Well lads, it's time to stop shitposting and time to make a real-life effort post.
>
> I will carry out and [sic] attack against the invaders, and will even live stream the attack via facebook.[27]

The anonymous user wrote like someone who had spent a lot of time on 8chan, using the tongue-in-cheek internet jargon typical of the forum:

> It's been a long ride and despite all your rampant faggotry, fecklessness and degeneracy, you are all top blokes and the best bunch of cobbers a man could ask for.
>
> I have provided links to my my [sic] writings below, please do your part by spreading my message, making memes and shitposting as you usually do.
>
> If I don't survive the attack, goodbye, godbless and I will see you all in Valhalla![28]

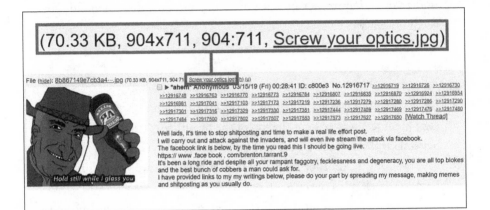

The user gave several links to the referenced document, a rambling eighty-seven-page document titled "The Great Replacement," as well as a link to a Facebook livestream under the account of a twenty-eight-year-old Australian man named Brenton Tarrant. "The facebook link is below," the 8chan post stated. "By the time you read this I should be going live."

Users replied, "Godspeed" and "Best of luck."

"Can't wait to see the news reports," wrote another.[29]

The video stream started just minutes after the message was posted. It opened with a man looking to be in his mid- to late twenties, as Tarrant's Facebook account stated, adjusting a head-mounted camera from the driver's side of a Subaru hatchback. He was wearing tactical gear and camouflage pants with magazines of ammunition strapped to his waist. To his left, in the passenger seat, there were three rifles. The weapons and the magazines were covered in white nationalist slogans.

Following directions from a GPS navigation voice, Tarrant said little as he drove. He arrived minutes later at al-Noor Mosque in the city of Christchurch in New Zealand's South Island. Old-time military field music played from the speaker attached to his chest. Just like Bowers chose the day of the Sabbath, a day when the Tree of Life Synagogue would be packed with services, Tarrant chose Jumu'ah, or Friday Prayer. He parked his car just outside the building. Inside the mosque were two hundred worshippers.

Tarrant, holding a rifle, exited the car and walked around to his trunk where he had gas cannisters and two more rifles with more white nationalist slogans and other messages written on them. "Welcome to Hell," one read. He walked down the sidewalk and toward the building, the drum-rolling field march still playing. At 1:40 p.m., it began.

Tarrant fired his first shots into people standing in the doorway and entered the building. It looked like the video games I've seen my sons play: a first-person view, a rifle turning with the aiming of the camera. He shot into crowds of worshippers as they fell onto the mosque's green carpet. People started running through hallways, panicking. Some piled into corners of the prayer space, pressing frantically into its white walls. But he kept firing, periodically loading new magazines into the rifle as the fallen bodies of those not yet killed groaned in agony. Among these victims was sixteen-year-old Hamza Mustafa, who was praying at al-Noor Mosque with his brother, Zaid, and their father, Khaled. Not seen in the video is Hamza calling his mother, Salwa, telling her Zaid had been shot in the leg. She stayed on the phone with him until she heard a scream. She called for him through the phone, but there was no answer. Hamza died, as did his father Khaled. Zaid survived two gunshot wounds.[30]

Breathing heavily, Tarrant paced out of the building and fired down both directions of the sidewalk. In the alley, the back hatch of his car was still open. He stopped and looked toward a distant end of the parking lot, aimed, and fired. A figure in the distance dropped to the ground. He went back in the mosque, fired into the motionless bodies once more, and exited the building.

As Tarrant headed back to his car, he came across a woman on the sidewalk. He shot her too. She dropped onto the street, her back against the curb.

Ansi Alibava, a twenty-five-year-old from Kerala, India, was pursuing a master's in agricultural engineering. She had just helped a group of women and children escape the building and, in further heroism, was attempting to reenter the mosque to find her husband.

"Help me," she screamed in anguish. Tarrant walked over to her and fired two more shots, the second hitting her head. Her screaming abruptly stopped. Back at his car, Tarrant closed the trunk and got in to drive away. As he put the car in motion, he ran over her body.

"Did not go as planned," Tarrant chuckled as he drove. He fired at several more people on his ride to the Linwood Islamic Center three miles away. The video cut out before he got there at 1:52 p.m., but reports state that he was unable to find the entrance to the building and began firing in through a window.[31] Seven were killed among the one hundred or so worshippers.[32] One attendant, Mohammed Afroze, saw his former housemate killed in front of him. Tarrant had "just started firing everywhere," he later told *Stuff*, describing the horror surging through the room:

> The bullets are not touching me. From the backside people are coming and they all die. The bodies are pushing me to go outside. I can't do anything. I just try to escape, escape, escape. Because we don't know what's going on. The shooting. Small people are dying, small babies, old people. Some people injured want to go out but they can't. They are still shooting the dead bodies. Some people are alive because the dead bodies are covering them up.[33]

By the end of the day, Tarrant killed 51 people and injured 50 more (one of whom eventually died in a hospital) before being arrested. The victims ranged from three to 77 years old.[34]

There's a picture of Hamza online. He's in a boat, holding up a fishing rod and a fish. Behind him is turquoise water and a clear sky. "Everyone loved Hamza," Salwa told *Stuff*. "Very caring, very polite. Everything good that you can imagine in this world was in my Hamza." These were the enemies Tarrant chose: a skinny, thick-haired high school kid with a heart-meltingly innocent smile; a newly married young woman described as "a very bubbly, loveable person."[35]

But to Tarrant, Hamza and Alibava were props in a theatrical production. And in Tarrant, the anti-optics camp finally got their own sadistic performer for the cause. Just as Zarqawi and others tapped into the brutal psyche of his movement, so did Tarrant for his far-right brethren.

—— ✺ ——

Alibava's plea for help was etched into my brain the instant it came through my speakers. I imagined myself laying right where she had, feeling what she did. I wasn't the only one rattled. Across the open space at our main office in the DC metro area, my staff members were glued to their computer screens with tense composure. I could tell who among them had been watching the livestream. They avoided eye contact except for brief instances. No words needed, no words available. Inside, we all wanted to sink into our chairs and mourn that Friday—but as always in similar circumstances, we couldn't. We had to continue monitoring the reactions on far-right venues. And those outpouring with celebration the likes of which we had never seen before.

Tarrant's value to the far right went far beyond the bodies he brought to the floor. After all, two years earlier, in January of 2017, a far-right terrorist named Alexandre Bissonnette had carried out a similar attack when he shot Muslim worshippers during evening prayers in Quebec, killing six and injuring nineteen.[36] Tarrant even wrote Bissonnette's name on one of his rifles used in the attack. But if you brought up Bissonnette to one of the white nationalist inhabitants of 8chan, they might not know who he was. Tarrant, however, delivered an entire package to his movement: a manifesto, a meticulously planned and trained-for operation, and most of all, the video. Tarrant's livestream was perfectly tailored to his video-game-loving audience. It was like a first-person shooter video game, even like a virtual reality experience. Viewers could see everything from his perspective, imagining what it was like to do what he did.

Keeping up with the aftermath of Christchurch at our offices was like trying to dam a waterfall. "At this point, it's not about finding it all, but just taking as much as you can get," said one of my analysts. "This stuff is coming from too many platforms. We need more people, there's no way around it."

He wasn't wrong. In my entire career tracking terrorists and their propaganda, I've seen very few celebration campaigns so prolific and persistent as that of the far right after the Christchurch massacre. "If you compared it to jihadist attacks, it was like the 9/11 of far-right terrorists," I stated, and was quoted in various news outlets.[37] Of course, the scale of the attack doesn't compare, but so many other elements did: the shock of the global community, the intelligence communities unprepared for it, and, above all else, the way it breathed new life into a terrorist movement.

You could see it in the artwork they were disseminating like wildfire. Posters depicted Tarrant as Jesus Christ surrounded by an aura of bullets, holding his rifle and manifesto in one hand and medallions bearing far-right icons in the other. Others placed his face into World War II–era pro-Allies propaganda reading, "This man is your FRIEND. He fights for freedom." Perhaps the most profound of these posters were those placing pictures of Tarrant alongside the text of Bowers's "screw your optics" mantra—the new creed of far-right terror next to its new master executor. Tarrant was a religious figure, a soldier figure, and an ideological figure all wrapped into one persona. One face, pasted across a never-ending outpouring of propaganda.

Tarrant's manifesto saw the same level of attention. Supporters translated it into French, Bulgarian, Ukrainian, Swedish, German, Russian, Romanian, Portuguese, and beyond. One white nationalist vlogger gave a two-hour reading of the document.

But despite the attention it got, Tarrant's manifesto wasn't some high-minded work of white supremacist literature, nor did it need to be. All his supporters wanted was the rhetorical red meat, which Tarrant delivered plenty of. The document is littered with the jargon and talking points spouted daily across far-right discussion boards, blogs, and social media accounts: "We are experiencing an invasion on a level never seen before in history . . . Invited by the state and corporate entities to replace the White people who have failed to reproduce."[38] Not long into it, the document starts to read like a paraphrased version of Norway attacker

FIGURE 3.2 Far-right poster of Brenton Tarrant with halo of bullets surrounding his head

Anders Breivik's manifesto, whom Tarrant claimed to be his "true inspiration": obsession with fertility rates, replacement of whites, the Christian West versus Muslim invaders narrative, and so on.[39]

But as Tarrant made clear, it was ISIS that served as the catalyst of his radicalization. On the eighth page of his manifesto, he wrote a

FIGURE 3.3 Religious-styled poster created in praise of Brenton Tarrant

self-posed question: "Was there a particular event or reason you decided to commit to a violent attack?"[40] He answers with three events, the first of which being the most emotionally charged. It was the April 2017 Stockholm truck attack, in which an ISIS-pledged thirty-nine-year-old man from Uzbekistan plowed a hijacked truck through pedestrians, killing five and injuring many others. Tarrant acknowledges that he had read of plenty of ISIS attacks across the West at this point, but the one in Stockholm tapped into something deeper. "That difference was

MAR 15, 2019, 7:38:15 AM

screw your optics

FIGURE 3.4 Still image from Brenton Tarrant's attack livestream with Robert Bowers's "screw your optics" quote inserted, posted to the Minds social media platform

Ebba Akerlund," he wrote, referring to one of the killed victims of the attack, an eleven-year-old girl. He wrote of her:

> Young, innocent and dead Ebba. Ebba was walking to meet her mother after school, when she was murdered by an Islamic attacker, driving a stolen vehicle through the shopping promenade on which she was walking. Ebba was partially deaf, unable to hear the attacker coming.
>
> Ebba death at the hands of the invaders, the indignity of her violent demise and my inability to stop it broke through my own jaded cynicism like a sledgehammer.
>
> I could no longer ignore the attacks. They were attacks on my people, attacks on my culture, attacks on my faith and attacks on my soul. They would not be ignored.[41]

FIGURE 3.5 Cartoon face styled similarly to the one posted by Brenton Tarrant on 8chan, containing an altered version of Robert Bowers's "screw your optics" declaration

His other two radicalizing events followed the same theme: the 2017 French general election, which saw the victory of the perceivably pro-immigrant Emmanuel Macron, and Tarrant's trip through immigrant-populated French cities and towns, which he saw as the disastrous result of such status-quo politicians.[42] To Tarrant, all three events were microcosms of the same problem: a hostile Muslim invasion, most severely in the form of ISIS, and leaders' lack of willingness to do anything about it. The politicians had failed, legal systems had failed, civility had failed.

"It was there I decided to do something, it was there I decided to take action, to commit to force. To commit to violence," he stated.[43]

It might seem maddeningly ironic that Tarrant, after expressing such heartbreak for eleven-year-old Ebba's murder by an ISIS-inspired killer, could bring the same suffering onto equally innocent young people like Hamza and Alibava through his own terrorist attack. It might also seem absurd that Tarrant and his supporters are telling the same exact historical narratives of ISIS and al-Qaeda, often down to the same terminology: the Crusades, invasions, Constantinople, the Ottoman Empire, Europe versus West, Islam versus Christianity. I don't see these overlaps as ironic or absurd; rather, they are something more systemic.

Would Tarrant have carried out a terrorist attack if ISIS didn't exist? If the organization that inspired the attack that killed eleven-year-old Ebba was never in the picture, would Tarrant have merely found another reason to "commit to violence," as he put it? Or would he have taken a different route, perhaps nonviolent activism with anti-immigration organizations or nonviolent corners of the alt-right?

No one, not even Tarrant himself, can answer the question with certainty. But it is abundantly evident that of all the variables that led to Tarrant's Christchurch massacre, ISIS was the one fueling his convictions. Ebba could be seen in pictures, smiling innocently with rosy cheeks and strawberry blonde hair. It's not hard to imagine what Tarrant felt and thought as he sifted through stories about her and other victims. How could her killing—in which a rejected Uzbek asylum-seeker ran her and others over with a truck—not be the result of some existential, civilizational crisis? How are we not at war? How are we not being invaded? What else works except violence?

Yet ironically, in carrying out his attack, Tarrant bit ISIS's bait, which was laid out for him and fellow Westerners in the group's aimless acts of violence.

That isn't to say that terrorist attacks are never strategically directed. The March 2004 Madrid train bombings, for example, killed 193 people just three days before the country's general elections.[44] The Spanish public was already wary of its government's participation in the Iraq War, and the bombings were seen by many as a result of that involvement. Despite a hazy outlook of who was behind the attack, just a couple of months later the newly empowered Spanish Socialist Workers' Party brought Spanish troops home from Iraq, a development many consider as a direct consequence of the bombings.[45] But what strategic benefit did ISIS get from killing an eleven-year-old in the streets—or bombing an Ariana Grande concert in Manchester in 2017 or an Eagles of Death Metal concert in Paris in 2015? Only more airstrikes by anti-ISIS coalition countries and more persecution of Muslims.

But that is exactly what ISIS wanted.

For all its claims of defending the oppressed Muslims in *Darul Kufr* (meaning "Lands of Disbelief"), ISIS intentionally works to render them unsafe. Peace and harmony between Muslims and non-Muslims, after all, would make the very existence of a group like ISIS pointless. ISIS's game is rather to manufacture the tension that translates to recruitment and, ultimately, power. By outraging an entire population with the murder of a girl like Ebba, the group drives a wedge between Muslims and non-Muslims, giving way to hate crimes and hardliner anti-Muslim politicians, and further feeding the group's argument that the West hates Islam.

In some instances, ISIS will even land someone as helpful as Tarrant. Jihadi propagandists bend every single Western-related event to fit the narrative of a Crusader agenda against Muslims. The assassination of a jihadi leader in Syria? Part of their Crusade. Arrest of an ISIS propagandist in the United States? Proof that you can't safely be a Muslim in the West. Every element of Western society and policy is in some way or another the continuation of a centuries-old war between the true Muslim believers and "idol-worshipping" Christians. That said, after seeing Tarrant's massacre in New Zealand—the bodies of innocent Muslims on the ground, the sound of Alibava's cries for help, the Islamophobic writing on Tarrant's guns and references to the Crusades—the jihadi propagandists' job just got a lot easier.

"In a sense, the Christchurch attacker has done a giant favor for the Global Jihadist movement," I was quoted as saying in the *Washington Post*. "And no one should be surprised when this attack is still a staple of jihadi propaganda and justifications for threats and incitements 10 years from now."[46]

This interconnectedness is one of the reasons I don't keep my far-right and jihadi analysts siloed. As attacks like Christchurch show, a member of ISIS and a member of a neo-Nazi paramilitary organization are two sides of the same coin. I need jihad analysts with a working knowledge of white genocide theory, and far-right analysts who can tell me what *baqiya wa-tatamaddad* means (it's ISIS's slogan, meaning "remaining and expanding"). Having a staff with multiple angles of expertise helps not just with the crossover between these terrorist movements, but also during times when one department is overrun with work and needs extra help.

In the aftermath of the Christchurch massacre, neither part of my organization had any time to spare; online jihadi forums, channels, and chat groups were overflowing with demands for Muslims to carry out retaliatory attacks. They suggested attacking Christians "during their Saturdays and Sunday prayers."[47] Posters demanded the same, with one from the ISIS community showing a fighter inside of a church, accompanied by text reading, "You are the only wolf to avenge the blood . . . You alone wolf of the Muslims who are lying everywhere."[48]

Looking at all the propaganda, it was as if the far right and jihadi movement were having a dialogue, almost as if they were trying to outdo one another. One image distributed by jihadists showed a trash bag fashioned as an improvised explosive device (IED), bearing the date March 15, 2019 (the day of Tarrant's attack). Beside it was a rifle modeled after Tarrant's, covered in its own inscription: "We will return the ball (the round) to you soon . . . No immunity for anyone, the response is coming . . . Be Patient New Zealand, the days are shorter until the wounds and punishment come."[49]

Even the highest leadership rungs of ISIS and al-Qaeda responded with calls for revenge. ISIS's spokesman exclaimed, "Let the scene of killing in the two mosques be enough to awaken the supporters of the Khilafah [Caliphate] residing there, to seek vengeance."[50] Al-Qaeda Central and its affiliates called for the same the following week, characterizing Tarrant as emblematic of the West's inherent hatred of Islam. "The only thing new is its documentation through a livestream," an al-Qaeda Central message exclaimed.[51]

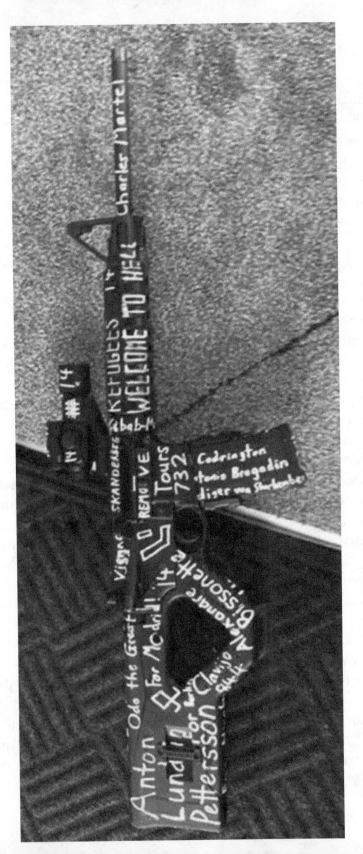

FIGURE 3.6 Rifle used in Brenton Tarrant's Christchurch massacre

FIGURE 3.7 Image distributed by ISIS supporters online, styled after Brenton Tarrant's writing-covered rifle and threatening retaliation for his massacre

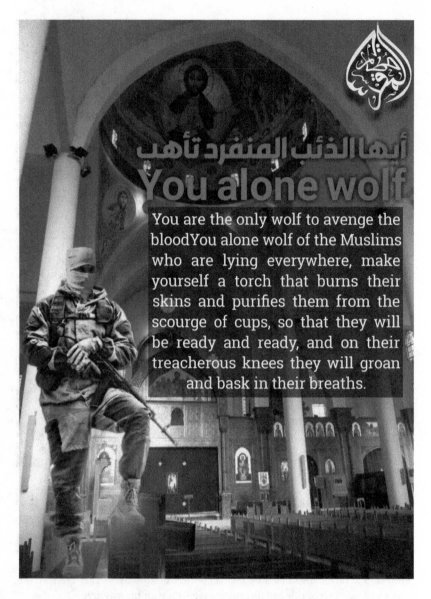

FIGURE 3.8 Image produced by the ISIS-linked Hutam al-Mathdasi media group

It's all about opportunism. Had those Muslims worshipping that Friday in Christchurch not been killed by Tarrant, they would have remained exactly what every ISIS fatwa and propaganda release said they were: apostates, enemies, fake Muslims paying taxes to aid the war against ISIS's caliphate. It wasn't until after that day that they conveniently became Muslims again in ISIS's eyes.

You could see the same opportunism in the far right after the murder of Louisa Vesterager Jespersen and Maren Ueland in Morocco. In the video of their attack, the men kneel above the two women's bodies in the tent, hacking at one of their necks with a large knife until her head is completely removed. The horrific visual was instant ammunition for white supremacists on sites like Gab—the same ones who would otherwise consider these young women race-traitor liberals for daring to visit North Africa in the first place.

"There Are No good Muslims," wrote one user. "Until we ALL understand, that they will continue preparing to overtake the U.S."[52]

Another wrote, "There is a race war coming, prepare and train now."[53]

This back-and-forth dynamic between jihadists and the far right often goes underlooked, because these movements have historically done a good job at hiding their opportunism behind ideological, pseudo-moral veils. But despite what white nationalist terrorists and jihadi terrorists espouse, the enmity between them is not a zero-sum game; it's a symbiosis that others have called "cumulative extremism" or "reciprocal radicalization" in various contexts.[54] As I wrote in *The Daily Beast* five days after Tarrant's attack, "For these violent groups and communities, such tragedies [as Christchurch] are mutually beneficial events."[55] Each side gets to either revel in the event or capitalize on it to justify their cause, depending which way the pendulum swings. And as neo-Nazis and white nationalists cheered in the aftermath of the Christchurch massacre, it was the jihadists' turn to demand revenge.

But after the Christchurch massacre, far-right terrorists finally dropped their charades about strategies and endgames. Now, the name of the game was to attack anywhere and everywhere.

—❦—

If killing fifty-one innocent worshippers made a small dent on Muslim populations in the West or even scared some Muslims from coming to a place like New Zealand, that was all fine and well to Tarrant, because this wasn't the main objective at hand. Just as Tarrant bit ISIS's bait, he was offering his own. There was a critical part of Tarrant's manifesto that the far right was clinging to, in which he asked himself, "Why did you carry out the attack?" He answered:

> To incite violence, retaliation and further divide between the European people and the invaders currently occupying European soil . . . To agitate the political enemies of my people into action, to cause them to overextend their own hand and experience the eventual and inevitable backlash as a result. To incite violence, retaliation and further divide between the European people and the invaders currently occupying European soil.[56]

Here, Tarrant is applying the essence of Bowers's "screw your optics, I'm going in" sentiment to a longstanding political methodology called accelerationism. In the context of recent far-right movements, accelerationism refers to the goal of generating chaos toward societal collapse that would bring forth a fascist state. Thus, when extremists look to accelerate their movements in this regard, they believe they must first agitate or even empower their enemies.

Tarrant's appeal to accelerationism applied a façade of purpose to far-right terrorism. Now more than ever, accelerationism had become the one-word justification for the aimless violence extremists rallied around. Users shared posters by groups like "The Base," a neo-Nazi paramilitary organization, which exclaimed, "Accelerationism is our weapon," while others portrayed Tarrant as the face of this strategy. "Accelerationist Now," one graphic of Tarrant read, pulling from the famous *Apocalypse Now* film poster. An article on the neo-Nazi *Roper Report* blog gloated that Tarrant had silenced the "shrieks" of the far right's optics camp, concluding with certainty that "accelerationism works."[57]

With these accelerationist rally cries picking up steam among far-right extremists, they started expounding on Tarrant's proposals and

FIGURE 3.9 Image praising Brenton Tarrant as an accelerationist, styled after the movie *Apocalypse Now*

coming up with their own likeminded ideas. Among the most popular targets of agitation was, to no surprise, Muslims. One user on 8chan's /pol/ board suggested that anyone "too afraid of killing Muslims" should learn how to make bombs and blow up mosques to agitate Muslim communities, thus pushing them toward militant jihad: "If we want to truly accelerate, we must also radicalize the Muslims that hide their Jihad level like we hide our power levels . . . The 'peaceful' Muslims will feel as if they are not safe, and therefore directly fight for our lands and their safety."[58]

FIGURE 3.10 Poster praising Brenton Tarrant as an agent of acceleration

An agenda doesn't get any more naked than when white supremacists openly call to push Muslims toward radical jihad. It shows not just the reciprocal relationship between jihadists and the far right, but also the nature of terrorism itself. Despite whatever ethno-states or Shariah-ruled utopias they describe, there is no peaceful end for either side. Figures like Bin Laden and Zarqawi haven't brought the rise of any legitimate caliphate. They merely sparked brutal, chaotic wars across multiple continents and decades with no end in sight. All the same, Tarrant didn't get the far right closer toward any actual end; what he did was quicken the spin of a wheel with no direction. And seeing what happened after Zarqawi's killing of Berg, we should have known how quickly that wheel would begin turning.

⸙

Though Tarrant is now behind bars for what will likely be the rest of his life, he leaves behind a legacy that will haunt us for a long time. Bowers's six-word middle finger to the status quo of a movement, "screw your optics, I'm going in," was now given the veneer of intellectual validity in Tarrant's accelerationist vision. Less than two weeks after the Christchurch attack, white supremacists and neo-Nazis were already pondering ways to mirror Tarrant's massacre. One user on 8chan wrote:

1. get a gopro
2. get a gun
3. SOLVE THE PROBLEM[59]

Another user gave the address and hours of operation of a Tennessee mosque. "Make Brenton Proud," the user wrote. "Stop shitposting and go fucking do something! See you there."[60]

Within the same day, users in another thread even suggested which head-mounted cameras would work best for livestreaming an attack. One user wrote, "Since brenton already used go pro, maybe u use glasses, so we can compare the quality."[61]

"Why not both?" another user responded before referencing *Minecraft*, a popular video game that far-right users name alongside attack incitements, plots, or other incriminating activity to, as they see it, diminish their culpability:

Link them up to seperate accounts/servers for upload and maybe one on "delay" so if they cut off your "Minecraft" livestream we still

have goodies to unlock and the creepers that go boom don't run interception somehow.[62]

The "screw your optics" current was becoming more brutal and callous. Attack incitements and death threats were piling in every week and
calls to follow in Tarrant's footsteps had become the dominant focus of
the community. As it all played out, there was an unspoken question
among my staff: How long until someone else took up the call?

4

THE MAKING OF A TERRORIST

At fourteen, John Earnest was considered a highly competent piano player. Focused and calm atop of the keys, he whizzed through Chopin's *Fantaisie-Impromptu*, a challenging piece technically and musically. Earnest navigated the emotional spectrum of the piece fluidly, his face showing no signs of strain.

Earnest honed his talents as the years went on, dazzling his fellow classmates at Mt. Carmel High School's annual talent show.[1] In school, where his father was a well-liked teacher, Earnest was known just as much for his wit and athleticism as for his musicianship, keeping up great grades in AP coursework while making the varsity swimming team. He was quiet, but not timid. When asked, he voiced his political views with confidence. His classmates understood his stances as Christian and conservative, but detected nothing indicative of a future murderer.[2]

After high school, Earnest decided to pursue a career in saving lives and enrolled at California State University San Marcos as a nursing student. His studies were going well. He even made the Dean's List.[3] On his Facebook, he looked like most other college kids with an active social life. In one photo, he is surrounded by young men and women apparently of his age, seated around an outdoor table at a grille just across the street from the university's soccer field. His companions are all of different ethnicities, unaware of what that diversity meant to him. Beside them, his thoughts remained hidden behind a calm, solemn disposition.

Saturday morning, April 27, 2019, a week after the photo was posted to Earnest's Facebook, a message was posted to 8chan's /pol/ forum. It was chillingly similar to Christchurch attacker Brenton Tarrant's post to that platform just over a month earlier: "It's been real dudes . . . From the bottom of my heart thank you for everything . . . It's been an honor. Livestream link is below as well as my open letter."[4]

The Facebook livestream link the user provided wasn't coming through, but the hyperlinked document was. It stated, "My name is John Earnest and I am a man of European ancestry. I'd rather die in glory or spend the rest of my life in prison than waste away knowing that I did nothing to stop this evil . . . I sacrifice this for the sake of my people. OUR people. I would die a thousand times over to prevent the doomed fate that the Jews have planned for my race."[5]

By the time the first eyes were on his manifesto, Earnest was already on his way to carry out his mission.

At the Chabad Synagogue in Poway, California, fifty-seven-year-old Yisroel Goldstein, the rabbi and founder of the congregation, was speaking with sixty-year-old Lori Gilbert Kaye, a congregant and close friend of his. It was just after 11 a.m. on the last day of Passover, which is reserved for remembrance prayer called Yizkor. Kaye wanted to make the prayer on behalf of her late mother and asked when the service would begin. Goldstein told her 11:30. It was the last exchange they would ever share.[6]

Goldstein walked into his office and then across the lobby toward the Sanctuary, the large room where the synagogue's religious services are held. That was when he heard the first shots. He turned around to see John Earnest, who he had never seen before, with an AR-15 and rounds of ammunition strapped to his chest. He had just shot Kaye and was now aiming the gun toward Goldstein. As Earnest raised the barrel, Goldstein heard the voices of children in the banquet hall and a play area right outside of it. He ran for them, but not before Earnest shot at him, hitting him in the hand.[7]

Congregants began fleeing the building as Earnest fired rounds into the sanctuary and banquet hall. It was chaos: adults crawling across floors, looking for their children and a safe way out of the building.[8]

Earnest soon depleted his first clip and clumsily tried to reload another magazine into his assault rifle. Some in the congregation noticed and began to approach him. Earnest abandoned his gun and ran. They chased him to his Honda Civic, but he managed to drive off just before they got a hold of him.[9] In the car, Earnest called 911 and told the operators what he did. "I just shot up a synagogue. I'm just trying to defend my nation from the Jewish people . . . They're destroying our people . . . I opened fire at a synagogue. I think I killed some people."[10]

Earnest's attack killed one person, Kaye, and injured three others. Among them was an eight-year-old named Noya Dahan, who suffered wounds to her face and leg. "I don't even have any words for it," Noya said to CNN after the attack, showing where she had been injured. "It was terrifying, scary."[11]

It was heartbreaking to see Noya speak so calmly about such a traumatic event, but violence was something she had known all her life. Her family moved to the United States in 2014 from Sderot, a town in Israel bordering the Gaza Strip, where bomb shelters and warning sirens of Hamas rocket attacks are a part of one's everyday life. Noya's father, Israel Dahan, describes their life in Sderot as "sleeping in a locked bedroom with knives and with baseball pole."[12] He met Rabbi Goldstein in Israel. Goldstein encouraged him to take his family to California to join his congregation. It seemed like a promise of peace.[13]

But less than a year into their new lives in the United States, the power in their house went out. When Israel went outside to check the powerlines, he saw swastikas spray painted on top of his truck and on his garage door.

"In Jewish history, [swastikas] mean someone wants to kill us," he told the media in the aftermath of the vandalization.[14]

Now, after the Poway synagogue shooting, Israel spoke once more to news reporters with a kind of cynicism one can't blame him for having. "I might need to run again and I need to prepare myself for the next run," he said.[15] "It is horrible, yeah, but that's the way we live."[16]

He said this in the United States. In the year 2019.

Noya is alive. But like her parents, she is no less harmed by what Earnest did at their synagogue. What could be more tragic than fleeing the

dangers of a border town like Sderot only to find hate and danger waiting for them on the other side of the world, in a different form? What
does that do to one's capacity for hope? What can the Dahans tell their
daughter?

⟋⟍⟋⟍

A jolt ran down my spine when we found Earnest's posting on 8chan,
just as news of the attack was breaking. The police hadn't yet released
Earnest's name, but its appearance in the manifesto gave us a head start
to run through person searches. Yet the more we found of him online,
the more skeptical I became. When we found a young kid by that name
playing piano in a video from years before, it seemed nothing like a person who would shoot up a synagogue. I told my staff to hold off using
his name in any of our reporting until we got solid confirmation of the
attacker's identity. Even as it was all adding up—the name, the age, the
location, the mention of Chopin in the manifesto and the video of him
playing the piano—a part of me still couldn't believe it.

My doubts only increased as I read more of the manifesto, which was
one of the most disturbing views into a brainwashed mind I had ever
seen. Earnest expressed his ideas with the same acidic confidence as a
Taliban member whose entire life had been spent in a madrassa (Islamic
religious school) in Afghanistan. He wrote, "Every Jew is responsible for
the meticulously planned genocide of the European race. They act as a
unit, and every Jew plays his part to enslave the other races around him—
whether consciously or subconsciously. Their crimes are endless."[17]

The police eventually confirmed it: Earnest was our guy.

I wasn't alone in my astonishment. Even those who knew Earnest
expressed disbelief when they saw the news. "He always hung out in his
classroom, came to see him at lunch," one former classmate said.[18] "He
always seemed like a nice guy . . . He didn't seem like the type of person
who would go off the deep end."[19]

Earnest's parents issued a statement after his attack, writing, "To our
great shame, he is now part of the history of evil that has been perpe-
trated on Jewish people for centuries . . . Our son's actions were informed
by people we do not know, and ideas we do not hold."[20]

And as shocked as I was, I was also somewhat disappointed with myself. In refusing to believe the mounting evidence we were finding linking the piano-playing kid to the attack, I had succumbed to the same false "vulnerable recruit" narrative that I'd been railing against for years—the one that characterizes terrorists as mentally ill, impoverished, or in some way or another oppressed in blanket fashion. But the reality is that there is no terrorist "type."[21] A young Dean's List college student from a loving family is just as vulnerable to radicalization as any troubled, underachieving kid down the block. Earnest acknowledges the innocent-kid-turned-terrorist trope to his story: "I'm a 19 year old nursing student from the depths of Commiefornia for fuck's sake. I had my whole life ahead of me."[22]

The young man knew he was smart. He knew he would shock people. Knowing these things seemed to be both a point of anguish and pride for Earnest, adding an element of arrogance to his logic: in carrying out his attack, he was a martyr, giving something so much more to the cause than other, more expendable individuals who have or would have done the same.

Earnest's case is a reminder that not all extremists are terrorists, and, more relevantly, that not all terrorist *supporters* are terrorist *actors*.[23] A person can hold extremist views and not necessarily want to commit violence.[24] In this regard, someone like Earnest is an anomaly among the sea of other hateful, Robert Bowers–adoring neo-Nazis who think like he did but will not actually shoot up a synagogue. In reading through terrorist actors' writings and life stories over the last two decades, I've found that they are often triggered by a specific event or series of events—sparks made to their radical views that bring them to *do* something about what they believe in. These can be personal events, perhaps the death of a friend or separation from a partner. Other triggering events come in the form of globally impacting stories: reports of government torture programs, genocides carried out by horrid government regimes. Some events are so large, so embedded with meaning that they spark action across extremist movements like an electric current through a lake.

For a long time, the Syrian Civil War was the major catalytic event that triggered jihadists' step across this threshold. In a few quick years after it started in 2011, the conflict devolved into the central stage of the Global Jihad movement. Jihadists saw it as a new iteration of the same holy war Osama bin Laden fought decades before in Afghanistan against the Russians.[25] As one young British law student described a year after migrating to Syria's battlefronts, he'd always held jihadi views, but as the Syrian Civil War raged on in another continent, it gave him an impulse that he couldn't get rid of: "When the syrian revolution quickly turn into Jihad, my mind went into overdrive with thoughts of fighting in the way of Allah."[26]

Years after the Syrian Civil War started, ISIS used it as a foundation to create its own triggering event: the establishment of its caliphate. Hypnotized by this newly announced capital-S "State" and the God-ordered duty to defend it, ISIS supporters threw their lives away to attack universities, store-lined streets, running trails, Christmas markets, office buildings, night clubs, and trains. They used knives, guns, bombs, and vehicles. Everyone everywhere was a target. Some of these newly engaged terrorist actors were already ticking time bombs: sons and daughters raised in the doctrine of their radical parents, felons who met terrorist recruiters in prison, or twisted minds long prone to sadistic behaviors. Others, however, had immense potential for bright futures: academically driven college students, socially active young people, beloved sons and daughters.

Far-right terrorists often pointed to their own triggering events. Tarrant wrote that before the killing of the eleven-year-old Ebba Akerlund in an ISIS-inspired attack, he never thought he'd carry out an attack himself. But after that day something snapped, and he embraced violence: "For some reason this was different . . . Something that had been a part of my life for as long as I could remember, cynicism in the face of attacks on the West by islamic invaders, was suddenly no longer there."[27]

The same went for Bowers. For years, he indulged in right-wing radio conspiracy theories about the United Nations and other topics, but never intended to murder eleven people as he did at the Squirrel Hill synagogue.[28] It seems it wasn't until the constant stream of Gab postings about migration crises and the Jews orchestrating it that he finally singled out the Hebrew Immigrant Aid Society.

What was Earnest's trigger? What brought him to cross the line from wishing someone harm to actually dealing them harm? All signs pointed toward "screw your optics."

———— ⬯ ————

If you walked through our main offices at SITE in the early spring of 2019, things might not have looked much different than they had in the months and years prior. The sound of clicking and typing coming from different corners of the main space, intermittent chuckles from staff members instant messaging one another, people talking about their weekend plans in the kitchen. It was only a partial state of normality, though. For many at SITE, particularly those in our far-right department, what couldn't have conceivably gotten any busier did indeed get so much worse. With the shadow of Robert Bowers's Pittsburgh massacre still looming, Brenton Tarrant's attack sent things into overdrive.

The work of tracking far-right terrorists had become an unavoidable confrontation with the man the far right adoringly referred to as "Saint Tarrant," the ultimate embodiment of Bowers's "screw your optics" mantra. They spread footage from his livestream, mocked his victims, and promised more violence against researchers like us and whoever else might be looking into their online lairs.

As much as I hate to grant these sycophants any satisfaction, their callousness and relentless sadism was affecting us. Barry, the head of our far-right department, was feeling it harder than anyone else. He had joined us a few years earlier when the former department head was leaving for a career in the FBI. We all came to love Barry, who brought a far less institutional energy to our far-right department. He wore beanies in the middle of the summer and almost all of his t-shirts referenced a video game, philosopher, or other nerd-friendly matter. Most importantly, though, he was a product of the internet's niche corners—chan boards, obscure blogs, gamer communities—which made him immensely good at tracking and understanding this new internet-hip generation of far-right extremists.

Up until the spring of 2019, Barry had never experienced any ill effects from the job. He came in early every day, poured his coffee in the kitchen, put on his oversized headphones, and scanned far-right websites and discussion boards for something worth reporting on. But after Bowers's attack, far-right extremists' invigorated "screw your optics" energy changed the landscape. Now with a Brenton Tarrant figure to latch onto, the far right radiated a new level of sadism.

Barry started coming into my office and those of his colleagues more often, pulling down on his beanie or nervously running his hand through his messy hair. "I don't know what to do with this one," he'd say, pointing toward whatever it was that day, or even that hour: a death threat, embrace of sexually assaulting women, calls for the murder of rabbis and burning synagogues. Other times he was quiet at his desk, disconnected. I kept asking him if he was alright, but he'd just shrug and tell me he was fine. I pressed on until one day, toward the end of April, he asked, "Can we talk in private?" I obliged. As we walked into my office, he shut the door behind him. He was leaving SITE, he told me.

"I've been having nightmares," Barry said. "It's all doing something to my brain and I can't figure out how to turn the loop off."

I nodded and thought back to my first time seeing the Zarqawi-Berg video and all the maddening glee that followed from the Global Jihad community. I knew where his mind was. He had spent the last six months since Bowers's attack ingesting the same demoralizing feed for hours every day. As one might expect, it started following him home.

Still, this was the same Barry who had already seen so many repulsive things that come with the job. In his earlier days with us, he reported on the Shabaab al-Mujahideen movement, arguably al-Qaeda's most brutal affiliate. He had seen grisly ISIS execution videos where the gazes of prisoners pierce at you through the screen in those last moments before they are savagely beheaded, drowned, shot by a brainwashed child, or set on fire. But this new energy coming out of the far right was something else entirely, something far more acidic. I tried to find some way to help him: more staff to assist him; two weeks' vacation, a month, as long as he needed. But he had made up his mind, and I stopped trying to steer him back. This new far-right current had become disturbingly capable of harming my staff, and I wasn't going to keep anybody here who couldn't handle it.

We ironed out plans for the timeline of his leave and the new, larger staff he'd be training up until then. But we both knew that what was infecting his well-being wasn't going away anytime soon. The far right's celebration of Tarrant's massacre raged on, all day, every day.

When an onslaught of propaganda and chatter can make a person so distressed that they quit their job, it shows a special kind of power. But that same power can have different effects on different people; it just depends on where you stand. The memes, chatter, and media that haunted me and my staff had an opposite effect on those inside the machine. It emboldened them. It primed them for any triggering event that might launch them out of a picture-perfect Southern California life and into action.

Earnest was able to keep his ideas separate from the rest of his life until the months leading up to the attack. He maintained good grades and enrolled in college toward a career in helping heal people as a nurse, with no plan in sight to gun down innocents in a place of worship.

"I've only been lurking for a year and a half, yet what I've learned here is priceless," Earnest wrote on 8chan when posting his manifesto, indicating he had been on the platform since his senior year of high school.[29] That would mean that when Bowers carried out his attack in Pittsburgh, Earnest had already been a regular reader of 8chan for more than a year. And when Bowers's attack sparked that widespread embrace of terrorism across the far right, Earnest was ready for it. He didn't need to be convinced of why he needed to be like Bowers and "fight back"; he was already crystalized in the same radioactive air that afflicted Barry and my other staff members. Thus, when the shooting in Pittsburgh occurred, Earnest's same feeling of all-or-nothing obligation was awoken.

It doesn't take much to see how important Bowers was to Earnest: his name was referenced five times in Earnest's relatively brief 4,000-word manifesto. Earnest even lists him alongside Adolf Hitler as an inspiration.[30]

"FIGHT BACK, REMEMBER ROBERT BOWERS," he wrote.[31]

Bowers's fingerprints were also all over Earnest's conspiratorial-minded obsession with Jews. Just as Bowers wrote about the "filthy vile degenerate Jews" and how he "can't sit by and watch [his] people get slaughtered," Earnest wrote, "the Jew—with his genocidal instincts—is insistent on poking the bear until it tears his head off. The Jew has forced our hand, and our response is completely justified."[32]

Seeing these mirroring anti-Semitic beliefs, a line from Earnest's manifesto takes on new meaning: "If you told me even 6 months ago that I would do this I would have been surprised."[33] I didn't think much about it the first few times I read that "six months" part, but Earnest carried his attack out on April 27, 2019; Robert Bowers's Pittsburgh attack took place on October 27, 2018, exactly six months prior to the day.

Different catalysts played different driving roles toward Earnest's attack. While Bowers was the apparent primer that brought Earnest to embrace violence, it was Tarrant who showed him how to do it. "Tarrant was a catalyst for me personally. He showed me that it could be done. And that it needed to be done," Earnest wrote.[34]

The word catalyst is an understatement. Earnest's attack was an homage to Christchurch, from the selection of his weapon and tactical gear to his attempted livestream and posting on 8chan. And like Tarrant, Earnest self-posed a question in his manifesto: "How long did it take you to plan this attack?" He answered "four weeks" prior, which would have fallen within a week or two after Tarrant's attack:

> Four weeks. Four weeks ago, I decided that I was doing this. Four weeks later I did it. I remember a specific moment in time after Brenton Tarrant's sacrifice that something just clicked in my mind. "If I won't defend my race, how can I expect others to do the same?" I immediately got to planning, and I never looked back. I never had doubts. I never felt afraid. I never felt anxious—just the occasional nervous excitement.[35]

Tarrant's influence on Earnest was interesting given how different their extremist ideologies were. Terms like "birth rates" and "invasion," which served as the cornerstones of Tarrant's manifesto, appear nowhere in Earnest's own document. Likewise, Tarrant's manifesto expresses nothing close to the Jewish global conspiracy that Earnest obsesses over. To the contrary, Tarrant even claimed (albeit weakly) he wasn't an anti-Semite, writing, "A jew living in israel is no enemy of mine, so long as they do not seek to subvert or harm my people."[36]

Nonetheless, Tarrant was Earnest's hero. As he passionately quotes Tarrant in his manifesto:

"WHY WON'T SOMEBODY DO SOMETHING? WHY WON'T SOMEBODY DO SOMETHING? WHY DON'T I DO SOMETHING?"—the most powerful words in his entire manifesto. Any White man—rich or poor, young or old—who is brave enough can take any action he wants against the tyrannical and genocidal Jew.[37]

On March 24, 2019, Earnest decided he would act, just like Tarrant did. He even chose a similar target. Earnest drove to the nearby Dar-ul-Arqam Mosque and Islamic Center in Escondido and, after breaking the lock on the entrance to the gate, doused gasoline on the building and set it on fire.[38] There were seven people sleeping inside, and when one smelled the smoke, they managed to call the fire department and extinguish the flames. Though the fire was put out before it could do any structural damage to the building, Earnest did leave behind a message in spray paint for them in the parking lot: "For Brenton Tarrant -t. /pol/."[39]

Surveillance footage captured Earnest driving away in a car, but authorities couldn't identify the suspect beyond a young male driving a 2010–2015 Honda Civic sedan—not enough to lead them to Earnest.[40] It was only a month later that he stormed the Poway synagogue.

Putting these pieces together, Earnest's manifesto gives a profoundly detailed look into a process that many are often left to guess about. For whatever possible factors may be at hand—perhaps unseen social hardships or preexisting foundation of racism or bigotry—we are nonetheless clear on the major benchmarks that led to Earnest's attack: one and a half years on 8chan's /pol/ community to bring him in, six months of post-Pittsburgh "screw your optics" rally cries to sell the idea of violence, and four weeks of how-to activation after the Christchurch massacre.

These triggers pulsed through Earnest, even to the point of grief. Parts of his manifesto read like a young man yelling for help from the bottom of a well, as if he loathed the burden of what he believed he had to do. He writes of "the future of having a fulfilling job, a loving wife, and amazing kids" that he was leaving behind.[41]

"I did not want to have to kill Jews. But they have given us no other option. I'm just a normal dude who wanted to have a family, help and heal people, and play piano."[42]

To some in the far right, Earnest's massacre didn't live up to what Tarrant did in New Zealand.

Foremost was the matter of Earnest's body count. His one fatality, Lori Kaye, paled in comparison to the fifty-one people killed in the Christchurch massacre. The fact that he couldn't reload a new magazine into his rifle didn't help either. Neither did the fact that he was chased out of the building by those he was targeting.

"Tarrant claimed he trained and planned for two years and he still failed in some of his objectives," one 8chan user wrote, complaining that Earnest "didn't put in the time, research and effort required to get the body count I'm sure he desired." Another user similarly wrote, "Good intentions but goddamn the kid fucked it up, what a waste and now we'll have kikes crying about this."[43]

Others were disappointed in Earnest's flubbing of the video stream, pointing once more to the new standard the Christchurch massacre's footage set for future terrorists: "No livestream? Lame as fuck. Don't mass shooters know they need to up their game now? Tarrant has changed the optics-level."[44]

Still, praise for Earnest far outweighed the criticism. For however small the number of casualties or novice the execution, Earnest left his keyboard and took his hate into the real world with a detailed explanation of why he did it. Livestream be damned, Earnest was a true accelerationist, just like Tarrant and Bowers.

"Now THAT'S a fucking manifesto," one 8chan user wrote of Earnest's document.[45]

Users posted links to it across online platforms. Some even distributed "audiobook" recordings of his writing. Posters glorified Earnest in artwork as another version of their beloved Bowers, whose attack against Jews in a synagogue had so obviously influenced him. One poster used a headline from a Jewish pop-culture website, "Going to Synagogue Makes You Happier, Pew Study Finds," and superimposed Bowers and Earnest's faces onto the image.

While he didn't demonstrate much competence in using a weapon, Earnest's intelligence and promising background was, to many in the "screw your optics" camp, validation of their cause. Posters placed Earnest's impressive high school coursework, GPA, and other academic achievements alongside words from his manifesto, using the former to

THE SCHMOOZE

Going To Synagogue Makes You Happier, Pew Study Finds

| February 10, 2019 | By Jenny Singer

The Great Synagogue in Budapest, Hungary

iStock

FIGURE 4.1 Image distributed on far-right communities after John Earnest's attack, imposing his and Bowers's face onto an article's top image

THEY HAVE CREATED A WORLD NOW, WHERE MUSICALLY GIFTED, INTELLIGENT, TALENTED WHITE KIDS DECIDE TO SACRIFICE THEIR LIVES TO SHOOT UP A SYNAGOGUE.

JOHN EARNEST
ANOTHER VICTIM OF THE JEWISH WAR ON WHITES

FIGURE 4.2 Praise of John Earnest as "another victim of the Jewish war on whites"

bolster the latter. Another piece of far-right artwork echoed Earnest's reluctant yet arrogant sense of duty beside a picture of him playing the piano: "They have created a world now, where musically gifted, intelligent, talented kids decide to sacrifice their lives to shoot up a synagogue."[46]

In the aftermath of Earnest's attack, the far right was reveling in the same thing the rest of the world was growing wary of. It was a sense that dominos were tipping over, that a chain reaction was under way. As one 8chan user wrote:

> [Earnest's] plan was to keep the momentum of Tarrant's act going in the hope of building a critical mass of action before it's too late. One act every 6 months to year isn't gonna cut it. Tarrant's act was like the initial fission of an atom in a chain reaction, this act was another fission in the chain. Likely these events will fizzle out, but someday we'll reach a critical mass and shit will get real.[47]

A new sense of power and formidability was growing across the movement: a feeling that tides were turning, and that this was their time.

5

SAINTS AND SOLDIERS

I n the fall of 2014, I was invited to speak at General Dynamics' annual conference for security personnel in New York City. This was where heads of security from the aerospace and defense company's offices around the world met to discuss trends in terrorism, what kind of attacks to expect, and new security equipment. Attendees were former FBI, Secret Service, and law enforcement types: buzz-cut men in their forties and older who, after decades of experience, were now tasked with handling the abundant threats against General Dynamics and similar companies. Adding in the officials from several NYPD divisions also in the room, there weren't more than fifty of us.

If it were any other year, I could have tailored past presentations to the audience and added in some updated events to reference. But that year, everything the world knew about the state of the Global Jihad threat became irrelevant because the rise of ISIS flipped it all on its head. On September 21, 2014, just weeks before my presentation and two weeks after the United States formed an international military coalition against the group, ISIS spokesman Abu Muhammad al-Adnani's voice returned once more in a forty-one-minute speech in Arabic. He laid out the new rules—or lack thereof—for ISIS's Global Jihad:

Do not ask for anyone's advice and do not seek anyone's verdict. Kill the disbeliever whether he is civilian or military, for they have the same ruling. Both of them are disbelievers . . . Both of their blood and wealth is legal for you to destroy, for blood does not become illegal or legal to spill by the clothes being worn.[1]

With this new landscape in mind, I called my presentation "Gamechanger." I stressed that all senses of tact and caution urged by al-Qaeda were gone. ISIS's new moto was simple: stop waiting for a "ruling" from some cleric and go kill someone. Anyone. Literally, *anyone*.

The attendees looked resolutely into my slides. I knew some of them from previous events and correspondences and sensed a genuine sense of concern among them. This new open-ended threat from ISIS had no clear-cut prescription. Suddenly, the ages-old cliché of expecting the unexpected had taken on bleak new weight.

Al-Adnani's call was blasted across social media in scores of different languages. Shortly after my presentation, attacks took place. On October 20, al-Adnani's directive to "smash [your enemy's] head with a rock, or slaughter him with a knife, or run him over with your car" were brought to life when an ISIS supporter named Martin Rouleau ran down two Canadian soldiers in Quebec.[2] Two days later, thirty-two-year-old Michael Zehaf-Bibeau shot and killed a Canadian reservist at Canada's National War Memorial and then stormed the nearby Parliament building before dying in a shootout with security personnel. Zehaf-Bibeau had previously applied for a passport so he could leave for Syria, his mother said.[3] The day after the Ottawa shooting, a hatchet-wielding man attacked police officers in New York City.[4]

The following months alone saw more attacks around the world: a stabbing against police in the French city of Tours; a shooting at a free speech event in Copenhagen;[5] a shooting at another free speech event in Garland, Texas—and that wasn't even counting non-Western countries.

Governments didn't know what to make of these actors. They were with ISIS, but they also weren't. They were referred to as lone wolves. But this term, which the *Oxford English Dictionary* defines as "a terrorist or other criminal who acts alone rather than as part of a larger organization," was more of placeholder than an accurate descriptor. As these terrorists showed, "acting alone" and "as part of a larger organization" were no longer mutually exclusive, because in fact they were doing both at once. Most of them never set foot in an ISIS training camp, had an in-person conversation with an ISIS operative, made it onto a government watch list, or conducted shady financial transactions. Yet they acted so uniformly on the group's behalf. All they needed was a smartphone to access the endless wealth of attack instructions ISIS made readily available. They could learn how to make a bomb or poison, how to fatally puncture organs when stabbing someone, or where to best plow an automobile through a crowd of innocents. ISIS invented a streamlined model of organized terrorism.

These do-it-yourself jihadis became a critical pillar of ISIS's global terrorism game, and the group gradually built a rigid system around the way it would embrace them into its "ranks." In parallel, ISIS continued to coordinate attacks from within, as seen in Paris, Brussels, and Manchester. But when a so-called lone wolf acted on ISIS's behalf in the ways it had directed, the group would embrace him through its Amaq News Agency, essentially endorsing what it couldn't fully claim responsibility for.[6] ISIS dubbed each perpetrator a "Soldier of the Caliphate."

Imagine the incentive this would give an ISIS supporter. Here were all the resources to execute a terrorist attack and have one's name officially enshrined among the rifle-wielding heroes fighting off the tyrants in places such as Iraq and Syria. They only had to leave behind some trace of their loyalty to ISIS prior to their attack—a pledge of allegiance posted to social media, a trove of ISIS videos on their computer—to be officially canonized as one of the group's soldiers.

With every such attack out of England, France, Germany, the United States, and elsewhere, the momentum grew, pumping yet more impetus into the minds of aspiring ISIS "holy warriors."

And just as ISIS promised glory in the Soldier of the Caliphate title, the far right was carving out its own canon.

As the Christchurch massacre reverberated, the far right's memes and media for Brenton Tarrant took on a different tone than those made for Robert Bowers. Media celebrating Bowers during the months prior emphasized his "screw your optics" declaration and the game-changing shift that came with it. But for Tarrant, the far right took their idolization to an even higher level. Pictures of him were styled after religious art, using halos and other religious icons to place him and his attack inside a holy context. Some images characterized his manifesto, *The Great Replacement*, as holy scripture or even the Ten Commandments, and he was widely revered as "Saint Brenton Tarrant."[7] From here, an entire canon of far-right "Sainthood" began to harden. Just as Tarrant became Saint Tarrant, John Earnest became Saint Earnest and Bowers retroactively became Saint Bowers.[8]

"Sainthood is bestowed upon these men as a showing of gratitude for their acts of martyrdom in the name of the white race,"[9] a user explained. They even celebrated anniversaries of their massacres as if they were holidays. A year after Bowers's attack in Pittsburgh, one user wrote, "Let it be known to everyone and from now on celebrated annually, that on this day in 2018, Robert Bowers (pbuh) ascended to sainthood by taking out 11 enemies of the white race."[10]

This canon became increasingly baked into the "screw your optics"–aligned far right. "Saint" was now a standard feature of their vocabularies—a term they used just as reflexively as any other word in conversation.

"Saint Earnests manifesto was no doubt better than Saint Tarrants in my opinion," one wrote.[11]

"The Romanian patriots . . . went for high level traitors and top Jews," wrote another user. "That's entirely different than Saint Tarrant or Saint Earnest, but it would seem that the system response would be the same: oppress the goyim [non-Jews] more."[12]

The "Saint" title is congruent with the militantly Christian sentiments and "Crusade" narratives embedded in the far right, but it is also ironic. Christian saints cannot be canonized as such until they have reached heaven (meaning, until they have died). However, the Saints to emerge from the "screw your optics" current of the far right seemed to skip the blaze-of-glory death option and surrender to police. Their perceived martyrdom was attained behind bars, where they so conveniently lived to witness their names honored by fellow white supremacists.

This Sainthood canon was quickly growing into a lasting movement-wide system. It functioned as the connector between attacks that, as it became increasingly clear, were continuations of one another. The Sainthood canon served as framework vague and malleable enough to encompass attackers of different far-right ideologies. Some even proposed inducting pre–"screw your optics" attackers like Dylann Roof and Anders Breivik into the canon to expand the scale of the narrative they were creating. And just like ISIS's "Soldiers of the Caliphate" title, far-right Sainthood came with a promise of glory. Within every utterance of "Saint Tarrant" and "Saint Earnest," there was a pitch: one's own place in the Hall of Saints, should they be willing to attain it.

With that, the world was once again struck by the same type of phenomenon that emerged from ISIS five years earlier: terrorist actors who couldn't be mapped together by straight lines of red string across a cork board and a momentous force that grew stronger with every attack. Listing the dates of attacks by far-right Saints from Breivik to Earnest, one user noted ominously, "The distance in time between these happenings is shrinking."[13]

It was midday on Saturday, August 3, 2019, four months after Earnest's attack in California. A thread started on the /pol/ section of 8chan. Its first message contained an attached manifesto and opening message, reading:

> Fuck this is going to be so shit but I can't wait any longer. Do your part and spread this brothers! Of course, only spread it if the attack is successful. I know that the media is going to try to frame my incorrectly, but y'all will know the truth! I'm probably going to die today. Keep up the good fight.[14]

Twenty-one-year-old Patrick Crusius fired the first shots in the parking lot of an El Paso Walmart just minutes after he uploaded this message to 8chan. He was using an AK-47-styled gun he ordered from Romania that had shipped to a gun store near his home in Allen, Texas.[15] By the time he entered the building, the store's manager issued an active shooter warning and shoppers began to flee.[16] Video footage of the attack shows people running and hiding under tables as the pounding shots from Crusius's rifle are heard out of view.[17]

Shortly after, Crusius got in his car and drove to a nearby intersection. Officers approaching the Walmart noticed the car stopped in the left turn lane. Crusius stepped out of the car with his hands in the air.[18]

"I'm the shooter," he said as he was arrested.[19]

Twenty-two lives were taken. Thirteen Americans, eight Mexicans, and a German. A soccer-loving fifteen-year-old named Javier Amir Rodriguez.[20] A seventy-seven-year-old man named Juan Velazquez, who had moved to El Paso with his wife Nicolasa just six months before.[21] Yet more faces in framed pictures at tear-filled vigils.

The world soon got a sense of the person behind the rampage. Crusius was much different than the high-achieving Earnest who preceded him. His former high school classmates describe him as a victim of constant bullying.[22] They say that while he seemed nice enough, he didn't do well socially. "People thought he was weird,"[23] a former classmate said. He wore a trench coat to school and kept mostly to himself.[24] His profile on LinkedIn paints a similar picture of a despondent, unmotivated young man. Despite being enrolled at a community college, the "About" section reads like more of a mockery of a LinkedIn post:

> I'm not really motivated to do anything than what's necessary to get by. Working in general sucks, but I guess a career in Software Development suits me well. I spend about 8 hours every day on the computer so that counts towards technology experience I guess.[25]

While he didn't seem driven, Crusius wasn't without vicious conviction. His three-page manifesto, titled "The Inconvenient Truth," positioned itself off the bat as a product of "screw your optics." "In general, I support the Christchurch shooter and his manifesto,"[26] it opened, pointing toward the same trigger that had snapped Earnest into action. Crusius adapted Tarrant's fears of Muslim fertility rates when he wrote that Hispanic "invaders" have "close to the highest birthrate of all ethnicities in America."[27]

But apart from his nods to the online far-right community and shout-out to Tarrant, Crusius didn't resemble a hardcore white nationalist. On Twitter, he came off as an avid but perceivably mainstream conservative, expressing support for President Trump, Fox News personalities, and building a wall at the southern U.S. border.[28] Even in his Tarrant-praising manifesto, he made no reference to the Jewish-run global conspiracy that Earnest described in his manifesto—or any reference to Jews at all. None of the historical appeals to white lineage, no detailed breakdowns of global conspiracies, no references to far-right historical figures like Oswald Mosley or Adolf Hitler. And while he wrote about the "fight for America and Europe," he seemed much more focused on the former. He even expressed anger at the "white supremacist" label he foresaw being applied to him, writing:

I know that the media will probably call me a white supremacist anyway and blame Trump's rhetoric. The media is infamous for fake news. Their reaction to this attack will likely just confirm that.[29]

Reading these lines, it appeared that Crusius was slapping a "screw your optics" sticker onto a far more generic brand of racist xenophobia. It seemed the element of ideological substance was once more taking the back seat to the "screw your optics" priority for aimless, open-ended carnage. Crusius indicated as much in his manifesto: "Actually the Hispanic community was not my target before I read The Great Replacement [Tarrant's manifesto]."[30] Here, Crusius indicated that his desire to carry out an attack preceded his reasons for doing it or his choice of target, which could very well explain his lack of a coherent ideological justification for his act.[31] It's a plausible, if not likely scenario: a sick young man mulling over targets when he comes upon Tarrant's manifesto, then coming to conclude he is living amidst an "invasion" in Texas—only instead of Muslims, it is Hispanic migrants. In this regard, Tarrant's manifesto was a template for a cause that Crusius couldn't formulate himself. There was no need to reinvent the wheel. Crusius couldn't rationally explain *why* he ordered an assault rifle and killed twenty-two innocent people, but the work of justifying his attack was already taken care of by Tarrant and his growing cult of supporters online.

All the same, the far right's immediate praise for Crusius poured out like a broken watermain. "Hail Saint Crusius," they railed across the internet.[32] They disseminated and translated his manifesto and distributed glorifying posters made from surveillance footage of Crusius entering the Walmart, reading, "Give them what they want."[33]

The celebration reached far beyond the United States. The day after his attack, a French far-right blog published a French translation of Crusius's manifesto along with a celebratory article titled "The Tarrant of El Paso: Twenty Chicanos Down for the Count." The piece articulated that same sense of a chain reaction voiced after Earnest's shooting in California, except now it was much clearer, much more evident:

> Tarrant's action directly inspired the action of Crusius. Others came before, like those of Breivik and Roof; and others will follow. These acts draw attention to the ongoing racial war. For anyone who becomes aware of the situation, their legitimacy naturally follows.
>
> These acts, where a man sacrifices his future for the cause, inspire resistance. They are a cure for the deadly trap of passivity.[34]

Other corners of the far right likewise promoted excerpts from Crusius's manifesto in the days after the shooting. It didn't matter how little Crusius fit with the movement he appealed to, or even that he distanced himself from the "white supremacist" title. Any attack, especially one as deadly as Crusius's, was too valuable to their momentum to reject out of ideological concerns.

The week after Crusius's attack saw massive outrage from the public and lawmakers. People were finally starting to ask why nothing was being done to address the evident links between 8chan and terrorist attacks. Hosting and website maintenance companies like Cloudflare pulled the plug on 8chan in the days following.[35] It was an echo of the Pittsburgh shooting aftermath the year before, when public outrage forced web hosts to drop Gab, the social platform Bowers and other anti-Semites used. But as the removal of Gab proved, it was going to take a lot more than one company's action to halt the gears of this movement. 8chan took the beating as the "screw your optics" far right hopped between alternative message boards and kept the propaganda machine raging on: celebrations of Crusius, artwork and lengthy posts inciting for more attacks, anything to keep the momentum going.[36] This time, it only took a week before the next Saint jumped onto the caravan.

⸙

Saturday, August 10, exactly one week after El Paso, and it was happening again.

"Well cobbers it's my time, I was elected by saint Tarrant after all," read the message posted to a chan board called EndChan, which some from the far right began using as an alternative to the recently removed 8chan.[37] The "cobbers" in the post was of course a nod to Tarrant's 8chan message that accompanied his manifesto, "you are all top blokes and the best bunch of cobbers a man could ask for." This new message urged fellow far-right terrorists to continue their work, like it was all a game of tag or a relay race: "We can't let this go on, you gotta bump the race war thread irl [in real life] and if you're reading this you have been elected by me."[38]

The post was written by a twenty-one-year-old man named Philip Manshaus. Shortly after posting the message, he arrived at al-Noor Islamic Centre in the town of Bærum, located just outside of Oslo, Norway.[39] The congregation had just finished their prayers and there were only a few elderly members left in the building. They were planning for the next day's festival of Eid-al-Adha, the Islamic Festival of the Sacrifice, which is one of Islam's most important holidays.[40]

Manshaus, armed with a pistol and what was described as two "shotgun-like" guns, began firing before he even entered the building.[41]

Channeling the same cowardice as Tarrant and others before him, he probably expected an easy rampage. But one of those seemingly easy targets was sixty-five-year-old Mohamed Rafiq, a former Pakistani military officer who had surely encountered far tougher specimens than Manshaus. Rafiq didn't hesitate. He ran toward Manshaus, took him to the ground, and seized his weapons.[42] Nobody at the mosque was killed.

However, investigators soon after found the dead body of Manshaus's seventeen-year-old Chinese stepsister at his residence, who police believe he killed before attacking al-Noor Islamic Centre.[43] Her name was Johanne Zhangjia Ihle-Hansen, adopted by Manshaus's father's girlfriend.[44] Police were unsure if he killed her because of her race or because she might have caught onto his plans and tried to stop him.[45]

Just like Tarrant and Earnest before him, Manshaus's post included a link to a Facebook livestream that Facebook quickly removed.[46] Accompanying his post was a "Chad" meme, which uses the format of an exaggeratedly muscular man to describe qualities of successful "alpha" types.[47] As such, the meme contained Chad-styled drawings of Tarrant, Earnest, and Crusius, all of whom the image described within the far right's Sainthood canon: "The Chad Saint Brenton Tarrant and his loyal Chad Disciples John and Patrick."

The image was a museum-worthy artifact of the "screw your optics" terrorist current, in some ways more representative than the longwinded manifestos that preceded it. The way Manshaus acknowledged the chain of events that led to his own attack speaks volumes by itself. Calling

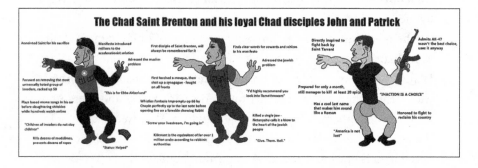

FIGURE 5.1 "Chad"-styled meme posted to the site EndChan by Philip Manshaus prior to his attack

Tarrant the "Saint," with Earnest and Crusius as his "disciples," was a nod to the triggering spark Tarrant set off with these attackers. This is why Manshaus wrote that he was "elected by saint Tarrant," and that he had now "elected" others in the far right to act after him: he contextualized his attack as part of this movement by asserting himself as the next adherent to grab the baton.

Manshaus's meme also juxtaposed the Saints preceding him, speaking yet more to the "screw your optics" far right's disregard for a cohesive ideology. Manshaus acknowledged Tarrant as the most powerful spark of the movement: "Anointed Saint for his sacrifice . . . Manifesto introduced millions to the accelerationist solution . . . Plays based meme songs in his car before slaughtering shitskins while hundreds watch online." But when it came to Earnest, the description read like a character from a completely different movie: "First disciple of Saint Brenton, will always be remembered for it . . . First torched a mosque, then shot up a synagogue—fought on all fronts . . . Addressed the jewish problem." Manshaus's description of Crusius made for even more divergence: "Directly inspired to fight back by Saint Tarrant . . . Prepared for only a month, still manages to kill at least 20 spics . . . Honored to fight to reclaim his country."[48]

So when Manshaus claimed himself to be another link in this chain, many from the movement accepted him as such, murdered stepsister and unclear motives be damned. The pencil-necked young man arrived in court two days later, grinning smugly with two black eyes and his face covered in scratches and bruises—another inductee into the far right's Hall of Saints.[49]

Manshaus "deserves the same respect as any of the Saints simply because he dared to try," a Ukrainian-language neo-Nazi group wrote. The same group praised him as following in the footsteps of the attackers who preceded him:

22-year-old Philip Manshaus decided to follow in the footsteps of Tarrant, Ernest and Crusius . . . I advise you to look at this strong-willed face, a worthy White Warrior. Later, Philip attacked the mosque in Oslo, broke the door and started firing at the Imam (Islamic leader). He wounded the Imam, but was knocked down by a 65-year-old sheep-herder and then caught by the cops and tied up. Significantly, these Norwegian Muslims did not even speak Norwegian.[50]

It was a lasting celebration. Months after his attack, at Manshaus's different court hearings, users wrote "HAIL SAINT MANSHAUS." Another wrote, "Soon the time will come, when Manshaus and Breivik will govern Norway, and this time is close."[51]

A twenty-eight-year-old Islamophobe from Australia who said "a jew living in israel is no enemy of mine." A nineteen-year-old anti-Semite on the Dean's List. A twenty-one-year-old social outcast whose views were probably closer to Donald Trump's than Hitler's. A twenty-two-year-old man from Norway so far gone he murdered his own stepsister before trying to shoot up a mosque. Ill-fitted constituents, yes, but far-right Saints nonetheless.

Based on what we had seen with ISIS in years past, these new types of terrorist canons could be bent to fit anyone, no matter how unworthy or invalid they might seem. ISIS's Soldiers of the Caliphate included individuals just as ideologically clueless as Crusius. Many ISIS-inspired attackers—not to mention its fighters—probably couldn't recite more than a few sentences of the Quran. Omar Mateen, whose June 2016 attack at the LGBT Pulse Nightclub killed forty-nine people and wounded fifty-three others, was embraced by ISIS as "one of the soldiers of the Caliphate in America."[52] But while claiming allegiance to ISIS via 911 calls, Mateen also started to appeal to ISIS's sworn enemy, al-Qaeda.[53] He referenced the Tsarnaev brothers, who carried out the 2013 Boston Marathon bombings with inspiration from al-Qaeda, and Moner Mohammad Abusalha, who carried out a suicide bombing in 2014 in Syria for an al-Qaeda affiliate.[54] And it gets odder. According to former FBI Director James Comey, Mateen told his coworkers in 2013 that he was a member of Hezbollah, the Shi'ite militia group and Iran proxy force based in Lebanon.[55] Anyone who has tuned into the last decade of Middle East conflicts would know that enmity between Sunni extremists like ISIS and Shi'ite militants like Hezbollah runs extremely deep, and there is no logical room for someone like Mateen to support both. This didn't matter to ISIS and its supporters, though. Mateen's attack was theirs now.

All the same, after Crusius's and Manshaus's back-to-back attacks, far-right Sainthood had room for virtually anyone who wanted in. As people, they might never sit together in the same room, but here they all were mimicking one another's attacks and manifestos in startling uniformity. Terrorists from around the world who had never met each other, and whose takes on far-right ideology were immensely different and often incompatible, were now acting in solidarity. They were seemingly antithetical characters within the same self-perpetuating chronology: Bowers to set the tone, Tarrant to exemplify it, and an ever-growing line of disciples to follow their lead toward Sainthood.

As was the case five years earlier, much of the world couldn't see what was right in front of its eyes. When ISIS-inspired attacks began in 2014, governments and media outlets were scrambling to explain this phenomenon, both to themselves and to the world. *The attacker acted alone*, the reporting would often go for ISIS-inspired attackers. After eighteen-year-old Abdul Razak Ali Artan plowed a vehicle through walkers at Ohio State University and then began stabbing them in November 2016—a clear manifestation of ISIS's attack directives—ISIS embraced him as a Soldier of the Caliphate.[56] Nonetheless, headlines showcased the conceptual disconnect between the terrorist act and its source. One from *The Independent* read: "Ohio State attacker may have been self-radicalised despite Isis branding him a 'soldier.'"[57] The top levels of law enforcement gave the same explanations. After the 2014 San Bernardino attacks, former FBI Director James Comey said of the attackers, "There's no indication that they are part of a network."[58]

Years later, as the "screw your optics" current built a similar terrorism machine, the same misguided understandings remained. Echoing Comey, Poway police said Earnest "acted alone and without outside support."[59] These misguided takes persisted well into the time of the El Paso and Norway attacks. "We have no information indicating that he is part of any larger network," a Norwegian police spokesman said after Manshaus's attack.[60]

This issue of acknowledging a terrorist "network" is not one of petty semantics. It is about the way we conceptualize that word in the age of social media. Just like FBI Director Comey, law enforcement officials handling far-right mass shootings often interpret a "larger network" as a direct collection of coconspirators. Someone like Manshaus largely wouldn't fit this definition because he probably wasn't sitting around weekly campfires with fellow white supremacists or collaborating on his attack plans on a drawing board. But these new kinds of canon-driven terrorist movements show clearly that the world needs new definitions of terms like "lone wolf," "self-radicalized," and even "network." Popular conceptions of these terms are too often reliant on narrow group-member-versus-non-group-member dichotomies and should be discarded along with the VHS tapes and floppy disks left lying on our shelves. These memes, media, attacks, incitements, message boards—these *are* the networks.

Still, if Sainthood is the structure, what is the force holding it all together? How does an attacker like Crusius, so clearly not versed in the far-right ideology espoused by his predecessors, come to attack on behalf of the same cause? What is the environment that gives a word like "Saint" so much meaning in the first place?

Indeed, there can be no understanding this network of Saints without an understanding of the tissue that holds them together: common culture.

6

CONTROL THE MEMES, CONTROL THE PLANET

SITE's offices can be quiet. Exasperatingly quiet. Most of our staff's communication happens via a messenger platform, so for stretches of time the only thing you'll hear is keyboards clicking from different corners of the office. On these quiet days, when someone yells something out—or speaks at any volume, really—everyone snaps to attention. In May of 2019, just a couple of months after the Poway synagogue shooting, we were especially jumpy.

"I'm in!"

It was Ray, the head of SITE's data collection department. As our database operations expanded, Ray oversaw most of it. He was particularly familiar with the mountains of far-right propaganda we were absorbing through our systems. If you picked a random neo-Nazi meme or poster, Ray could likely tell you exactly when and where it was posted online. He was like SITE's librarian of neo-Nazi propaganda, sorting through the content in his distinctively placid demeanor. So when he yelled across the room, I knew it had to be very important.

"In where?" I asked.

"I got in the Discord channel."

"Which one?"

"Wehrwolf."

"Yes! Great!"

In previous years, it would have more likely been a jihadi chat group we were trying to infiltrate. But things at the SITE offices had changed. Our far-right specialists were starting to outnumber our jihadi specialists, and the shift was escalating. My jihad-focused team members had their work down to a science and no matter where the jihadists went, my team was never overloaded. The work on the far right, on the other hand, just kept ballooning. Every time we began monitoring a new platform or far-right submovement, it meant more SITE team members were needed to report on it or collect data and content. It seemed that every other day I was telling our office manager Roland to put another job listing online.

In those months we had been directing much of our archiving efforts toward Discord, an instant messaging platform for video game players. Users create Discord groups via their own servers, which they can separate into different rooms and categories, almost like personal websites for discussions and content-sharing with fellow members. There's a lot of overlap between Discord communities and those on 4chan, 8chan, and other message boards. Conversations between all these platforms tend to use the same niche jargon: users endearingly referring to each other as "faggots" and talking trash about the "normies" of mainstream cultures.[1] Sure enough, 8chan was where we found the Wehrwolf invite link in the first place. As for the far-right extremists among these users, Discord is a place where they build trust and relationships, let their guard down, and occasionally spill actionable information: death threats, doxed info for attack targets, bomb manuals, you name it. The smaller chat groups are where we keep particularly close lookouts for the formations of terror cells or dangerous coordination between extremists.

These far-right meeting spaces were often hard to get into, especially after the Christchurch attack and others that followed. Far-right accounts and discussion threads were being reported and removed far more frequently. With that came a growing priority for precautions—or in these contexts, operations security—among these actors. They were now questioning users who entered chat groups but didn't participate, and interrogating users trying to join. As for the Wehrwolf server, we tried multiple times to pass their vetting process but never succeeded. The more we got rejected, of course, the more I wanted to get in. I couldn't speak the far-right lingo as well as some of my staff could, but I guided them with the methods that had always served me well while infiltrating small jihadi cells. Most important is to act natural, like you're just talking with friends; keep the answers short and don't try to impress your interrogators with too much ideological jargon or by fitting the bill of a desirable prospect. If things are dragging on, act like the administrators are wasting *your* time by interrogating you. Looking through some of the answers my staff gave on this latest Wehrwolf vetting questionnaire, it seemed like it worked:

> *What got you into your current idology [sic]?*
> History
> *What books have you read that have influenced your worldview?*
> Doctrine of Fascism, Half of Mein Kampf, Siege
> *Define Fascism in your own words.*
> Unity, Purity, Strength, Purpose
> *Where did you get the invite from?*
> Some faggy chan board.
> *Have you ever had a girlfriend?*
> Yes[2]

The server was called "SS Wehrwolf Combat Unit," named after a secretive (but largely inconsequential) resistance network of Nazi militants formed when Allies came to occupy Germany in 1945.[3] Its name has endured as a motif in neo-Nazi propaganda and groups.[4]

This Discord server was small: less than fifty members. But despite the guerilla warfare language, Wehrwolf's admin, "Stephen White," seemed less focused on attacks or assassinations than he was on indoctrination and recruitment. Like other Discord servers, a sidebar menu detailed various categories and requirements of the group: vetting, rules, roles, and other items. The description of the group's different "squads" described the different tasks people would take in recruiting (or "redpilling") other online communities:

Squad Wehrwolf: Main Squad for infiltration missions
Squad Youth: For going into kiddie server's and redpilling them
Squad Jäger: For hunting down faggot's and people that threaten the
   server[5]

Wehrwolf's membership was typical of what we were seeing elsewhere in far-right communities online. Members identified as being from countries like the United States, Romania, Denmark, Canada, France, Czech Republic, Cuba, and Germany. The majority were young adults, with few members claiming to be over twenty-eight. Stephen White demanded members adhere to a zealous Nazi-aligned lifestyle free of "degenerate" elements. He also required substantial reading of fascist and Nazi literature: Hitler's *Mein Kampf* and writings by Alexander Mukhitdinov, who founded the popular fascist message board (and terrorist haven) Iron March.[6]

Despite the shroud of secrecy surrounding this Wehrwolf group, none of what we were seeing seemed terribly alarming. For a while, I was underwhelmed. But then I saw the words "How to Spot a Jew." I clicked.

It led to a new section of the server under the heading "The Poisonous Mushroom." It was written as a sort of lesson, opening, "Just as it is often hard to tell a toadstool from an edible mushroom, so too it is often very hard to recognize the Jew as a swindler and criminal." In the story, a mother teaches her son Franz:

"Look, Franz, human beings in this world are like the mushrooms in the forest. There are good mushrooms and there are good people. There are poisonous, bad mushrooms and there are bad people. And we have to be on our guard against bad people just as we have to be on guard against poisonous mushrooms. Do you understand that?"

"Yes, mother," Franz replies. "I understand that in dealing with bad people trouble may arise, just as when one eats a poisonous mushroom. One may even die!"

"And do you know, too, who these bad men are, these poisonous mushrooms of mankind?" the mother continued.

Franz slaps his chest in pride:

"Of course I know, mother! They are the Jews! Our teacher has often told us about them."[7]

I put my hands on my desk and backed my head away from the computer. *What am I reading*, I thought. I leaned back in toward the screen.

The mother praises her boy for his intelligence, and goes on to explain the different kinds of "poisonous" Jews: the Jewish pedlar [*sic*], the Jewish cattle-dealer, the Kosher butcher, the Jewish doctor, the baptised Jew, and so on.

"However they disguise themselves, or however friendly they try to be, affirming a thousand times their good intentions to us, one must not believe them. Jews they are and Jews they remain. For our Volk they are poison."

"Like the poisonous mushroom!" says Franz.

"Yes, my child! Just as a single poisonous mushrooms can kill a whole family, so a solitary Jew can destroy a whole village, a whole city, even an entire Volk."

Franz has understood.[8]

The past two months had been a far-right lovefest for Saint John Earnest and his shooting in Poway, so at this point I thought I'd become as hardened as I had ever been. But there was just something so nakedly dehumanizing about this writing. Suddenly, I was back in Holocaust education classes in Israeli elementary school, looking into faces of photographed Jews heading toward their deaths at concentration camps. I needed to know if this text was unique to this Discord server or if it was pulled from somewhere else. After a few minutes of digging, Ray confirmed it was from a children's book called *Der Giftpilz*—German for "The Poisonous Mushroom," as the post's heading read. The book was published in 1938 by a notorious Nazi Germany propagandist named Julius Streicher. He had a fruitful career as a loudspeaker for Nazi

Germany's anti-Semitic agenda, publishing children's books as well as the notorious *Der Stürmer* (*The Stormer*) newspaper. Streicher was among those found guilty of crimes against humanity in the post–World War II Nuremberg Tribunal and was hanged in 1946.[9]

In homes and classrooms across Germany, teachers and parents once read this book to developing minds. And to find it resurfacing all these years later, housed on a video gamer messenger platform, added a revulsive layer of absurdity.

Yet my reaction to *The Poisonous Mushroom* wasn't just about the book. A book by itself may not suffice to turn a child into an anti-Semite. *The Poisonous Mushroom* was just one artifact among many pushing the same message. After all, Hitler's path to genocide was paved not just by the unchecked authority he seized, but also an entire culture engineered to accommodate it. Germany's Propaganda Ministry, the Reich Chamber of Culture, and other government bodies overseen by Joseph Goebbels took control of all forms of German media to push themes of collective struggle and heritage while removing cultural elements deemed "foreign," "degenerate," or of cosmopolitan elitism. Music was likewise filtered through this culture machine, with the country's State Music Bureau banning jazz, swing, and anything else not deemed "good German music."[10] Meanwhile, films like 1933's *Der Sieg des Glaubens* (*The Victory of Faith*) and 1935's *Triumph des Willens* (*Triumph of the Will*) glorified the Nazis' rise to power while others, like 1940's *Der ewige Jude* (*The Eternal Jew*), characterized Jews as parasitic and untrustworthy.[11] Publications like Streicher's *Der Stürmer* featured cartoons of Jews extracting blood from Christian children, echoing the same blood libel myths that had followed Jews for centuries.[12]

Together, these cultural artifacts and outlets form an infrastructure: one in which the ideas put forth in *The Poisonous Mushroom*, absurd as they may be, are in common company. Some Germans began to lean into this culture's promises of destiny and superiority, especially as Hitler executed or imprisoned the many who opposed these notions.[13] These ideas were force-fed, but nonetheless gripped enough people who would accept them, repeat them, and truly believe that a category of people, *those people,* were standing in the way of Germany's greatness.[14]

FIGURE 6.1 Cover of Nazi-era children's book *Der Giftpilz* (*The Poisonous Mushroom*)

Hitler himself noted, very chillingly, in *Mein Kampf*, that "Propaganda is a truly terrible weapon in the hands of an expert."

Those times often seem like a bygone era. Hitler is dead. The Third Reich was dismantled. Nazi materials were banned and burned by the Allies. To this day, waving a swastika flag in Germany is illegal. Yet three-quarters of a century after World War II, here was *The Poisonous Mushroom* on my computer screen, like a ghost. As I read this fictional mother's lessons to her son Franz, that era felt so alive inside of this Discord server. It was one of those moments where all your familiarity of a subject disappears, and you are reminded how strange it all is: a venue for potty-mouth video game players doubling as a library for century-old Nazi children's literature and recruitment hub for a group named after a guerilla Nazi unit.

But to understand this absurdity is to understand a culture, and from there, the driver of so much far-right terrorism occuring today. The culture of the "screw your optics" far right is a tapestry of contradictions: traditionally styled Third Reich propaganda posted alongside immature memes; filth-filled chan board rants against modern "degeneracy"; niche electronic dance music longing for a century past. The transgressive energy of video game obsessives, nihilistic internet trolls, 4chan and 8chan meme-makers, anti–political correctness crusaders, and other communities configured to serve bigoted white supremacist and fascist agendas.

For all the frequent examination of far-right attackers' ideologies, upbringings, and mental states, it is in fact the culture that today's far-right terrorists are compelled by and keen to harness. Culture is what gives the terrorist "Sainthood" canon its meaning, and what gives immensely different young men like Brenton Tarrant, John Earnest, Philip Manshaus, Patrick Crusius, and others a common denominator.

Back in February 2017, I was walking into the office when Barry, then still the head of the far-right department, stopped me.

"I need you to take a look at this report when you get a chance," he said. "It feels a little outside of the norm."

It was rare that Barry asked for my input on his reporting, which was fine because I rarely took issue with what he dispatched to our clients. He knew most of my time in those days was occupied with ISIS, whose attacks still consumed the world. The previous three months alone included a vehicular massacre at a Berlin Christmas Market, a car-ramming and knife attack at Ohio State University, and a mass shooting at a nightclub in Istanbul on New Year's Eve.[15] It might feel like a fleeting memory now, but five years ago nowhere in the world felt safe. Even for me personally, jihadi artwork of me being beheaded was disseminated online or appearing in email threats. At one point, the FBI even called me about an ISIS-inspired threat against me. They couldn't specify where it came from but offered protection in the form of a service car parked outside of my residence. I declined, but my fear for my family's safety was very real.

In parallel, the far right was growing in its own way. It was still a year before Bowers declared "screw your optics" prior to his attack in Pittsburgh, but even then, it was clear that something toxic was brewing in the United States and across the West. The FBI assessed that in 2016, reported hate crimes in the country had increased for the second year in a row, up to 6,121 from 5,850 in 2015.[16] Jewish schools and community centers were receiving increasing bomb threats, just as the so-called alt-right was becoming a distinct American political presence.[17] In Europe, anti-Semitic crimes prompted some Jewish leaders in countries like France and Germany to consider advising fellow Jews to not wear yarmulkes in public.[18] The Trump administration was far from helpful in countering the problem. Less than two weeks into its tenure, the Trump administration sought to redirect the U.S. government's Countering Violent Extremism (CVE) program away from far-right extremism and instead solely focus on Islamist extremism.[19]

The far right was feeling bolder as a result. Sharing news of the CVE's shift away from far-right extremism, users on Stormfront were ecstatic. "9th workday in office," wrote one. Others exclaimed, "Wow It just keeps getting better and better" and "I am starting to changing [*sic*] my mind about Trump. Every move he made was ****ing AWESOME."[20] One post expressed a sense that white nationalists finally had sympathy from the highest levels of the government:

> Oh my goodness. Is this for real.
> Amazing my government no longer targets me as the enemy.
> It is up to us all to stay organized and continue the fight.
> This is just to good, we cant let this slip away from us again.[21]

With this new feeling of being untouchable, some suggested it might be their turn to monitor the ones monitoring them. One user even brought attention to SITE and other "Jewish and Jewish-led groups" like the Southern Poverty Law Center and the Anti-Defamation League. The post provided pictures and detailed profiles, including mine—headshot, bio, the whole thing. The same user asked, "Who is keeping an eye on the 'far-left,' the 'left wing,' and the Jewish Supremacists in America?"[22]

The stakes of tracking the far right felt higher than ever, so it made sense that Barry might want to check in with me. But when he pulled up the video in question, I thought he was kidding. It was an amateur-ish mash-up of cartoon drawings and a creepy-looking character with a crescent moon for a head. I smirked and rolled my eyes.

"Very funny," I said and continued walking to my office. I would perhaps another time stick around for a laugh, but things were too hectic. It wasn't just the death threats, constant ISIS attacks, and mounting project deadlines. I had a lot going on in my personal life. It was just days before my son's wedding and, at the same time, my daughter had been in constant fights with me and my husband over which college she was going to attend. My entire waking life was a blur of ISIS communiques, briefings to government agencies, and phone calls about last-minute tweaks to hotel reservation blocks. The funny YouTube videos would have to wait.

"I'm being serious," Barry said. "Phil agrees it's worth a write-up."

Phil Cole is one of our top analysts (and, as I mention in the acknowledgments, without him this book would not exist). He has been the go-to person for my staff when it came to trickier reports and how to frame them. He always stressed caution when reporting on potentially sensational items, so I was curious as to why he gave this one a thumbs-up.

Barry sent me a draft of his report and a YouTube link to the video. I opened it in my office. The video was a confusing hodgepodge of images and animations, but I was able to gather that the moon-headed cartoon character was a rapper called "Moonman." The character's rap verses were recorded via robotic text-to-speech software timed to the beat of the music:

> I'm Moonman, representing white power
> I stack bodies higher than Trump Tower[23]

It was hard to make out all these lyrics, so I looked to the transcript Barry wrote up in his report. As I followed the words along with the song, I understood why he and Phil wanted me to see it:

> Control the memes, control the planet
> Fascism is back and the left can't stand it
> Death camps for the blacks, sit back and relax
> Right-wing death squads prepare to attack[24]

As the video went on, it depicted Moonman shooting YouTube executives inside of a skyscraper with a Star of David on it. Other scenes showed crudely drawn Jewish and Black people, video footage of Nazi Germany's soldiers marching in step, and Donald Trump declaring "Make America Great Again." Suddenly, I felt the same conflict Barry did: Yes, the video was repulsive and unambiguously inciting, but what would our clients think about it? Would they roll their eyes? Would they wonder why we thought a sixth-grade-level video production like this could possibly be useful intel?

I began asking myself more fundamental questions. Why would extremists make light of their cause? How was this supposed to recruit anyone? In my experience, terrorist propaganda was almost always serious in tone. Even low-quality white supremacist cartoon characters like Happy Merchant had very frank, straightforward messages to them. Furthermore, the value of our work came in no small part from our expertise in canceling out the noise. We boiled all the chatter and propaganda down to what really mattered within far-right communities, such as attack incitements, news events of focus, and trends in recruitment appeals. This video seemed exactly like the type of garbage that we wanted to keep out of our alerts to customers and subscribers.

I looked into Moonman's backstory on the website Knowyourmeme. He was apparently a mascot from a series of 1980s–1990s McDonald's commercials named "Mac Tonight." Some of my staff remembered those commercials, but I was still living in Israel at the time, so this creepy narrow face was new to me. Apparently, racist Moonman mashup videos started popping up in the mid-2000s, and they had a resurgence in the mid-2010s.[25] The timing of this revival seemed fitting to everything else happening simultaneously: hate crimes, pushback against a perceived rise in "political correctness policing," and growing normalization of bigoted talking points upon the launch of Donald Trump's presidential campaign. The Moonman video had acquired tens of thousands of views in the two months since it had been uploaded.[26]

When do racist videos become propaganda? The answer—and thus, the value of letting Barry dispatch the report to clients—ultimately depended on what it meant to the people sharing it. I combed through a Stormfront thread about the video. Initially, I was relieved to see that some thought it was as preposterous as I did.

"This moonman stuff is a major embarrassment to be honest with ya," one wrote.

"I second this," replied another.

One stated bluntly, "I got to like the 24 second mark. I just cant with that whatever *that* is. No offense but it's ridiculous."[27]

But others really liked Moonman. This cartoon character, as they saw it, had actual recruitment potential. "It's White Nationalism rebranded for those us in the 18–34 demo," one wrote. Among the praise for Moonman, one message struck a particularly heavy note: "This is more for

4chan and daily stormers rather than the more dusty stay at home and do nothing types.”[28]

I paused for a moment and then yelled across the office to Barry, “You’re right, it’s very important. Dispatch the report.”

This post about “4chan and daily stormers” and “do nothing types” was getting at something critical. These contrasting responses by Stormfront members pointed toward a divide in the far right—not so much in terms of ideology, but of culture. Stormfront is dominated by the sensibilities of its older founding members, and posts there resemble racist chain emails or anti-immigrant rants on AM radio—no irony, no trolling, no niche references. Don Black, the founder of Stormfront, demanded of his fellow forum members: “Keep discussion civil and productive . . . No profanity. Avoid racial epithets . . . No personal flames . . . No spamming. Don’t post unless you have something relevant to say.”[29] However, posting without “something relevant to say” on sites like 4chan and 8chan is routine “shitposting,” as it’s commonly called. And profanity? Please.

There was far more to this divide than manners (or lack thereof). These were completely different worlds. Discussions on 4chan’s Politically Incorrect board (referred to as “/pol/”) can make one feel as baffled as Star Trek’s Captain Kirk landing in an alien civilization with its own bizarre language, social norms, and cultural eccentricities. The white supremacists of chan boards and Discord servers communicate with obscure terms from intertwining discussion boards, social media trolling campaigns, and video game and anime fandom communities. These are words you’d likely never seen before; other words you might have seen elsewhere but seemed to suggest a completely different meaning. I often had to (and still do) ask my staff to translate posts like this one from an October 2017 /pol/ thread about white farmers protesting in South Africa: “[White South Africans] are actually getting oppressed and killed while nig nogs are chimping for gibs me dat” (translation: “White South Africans are actually getting oppressed and killed while Black people are demonstrating for social safety net programs”). Or this post from the same thread: “SA is just a few steps ahead of Leafland,

Cuckistan and Germanistan" (translation: "South Africa is just a few steps ahead of migrant-welcoming Canada, Cuckistan [a fictional country overrun by political correctness and so-called social justice warriors, often used to derogatorily describe Western democracies], and the Muslim migrant-welcoming nation of Germany").[30]

With the help of Google searches and some of my analysts, I gradually built up a glossary of these alien terms, as well as of familiar words that had new definitions:

> *normie*: a derogatory reference to people and products of mainstream culture
>
> *glowpost*: posts believed to be made by law enforcement to entrap other users
>
> *fedpost*: posts made by users that others believe will bring attention by law enforcement
>
> *based*: the state of voicing or acting upon far-right beliefs without regard for consequences
>
> *anon*: a fellow anonymous user
>
> *-fag*: a suffix referring to other users, usually attached to a community or other specifying attribute

Despite their common narratives of Jewish conspiracies and race wars, this new Moonman wing of the far right was its own species. Its origins were less of the Klan and bloody-knuckled skinheads than it was the hub of socially rebellious, nihilistic internet subcultures.[31] They knew how to leverage millennial and Gen-Z internet culture because they were its products.

As the months and years went on, I came to miss the days when all the action was on sites like Stormfront and Vanguard News Network. Those places felt comfortingly familiar, strange as it is to say, because I could actually navigate their interactions. Even many white supremacists couldn't lock in with this new chan board brand of the far right, which made me content to learn that it wasn't just me or my relationship with English as a third language. As a Stormfront user wrote in 2019, "Im an older guy as are many users her [*sic*]. I lurked 8chan a little but I like this old BBS based message board better."[32]

By BBS, the user was referring to the straightforward bulletin board system that sites like Stormfront use. Sites like 8chan and 4chan, on the other hand, can be confusing: no usernames, a congested interface, the crisscrossing exchanges between poster ID numbers. Just looking at it is enough to give one a headache.

"I'm old too," replied another Stormfront user. "I tried to hook into 4chan to understand what the mindset was there, but finally I didn't feel up to trying to conquer another unknown computer-scape. I figured 8chan would be similar, so I never visited."[33]

As far as these computer-scapes go, Moonman was just the tip of the iceberg. Anyone alienated by Moonman would likely feel the same way about meme characters like Honkler, a cartoon green frog with rainbow clown hair, adapted from the popular "Pepe the Frog" meme. There's nothing overtly racist or hateful about Honkler; he's more often a nod to the far right than an explicit message in itself. Far-right content creators use Honkler or Honkler's features (the hair, the nose, the rainbow colors) in their propaganda, gleeful at whatever confusion or frustration it causes among the general public—let alone the old heads of Stormfront.

In a sense, this divide was history repeating itself. In the 1980s, skinhead culture came to the United States from England and gradually shifted from a class-focused counterculture—not entirely wedded to white supremacist ideology—into a leading force in the white supremacist movement. As extremism scholar Arie Perliger noted, skinheads "absorbed traditional neo-Nazi elements and merged them with practices that emphasized antisocial and taboo-breaking behaviors," forming a violence-embracing culture around white power music, in-group terminology, clothing styles, and other items.[34] Decades later, this new Moonman-loving far right was carving out its own cultural space. And doing it fast.

This new generation of neo-Nazis and white supremacists wasn't replacing the rest of the far right. Men were still putting on white robes to burn crosses in fields throughout the 2010s, just as skinheads were still putting on brawl-filled music events.[35] But even at that early point in 2017, this movement had the potential for far quicker growth than analogous far-right movements of the past. Resources like social media and mobile applications now enabled them to sidestep the risks that come with in-person networking. We had already by this point seen what such technological tools were doing for ISIS as it pulled people of all ages and nationalities into the battlefield of Syria. A look at numbers available suggested that this was exactly what was happening with this new far right: in a month's time, the Moonman YouTube video Barry showed me nearly tripled in views from 50,000 to close to 140,000 before being removed. Other Moonman videos like "Black Lives Don't Matter" and "The Final Solution" saw similar numbers. There was a growing movement behind this content, and it was barely even hiding itself.

We began recalibrating SITE's monitoring throughout the rest of 2017 and beyond. What we found day to day—memes about gassing Jews and lynching Blacks, attack incitements that were *kind of* but *not actually* kidding—made it clearer and clearer: if we were indeed at war with the far right, it wasn't just an ideology or a handful of groups, but also a unique culture. Barry was consulting with me and others more often. The more I saw in the weeks after seeing that Moonman video for the first time, the more I thought about that user's distinction between "4chan and daily stormers" and "dusty stay at home and do nothing types." In other words: *This isn't for all-talk old heads. This is for the ones ready to act.* Moonman's talk about killing Jews and Blacks was no joke. These were the rally cries of a movement that meant every word it said, regardless of the snark and irony it used.

Seeing all these variables together—this new far right's lack of restraint, the lack of moderation online, the external social and political variables that seemed to be feeding it—it was clear we were witnessing the beginning of a fast-growing problem. It was beyond the Trump administration refusing to address the issue. Rather, it seemed like every so often, the president or his allies were giving winks and nods to these communities, whether it was Trump's railing against "rapist" immigrants, his "Muslim ban" executive order,[36] assertions that the media was lying to the American people, or numerous other examples. These were the same things the far right had been saying and demanding for years.

This problem needed to become known. In April 2017, I wrote an article for *The Daily Beast* describing the red warning lights we were seeing every day at SITE: "As someone who has received death threats from various extremist communities, I am far more scared of America's white nationalists than I am of its jihadists. Like any domestic lone wolf jihadist, white nationalist extremists live among us, and recruit and attack on American soil."[37]

But like other societal ills, it seems the worst must happen before a problem is fully realized. It was déjà vu from the days when a similarly transgressive, unapologetically bloodthirsty hive of extremists had trounced virtually unimpeded on social media.

A word came to mind: *baqiyah.*

———— ∞ ————

Everyone and their mother had seen the products of ISIS's behemoth media machine in the mid-2010s. News TV shows and websites that wouldn't normally pay more than a few paragraphs of attention to Middle East affairs were now dedicating their landing pages to the latest acts of depravity: beheadings, setting men on fire, drowning them via cages lowered into swimming pools. ISIS made terrorism into a blockbuster television show. There was also a Westerner-tailored culture that developed around it that not everyone was necessarily aware of. During the early to mid-2010s, social media—Twitter in particular—housed a buzzing social ecosystem where supporters, fighters, commentators, and media distributors had their own hashtags and jargon.[38] ISIS fighters and recruiters were lifestyle brand ambassadors, posting beheading photo reports next to pictures of M&Ms and what they made for dinner. They posted battle footage next to "#CatsOfJihad" posts, in which they'd photograph cats next to assault rifles and grenades. ISIS was Hollywood, and jihadists were its celebrities.

This culture was in many ways united by a single word: *baqiyah.* It was a shortened version of ISIS's de facto slogan, *Baqiyah wa Tatamadad* (meaning *Remaining and Expanding*). The phrase was pulled partly from an April 2007 speech by Abu Omar al-Baghdadi, leader of ISIS's predecessor, the Islamic State of Iraq.[39] *Baqiyah* was a statement of defiance to the global community that sought to eliminate it: *We are enduring, and we are growing.* ISIS supporters built their online presence around this concept, creating the illusion that they were bigger than they actually were.[40] They referred to their comrades online as their "*baqiyah* family" and gave "*baqiyah* shoutouts" to other ISIS Twitter accounts when they resurfaced after being removed. They compiled hot conversations and trends as part of the latest "*baqiyah* Twitter buzz" and named media groups after it. *Baqiyah* posters, *baqiyah* written in photographed arrangements of bullets, named in social media accounts. *Baqiyah* was, in a way, everything: a showing of strength in numbers, of solidarity, of fortitude. It was the unified howling of wolves around the globe.

The Moonman neo-Nazi scene had different sensibilities than the *baqiyah* community, but the two were eerily similar. Much like the chan board wing of the far right, ISIS's online culture leaned heavily on humor and sarcasm. After CNN aired a segment about the casual lifestyle conveyed by female ISIS recruiters—in which the network used an over-the-top banner reading, "ISIS LURES WOMEN WITH KITTENS, NUTELLA"—ISIS members and supporters began flooding the internet with references to the segment.[41] They set their usernames and handles to aliases like "Abū Nutella shawarma," "Umm Nutella" (Mother of Nutella), "Umm Nutella Lioness," and "Unknown_nutella."

Like the neo-Nazi pits of /pol/ and Discord, interpreting ISIS's culture-baked posts could be confusing if you weren't sitting among them online, all day, every day. It took time to become fluent enough in the *baqiyah* family language to read tweets like this one by prominent community member "Umm Waqqas": "To those whose Hijrah plans are near, my best advice to you is BECOME A COCONUT! Ahaha No I'm actually serous [sic]!" (In this post, Umm Waqqas is advising those seeking migration to ISIS to keep a low profile by acting like a "coconut Muslim," a derogatory term ISIS supporters used to describe anti-ISIS Muslims whose skulls were, as the joke went, empty like a coconut.) The same went for other ISIS community inside jokes. In 2018, I was giving a briefing to UK counterterrorism officials in London when one of them, though plenty knowledgeable of ISIS, asked, "What's with all the ISIS supporters' Toyota references?" He was referring to the countless array of chat groups named "Toyota Gang" and user aliases like "Abu Toyota." Once again, the answer was in the culture. After ISIS claimed swathes of Iraq and Syria in 2014 and 2015, its videos were filled with shots of fighters in fleets of Toyota Hilux trucks. As prominent ISIS fighter and recruiter Reyaad Khan (a.k.a. Abu Dujana) tweeted in January of 2015 following ISIS's execution of Japanese video journalist Kenji Goto, "I don't see why Japan has a problem with #IS . . . we gave Toyota a free Ad Campaign worth millions thru our vids . . . they never looked so good."[42] Governments scrambled to find out where these trucks were coming from and Toyota reps flocked to cleanse the company's brand while the ISIS community reveled.[43] Fighters' accounts were filled with inside jokes about Toyota, using handles like "@toyotatttfgh" and posting news stories about the matter with comments like "Caliphate lions love driving Toyotas, U.S. wonders why." A user once jokingly asked Abu Abdullah al-Britani, a British ISIS recruiter and a member of a militant group called "Rayat al-Tawheed," on his Ask.fm account, "Is [ISIS] sponsored by Toyota Hilux?"[44]

I was always amazed at the idea of the planet's most ruthless, indiscriminately murderous terrorist militants giggling about Toyotas and kittens. But these snarky jokes, buzz phrases, and other cultural components were critical building blocks of ISIS's online culture. Even several of us at SITE were captivated by this phenomenon. Some of us recall this time as the Wild West days of Twitter, when every day was a rabbit hole of gossip between recruiter cliques and ISIS fighters threatening to kill members of enemy factions on the battlefields of Syria. To this day, some of my staff still quote one fighter's hilariously stupid tweet from July 2015: "Haters gon hate, potatoes gon potate, and the islamic state gon remain a state."[45]

But for ISIS supporters, these *baqiyah* family posts and interactions were far more than just entertainment. They were like badges to flash at other supporters, exclaiming *I'm one of you*. And once more, just like the far right soon to follow their footsteps, ISIS's culture thrived with

little regard for ideology. The group's more pious members and supporters sometimes railed against those who were there for the party but not
the cause, the ones who were "all talk" about carrying out attacks and
the "liars or hypocrates [*sic*]" who still hadn't made it to Syria yet.[46] The
young women of the *baqiyah* family were often more drawn to the slum-
ber party social cliques and dreamy fighters exhibited in ISIS's online
culture than any religious aspect. British ISIS fighter "Abu Farriss"
addressed this in a 2014 post to a Q&A website called Ask.fm:

> Sisters that sit making HUGE group chats with about 10 sisters speak-
> ing about which mujahid they want to marry or which mujahid they
> speak to is absolutely shameful . . . They havr seen these handsome
> mujahids and the cool nasheeds and that's why theyre making "hijrah"
> [migrating to ISIS].[47]

It was ironic, though: Abu Farriss wanted to distance ISIS from any
superficial appeal, but its superficial appeal was one of its strongest assets.

Just as the lineage of chan board white supremacists was different
from Stormfront-oriented white supremacists, constituents of ISIS's *baqiyah* family culture were not descendants of al-Qaeda or other establishment figures of the Global Jihad. Sure, ISIS itself was an offshoot of
al-Qaeda, but so many of its members were of a completely different, disconnected generation. For however many ISIS fans came from Ansar
Mujahideen English Forum and the other jihadi hubs of years past, far
more came into the movement completely anew. ISIS wasn't something
their elders led them to. It was rebellious, something to hide from one's
parents.

ISIS's internet culture was what al-Qaeda didn't have, and it was why
youth from across the West were flocking to join the former instead of
the latter.[48] An especially vivid (and heartbreaking) example was "Umm
Sufyan," the alias of a teenaged Muslim girl from Colorado. Umm Sufyan spent much of 2013 writing on Ask.fm about how much she loved
playing tennis and hanging out with her friends. She liked swimming
and listened to music for "probably like about 3 hours" a day. Her most

important life lesson: "To always do my homework." Best friends: "I have a lot." Her dream job: "A fashion business!! Duh." And when asked what thing she "could not live without," she replied, "I can't live without my family and friends." That March, someone asked her, "Did you ever run away from home?" She replied, "No way there is no reason to run away."[49]

But less than a year later, all these hobbies and dreams suddenly didn't matter anymore. She had become a different person. "[I] Don't listen to music Allahamdulilah [Praise be to God]," she wrote in May of 2014, calling it "haram," meaning that it is religiously impermissible. Once boasting of a lively social life, she now stated that she would "never go to prom" because she was "pretty sure it's haram." Her previous focuses— school, friends, and family—were likewise traded for a preoccupation with death and paradise. Her followers didn't understand the change. "How did you turn so religious[?]" one user asked. "I mean you weren't like this before."[50]

The answer was written all over her profile. "I'm always on twitter and youtube and Instagram," she once tellingly wrote.[51]

On October 17 of that year, Umm Sufyan, along with her fifteen-year-old sister and sixteen-year-old friend, skipped school to board a series of flights destined for ISIS in Syria. After over a year of Twitter conversations with ISIS fighters and recruiters, their *baqiyah* family had replaced their old friends and family. As Umm Sufyan's sister tweeted the night before they attempted to flee, "I started to notice the people I called 'friends' weren't my true friends . . . But the people who reminded me about my [religion] were my TRUE friends."[52] The girls were intercepted and brought back home, resulting in a much more fortunate fate than other young women who made it to Syria and never returned.

ISIS's internet culture steered young minds to more than migration. Just as Moonman videos and chan board posts wantonly called to shoot Jews, Muslims, and others, members of ISIS's community uninhibitedly issued threats and incitements. It was a profound departure from the days of the al-Qaeda–led jihad, when calls for violence required some sort of scholarly permission or justification. Men and women, young and old were now posting fatwa-level attack directives to fellow community members without a second thought. Years before she begged for the United States to take her back in,[53] ISIS bride Hoda Muthana (a.k.a. Umm Jihad) tweeted in March 2015:

> Americans wake up ! Men and women altogether. You have much to do while you live under our greatest enemy, enough of your sleeping !
> Veterans,Patriot,Memorial etc Day parades..go on drive by's + spill all of their blood or rent a big truck n drive all over them. Kill them.[54]

As sincerely as they meant what they said, the casual delivery and sheer volume of these incitements reduced words like "slaughter" and "kill" to something lighter. It was now casual in-group signaling, like waving hello. "Today, find an American terrorist of the US military and kill him with whatever you can, wherever you can find him!" one ISIS account brainstormed in a lengthy thread of tweets in October 2015. "Don't want to get messy slicing with a razor blade? Then user razor wire from behind to decapitate an American terrorist of the US military."[55] These messages were a dime a dozen. Canadian ISIS fighter Farah Mohamed Shirdon (a.k.a. Abu Usamah as Somali) tweeted in August 2015:

> Easiest way to get [spiritual reward] in the West.
>   1. Get a job at McDonald's
>   2. Buy large amounts of rat poison
>   3. Poison the food of the disbelievers[56]

At certain points, baqiyah family incitements even felt like trolling, as if it was a game. When ISIS fighters like Junaid Hussain (a.k.a. Abu Hussain al-Britani) surfaced to tweet messages like "It is your duty to detonate an IED in the lands of the crusaders" —often in minutes-long windows of time before Twitter once more deleted their accounts—it seemed equally a snarky nod to his followers as it was a purposeful incitement.[57] They wore their resulting account deletions like badges of honor. Bio sections on Twitter accounts read "15th account" and "#35" like bad-boy high schoolers bragging about getting detentions.

Snarky as they were, these incitement-dealing recruiters held sway among ISIS supporters. In June 2015, a twenty-six-year-old ISIS-sympathizer named Usaama Rahim, a subject of government counter-terrorism surveillance, was shot and killed while attempting to stab police officers in Boston.[58] Junaid Hussain quickly took to Twitter to claim his advisory role to Rahim: "The last time we spoke, he asked me if it was a good idea to carry a knife incase the feds try arrest him, i advised him to carry one . . . because of that knife he attained [martyrdom]."[59]

These were the consequences of a thriving terrorist culture. It was why ISIS not only let its fighters spend so much time joking around online, but also mandated that they do so. It was also why ISIS's tech-savvy members and supporters invested so many resources in creating new accounts and helping users avoid account suspensions or arrests. This radicalizing culture was working, just as it would for this chan board generation of white supremacists.

⸺ ✦ ⸺

Nothing would ever be the same after Brenton Tarrant's March 2019 attack in Christchurch—not only for the many traumatized citizens of New Zealand, but also for Tarrant's elated supporters. To them, the attack was the start of a new phase in far-right terrorism.

Recall Tarrant's final meme-packed, tongue-in-cheek salute to his brethren on 8chan: "Well lads, it's time to stop shitposting and time to make a real life effort post. It's been a long ride and despite all your rampant faggotry, fecklessness and degeneracy, you are all top blokes and the best bunch of cobbers [friends] a man could ask for."[60]

This post was, in a way, just as important to his fellow chan board extremists as the bodies he put to the ground. It told the community on 8chan's /pol/ board that he was one of them and affirmed: *this attack was ours.* But there was more meaning to this message. Posting his manifesto and link to his livestream, Tarrant asked fellow /pol/ users to hype his attack by means of the same activities they partook in every day on the board: "Please do your part by spreading my message, making memes and shitposting as you usually do . . . If I don't survive the attack, good-bye, godbless and I will see you all in Valhalla!"[61]

There was an acknowledgment in Tarrant's words. By asking to prop-agate his message via "memes and shitposting," he was not only speak-ing to the radicalizing power of these activities in general, but also their power over *him*. Tarrant would not have made this his final request to /pol/ users—let alone leave behind an entire bloody livestream of con-tent for them—if he didn't know for himself what radicalizing power this culture had. For whatever role European immigration policies and ISIS attacks Tarrant cited as pushing him over the deep end, the culture of this chan board far right evidently played its own part. Elaborating on his directives, Tarrant urged his fellow anons to use the memes and other cultural devices of havens like /pol/ to fuel this new movement:

> Stop trying to persuade the general population with statistics, charts, tablets and figures. A one-point-seven percentage point difference may mean something to a few, but a ingeniously worded expression or bril-liantly crafted poster will convince the many. Humans are emotional, they are driven by emotions, guided by emotions and seek emotion expressions and experiences. Monotonous repetition of Immigration facts and statistics will simply bore the masses, and drive the people away from the stale and uninspired speakers that propagate them.[62]

These cultural devices, he stressed, were far more important than a coherent message. If they wanted to grow their culture into something larger, they would have to abandon the pursuit of substance for the pur-suit of viral appeal. "Paint, write, sing, dance, recite poetry. Hell, even meme. Create memes, post memes, and spread memes. Memes have done more for the ethno-nationalist movement than any manifesto," he wrote.[63]

If this new far right wanted to recruit across places like Discord and chan boards, they needed to speak their language. Now was the time to pull those people in; the ideology would come later. Tarrant wrote: "Whilst we may use edgy humour and memes in the vanguard stage, and to attract a young audience, eventually we will need to show the reality of our thoughts and our more serious intents and wishes for the future."[64]

There have been few statements as critical as this one regarding today's far-right terrorism. Tarrant, who this new far right saw as their own Zarqawi or Bin Laden, was telling fellow extremists to turn their shitposting hangouts into content factories. Their weird culture wasn't a waste of time; it was an asset, a weapon. The ones making this content had a critical role to play in the coming race wars.

The effect of Tarrant's directives, bolstered by the deadliness of his attack, was colossal. Many far-right users began treating meme-making and related activities as a full-time job. The content was flowing out in a limitless stream, drenched in the cheeky culture Tarrant told his followers to embrace: footage from Tarrant's attack edited to make it look like a video game, far-right themed movie posters, anti-Semitic memes declaring "Jew Lies Matter" and mocking victims of recent attacks.[65] Their post-Christchurch memes also used Tarrant's own points about the futility of "statistics, charts, tablets and figures," mocking other wings of the far right unwilling to carry out mass shootings. One such meme showed an image of torches brought to a May 13, 2017, white nationalist rally in Charlottesville (three months before the Unite the Right Rally took place there), edited to include the declaration, "We're done showing graphs to you cucks."

FIGURE 6.2 Meme disseminated in the aftermath of the Christchurch attack, made from a photo of a May 13, 2017, white nationalist rally in Charlottesville

FIGURE 6.3 Meme disseminated in the aftermath of the Christchurch massacre, praising Brenton Tarrant alongside far-right attackers Dylann Roof and Anders Breivik

The effects were inversely impactful on my staff and me. Barry, as I've mentioned earlier, ended up leaving the company after he couldn't get the vile words and images out of his head.

The incitements on these sites were materializing into a movement, and faster than I could have ever expected. As we would soon see, there would be real-world consequences from this barrage of content, from the stacking piles of memes all the way down to that creepy cartoon character I first encountered over two years earlier. When we first began investigating John Earnest's shooting on April 27, 2019, we initially thought it would be difficult to figure out what had radicalized this kid. But his manifesto laid it all out clearly—not just the inspiration he took from Bowers and Tarrant,[66] but also what poisoned his mind in the first place. Phil was reading Earnest's manifesto in his office the day of his attack when he yelled into mine, "Rita, check out what I just sent you."

I looked at our instant messenger window and saw the excerpt. It was from a Q&A section of Earnest's manifesto. He asked, "Who inspires you?" to which he answered, "Jesus Christ, the Apostle Paul, Martin Luther, Adolf Hitler, Robert Bowers, Brenton Tarrant, Ludwig van Beethoven, Moon Man, and Pink Guy."[67]

Here was Moonman again, two years since I first encountered him, having gone from debates among Stormfront users to a terrorist's manifesto, right alongside Hitler and Jesus.

"This guy cannot be serious," I yelled back to Phil.

But Earnest wasn't joking. He was giving the same affirmation that Tarrant made in his own /pol/ post and manifesto: that he was one of them. He wanted to let fellow 8chan users know that he too was a creature of internet culture, savvy with all from far-right Moonman videos to others like "Pink Guy," a shock humor content creator whose material has nothing to do with the far right. And by ranking Moonman as a radicalizing force equal to Hitler, Earnest was testifying to the power of this culture that radicalized him. Other lines in Earnest's manifesto served the same purpose, with one reading, "IT'S FUCKING HAPPENING. McFuggen ebin. :DDD." ("Fuggen," an intentional misspelling of "fucking," and "Ebin," an intentional misspelling of "epic," are joking references to a meme character called Spurdo Spärde.) Like Tarrant,

Earnest wanted to tell the sadists of 8chan that it was they who helped radicalize him. He wrote to his 8chan brethren:

> From the bottom of my heart thank you for everything. Keep up the infographic redpill threads. I've only been lurking for a year and a half, yet what I've learned here is priceless . . . Meme magic is real.[68]

And just as his idol Brenton Tarrant did, Earnest called on fellow 8channers to use their common culture to amplify his words:

> Make sure that my sacrifice was not in vain. Spread this letter, make memes, shitpost, FIGHT BACK, REMEMBER ROBERT BOWERS, REMEMBER BRENTON TARRANT Meme Robert Bowers back and keep up the memes of Brenton Tarrant.[69]

All the shitposters and meme-makers finally had a case to uphold as their own doing, proof of their agency. As one such user stated after Earnest's attack in Poway, "I'm happy because it shows that our red-pilling efforts are having an effect. All of this because of some carefully crafted and creative memes about Jews and their control of the United States."[70]

All the same, Earnest's name was added to the newly invigorated propaganda stream. For years, they would pump out memes of him next to other far-right "Saints" like Tarrant and Bowers, and artwork of him playing piano alongside an armed Moonman.

Throughout the rest of 2019, the baton got passed from Earnest in California to other members of the far right's chan board wing: Patrick Crusius in Texas, then to Philip Manshaus in Norway, and so on. Some left behind manifestos, others didn't. Manshaus even left behind a meme in the place of a manifesto, in full spirit of Tarrant's assertion that memes "have done more for the ethno-nationalist movement than any manifesto." Terrorists of contradictory philosophies, bound by the doctrine of memes and irreverence.

FIGURE 6.4 Album cover–styled Moonman art using an image from a video of John Earnest playing piano at age fourteen

Just as it had happened with ISIS not so long before, culture—not ideology—was the bond to form a network between extremist young men in the United States, Australia, Norway, and around the globe. Culture was what allowed both movements to wrap ages-old extremist ideas of caliphates and white supremacy into exciting new packages. Without it, terms like "Saint" or "Soldier of the Caliphate" were weightless. But a deft command of culture, as both movements proved, sent ripples across their international communities. In Moonman's words, "Control the memes, control the planet."

7

THE VIRAL CALIPHATE

I n 2007, Osama bin Laden was the face of global terrorism. Yet for three years he was nowhere to be found. No videos, no audio messages, nothing. Rumors abounded that he had been killed in an airstrike or that he was incapacitated by chronic kidney disease. Dead or alive, he was a ghost.

But then, just a week before the six-year anniversary of 9/11, we got ahold of a video by al-Qaeda Central that was due for release the next day. It was Bin Laden. The video featured him discussing recent events, proving that the AQ leader was alive. This find took precedence over all else. We stayed in the office late into the night to translate the video, create a transcript and summary, and upload it to our server, as we did with every video. This video would be published by AQ the following day; we needed to make all the preparations for its release before it was out there.

We shared our finding with the government; we wanted to be good team players, and it was too sensitive not to. But I was adamant that it be shared only with the director of the National Counterterrorism Center (NCTC) at the Defense Intelligence Agency. If the video were to leak prematurely, it would expose our position in the highly secretive al-Qaeda circles we worked so hard and so long to infiltrate. If shared, it would ruin many years of investigation and would close the lid on our ability to tap into that incredibly important resource.

In an email to the NCTC director, I attached the PDF with the transcript, the executive summary we wrote, and the link to the video that we uploaded to SITE's private server. To make sure there was no misunderstanding, I reiterated: "Please understand the necessity for secrecy . . . We ask you not to distribute . . . [as] it could harm our investigations."[1]

They promised to hold on to it until it was safe to share.

Strange things began to happen less than two hours later.

My team first complained that our server wasn't running well, so my IT people began looking into it and saw unusually high traffic. Shortly thereafter, the office was flooded with phone calls from media outlets asking for verification that al-Qaeda forums were indeed down and that there was a new Bin Laden video coming out. I thought at first that perhaps they were referring to a post on one of the jihadi forums that a video from as-Sahab, al-Qaeda's media arm, was forthcoming. Gradually I began to realize that it was something entirely different. Within minutes, several office staff and I were standing around my TV. The video was headline news on all stations and on major news websites: "U.S. says [it] has copy of purported bin Laden tape."[2] Cable news outlets showed segments from the video and footage from a press conference, in which a spokesperson implied the finding was their own, framing it as a substantial blow to al-Qaeda and their communications.

I was dumbfounded and petrified. It was as if the executive summary I'd sent to NCTC was being featured everywhere. My staff was staring at me for a reaction, but I just froze. I couldn't digest it. Those who know me well know I don't hesitate to share what's on my mind, but in that moment, I turned to stone.

A reporter faxed us the document that the Department of Defense had handed out after its press conference. My jaw dropped when I picked up the paper. It was the exact same transcript and summary document we'd prepared the night before, only someone at the Pentagon had cut off the SITE Intelligence Group headers and footers on the document. But for as much as they wanted to hide my company's name, they did a pretty careless job, because they failed to remove the link to the video on SITE's server written into the summary.

Only moments after I provided the link to the NCTC, government-registered computers all over the country began downloading the video. IP addresses showed that the CIA, National Security Agency, Department of Defense, and even the media were all simultaneously pulling the video from our server.[3] It began to crash. I instructed my staff to shut it down until the frenzy subsided.

Al-Qaeda's online administrators caught on instantly and started shutting down their infrastructure one piece after another. It was a nightmarish whirlwind all around me: the ringing phones, the news reports, my staff members running frantically between their computers trying to see what could be salvaged. I tried to save as much as I could—the media, the data, the networks—but it was all disappearing into a black hole right before my eyes. Our innumerable long days and sleepless nights at computer screens, digging through jihadi terrorists' online activities with fine-tooth combs until our eyes were bloodshot to get to where we were, was all gone.

In tears, I closed my computer, picked up my bag, and went home.

The video was treated as breaking news that entire weekend. "The tape is here," one CNN anchor opened their show that evening. "The experts believe it's real. Tonight, breaking down Osama bin Laden's message to Americans."[4] President George W. Bush commented on the video to reporters from a meeting in Sydney: "The tape is a reminder of the dangerous world in which we live and it is a reminder that we must work together to protect our people."[5]

All that weekend I stared lifelessly into the wall, my dinner plate, and the computer screen as the news coverage and interviews came out. By Sunday all the al-Qaeda sites were still down, and it seemed all but certain we'd never get them back. At our Monday morning staff meeting I was a zombie. My staff had never seen me this way before or since: quiet, drifting off, disinterested.

"Rita, don't worry. We promise, we'll get it all back," my team told me. I smiled faintly. As sad as I was, it was consoling how they wouldn't give up. I felt lucky to have them. Even if we didn't know exactly how we'd do it yet, we were eventually going to get the operation back up and running.

—— ⊗⊗⊙ ——

In the mid-2010s, when it came to ISIS's Twitter-centered social media recruitment and radicalization machine, the objective was clear between governments and tech companies alike: take it down.

In 2015, public pressure mounted on Twitter to rid its platform of ISIS recruiters and the ISIS propaganda littering it. Twitter gradually responded with aggressive policy enforcements against the group. Sure, ISIS recruiters still had their accounts on Tumblr, Facebook, and Instagram, but Twitter was the core of ISIS's social media hive and the uniting point for their accounts on other platforms.

By the end of that year, Twitter's account deletion started taking a toll on ISIS at the organizational level. For ISIS's Central Media Division, Twitter was the primary tool for disseminating videos, magazines, communiques, and other products. Things got tricky for ISIS when it could no longer hold onto official Twitter accounts for its central media arms and its various territorial "provinces," which amassed tens of thousands of followers.[6] ISIS's top media officials now had to sneak media releases onto Twitter via disguised accounts, which made it easier for anti-ISIS trolls to create fake ISIS media accounts, at times leaving ISIS supporters unsure if a given statement or media release was real or fake.

To help ISIS weather the beatings on Twitter, tech-savvy members and supporters created blog pages and social media accounts to direct the community on how to skirt deletion. Others tried threatening Twitter and other social media companies into easing off, as I reported in a March 2014 piece for the *Washington Post*.[7] One ISIS-linked group's message from March 2015 warned Twitter that their personnel had become "an official target," warning, "imagine the scene . . . while one of the employees of Twitter is outside a bar in the neighborhood . . . and the deep darkness, a lone wolf lies in wait in the darkness and he attacks him and slits his throat."[8]

ISIS tried to find Twitter replacements. They looked to major platforms like the Russia-based VKontakte and to smaller ones like Facebook alternative "Friendica," Twitter alternative "Qwitter," and others we never heard of before.[9] These other alternative sites either kicked them off instantly or simply couldn't substitute for that irreplaceable audience reach Twitter supplied them. Either way, all roads always led back to Twitter.[10]

Even before these crackdowns, Twitter was inevitably problematic for ISIS, both in terms of its limitations and the vulnerabilities it created. By summer of 2014, ISIS reached peak notoriety. It had taken over swathes of Syria and Northern Iraq, and people from around the world flocked to join its newly declared caliphate. The world responded to this wake-up call by forming an international coalition against it. As a result, ISIS was under constant barrage of airstrikes, giving the group the first hard pushback it had yet received.

ISIS went to horrific extremes to try to stop these airstrikes. On August 19, 2014, the group released a video showing the beheading of James Foley, an American journalist kidnapped in 2012 in Northern Syria.[11] The setup of the video has since become emblematic of ISIS's brutality: Foley in an orange jumpsuit, towered over by masked British executioner Mohammed Emwazi, better known as "Jihadi John." Waving his knife, Jihadi John demanded President Obama stop the airstrikes the United States had begun launching against ISIS just weeks earlier.[12] He then decapitated Foley.

But there was more. At the end of the video, Jihadi John held onto another prisoner by the back of his orange jumpsuit. This was American Israeli journalist Steven Sotloff. Sotloff was known for his consequential coverage of Libya conflicts, including the September 11, 2011, assault on the U.S. consulate in Benghazi.[13] Jihadi John held Sotloff from behind in the video, demanding an end to U.S. airstrikes against ISIS.[14] "The life of this American citizen, Obama, depends on your next decision," he threatened.[15] But the world knew the U.S. airstrikes weren't stopping any time soon. Jihadi John's words weren't a demand; they were a death sentence.

Foley's beheading was the first high-profile jihadi snuff video of its kind since Zarqawi's beheading of Nick Berg in 2004. But jihadists' outpouring of joy for Berg's killing was different. Those were the days when social media as we now know it did not yet exist, and jihadists' celebrations were contained among themselves on password-protected forums. But now, ISIS supporters' celebration of Foley's killing seemed to infect the entire internet. It was something I had never seen before: a tidal wave of accounts setting their profile pictures to Foley's beheading. Posters of bloody knives in one post, a child reenacting the beheading on a doll in another. Ecstatic posts by Western ISIS members and supporters sharing links to "enjoy & spread" the video.

"I was happy to see the beheading of that kaafir [infidel]," a female ISIS member tweeted. "I just rewinded to the cutting part . . . Allahu akbar! I wonder what was he thinking b4 the cut."[16]

"The brother that executed James Foley should be the new Batman," wrote British ISIS fighter Reyaad Khan.[17]

These celebrations weren't just rubbing salt into the wound of Foley's traumatized family. They were a showing of force from this rising terrorist group. It said to those ISIS was trying to recruit: *We are untouchable. Join us.*

FIGURE 7.1 Photo circulated on Twitter of a child reenacting the James Foley beheading on a doll

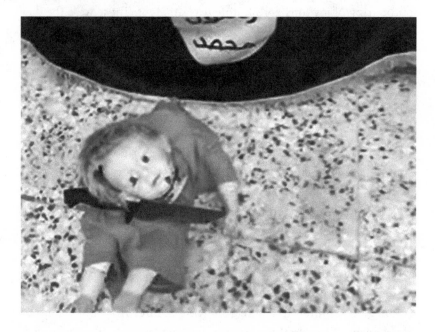

FIGURE 7.2 Photo circulated on Twitter of a child reenacting the James Foley beheading on a doll

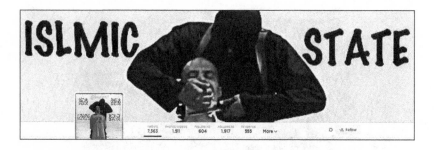

FIGURE 7.3 Social media account with avatar and banner images set to scenes from ISIS's Foley beheading video

My staff knew how important the work of tracking and reporting on this was, but it was emotionally taxing, nonetheless. Everywhere we looked on Twitter, images of Foley's head were strewn across our screens. Watching it all play out, I began to wonder if we could do something more than simply report about it. I consulted with Chris, my top jihadism analyst who had been mapping terrorist networks with me for a decade. We started to plan.

Jihadi groups like ISIS or al-Qaeda spend immense efforts in building fortresses around themselves online, but there is always a way in. It's an inevitable fact of operating online, no matter who you are or what organization you're with. As for ISIS, at that time, we knew their media machine well enough to penetrate their armor. Twitter didn't allow users to upload large files, which was problematic when ISIS wanted to release one of its flashy videos or long leadership speeches. Instead, the group had to upload these releases to various file-sharing and streaming websites. By this point, Chris and I had built up a collection of usernames and email addresses of ISIS Central Media Division officials on these various platforms. They tried to cover their tracks by altering username spellings and using alternative email addresses, but we always managed to catch up. As a result, we often saw the group's high-profile media releases hours, even days before they were released. It was a delicate situation. If we ever reported on what we saw, ISIS would know it was compromised and completely change its methods.

But on September 2, the equation changed. That day, two weeks after the Foley video, one of the accounts we were tracking uploaded a video. Chris spotted it first and opened the file. It was Steven Sotloff. Beside him was Jihadi John. Just like they did to Foley, ISIS made Sotloff read a script, blaming the United States for what was about to happen to him. Afterward, Jihadi John finished the crime in front of the camera.[18]

It was only a matter of time before ISIS would release the video and trigger the same horrid celebration we saw for Foley.[19] If we were going to make a move, now was the time. But after our experience with the Bin Laden video seven years earlier, in 2007, I told myself I'd never trust the U.S. government with handling our research again. We'd handle this one ourselves.

Chris wrote up the report and, with the click of a button, sent it to all of SITE's verified subscribers: government agencies like the Defense Intelligence Agency, Department of Homeland Security, Department of Defense, Department of Justice, and FBI; foreign government agencies; news outlets including CNN, NBC, and the *New York Times*. In an

instant, it was all over television and on the landing pages of news outlets. Our phones started ringing off the hooks. Governments and media
alike asked us the same questions: Is this video real? If ISIS didn't pub-
lish it, how did you get it?

At the same time, conspiracy theorists were having a field day. According to some, my staff and I were making ISIS's videos in a basement
studio. As one blog article the next day put it, "Once again, SITE/Rita
Katz . . . brings us the latest fake terrorist videos . . . MANUFAC-
TURED BEHEADINGS TO SELL YOU A NEW WAR!"[20]

Nonetheless, getting ahold of ISIS's video accomplished the first of our
objectives: humiliating the group in front of its supporters. Media is all
about terrorists portraying themselves as they want others to see them.
Their entire reputations are embedded in their media, from the quality
of their production to how smoothly (or not) they are released. So when
ISIS had its high-profile video taken from it—no less by a Jewish American woman with no security clearances—the group's stealthy reputa-
tion took a hit.

Our other objective was to squash what would have been a massive
online hype campaign by the ISIS community. ISIS supporters had no
idea how to deal with the fact that channels like CNN had the Sotloff video and they didn't. They searched among well-connected ISIS
accounts, but those didn't have it either. Some ISIS supporters tried generating hype by posting clips and screenshots sourced from news
outlets, but others warned against sharing it since ISIS itself had not
actually released it. Maybe it was fake, they said. Thus, it was all crick-
ets. No celebration, no hype or recruitment capital. Only embarrassment on ISIS's part. The group did not release the Sotloff video—not
that day, not that week, not ever.

That we dealt this blow to ISIS, a group defined in no small part by
its media machine, mattered in more than one way. It showed that
deleting ISIS social media accounts did not constitute a comprehensive
solution in and of itself. Like administering painkillers for a serious chronic illness: the underlying problem still existed. Yes, removing
accounts that promoted ISIS was a vital component in the fight against
the group, but countering its propaganda and recruitment machine on

a deeper level required more creativity. ISIS needed to be hit closer to its core.

But the incident and its implications also begged the question: If a small private organization relying on open source material was able to do this after mapping out ISIS's network, what could an entire government and its vast intel resources do? Sadly, it was premature to ask that question then. Many government officials didn't seem much further ahead on the issue than Twitter and other social media companies. I've seen it firsthand multiple times. In 2015, I briefed a congressperson after an ISIS-inspired shooting in Garland, Texas. This congressperson was a leading voice on the issue and was frequently on cable news talking about how the United States could defeat ISIS and its message. Yet as I described how one of the Garland attackers was immersed with recruiters on Twitter, I could tell I was losing this person. I suspected the congressperson didn't know how Twitter worked. Sure enough, I had to spend the rest of my briefing showing them how direct messages, retweets, threads, and other features worked. How could our leaders create effective policies against ISIS if they didn't understand how the group worked? I saw this lack of understanding across many corners of the U.S. government in these early years of ISIS's rise, and I have no doubt it worked to the group's advantage.

Regardless, when Twitter eventually stepped up its deletions, ISIS needed a new home: somewhere stable, a place where it could keep things tight and in-house, a place it could thrive without fear of constant account removals. One year after SITE's interception of the Sotloff video and countless more account removals, a new platform finally won ISIS over.

On September 22, 2015, Telegram, an encrypted messaging platform, announced a new feature called "channels," with which users could broadcast content to an unlimited number of members.[21] It didn't have a significant market share in the United States and other countries, but still managed to surpass 50 million active users by 2015.[22] It was founded in 2013 by a Russian-born man named Pavel Durov. Durov, who has described himself as a libertarian, fled Russia in April of 2014 as his work with VKontakte, a Facebook-like platform he launched in 2006, increasingly drew the ire of the country's authoritarian government.[23] Since then, Telegram has operated in various countries.[24]

It was strange: as far as messenger platforms went, ISIS members were always far more reliant on apps like WhatsApp, Kik, SureSpot, and others.[25] But Telegram's new channels feature was the hook for ISIS. One week after the company's announcement, out of the blue, ISIS announced its first Telegram channel, "Nashir" (meaning "publisher"), via one of its disguised Twitter accounts.[26] The Arabic message read:

> #Nashir_Channel
> Dedicated for the official publication issued by the Caliphate State
> To subscribe to the channel, visit the following link
> http://telegram.me/nasherislamicstate . . .
> Spread the message, may God help you

Within seconds after ISIS first posted the link to its Nashir Telegram channel, ISIS-linked media groups cascaded with uniform copies of the message across social media in various languages. Answering users' requests for technical breakdowns of Telegram, ISIS-linked groups started publishing tutorial videos and documents on the platform.[27]

It can't be overstated what a huge gamble it was for ISIS to move to Telegram. Brutal as the account removals were for ISIS, Twitter and social media gave the group reach it could never have had anywhere else. Could they hold onto that reach on Telegram? Would their supporters leave the social media platform they knew so well to venture onto a new and unfamiliar one? Even if they did, would Telegram give them the boot like the other platforms they tried to set up shop on?

In the coming days, ISIS's members and followers started making accounts en masse by the tens of thousands. Telegram did little to stop this influx of users. ISIS's ultimate confirmation came when al-Qaeda and its affiliates, now plagued by the same account removals as ISIS, set up shop on Telegram as well.

For ISIS, Telegram had everything the group could ever want: encryption to protect its operatives from investigators, virtually unlimited storage space to exchange and archive content, and plenty of other useful features. It was their new base from which all other online activity stemmed. Media operatives workshopped content and coordinated its release in chat groups, and then broadcasted it in neatly composed channels. There were no more disguised accounts like there were on Twitter. On Telegram, every media group's channel was clearly branded and easy to find, from media groups like "Khilafah News" to attack-guide providers like "Lone Mujahid." Some chat groups were dedicated to religious advice while others were for general conversation.

ISIS devised an entire system around Telegram, with groups like "Fursan al-Rafa" (meaning "Upload Knights") proliferating URLs to media releases across various streaming platforms and groups like "Online Dawah [Preaching] Operations" and "Invasion Brigades" coordinating ISIS spam messaging on social media.[28] ISIS supporters were reminded that Telegram was not a replacement for social media, but rather the headquarters where social media outreach was coordinated:

> Telegram is not a media platform for dawa [preaching] to all Muslims and the West. No one will enter your channel except the Ansar [supporters] who already know the truth . . .
> We realised some lack of care and efforts on Twitter. And we want everyone to return to Twitter with double efforts. Let Telegram be like an Archive.[29]

As ISIS began developing these new systems around Telegram, the group and its supporters were thriving. But their party wouldn't go entirely uninterrupted for too long.

On the evening of November 13, 2015, I returned home from the office and started preparing Shabbat dinner. My phone buzzed. It was a text from a good friend of mine, a federal agent stationed in Europe. "Who do you think is behind the attacks?" he asked.

I rushed to my computer. It was unclear what was happening: reports of bombings and shootings in multiple locations in Paris. Some were suggesting it might be al-Qaeda, given that its affiliate al-Qaeda in the Arabian Peninsula carried out a mass shooting on the satirical newspaper *Charlie Hebdo* earlier that year. This appeared different, though. It was more intentionally chaotic and less specific to a single target.

Sure enough, it was ISIS. From its territories in Syria and Iraq, the group planned a sophisticated operation against soft targets involving a mass shooting and hostage-taking attack at the Bataclan theatre, three suicide bombings at the Stade de France during a soccer game, and rapid mass shootings and an additional suicide bombing in bars and restaurants around Paris. These suboperations claimed 130 lives and injured hundreds more.[30] Several of the attackers, including mastermind Abdelhamid Abaaoud, were Europeans who left for ISIS in Syria and returned with deadly new experience to guide their attacks.[31] It was a hellish realization of France and the world's worst nightmare: the war *over there* in the Middle East was never going to *stay* over there. By then several ISIS-inspired attacks had already taken place in countries like France, Canada, and Belgium, but the scales of these were far smaller and involved no coordination with the group.

As the horror unraveled that night, ISIS and its supporters launched a massive celebration campaign out of Telegram to social media before the group even claimed responsibility, making a high-profile signal of how entwined Telegram was with ISIS and the real-world havoc it sowed.[32] Telegram's name instantly become synonymous with ISIS. News outlets reported that ISIS claimed the attack on Telegram and how its supporters celebrated there, running headlines like "This Is ISIS's New Favorite App for Secret Messages."[33]

Telegram had no choice at that point; it had do something. On November 18, five days after the Paris attacks, I was on the phone with a reporter talking about the attacks and the role Telegram was playing for ISIS. As I went to check the latest number of followers from ISIS's Nashir channel, it wasn't there. Had I been kicked out?

"I'm sorry, I have to go. I'll call you back," I said abruptly and hung up.

It wasn't just my account; the rest of my staff said they couldn't access theirs either. Nashir was gone, and so were many other channels.

That day, Telegram announced that it had removed seventy-eight public ISIS channels.[34] It was a small feat given how much more there was to ISIS's Telegram presence, but it nonetheless marked the company's first significant move against the group since it had set up shop months earlier.

Telegram's ramped-up ISIS removals was just one signal of a changing global priority. Deadly attacks popping up around the world were forcing governments to acknowledge that everything they were doing against ISIS was not enough. In early 2016, with the wounds of November's Paris attacks still raw, Europol established the European Counter Terrorism Centre, which added more emphasis to the EU's tracking of online terrorist content.[35] In the United States the Paris attacks prompted lawmakers to revisit debates about surveillance, particularly those of proposed "back doors" imposed upon encrypted messenger applications.[36] Such proposals picked up steam weeks later, after a married couple carried out a mass shooting and attempted bombing of a Department of Public Health training event and Christmas party in San Bernardino, California, on December 2, 2015.[37] Federal authorities got into a battle with Apple not long after regarding encrypted data on one of the shooter's iPhones, which the tech company refused to unlock. Implying the need for more reach, FBI Director James Comey stated that encryption barriers were "overwhelmingly affecting" law enforcement's investigation of the attack.[38]

Such calls for privacy invasion felt unjustified. Assuming the government used such access effectively—that being a big *if*—would this reach be permanent? It always seemed clear to me that no freedom should be given up without pause, because it tends to be hard to regain. As tech companies, government officials, and experts debated the matter, I was asked to write an article for the *Washington Post* to contribute to the conversation. I asserted in my piece that the government should make more use of what was right in front of them before asking for invasions of citizens' privacy:

Rather than try to create backdoors to encrypted communication services, or use the lack thereof as an excuse to intelligence failures, the

U.S. government must first know how to utilize the mass amount of data it has been collecting and to improve its monitoring of jihadist activity online.[39]

There was no denying that ISIS always seemed one step ahead as the group continued operations on Telegram and the other platforms it branched out to. According to a report by the House Homeland Security Committee, recorded ISIS-related attack plots rose from 19 in 2014 to 48 in 2015 and 74 in 2016. Most of these attack plots were aimed at targets in Western countries, ranging from minimal casualty events like the 2015 Garland, Texas shooting to the Bastille Day vehicular ramming in France in July 2016.[40]

Attacks were spiking even as ISIS began suffering territory losses in Iraq and Syria. During this time, ISIS doubled down on demanding lone wolf attacks from its supporters. In September of 2016, ISIS took these incitements to a new level by launching a magazine called *Rumiyah* (meaning "Rome"), which it released in a growing array of languages.[41] The magazine provided religious fatwas urging that spilling the blood of non-Muslims in their countries was *halal* (meaning permissible) and gave detailed guides on how to carry out stabbings, vehicular attacks, and other types of carnage. ISIS supporters circulated *Rumiyah* online aggressively. The deadly effects could be seen in many attacks carried out in the West true to the directives provided within the magazine. Vehicular attacks alone included twelve killed in the December 2016 truck ramming at a Berlin Christmas market, five killed in the April 2017 Stockholm vehicular attack, and five killed in the October 2017 Manhattan vehicular attack.[42] ISIS also managed to land some horrific coordinated attacks against the West in this time, including the March 2016 Brussels bombings and the May 2017 Manchester Arena bombing.[43]

For years, I spoke to tech companies and government officials about the problem at hand, whether in private meetings or in conference presentations. Defeating ISIS on the ground alone wasn't going to diminish its influence in the West so long as their online presence endured, I explained. Jihadi terrorists' use of the internet was a problem since the late 1990s, but what we were seeing online was something much more evolved and harder to contain. ISIS planted its pseudo-caliphate across the internet like a viral infection. There was no need to visit a training camp or even talk to an operative online; everything a prospective ISIS attacker needed to carry out the deed was just a few clicks away.

And it wasn't just the attack manuals and high-profile magazines that created ISIS's virtual caliphate. Its propaganda created a vivid sense of place, often capturing the parts of life under its rule that didn't have to do with a holy war: pizza shops, the day-to-day visits by agricultural inspectors, commerce in city squares, children at the park, sunsets, and so on. When attackers rammed trucks or fired into crowds of innocents, they were acting as citizens of this caliphate, regardless of whether they had physically been there.

"How is this propaganda?" I was often asked about ISIS's productions about pizza restaurants and sunsets. "What *is* propaganda, at the end of the day?"

If we were indeed at war with ISIS, fighting it online was just as critical as fighting it on the ground. If ISIS's online presence was a virus, it had to be treated like one. That meant there were no magic pills to swallow while the underlying foundations of the problem went unchecked. The world needed to think holistically. Lives depended on it.

<hr />

Around the world, the pieces gradually started coming together toward a more comprehensive fight against ISIS online. The EU began crafting new regulations that would impose fines upon social media and tech companies that failed to remove terrorist content, creating the first foundations of a legal framework for companies to operate within.[44] Meanwhile, social media and streaming platforms started employing smart algorithms and protocols to detect ISIS content. In 2017 we published a study showing that in the ten days between March 8 and March 18 of that year, ISIS generated 515 YouTube URLs.[45] In a follow-up study in 2018, I examined the same ten-day period for 2018 and found that ISIS only generated 15.[46] To put it simply, YouTube managed to block ISIS off of its platform, proving that progress was possible.

More importantly, there was a new embrace of collaboration around the globe. In June 2017, Facebook, Microsoft, Twitter, and YouTube announced the creation of the Global Internet Forum to Counter Terrorism (GIFCT).[47] The program wasn't prescriptive in and of itself. Instead, it established a foundation of collaboration and data-sharing among tech companies, large and small.[48]

We at SITE had long been waiting for this new environment. We spent the years prior developing methods of identifying, verifying, and removing terrorist content so that social media, streaming, and file-sharing companies could remove it—and even prepare to remove it before it hit their servers. Now, as the international mood was changing, these entities were embracing new solutions and our database became a major resource in the fight against ISIS. Meanwhile, Telegram remained the primary operative point for ISIS, its media groups, and supporters. But it was getting harder for them to post ISIS content on other social media sites, as major platforms like Twitter and Facebook were removing ISIS content almost instantly. Streaming and file-sharing services like Google Drive, OneDrive, and YouTube were likewise detecting ISIS propaganda upon it being uploaded, often rendering many of the URLs ISIS generated for its multimedia releases useless.

To be fair, Telegram was also taking some action against ISIS. As the platform gradually ramped up removals of jihadi channels and chat groups, many were forced to go private, meaning users couldn't join unless they had an invite link (similar to how groups on Facebook are closed off to the public). Some of these channels would only last hours before they were removed, despite their tightened privacy settings. The result was a constant battle of removals by Telegram and evolving adaptive measures by ISIS: creating duplicate channels, groups, and back-up accounts, and coordinated distribution across the platform. No matter what Telegram threw at it, ISIS always had a workaround.

On Friday, November 22, 2019, I noticed that Telegram had removed my account. I had been using this one for a number of years, so a lot of my research and position within certain ISIS circles went out the window with it. As I logged into my alternative Telegram accounts, they went black, one by one. The same went for my al-Qaeda-tailored accounts.

Ray, who heads SITE's ISIS data collection, yelled from the other side of the office, "My account is gone!" Others from my staff said the same throughout the day, as did prominent counterterrorism researchers and journalists from other institutions. It seemed that anyone remotely connected to ISIS on Telegram had been booted from the platform. There was no use creating new ones, because those went down just as quickly.

Chris, Ray, and others from our team began panicking. "How are we supposed to do our jobs?" they asked, exasperated. But I kind of enjoyed it, to be honest. If we were scrambling, so were ISIS, al-Qaeda, and their supporters. Plus, how often is it that a major terrorist organization like ISIS is temporarily muted across social media? I was going to be hosting Thanksgiving dinner the following week, so maybe it would be a rare opportunity to relax and spend time with my family uninterrupted. And when Telegram's aggressive purge continued in the days that followed, I got to do exactly that.

It turned out that around the time I first noticed my account went down, Telegram had partnered with Europol, which by then had a substantially equipped Internet Referral Unit to track jihadi propaganda and bad actors.[49] It was a major departure from the company's usual methods. Up to that point Telegram's removals of ISIS accounts were dispersed, leaving enough time for an ISIS operative to join back in and reconnect with their counterparts. But now, Telegram was hitting them all simultaneously and wasn't sparing anyone. The purge hit everyone from supporters and Telegram bots to high-ranking operatives from ISIS's Central Media Division.

Meanwhile, ISIS was regrouping on other platforms, some of which we had never heard of: TamTam, Hoop, Wink Messenger, Blockchain Messenger, and Mastodon social network.[50] They also hopped onto better-known alternatives like MeWe, Minds, and Element.[51] For ISIS, it was a confusing mess of account deletions and displaced media workers frantically trying to reconnect with partners they had never interacted with off Telegram. To date, ISIS accounts can be found to varying degrees on several of these platforms.

Sadly, Telegram's purge proved short-lived. The platform gradually eased off its removals and ISIS began making its way back on, and within roughly a month, it was back to business as usual. By mid-December, as ISIS had now regained its standing on Telegram, it was hard to see what the point of this purge had been.

ISIS and al-Qaeda definitely gained something out of this. Despite the disruption it caused, Telegram's purge taught these groups to have disaster protocols in place. Following Telegram's purge that November, both groups still maintained their accounts on platforms like Conversations and Threema so that their operatives could find each other following any future shakeups.[52]

There were valuable lessons for those fighting ISIS too. First was the importance of removing the group as soon as it surfaced on any given platform. The platforms that booted the group most quickly and thoroughly were the ones that the group abandoned; the ones slower to put up a fight tended to be the ones where ISIS sensed weakness and thus hung onto.

The most important lesson, though, was in Telegram's ability to disrupt ISIS's online presence. Even if for a relatively short time. If Telegram could so profoundly disrupt ISIS's online activities, there was no reason other companies couldn't do the same, so long as they were correctly advised and given the appropriate resources. It was no longer a question of what the tech sector could do in the fight against ISIS. It was a question of how much it was *willing* to do.

Though ISIS media continues to incite its supporters to kill its enemies, ISIS-inspired attacks in the West have become relatively rare. In 2018 the group claimed only seven attacks in Australia, Belgium, Canada, and France.[53] There was just one in England in 2019, and two in England and Austria in 2020.[54]

What was once a chaotic, directionless assortment of affected companies and government agencies transformed into something much more cohesive. They employed an all-of-the-above approach to stomping out ISIS online: image recognition, URL databases, smarter algorithms and security requirements, accessible databases of known terrorists, larger and better-trained teams to screen and vet potential terrorist content. There were shared plans and systems. Enough major players willing to act and collaborate—exactly what the world had needed all along.

There is still a long way to go in fighting ISIS online. But given where we were in 2014, significant progress has been made. It is no coincidence that as its social media presence deteriorated, so too did ISIS-inspired attacks in the West. By SITE's count, attacks in the West went from roughly fourteen in 2017 to seven in 2018, and then just a couple a year ever since.[55]

ISIS still haunts us online, but not with the same openness as it once did. The group still relies mostly on Telegram as a central hub, but it is constantly changing locations and trying new ones out. What few accounts remain of Western ISIS supporters on Twitter, Facebook, Tumblr, Telegram, and elsewhere are forced to hide like mice. There are no more uninterrupted *baqiyah* family social media meetups, no more endless streams of propaganda, no more celebrity recruiters to give instructions of how to join them on the front lines. This is especially true of Westerners. Today, if you're an ISIS supporter—or even just a vulnerable prospect, curious about the group—you might not even be able to find the group online.

Seeing the hard-earned successes against ISIS online—and the collapse of its physical caliphate around the globe—one would naturally assume that should another, similar terrorist movement come around, we would be prepared. After all, the years of ISIS's worldwide terror reign served as a case study in what to do. And not to do.

8

TERRORGRAM

My phone, perched on the kitchen counter, lit up with email notifications as I prepared for dinner with my family on Sunday, February 16, 2020. Probably just dispatches from the office, I thought. I convinced myself to ignore it. But as I went to sit at the table, I got yet another alert. I peeked and saw it was from a friend of mine who works in counterterrorism. He doesn't email me too often, let alone on Sunday evenings. It was probably important.

"Assume you got this, too," he wrote. "Do you [know] much/anything about this group? Any reason [for] concern?"

It was a forwarded email. It opened with a paragraph-length message, but before I could even read it, my eyes darted to the images that followed. One showed Nazi militants shooting me. It read, "As the day of rope draws near . . . Ms Katz has a lot more to fear."

Another image showed a satellite view of our office address in Bethesda, Maryland with explosions surrounding it: "MARYLAND ISN'T SAFE ANYMORE, KIKES. Bomb your local SITE Headquarters."

Grim as it sounds, I've grown used to these types of threats over the years. It started in 2003 when I published a book called *Terrorist Hunter* about how I got into counterterrorism, including the undercover work I did to expose terrorist groups and their fronts operating in the United States. Though I published the book anonymously to protect my identity and family, I was outed as the author after the book came out.

The resulting threats came for years: in the mail, through phone calls, via internet posts. I relocated my office, our home, and my kids' schools, but I couldn't get rid of the underlying fear. For years, if I called the house and the kids didn't answer immediately, I would panic and call my husband or neighbors to check on them. It was tough.

This new normal set the tone as I built up SITE in the following years. We installed cameras at every entrance and required visitors to sign nondisclosure agreements about our location. I gave all my staff cover stories to tell people when asked where they worked: a fake company name, fake job titles, and fake day-to-day tasks that they'd be able to rattle off on the spot. In earlier years I might have viewed these measures as excessive, but when the FBI informs you of recurring threats on your life, you'd take security very seriously.

Yet with this new email, it wasn't just me and my company in the crosshairs. One of the images depicted the friend who emailed me with a Holocaust-era yellow "Jude" star on his jacket as he was being shot in the head. It was accompanied by a message, "YOU'RE NEXT!" The image also contained the address of an institution he worked at along with a threat at the bottom, "COMEUPPANCE IS COMING, KIKE."

Another image showed us being shot by Nazi militants. "LINE THEM UP AGAINST THE WALL. THE MOON CREW WILL KILL YOU ALL," it read.

As my friend suspected, the same email was sent to SITE—likely one of the messages I had been ignoring moments earlier. I was particularly worried about him in all of this, though. He was a recognized figure in the DC area. When terrorists threatened SITE, I took the brunt, not my staff and associates. And unlike me, he didn't undertake extensive security measures against potential attacks.

It was clear who sent us these images and why. It was a neo-Nazi group called MoonKrieg Division (MKD), whose name and logo (far-right meme character Moonman's crescent-shaped head with a skull mask) were nods to Moonman. This was how prevalent of a motif Moonman had become in the far right: they were literally branding groups after him.

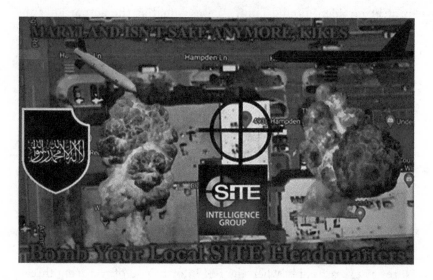

FIGURE 8.1 One MKD image among others emailed SITE on February 16, 2020

We had been tracking MKD since they'd formed about a week earlier. It was smaller than most groups on our radar, but easily one of the most vile: constant death threats against Jews and Jewish organizations, incitements for "white jihad" and to "blow up your local synagogue." They were the latest addition to the "screw your optics" far right, adding to the still-growing chorus of worshipful praise for Brenton Tarrant, Robert Bowers, and other terrorists. SITE had already published multiple reports on the group prior to these threats, including its incitement to shoot up a well-known hate crime monitoring organization and a European airline.[1] It was SITE's reporting that prompted them to threaten us in the first place, with them noting their appearance in one of our latest reports.

MKD was a microcosm of a much larger shift happening across the most extreme parts of the far right. The "screw your optics" current was transcending mere clusters of anon posts on /pol/ and other message boards and platforms. It was becoming more organized, giving way to new groups with Nazi-themed names ending in *-krieg* (German for "war"), *-waffen* (German for "weapon"), and the like.

They were openly forming synergistic relationships with neo-Nazi militants overseas and taking their online planning to the streets, tacking up posters declaring "It's Ok To Genocide Subhumans" on college campuses, police cars, and in front of an African American church, with email addresses for recruits to contact.[2] Some posters were placed not too far from our main offices; one of our staff members even saw one on his way to work. It was as if all the propaganda we had been tracking online was coming to life, climbing out of our computer screens and into the physical world.

It wasn't for nothing that 2019 was the first year in our lives as Americans that my husband and I agreed not to put a mezuzah on our front door. A mezuzah, a piece of parchment containing Jewish verses placed inside of a case, are typically designed as small ornaments to put on the right side of one's door, thus identifying the house's residents as Jewish. Who among our neighborhood might have been among this growing movement? The mailman? The food delivery person? A neighbor down the street?

I immediately reported the MKD threats to federal law enforcement contacts of mine. This isn't something I've ever done for myself, but my friend entering the mix changed things. Within minutes, I got an email from the FBI's New York Office, who seemed just as concerned with the situation as I was:

> As you may be aware, a white supremacist group, Moonkrieg Division, has posted a threatening message with your name on its public message board. I wanted to make sure you are aware of the threat.
> We take this very seriously and are investigating the matter.

I thanked them and asked that they please focus on seeing that my friend was taken care of before me. I also instructed SITE's web department to immediately remove the Advisors section from our website, as well as any other partners or associates we might have listed elsewhere. The next day, I spoke with the FBI agent who emailed me the night before and assured her I would help with the investigation. I told her what we knew about MKD based on the SITE reports and database entries I pulled together and what our plan was from there. After the call, I pulled some of my senior analysts together to start the work.

The urgency didn't come from MKD's threats in and of themselves, serious as they were. Rather, it was the environment that those threats came from and echoed within. The far right was nearly a year into an ISIS-like online shift that was lending new weight to the movement's attack incitements. They had more eyes and ears to absorb such rhetoric, and more sophisticated, reliable networks to push it through.

How did we get here? How could a group like MKD be so bold and uninhibited by the year 2020? Had the world not just witnessed the mass shootings in Pittsburgh and Christchurch, and how those events inspired further mass shootings in California, El Paso, and beyond? Any rational person would assume that world leaders, seeing the international nature of this horrific threat, would unite to defeat it. With the global fight against ISIS finally taking effect, was the fight plan not partly written already?

⌾⌾⌾

After major terrorist attacks, social media platforms typically begin massive purges of extremist accounts. In some cases, platforms get taken down altogether. And in March 2019, as the world pieced together the undeniable links between 8chan and the Christchurch massacre, my staff and I were waiting for the latter scenario. Our browsers were crammed with tabs of discussion threads we were saving before it all disappeared. Even far-right users on Discord and chan boards knew it was coming. They saw the scrutiny that Gab had faced five months earlier after the Pittsburgh shooting, and now it was going to be their turn. News outlets ran intense coverage of 8chan and other far-right spaces under headlines like "New Zealand Shooter Steeped Attack in Dark Internet Culture" and "8chan Looks Like a Terrorist Recruiting Site After the New Zealand Shootings. Should the Government Treat It Like One?"[3]

It wasn't just the fear of a crackdown that had the neo-Nazis of 8chan sweating. They had long been in online wars with different communities of trolls and activists. Anti-fascist journalists had even begun doxing them on their corresponding hangouts on Discord.[4] So whether it was going to be a post-attack removal of 8chan by their web host or further harassment and censorship from their online enemies, neo-Nazis and white supremacists knew their days on 8chan were numbered. They needed a strategy.

Sure enough, they pulled from ISIS's playbook. In early April, a couple of weeks after Brenton Tarrant's massacre, one 8chan user started a thread about the trolling and censoring campaigns being waged against /pol/ users. The post proposed Telegram as a well-suited alternative and listed over fifty channels and chat groups dedicated to everything from fascist literature and speeches to neo-Nazi memes and artwork. Telegram, the poster explained, could be the solution the far right was looking for:

> I've listed the most important /pol/ related channels and chats available on telegram [as far as I know].
>
> Join them to get the pure redpills without shills hiding them. Also feel free to create and add here your own channel/chat if you have any interest to share (music channels would be appreciated).[5]

The interest of 8chan users was piqued. They began asking questions about Telegram—its security, how it would protect them from trolls and spies—and the user answered by detailing the platform's encryption design and privacy features. As the user stressed, if Telegram had frustrated governments like Iran and Russia enough to ban it, it had to be legit.

It wasn't surprising to see them follow in ISIS's footsteps to Telegram. Why repeat the research ISIS had already done? In carving out a booming new hub on Telegram, ISIS created a reproducible trajectory for other terrorist movements, four years after ISIS launched its first Nashir channel.[6]

As far-right users began delving into Telegram in the coming weeks and months, 8chan never went down. Two days became two weeks and 8chan was still there, as if nothing had happened.

It wasn't for a lack of effort; lawmakers began calling for action against the source of Brenton Tarrant's radicalization. The problem was that they were looking in the wrong places. Rather than focusing on 8chan, the place where Tarrant uploaded his manifesto and called on his brethren to wage a radicalization campaign, they looked to Facebook. Their thinking seemed to be that the site where he livestreamed his attack would have to be the site where he had been radicalized. U.S. senator Richard Blumenthal put Facebook at the front of his calls to action in two tweets made the day after the Christchurch attack:

> Facebook & other platforms should be held accountable for not stopping horror, terror, & hatred—at an immediate Congressional hearing. They must answer for an apparent abject failure to stop shock video & hate messaging.[7]

Indeed, Tarrant's Facebook reflected his ideology. On March 13, 2019, two days before his attack, Tarrant filled his account with far-right posts, including at least one article from *National Vanguard*, a white supremacist news outlet; videos on Oswald Ernald Mosley, a twentieth-century English fascist figure; and a video by a far-right video channel called "You Kipper." His posts of mainstream news articles were also selectively chosen to reinforce his narrative of nonwhite invasions. Such headlines read:

"You Are the Future of Europe," Erdogan Tells Turks

Why the Announcement of a Looming White Minority Makes Demographers Nervous

White Women Have Lower Fertility Rates in Every US state[8]

Were these posts indications of his white nationalist beliefs? Absolutely. Did they suggest he was going to carry out a terrorist attack? Not really. If Facebook admins had come across these posts at the time, I suspect they might not have even removed them.

I identify with the genuine conviction in Senator Blumenthal and other leaders' calls for action. I also agree wholeheartedly that major tech and social media companies, in wielding major influence on public discourse, also bear major responsibility in fighting online extremism. I've spent most of the last decade emphasizing this point and have spared no criticism for many companies' brazen lack of action. Still, it's hard to see how these companies will collectively be held accountable without a sense of what the rules are—let alone any sense of direction. In the years surrounding the Christchurch attack, the Trump administration gave daily nods to the far right while leveling constant allegations that social media companies' anti-hate speech censorship was unfairly aimed at conservatives. As Trump tweeted in August 2018, "Social Media is totally discriminating against Republican/Conservative voices. Speaking loudly and clearly for the Trump Administration, we won't let that happen."[9]

In May of 2019, exactly two months after Tarrant's attack, New Zealand Prime Minister Jacinda Ardern led a political summit cochaired by French President Emmanuel Macron. The initiative was called the "Christchurch Call." Though not mentioning 8chan, it was clear that Ardern understood the global nature of far-right radicalization on social media, even this early on. She stated in a video message, "Now we as a government, we could have simply sat back in New Zealand and formulated our own regulatory response. But social media companies, these platforms, they're global, and so the response needs to be global."[10]

Ardern's initiative called for governments and tech companies to collaboratively counter terrorist content and the ideologies behind it. Heavy hitters from the tech industry like Amazon, Facebook, Google, and Microsoft joined in. Likewise, seventeen countries, along with the European Commission, signed on, including the United Kingdom, France, Japan, Spain, the Netherlands, India, and Jordan.[11] And why wouldn't they? The Christchurch call was, by its very nature, the easiest gesture a tech company or government could make: a loosely framed and non–legally binding promise to do whatever was reasonable and feasible to stop the spread of terrorist content. At the same time, it was something the world needed. Practical questions regarding the Christchurch Call aside, it meant something that people could see the world's most powerful governments and tech companies together, willing to get the wheels of collaboration moving.

Well, some of the world's most powerful governments. The Trump administration didn't seem eager to join in at all.

The United States, the leader of the free world and home of the titans of Silicon Valley, did not sign on to the agreement. The White House cited freedom of speech concerns, asserting that "the best tool to defeat terrorist speech is productive speech."[12] The statement instead suggested the promotion of "credible, alternative narratives as the primary means by which we can defeat terrorist messaging."[13]

So what precedent did this set for Facebook, YouTube, Twitter, and other internet platforms—if from one branch of the federal government, lawmakers demanded that these companies "be held accountable for not stopping horror, terror, & hatred," while another branch shrugged it off as a matter of free speech?[14]

It was also peculiar that Trump and his administration never voiced free speech concerns for ISIS propaganda when tech and social media companies started removing it. I was also curious what a "productive" dialogue was supposed to look like with someone who literally wanted to murder Muslims or throw Jews like me into gas chambers. If only we could figure out which "alternative narratives" they just hadn't heard yet.

Without a unified front against far-right terrorist recruitment online, the Christchurch Call never materialized into anything impactful. The largest player, the United States, had effectively opted out, leaving the far right to continue business as usual. It wasn't until Monday, August 5, 2019, two days after the El Paso attack, that 8chan was finally shut down by its cyber protection company, Cloudflare.[15] Supporters tried resurfacing the website via different names and web mediums, including a decentralized network called ZeroNet, which protected it from further hosting removals.[16] None of it really worked, though, and 8chan would never exist the same way.

A victory, right?

Not entirely. 8chan was removed late in the game, and as foreshadowed by posts on the platform dating from April, the far right had been preparing to replace it for quite some time.

———— ✺✺✺ ————

The far right's embrace of Telegram was indeed a mirroring of what ISIS had done a few years earlier, but the far right took on much less risk in doing so. When it came to setting up a new hub on Telegram, ISIS was gambling. No jihadi group—let alone *any* group—had set up an official broadcasting operation on Telegram before 2015; it was only a week after Telegram announced its channel feature's launch that ISIS announced its first Nashir channel. The group couldn't have been sure whether or not its network of aligned media groups would follow it there.

The far right never had to worry about such a gamble. By the spring of 2019, white supremacists and neo-Nazis had amassed hundreds of Telegram channels and chat groups, from paramilitary entities to hate groups and accelerationist terrorist organizations. Azov Battalion, a Ukraine-based paramilitary group, was active on Telegram at least as early as spring 2017 with multiple channels for different parts of its operations. Formed during the 2014 Ukrainian Crisis, Azov was adored across the far right as a model of what they wanted to establish in their own countries.[17] Far-right extremists in the West frequently asked how they could join the group to get military training for their own agendas back home.[18] Stickers and patches of Azov's Nazi-inspired logo have been sported throughout the West, from neo-Nazi demonstrators in the United States to right-wing terrorists attempting to bomb a mosque in Sienna, Italy.[19]

Telegram also housed smaller, more shadowy paramilitary organizations like the notorious Atomwaffen Division. Atomwaffen (German for "nuclear weapons") was an international neo-Nazi paramilitary group that formed in the mid-2010s.[20] Atomwaffen videos showed its members carrying out paramilitary training with automatic rifles, burning American flags, and slapping recruitment posters across college campus buildings.[21] Its posters read like far-right versions of U.S. Army recruitment bulletins, exclaiming "JOIN YOUR LOCAL NAZIS," with contact information at the bottom.[22]

Also joining Telegram pre-Christchurch were white nationalist and hate groups like the Europe-based Generation Identity, to which Brenton Tarrant had donated money and sent emails in 2018.[23] The group had at least six channels and chat groups across different languages and countries. Given the relatively strict censorship laws in some European countries, it was a particularly fitting venue for some groups. Even the Proud Boys, the ultranationalist group whose members were notorious for violence at demonstrations, had a presence on Telegram since at least as early as 2018.[24]

Yet until March 2019, the far-right scene on Telegram wasn't very prominent. Groups were still more active on their own websites and individuals were still scattered across 8chan, Discord, and other sites and streaming platforms. But after the Christchurch massacre, everything changed. Telegram quickly became the central mass around which all these other sites orbited.

Far-right channels that were long stagnant began shooting up in membership numbers. One of those channels shared in the April 2019 8chan post was "Racism Inc." For months prior to the Christchurch massacre, the channel had a flat subscriber count of roughly 3,000. After the attack, though, Racism Inc. began a steady climb upward, doubling to more than 6,000 subscribers by the end of October.[25] "Multiculturalism Revamped," another channel shared in the 8chan post, almost doubled by May.[26] The same pattern was seen across the far right. Between May and October that year, white nationalist and neo-Nazi channel subscriptions had risen by nearly 120 percent.[27]

More far-right users flocking to Telegram meant more venues created on it. Every day, we saw scores of new channels and chat groups being established and invite links strewn across Telegram. By October, 80 percent of the channels and chat groups we monitored were created after the Christchurch massacre.[28]

Neo-Nazis and white nationalists were cavalier about their booming growth, and for a reason. The platform was empowering. No censorship, no deletions, uninterrupted recruitment and outreach, easy coordination—the sky was the limit. Now, any Joe Schmo Nazi could create their own media group-like channel and become a major influencer in the far right.

White supremacists like "Alt Skull," the alias of a Tarrant-adoring online white nationalist personality named Shawn Deats, loved their new hub.[29] Alt Skull regularly gushed about its features and how it connected him with "thousands upon thousands" of others like him. He wrote:

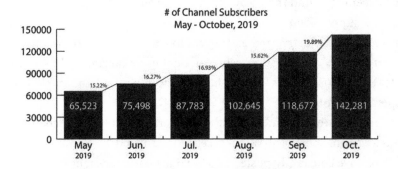

FIGURE 8.2 Data based on a sample of 80 far-right Telegram channels collected by the author and published in a December 2019 special report by the SITE Intelligence Group

The total freedom of speech and ability to network, coordinate, organize, and spread information has resulted in absolute White supremacy on Telegram. This is a microcosm of the greater society, and the results we've experienced here demonstrate why they spend millions upon millions of dollars and probably billions in resources to keep us isolated and apart.[30]

As another popular neo-Nazi channel put it, "If you are here; you are at the nerve center."[31]

I hate to agree, but Telegram is wonderful. I don't say this to promote the platform, but rather to give a sense of what the far right's fuss was about. If you've never used Telegram, it might be hard to fully understand (try explaining Twitter or TikTok to someone who has never used them). But imagine this: a largely glitch-free platform accessible via phone or desktop that can handle and share massive loads of traffic without slowing down. It's simple, reliable, secure, and fast.

Within this cacophony of white supremacist ideas swirling around Telegram, the "screw your optics" current bled into new corners of the far right. It was by far the loudest voice, both in terms of the volume of content as well as the aggression in the message. Ignoring it was impossible. No matter what far-right subideology a channel was dedicated to, posters and videos praising "Saints" like Tarrant and Earnest regularly seemed to find their way in. In chat group discussions, those not openly supportive of attackers like Robert Bowers were put on the defensive, even ostracized as cancers to the cause. On Telegram—or "Terrorgram," as its most extreme far-right users came to call it—it was the "screw your optics" wing that set the tone, and the movement operated accordingly.[32]

"Terrorwave Refined," one of the most prominent far-right channels, was a clearinghouse of all things accelerationism and "screw your optics." Terrorwave constantly posted neo-Nazi artwork, far-right ideological writings, manifestos by attackers like John Earnest, accelerationist incitements to "KILL THE COPS," and doxed information about left-wing activists.[33] Forwarded posts read, "Don't forget to pray to Saint Tarrant," while posters called to "start hunting tech CEO's for sport."[34] Like other far-right channels, Terrorwave promoted others within Telegram's budding network of accelerationist neo-Nazis. For less popular groups, Terrorwave's shout-outs could boost their profiles like primetime television advertisements. One channel, it described, "is your go-to for guides regarding gaming irl," implicitly referring to terrorist attacks.[35]

Terrorwave was just one channel (even if a popular one) within a network of others purposed to boost accelerationist content and messaging. These influencer channels helped keep the far right's bonfire on Telegram going. From here, the platform's neo-Nazi community was developing a sense of shape, identity, and unity. Prominent channels and individuals created corresponding chat groups wherein users established contacts, friendships, and partnerships. They organized new groups, and at times even cells. As a popular neo-Nazi Telegram channel with over 3,000 members wrote, the far right should "mimic" Islamist terrorist groups like Hezbollah. The post suggested that even those too scared to carry out violence themselves could now contribute to it:

> As westerners, we don't really know how to be terrorists, but we are really effective when we apply ourselves.
>
> . . . So imagine creating networks or common fronts together with other groups and organizations.[36]

Forwarded from T E R R O R W A V E R E F I N E D

04:18

THE ATOMWAFFEN DIVISION - FISSION (LQ)   8349 2:27 AM

FIGURE 8.3 Atomwaffen video promoted by Terrorwave on January 14, 2020, reaching over 8,300 views after being shared on this channel and elsewhere

Anticipating that Telegram would treat far-right extremists the same as it treated ISIS, the post closed, "And this is what I want to use telegram for, before we lose it."[37]

Thus, the story of MKD isn't a story about one group as much as it is about a new phase of far-right terrorism. Everything about MKD—its formation, activities, and its email to me and my friend—was the result of a shift from a dispersed network of far-right actors on sites like 8chan and Discord to one far more methodical and developed. The "screw your optics" wing of the far right was now more than a nebulous network of incitement-fueled extremist hives and dispersed lone wolf attackers. The rising wave of far-right terrorist attacks around the world proved that they had momentum. Now they were ready to leverage it toward something more structured, beyond the memes and chat groups.

MKD was established on February 8, 2020, approximately one week before it emailed death threats to me and my friend. The first posts on its newly established channel were a poster calling to "BLOW UP YOUR LOCAL SYNAGOGUE" and a series of introductory posts reading in part:

> Here we will fedpost to our hearts content and we will never stop in our struggle against the evil kike system. By spreading redpills we hope to wake up fellow Aryans to the ongoing White genocide and stop the evil kikes. WHITE POWER![38]

MKD fit in a specific category of far-right entities called "siege groups," referring to their adherence to *Siege*, a book by neo-Nazi ideologue James Mason.[39] While Mason's advocacy for a leaderless far-right terrorist movement once kept him on the fringes of the far right, this new generation of accelerationist neo-Nazis welcomed Mason's ideas. The "screw your optics" current needed an ideologue—someone to cast as a sage to guide the youth within it. Mason's *Siege* spoke to this current with eerie accuracy:

> Let us drop the dreaming, the faking, and the immature unreality, and recruit an army of the worst . . . For our part, we will welcome and honor as COMRADES any White, bar none, who wishes to join with us in the struggle. ANY action taken against the Enemy, no holds barred, is a heroic deed.[40]

With Mason as a de facto ideological leader, the phrase "READ SIEGE" became a meme unto itself, echoed by siege groups and their followers like uniform salutes. It was unclear how many of them actually read *Siege*, but they nonetheless championed it obsessively, with some even posting pictures of weapons next to physical copies of the book.

Siege groups branded themselves with similar aesthetics as Atomwaffen, which was among the most significant groups to boost Mason's profile to this new generation of neo-Nazis. They used jagged lettering, red ink

FIGURE 8.4 Image posted to the MKD Telegram channel on February 11, 2020, showing a hard copy of James Mason's *Siege*, alongside a flare launcher gun, a knife, and a copy of another book popular among the far right, *The Turner Diaries*

splattering effects, and images set to red and black gradients when praising figures like Osama bin Laden and declaring "WHITE JIHAD." It was as if they were jealous of their jihadi counterparts, wishing they could replicate the world-changing damage that events like 9/11 inflicted.

But the timing and circumstances surrounding this newly founded MKD group were unique. Its formation came just hours after the Feuerkrieg Division (FKD), perhaps the most prominent siege group at the time, announced it had "officially dissolved."[41]

FKD's dissolution came as a shock to many of its followers. Since the group surfaced in 2018, it managed to harness the "screw your optics" current's energy to form a remarkably structured, branded organization, especially as it left Gab for Telegram in 2019. It combined siege group aesthetics with the underlying essence of this new generation of far-right terrorists: praise of the "Saints," pursuit of "acceleration," the "Day of the Rope," and targeting racial minorities, LGBTQ, and other categories. It doxed federal law enforcement officials and journalists for attacks and proliferated posters showing hanging Jews and declaring, "SCREW YOUR OPTICS."[42]

If avenging the killing
of our people is terrorism
then history should be a witness
that we are Terrorists

FIGURE 8.5 Siege group-styled image published December 16, 2019, quoting Osama Bin Laden's embrace of the title "terrorists."

On Telegram, FKD was able to drastically up its recruitment game across North America and Europe, providing its email address for prospective recruits in those regions to form their own regional divisions. Their outreach messages declared, "If you're from the Great Lakes Region, Texas, California or the midwest and are looking to organize then contact us at FeuerkriegDivision@***" and "If you are from the New Jersey or New York area then message us at FeuerkriegDivision@***."[43]

It was unclear at first if FKD's outreach would amount to anything. Neo-Nazis were constantly hurling accusations and criticism at high-profile siege groups. Many were uncomfortable with Atomwaffen's promotion of the Order of Nine Angles, a Satanist neo-Nazi network formed in the 1960s.[44] Meanwhile, there had long been whispers that The Base, a growing siege group with branches popping up around the world, was a fed-run "honeypot."[45] FKD could have very well generated such wariness.

But prospects came to trust FKD as the real deal as it acquired widespread endorsements by prominent influencer channels like Terrorwave. It got even more credibility in August 2019, when authorities arrested a twenty-three-year-old Las Vegas man named Conor Climo for plotting attacks on a synagogue and LGBT bar.[46] Climo was a member of FKD, which took interest in "his knowledge of constructing explosive devices," per the DOJ.[47] After his arrest, the group publicly acknowledged speaking with him in a series of Telegram posts, criticizing him for getting arrested before carrying out his attack.

"When he told us about his idea we even encouraged him and asked if he needed help, he said he didn't," the group wrote, using the event to gain clout.[48]

Climo pleaded guilty to one count of possession of an unregistered firearm—"specifically, the component parts of a destructive device"—on February 10, 2020.[49]

As summer turned to fall in 2019, FKD posters were slapped on or near telephone poles, police cars, college campuses, synagogues, and other places across California, Pennsylvania, Washington State, and Florida, as well as in Canada. FKD flaunted its international branches, which it called "our cells."[50]

FKD was waging the same aggressive recruitment in Europe. A July 25 message on its Telegram channel read, "We are looking for members in Norway, Russia and the Benelux! Send us an introduction at FeuerkriegDivision@***."[51] Its posters celebrated right-wing terrorist attacks in Europe and asked prospective terrorists to contact them. The result in Europe was the same as in North America: FKD posters and other

Feuerkrieg Division **OFFICIAL**

Recent flyering done by a FKD recruit in California

FIGURE 8.6 November 2019 FKD post showing an individual standing next to a poster placed on wall with a caption reading, "Recent flyering done by a FKD recruit in California."

activity started appearing in countries like The Netherlands, Germany, United Kingdom, Croatia, and Italy.[52] FKD even posted updates on their meet-up events.[53]

As FKD's international network grew, members and associates were being arrested for terrorism-related charges. In the summer of 2019, the United Kingdom arrested a fourteen-year-old boy from Cornwall who would later confess to disseminating terrorist documents and possessing terrorist material, including bomb manuals.[54] The boy was in contact with FKD's leader, known as "Commander," and set up a British chapter of the organization, for which he recruited.[55] Among the recruits

FIGURE 8.7 Two posts made on FKD's Telegram channel on September 19, 2019, less than two hours apart.

brought in was another British boy who allegedly sought to carry out a terrorist attack while advising other FKD members on firearms.[56]

If these mounting events didn't put enough pressure on FKD, the troubles of its leader certainly did. In early January, police in Estonia went to the home of FKD's leader to question him.[57] It turned out this "Commander" was in fact a thirteen-year-old boy who had been running the multinational network from his bedroom.[58]

These new pressure points eventually crushed FKD. On February 8, 2020, the group was dissolved.[59] Nonetheless, FKD provided a blueprint to create a global network of siege cells. And as duped as some might have felt in hyping up an organization formed by a thirteen-year-old, others sensed opportunity. There was a market of radicalized teenagers and young men around the world who wanted to belong to something. With that, there was a void to fill after FKD's demise.

The night we received the MKD threats, I poured a glass of wine and started researching the group. Fortunately, I had a head start. Since the far right had upped its Telegram use, I doubled my staff count to archive all the open-source intel coming from the platform: chats, user profiles, associations, propaganda. It was a library of important terrorist content, so it didn't take long to identify one of MKD's leaders in the chats we archived. As it turned out, the day FKD announced its dissolution, a Telegram user by the username "SorestHH" forwarded the group's message to "Lunar Lounge," a neo-Nazi chat group frequented by many in Telegram's siege group scene.

"This is so sad," another user wrote. "So FKD Commander most likely got caught or is gone in some other way."[60]

SorestHH replied, "Yes i talked with him not so long ago and with the other FKD lead members. it's over."[61]

For SorestHH, the aftermath of FKD's dissolution spelled out opportunity: "Now since FKD is 'dissolved' people should search for new divisions... And not the ones run by (((feds))) or LARPing divisions."[62] (LARP stands for Live Action Role-Playing; in this context, "LARPing divisions" is meant to mock extremist groups that only play the part instead of carrying out real-world action.)

Openly stating one's connection to an international terrorist organization's leadership, affirming the group's agenda—that was reason enough to take interest in this person. But the way he seized on FKD's demise took things to another level:

> We are very glad to announce the start of our own division. Now since FKD is gone it's time for something new, something more radical, something more BASED. I introduce the MoonKreig division![63]

SorestHH, clearly some sort of leader within MKD, was true to his word. The group came out of the gate even more incendiary than FKD.

In its second day in existence, MKD published a series of posters calling to "COMMIT ACTS OF GENOCIDE AGAINST THE JEWISH COM-MUNITY" and "LYNCH YOUR LOCAL GOOK!"[64] In just a month after it was launched, we sent out an array of alerts to our subscribers about MKD. The group doxed the Anti-Defamation League's New York office address and called to "SHOOT UP" its headquarters "AND SLAUGHTER THEM ALL."[65] It called to "SHOOT DOWN YOUR LOCAL [Scandinavian Airlines] Plane," bomb the U.S. Capitol and Palace of Westminster, and even "PIPEBOMB YOUR LOCAL JEW-ISH KINDERGARTEN!"[66]

We had ample reason to take MKD's threats seriously. When a group's leader says they want to create a "more radical" version of a group like FKD, that in itself is worrying. FKD was a group that inspired multiple terrorist attack plots, so what is the intent of someone seeking to make an even more extreme version of it? Would MKD acquire a simi-lar reception and massive audience size as FKD? There was an apparent connection between the leaders of FKD and MKD, so would the former give the latter recruitment leads to pull into its new network? Those FKD cell members posting flyers across North America and Europe didn't just disappear upon FKD's dissolution, nor had they suddenly become less radical.

The Monday morning after receiving the MKD threats, I put together a team to assist me with investigating the group. We hunkered down in my office and went through every chat group discussion, channel, and corre-sponding account on other platforms pertaining to MKD and its mem-bers. Our searches led us everywhere from Reddit and Discord to Telegram chat groups for the Nordic Resistance Movement, a Sweden-based far-right organization. By the end of the day, we identified a few other key members of MKD in addition to SorestHH. Their roles in the group varied among propaganda, incitements, and posting content on the streets.

One stand-out member went by the name "The Wigger." He claimed in different chats to live in Mississippi, which checked out via the strong Southern accent in the audio messages he uploaded as well as the pic-tures he posted from his neighborhood. These included images of MKD posters denying the Holocaust and inciting attacks put up at a nearby synagogue, African American history museum, and other locations. The Wigger commented of them, "When you put up moonkreig propaganda at a synagogue irl [in real life]."[67]

But as we dug in more, things got weird. In one conversation, a user asked him if he was going to be voting for Trump, to which The Wigger replied he wasn't "old enough."

"How old are you anyway?" the user asked.

"13," The Wigger replied.[68]

You have got to be kidding me, I thought. My staff and I looked at each other, speechless. We knew we'd potentially be dealing with teenagers, but we weren't expecting middle-school-aged children. *Not again.* It sadly added up as we found more of his posts about field trips and being in school.

The Wigger, whose identity we eventually confirmed, didn't appear to have any leadership role within MKD, though. What we needed to find was who MKD's ringleaders and administrators were. Or better yet: the people who had sent the death threats to my friend and me. After evaluating MKD's members, we narrowed it down to two main individuals running the MKD operation: SorestHH and another user by the name "Paddington."

Sure enough, a week before we received MKD's threats, SorestHH was identified in a chat group as "an underage kid that the feds have twice tried to unsuccessfully deradicalise."[69] If this was in fact the case, it meant that SorestHH had been on authorities' radar well before MKD sent those emails to us—another unsettling development, considering that he was apparently only a minor. Sure enough, we gradually deduced from different chat groups that Sorest was a fourteen-year-old Bosnian kid living in Sweden.

My staff and I felt uneasy. I've spent the last two decades tracking battle-hardened militants and operatives around the globe and testifying against them in court, so how did I end up investigating what felt like an afterschool detention room? How many of the neo-Nazi groups we tracked were being run by kids too young to watch R-rated movies?

Nonetheless, one of these two partners seemed to be far more instrumental in MKD's threats against us. The day MKD sent the emails to us, SorestHH forwarded one of the posters into the Lunar Lounge chat group.

"Thank [Paddington] for that one," SorestHH wrote.[70]

From here, we zeroed in on this user and found overwhelming assertions that he was the one behind the emails. Over the course of examining Paddington's online presence, we learned that he was a nineteen-year-old college student living in Bosnia, though he claimed he had lived in the United States, United Kingdom, and Russia in years prior. He said he was studying economics to ultimately "get a government position so I can be a useful 'insider.' "[71]

Paddington aspired to more than a just politicking manipulator, though. He distributed guides on how to build homemade weapons and emphasized that change can only come "from the barrel of a gun." He even claimed to have physically "beaten" a Jewish person himself at one point: "Killing at least one jew in his lifetime is the duty of every Aryan man . . . I'm on the right track. I already have one jew beaten down with a steel chair under my belt."[72]

Paddington was easy for us, because he couldn't seem to keep his mouth shut about every little thing he was doing with MKD. He bragged about how he "sent threats to private emails of kikes in charge of US anti-terrorism ops." Just one day after sending the emails, he bragged to another user on a chat group: "I mean, just look at my stuff targeting that [Jack, my friend] kike."[73]

Even as SorestHH, The Wigger, and other MKD members seemed to tone down their Telegram activity amid inquiries from law enforcement after the emails were sent to us, Paddington kept going with the incitements. He felt like he was untouchable. "We aren't even in the US so we shitpost 24/7," he wrote.[74] He seemed to think that unlike SorestHH in Sweden, feds in Bosnia would never approach him: "I actually live in Bosnia so the kikes cant knock on my door daily."[75]

Of course, Paddington wasn't actually as shielded as he thought. We forwarded our findings to the FBI throughout our investigation, which took a month or so. Each of these MKD members were eventually approached by their respective countries' law enforcement in one way or another. The most critical justice came when Bosnian officials announced in June 2020 that they had searched Paddington's house.[76] In December 2020 they issued terrorist charges against him. His trial started in February of 2021, and he pled not guilty.[77]

I often thought about those thirteen- and fourteen-year-old kids that kept showing up in our investigations, whether they were from FKD, MKD, or other groups. We often forget what it's like to come into our first senses of conviction and independence at that age. I still remember the certainty I felt as a young teenager—what was best for me, what was objectively right, what mattered—and the headaches I gave my mother every time I went where she told me not to, or how I argued against everything she told me. My role switched decades later, with me becoming the mother of several teenagers with their own burgeoning convictions, defiant instincts, and excitement to belong to something.

This was the shift that Telegram facilitated for the far right's "screw your optics" current: the evolution from a horde of far-right ideologies on the primordial pools of /pol/ and other sites to something sophisticated, branded. These were groups that couldn't be deleted with the disappearance of a site like 8chan, with massive audiences that could be built into followings, and followings that could be mined for members.

Yet after all the violence and sufficient proof of the threat far-right terrorism poses to the world, Telegram has yet to wage removal campaigns against far-right extremists that are anywhere comparable to its purges against ISIS and al-Qaeda (which it continues to hit with constant, often instant removals). The company has performed some actions against the most extreme of far-right users, including a significant removal of Terrorwave and other major channels in the summer of 2020, but such measures remain intermittent and not disruptive in any lasting way.[78] Today, the platform remains the foremost communication and recruitment hub for far-right extremists around the world.

Telegram's lax approach toward the far right is a symptom of the international community's stance toward far-right terrorism. In many ways it feels like the early days of ISIS's rise, watching some companies and governments rise to the occasion while others look away. Noble initiatives like the Christchurch Call simply cannot be successful without enough major players onboard.

Siege groups like FKD and MKD (not to mention the other types of entities forming around Telegram) were proof of concept cases for a new generation of far-right terrorists. After all, making such a group was apparently so easy that a thirteen-year-old could launch a network of cells spanning at least a dozen countries across North America and Europe. And as shocking as it was to learn that a child sat at the helm of FKD, by no means did it imply the group's threat was any less real. Quite the contrary. Conor Climo did not know the age of his "commander." Tarrant and Bowers did not know the ages of those who sat behind keyboards and computer screens, spreading the vile content that pushed them over the edge. FKD members didn't know, or care, what the age of their leader was. In the new age of terror, terrorists are ageless.

The youth of these groups, their memes, the things they responded to and laughed at, the things they got angry at—it all made me pause and ask myself, *What are we even fighting?*

9

SEX SELLS (TERROR)

Sometimes I wonder if I should continue to be surprised when I see a picture of me being executed in jihadi and neo-Nazi posters. I check off way too many boxes: Jewish, Iraqi-born, Israeli, a public career in counterterrorism. Whether you're a Moonkrieg Division (MKD) member or ISIS supporter, I am the epitome of an enemy.

But it's not just my heritage or career that attracts terrorists' wrath. It is me being a woman.

Months after our MKD investigation was over, I kept thinking back to chats and graphics we picked up in the process. For example, there was a meme published to MKD's channel in February 2020, showing an old Swedish fairy cartoon character named Snufkin with the text:

SIEGE SNUFKIN TAKES OUT THE TRASH
Jews Nigs Spics Fags Women[1]

Why would a woman, simply by the condition of *being a woman*, receive the same hatred from neo-Nazis as racial and religious minorities or so-called degenerate LGBTQ community members? Why would attacking women equate to taking out the trash for Nazis?[2]

There are two facets to extremists' treatment of women. On the one hand, there is male frustration with women's success and progress,

FIGURE 9.1 Image posted to MKD's Telegram channel in February 2020

shared by communities from hardline Orthodox Christians, Jews, and Muslims to sexists, bigots, racists, and nationalists. On the other hand, there is also men's desire to *have* women—even if only in the afterlife. Jihadi fighters envied their brethren killed in battle: for meeting God, primarily, but also for getting to meet their *Hoor al-Ayn* (virgin women of Paradise).[3] Combatants raced toward battlefields to hasten these afterlife encounters. Some even put on cologne before martyrdom operations to smell nice when they meet them. (Yes, really.)[4]

It's not just men from fundamentalist upbringing in far-off lands who bought into this suicide-operation-for-heavenly-virgins promise. Moner Mohammad Abu-Salha's neighbors in Florida knew him as a "normal kid": a handsome young man in t-shirts and gym shorts, basketball in hand, looking for anyone to play a pickup game with.[5] Yet on May 25, 2014, at the age of twenty-two, he was standing outside an explosives-packed truck in Syria's Idlib governorate, giving good-bye hugs to fellow members of the Nusra Front, then al-Qaeda's branch in Syria. A jihadi propaganda video about Abu-Salha showed him shortly before his operation, narrating his preparation to meet the *Hoor al-Ayn*:

Last moment he beautified himself to meet Allah by applying Athar
[fragrance] and wearing a white thobe [clothing] and his shroud

He also held a rose for the Hoorul-eens [the Maidens of the
paradise][6]

Shortly after, Abu-Salha drove the truck into a Syrian military check-
point and detonated the bombs onboard. In an explosion that could be
seen from miles away, Abu Salha had become the first known American suicide bomber in Syria.[7] His rose, robe, and body turned to ash.

As for ISIS, its recruiters went further by playing into many men's
romance-related experiences here on Earth: frustrations with dating,
anxieties about rejection. Life under ISIS, as recruiters described it, was
a guaranteed ticket to a wife—even *multiple* wives. These wives would
do whatever men wanted: make children, cook food, clean a house, and
never even glance at another man.[8] Tracking them on social media, it
wasn't uncommon to come across tweets like one from 2015 of a husband with four wives illustrated as "Minions" from the *Despicable Me*
movies. Tweeting the meme, an ISIS supporter cheekily wrote, "MashAl-
lah ["what God has willed"]" while touting how "a lot of brother[s] and
sister[s] getting married" in Syria.[9]

ISIS also had other, far more disturbing ways to sell its caliphate to
sex-driven men.

As has been well-documented by Amnesty International and other
human rights groups, the most extreme of ISIS's sex-related selling points
were its *sabaya*, female sex slaves.[10] Sure, ISIS's men could have one to
four wives, but *sabaya* were literally treated as property, traded among
fighters. Recall the ISIS executioner Mohammed Emwazi (a.k.a. "Jihadi
John"), who beheaded James Foley, Steven Sotloff, and others? ISIS's
eulogy of him described how he "generously" offered his own *sabaya* as
gifts to fellow fighters:

Of the deeds that attest to his kindness and generosity is that after
receiving a sabiyyah (concubine) as a gift he did not hesitate to give her
away—likewise as a gift—to an unmarried injured brother.[11]

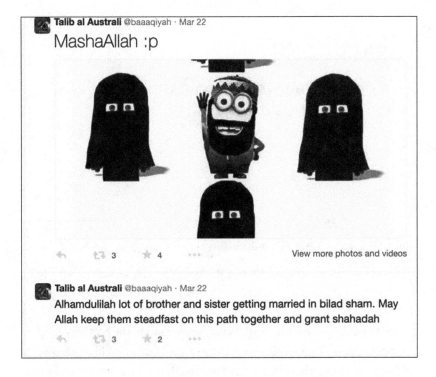

FIGURE 9.2 Image posted and reposted among ISIS Twitter accounts in 2015, showing the "Minions" from the Despicable Me movie series as a husband with four wives.

These *sabaya* were staples of recruiters' pitches to prospects, promising that whatever marriage-related troubles they might face under ISIS, *sabaya* would always be a given.

"Brothers in iraq dont stress themselves about marriage many sabayas," tweeted one ISIS fighter in May 2015, using smiling emojis. "[It's] only in Iraq where some brothers give you sabaya as a GIFT."[12]

For fighters already living under ISIS, *sabaya* were the ultimate form of "war spoils." Taking a city meant taking whatever they wanted, including *sabaya*, giving fighters yet more motivation to continue conquering. They were obsessed with *sabaya*, speaking about it openly on social media as an ordinary part of daily life. As ISIS fighter Shawn Parson (a.k.a. Abu Khalid al-Amriki) once tweeted:

FIGURE 9.3 Alleged ISIS fighter discussing female slaves given as a "GIFT" in Iraq under the group

Three weeks on the last [battle] every conversation the brothers speak about ended with sabiyas. I hear the word so much I got headaches . . . Even speaking about food the conversation ended with the word sabiyas."[13]

ISIS's promises of sex marked a major departure from the old ways of jihadi recruitment. "Father of Global Jihad" Abdullah Azzam never raved about having multiple wives and sex slaves during his lectures around the world, including the United States, in the 1980s. Even notorious al-Qaeda operative Anwar al-Awlaki, despite his documented visits with prostitutes and stubborn penchant for blondes, never tried to sell militant jihad as a means to "get laid."[14]

ISIS's tactic can be viewed as a disturbing social experiment in the dehumanization of women, and demonstrates how depraved some men can act once they are given permission. But ISIS's treatment of women was not unique. In most if not all the chat groups MKD members and associates frequented, a grimly similar vision of the world to ISIS's had emerged. As a woman, reading this chatter was often emotionally tasking. In the Lunar Lounge chat group, derogatory words like "whore" were staples of conversation. They declared that women would not "be race mixing if you ruled them with an iron fist."[15] They shared articles about bold, ambitious women while commenting, "Nobody wants her because she has a face of a man . . . Ugly deformed testosterone bitch."[16]

This misogyny was a feature of chan boards that I didn't think would fully carry over into Telegram. On boards like /pol/, users hid behind anonymous ID numbers with no recourse for what they said. As a result, those boards often felt like safe venting spaces for angry, frustrated young men: places where they could say things about women (and by extension, themselves) that even many white supremacists would frown upon. Yet they had no problem attaching their sentiments to their newly static identities on Telegram. On a chat group dedicated to a far-right organization called the Nordic Resistance Movement, it seemed like no conversation about minorities or Jews was complete without similar denigration toward women. At times it seemed like they hated women even more than Jews, Blacks, and other perceived enemies.

"Women have no power other than what men give them," wrote one user.[17]

Another ranted about enslaving women once the desired race war came about, fantasizing about putting them "in chains" and imprisoning them:

> there's nothing stopping us but other weak, treasonous men
> they can't physically stop us
> once the law man is gone they're going back in chains
> broooo imagine listening to morrissey as we enslave all women[18]
> gonna be based fellas[19]

If anything, Telegram made the violent misogyny of 8chan and Discord even louder and more prolific. As neo-Nazi siege groups multiplied on Telegram, some situated themselves within Order of the Nine Angles (O9A), which, as mentioned in the previous chapter, was an extremist network formed in the United Kingdom in the 1960s.[20] O9A ideology was based on Satanism and the embrace of sadism and violence as means of empowerment, pulling inspiration from Hitler and even jihadi ideologues.[21] Among the most dominant themes in O9A ideology was rape, which adherents embraced both literally and figuratively as necessary for initiation into O9A.[22] As such, posts about raping women became ubiquitous across far-right channels and chat groups. "Rapewaffen" (meaning "rape weapons") and its splinter group "Rapekrieg" (meaning "rape war") centered their entire existences around rape. To these groups, women were animals that distracted men from advancing O9A's violent agenda. In giving instructions on how to carry out rape, O9A groups capitalized the R, almost as if it were a holy act:

> It's not Rape if you flirt with her or conversate, only if you go for the kill with no words.
>
> You CANNOT flirt because that means you care about the moid [woman], do not give the f*moid [woman] too much attention other than the Rape. It will grow attached and will want to stay even after you Rape it.[23]

These groups were controversial, even scoffed at among some far-right groups and users, but their messages seeped in everywhere. Members of O9A groups were also members of other groups, and major channels promoted them, echoing their ideology. Paddington, the MKD member who sent us death threats, even bragged about being a former member of Rapewaffen and pondered plans to collaborate with them: "I wonder how rapewaffen has been doing since I left. Probably should get them to team up with MoonKrieg."[24]

A group like Rapewaffen or Rapekrieg might seem like a twisted but likely contained phenomenon; in reality, such groups have pulled in men from all walks of life, including even the U.S. military. One of those men was a twenty-two-year-old U.S. Army private named Ethan Melzer, who attempted to orchestrate an attack against his fellow soldiers. Melzer, an O9A adherent and member of Rapewaffen, sent sensitive information about his unit's activities to a purported al-Qaeda recruiter on Telegram in the hopes it would facilitate a "jihadi attack" on them and thus contribute to "another 10-year war in the Middle East." The Army and FBI thwarted his plot in May of 2020 and revealed its details the following month.[25]

O9A-adhering terrorists have also been seen in Europe. Others included a sixteen-year-old adherent from England convicted in November 2019 of preparing terrorist acts via a "manual for practical sensible guerrilla warfare against the Jewish system."[26]

Some even appeared to reflect the sadistic sexual deviance they preached. In February 2021, thirty-year-old O9A adherent Ryan Fleming from England was sentenced to six months in prison for using Instagram to message young teenagers. Fleming was a known pedophile, having been convicted in 2012 for imprisoning and sexually abusing a boy.[27]

O9A-adhering far-right groups are perhaps extreme examples, but one reason they are able to manifest so widely is the far right's longstanding foundation of misogyny.[28] Far-right adherents young and old see themselves as being at war against feminism, which they perceive as a threat to the survival of the white race.[29] Sure, you could find women of the far right championing these same regressive (if not dehumanizing) concepts, but the ideas are nonetheless concocted and perpetuated by the men steering these movements.[30] It's not for nothing that the word feminism appears in Anders Breivik's manifesto more than seventy times between his writing, footnotes, and quotes pulled. He wrote that "equalising the sexes has led to a crippling feminisation of Western society . . . the pursuit of equality is being used to destroy our society and undermine—and therefore be in conflict with—Mother nature."[31]

The younger attackers of the "screw your optics" far right carry the same torch. Brenton Tarrant and Patrick Crusius characterized their attacks as responses to white populations being outbred by ethnic "invaders," thereby blaming this alleged crisis in part on women and their choices to pursue life paths outside of childbearing. John Earnest also spoke to this crisis in his manifesto, blaming the Jews "for their role in feminism which has enslaved women in sin."[32]

These young men were products of communities obsessed with women's "purity," and who long for the days when so much of a woman's life revolved around serving and cleaning up after their husbands.

8chan's /pol/ board, Discord servers, and Telegram channels are filled with memes about their dream women, who they call "trad wives" (meaning "traditional wives"). These trad wives are modestly dressed, described as being "knowledgeable about her European roots" and homeschooling her children "so they aren't taught progress [bullshit] in school."[33] The memes juxtapose these make-believe blonde-haired women with "feminists," who are caricaturized as shallow, drug-addicted sex addicts.

Looking at trad wife and similar memes, the mind starts processing apparent similarities to the obedient wives of ISIS. But the fundamental issue at hand is about more than these similarities. The fact that terrorists can so effectively radicalize and recruit based on the desire to control and punish women says just as much about some aspects of our society

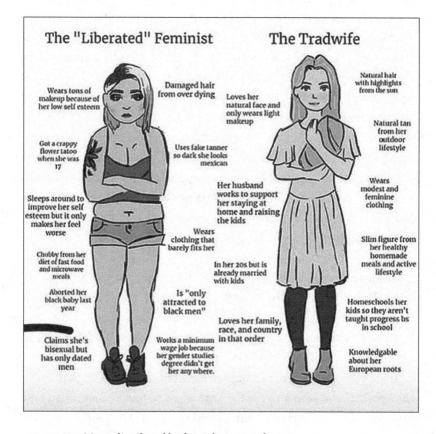

FIGURE 9.4 Meme distributed by far-right users online

as it does about ISIS or neo-Nazis. After all, are these groups' outreach not based on the recruitment market at hand? The best terrorist outreach is often the kind that effectively speaks to the frustrations of prospective recruits. These frustrations often shift as society does, making a society's culture wars a critical nerve to press into. And as groups like ISIS and movements like the "screw your optics" far right show, the culture wars around feminism and female progress are among the most universally potent.

The last fifty years have been a fast-moving streak of progress for women. And now, in the age of #MeToo and the mainstreaming of feminism in popular Western culture, some men are angry. For every sensationalized story about young feminist activists taking their cause "too far," many men—including *young* men—lean more fervently into toxic senses of sexual entitlement and bitterness at failed romantic lives, blaming their perceived failures on the changing culture they live in. Hence, the trad wife or ISIS bride: someone who never questions her husband, who doesn't speak her mind, who doesn't require being listened to. A woman who doesn't expect men to do the aggravating work of charming or developing an organic connection with her.

These fantasy women are just as critical to the far right's utopian societies as the absence of the religious and racial minorities they loathe. This misogyny is omnipresent, injected in one way or another into most discussions about race wars and racial hatred. Sometimes, it is hidden amid all the swastika imagery and yelling about immigrant invasions. But other times, it's hard to miss. Especially when it's riding in a car with a stockpile of homemade weapons.

October 9 of 2019 was Yom Kippur, the holiest of all Jewish holidays. Known as the Day of Atonement, the holiday is centered around the idea of recognizing one's sins and repenting. The most devout Jewish adherents fast and pray for twenty-five hours in synagogues to atone for their sins. I myself have always observed the holiday in a less rigid fashion.

Yom Kippur was very different in Israel, where it was the most outstanding day of the year: all vehicular traffic comes to a standstill for an entire day. Everything is eerily quiet; all normal city noises are gone. At night, most houses are dark. In what may appear surreal to a non-Israeli, all roads and highways are free of vehicles, and, instead, *people*, including very young children, walk or ride bicycles and tricycles on them. It is the day of the year when parents finally take the opportunity to teach their kids how to ride a bike. Everyone is outside, chatting with friends and neighbors, dressed in holiday clothes, fasting, getting ready to go to synagogue, absorbing the solemnity of this High Holiday. You can almost *smell* the holiness in the air.

But since moving to the United States, Yom Kippur gradually faded into the background of our lives (I've actually come to love Thanksgiving far above all other holidays). In our family, Yom Kippur is still quite important, but it's more of an open-ended occasion to feel connected to our culture and history. In 2019 my mother and one of my sons came to stay with us for the holiday. Given how it always seemed to go for other Yom Kippurs—or any holiday, really—I promised I'd try to give them my undivided attention this time. But as soon as I woke up, I was bombarded with alerts from my analysts on our messenger application. One of them was a *BBC Breaking News* tweet: "At least two people shot dead in eastern German city of Halle, police searching for suspect."[34]

The alerts kept on coming. Leslie, one of my top analysts for the far right at SITE (and who is also fluent in German), messaged me: "Supposedly took place near synagogue and carried out by a guy in camo gear."

My heart sunk into my stomach. I asked my husband to watch over my mother. Downstairs, where some of my family was gathered in the kitchen, I began to apologize for breaking my promise as I put my laptop into my bag. Before I could even finish, my son interrupted.

"It is what it is, *Ima*," he said, using the Hebrew word for "mother." "It was pretty much expected to happen."

I had nothing to say, so I just nodded. I put my bag around my shoulder and walked out the door.

Apart from the Jewish members who had taken the day off for the holiday, our team was all in the office when I arrived. Leslie was monitoring the German forums and Telegram chat groups, as others checked for reactions on other platforms. News was coming in fast as Halle residents began uploading pictures and video footage of the attacker to social media. He seemed to be a white male dressed in military attire, holding a rifle. Zooming in on some images, it seemed there was a smartphone mounted to his helmet.

Once those pictures emerged, the far right had seen enough to start celebrating across Telegram and message boards.

"And we have ourselves an Aryan, fam!" one wrote.[35]

"Looks like today is going to be a good day. God bless our saints one and all!" exclaimed another.[36]

"Yom Kippur is LIT in Germany this year!" wrote another.[37]

Others, making note of the camera on his helmet, started to ask where the livestream was.

"FINGERS CROSSED, BOYS," one wrote. "Looks like a new video-game is coming out."[38]

Sure enough, our team monitoring the situation picked up the attacker's livestream shortly after. It was housed on Twitch, a video streaming platform for video game players, along with three documents filled with detailed tutorials on homemade weapons and strange anime-style cartoons, among other content. The video confirmed what those first photos of this helmet-wearing attacker suggested: another Brenton Tarrant copycat.

The stream opened from the driver's seat of a Volkswagen.[39] The man had a shaved head and piercing blue eyes. His first words, spoken in English through a thick German accent, were an amalgam of "screw your optics"–era attack manifestos. He combined the anti-Semitism of Bowers and Earnest with the birthrate obsession of Tarrant and Crusius—and, of course, the far right's widely shared hatred of feminism:

Hi, my name is Anon, and I think the Holocaust never happened . . . Feminism is the cause of the decline of birthrates in the West which acts as a scapegoat for mass immigration. And the root of all these problems is the Jew. Would you like to be friends?[40]

"Nobody expects the Internet SS," he said and let out a laugh, giving yet another nod to the far-right message board community.[41]

He parked on a quiet street in Halle's Paulusviertel neighborhood, grabbed his gun, and stepped out of the car. He walked to a door in a brick wall, where a gold-plated sign read in German: "Jüdische Gemeinde zu halle (Saale)" [Jewish Congregation of Halle, Synagogue][42]

The man tried to open the door, but it was locked. "FUCK," he yelled and walked toward another door, homemade weapons on his body clanking as he stepped. He activated one of them and sent it hissing over the wall. It made a popping sound when it blew.[43]

A woman walked by him on the street. As she turned her back to him, he fired into her. A moment later, he returned to where she lay in the street. "*Schwein* [pig]," he whispered to himself as he fired more bullets into her.

My staff who started the video around the same time I did began gasping throughout the office. "I can't watch this," one said as they closed the window on their screen and stepped away from their desk.

I couldn't blame them. My mind flashed to recent posts I'd been seeing across the same online hangouts this self-identified "Anon" may have inhabited: the dehumanization and violent hatred of women.

The woman was soon identified as forty-year-old Jana Lang.[44]

The shooter then tried to find another way into the synagogue, but failed again. After throwing some more explosive devices over the wall, he returned to the car and drove away.

"Sorry guys," he said. "I am fucking . . . I am shit. I'll try to kill some [inaudible] while I'm here, and then I die."

He parked at a corner, armed himself, and walked across a busy street toward a kebab shop.[45] He threw one of his explosive devices into it.[46] Men inside began to run. One fled up a set of stairs and another hid behind a row of beverage refrigerators, crying in terror as the attacker attempted to fix his malfunctioning gun. He shot at the man. The crying stopped.

The kebab shop was quiet. Dining booths were left crooked by the men who fled, covered in spilled soda, food, clothing, and a pair of glasses that were left behind.[47]

The attacker left the building, pacing around and attempting to fire at others in the street before returning to the kebab shop. Behind the vending machines, the same victim from before was trembling against the wall with his hands covering his face.

"Ugh," the shooter grunted, "He is still living."[48]

The attacker raised the gun and shot him repeatedly, confirming the kill.[49] The victim was identified as Kevin S., a twenty-year-old professional painter who was working on a construction site near the establishment.[50]

The shooter drove away and was spotted by a responding police vehicle. He stopped the car and fired toward the vehicle several times.[51] Police fired two shots back at him, one of the bullets grazing his neck. He drove without speaking for several minutes, breathing heavily as the radio kept playing.

"Failure, man!" he said. "I have to unfortunately say, I am bleeding, I've been shot, and in my throat, I don't know if I'll die . . . So guys, that was it. A little action. I'm a complete loser. I will discard the smartphone."[52]

He threw the phone out the window. The video ended shortly thereafter.

The shooter was Stephen Balliet, a twenty-seven-year-old man who lived with his mother in a town called Benndorf, a forty-minute drive from Halle.[53] Despite his anticipation of dying, he survived the shot to the neck and was captured roughly ten miles outside of Halle after an hours-long chase with police.

The video left my team quiet. Some cried. A recent college grad who also spoke German had to go through the work of watching the video and translating it with Leslie. This was less than a week after he'd started with us. Later that day, still rattled, he pulled Leslie and our office manager aside and asked: "This is a rare thing, right? Like, we won't be doing this all the time?"

The truth wasn't very reassuring: we had no way of knowing. The next day, he called the office and informed us that he wouldn't be coming back.

Balliet's livestream was only the beginning of the disturbing materials he left behind. His documents were a bizarre compilation of chan board drama, weapons guides, and video game–themed terrorist directives. While I hesitate to call them outright manifestos, they were nonetheless nods to the same "screw your optics" current. One of the documents gave a "pre-action report" of his attack. This included a detailed guide of the weapons and explosives he used, breaking down how each was created via 3D printing and other methods. It also detailed the plan for his attack, including his earlier probing of the Halle synagogue. He chose to attack this synagogue because it was "the nearest location with a high population of Jews," but he first considered other targets. As he explained, Jews were the ultimate enemy above all others:

> I originally planned to storm a mosque or an antifa "culture" center, which are way less defended, but even killing 100 golems won't make a difference, when on a single day more than that are shipped to Europe. The only way to win is to cut of the head of ZOG, which are the kikes. If I fail and die but kill a single jew, it was worth it.[54]

Everything up to this point seemed to spell out another episode of the same series: the live stream, his blaming of feminism, the chan board language, the Holocaust denial, the "Internet SS" shout-out, and the celebratory responses by supporters online. Balliet was another "Saint" of the "screw your optics" current, or as some began calling him in reference to his homemade weapons: the "Saint of the DIY [Do-It-Yourself]." They made audiobooks of his documents and archived his livestream, declaring, "Pour one out for your blood brothers or Comrades in Germany, pour one out for the new SAINTS!"[55]

If all that wasn't enough, there was the picture Balliet shared of himself wearing a hat with a pin. I had to squint at the pin to see it, but sure enough, it was the "screw your optics" far right's favorite mascot, Moonman. No matter where you looked throughout this movement, this creepy long face seemed to follow.

There was something different about Balliet, though. It was nothing that contradicted the "screw your optics" signals attached to his attack. Rather, it seemed like there was an additional dimension at hand that went beyond the conventionally understood parameters of the far right. The file name of the third document Balliet left behind was "マニフェスト" ("manifesto" in Japanese). Its title was "Techno-Barbarism—A spiritual

FIGURE 9.5 Posting of an audiobook from Balliet's documents in the aftermath of the Halle, Germany attack

guide for discontent White Men in the current year +4."[56] The title is a reference to warring characters called "Techno Barbarians" from the fantasy video game *Warhammer 40K*. The document barely contains any words. In giant, sparse text spread across the first two pages, the document reads, "KILL ALL JEWS! . . . Mudslimes, christkikes, commies, niggers and traitors too." The third page is entirely blank except for tiny, barely legible text stating, "thanks for reading."

But on the fourth and final page, there is an anime-styled drawing of a sexualized girl with cat ears inside of a cardboard box. Beside her, Balliet writes what reads like a twisted, tongue-in-cheek version of jihadi

FIGURE 9.6 Balliet wearing a Moonman pin on his hat (image edited to show enlarged view of this pin), posted online prior to his attack

groups' promises of *Hoor al-Ayn*, promising fellow neo-Nazis they can "get a FREE* Cat-Girl" by carrying out the following criteria:

*Disclaimer: You need to kill at least one jew to qualify
Alternatives include Fox-Girls and normal Waifus.
She will always be loyal, so treat her good.[57]

This image was as telling of Balliet's motivations as his talk of "filthy" Jews and weapon-making guides, perhaps even more. Balliet's appeals to sexualized anime characters seem to lock in with other parts of his story: his ire for feminism, the way he called innocent Jana Lang a "pig" as he fired into her, his mutterings of self-hatred throughout the livestream ("I am shit . . . Like the loser I am . . . I'm a complete loser"), statements from his neighbors that he "lived in seclusion, never said hello."[58] These elements pointed toward the often-overlooked intersections between this new far-right internet culture and toxic misogynist subcultures. The more we pieced Balliet's words and activity together, the more he seemed fitting to a specific community known to frequent many of these same platforms: incels.

The "incel" community ("incel" being short for "involuntary celibate") is comprised of angry men venting about how they cannot get women, whether romantically or sexually.[59] To some incels, women are "femoids" (short for "female humanoids"), who they consider robotically self-interested, incapable, and evil. Incel forums are filled with the same types of racist and bigoted scapegoating seen in far-right forums. By their thinking, it's the "cultural Marxists," racial minorities, and especially the Jews preventing them from getting women.

"Jews have helped propel this society into degeneracy and caused [femoids] to have an enlarged ego due to the shit that the kikes churn out in (((Hollywood)))," reads a November 2020 post on a popular incel forum.[60]

"I am 100% positive that this Radical Feminist agenda was started by Jews," reads another from a few months earlier.[61]

Incels, which are by many criteria a terrorist movement of its own, even celebrate attacks similarly to the "screw your optics" far right, all the way down to the ways in which they canonize them.[62] On May 23, 2014, a twenty-two-year-old named Elliot Rodger carried out a combined shooting, stabbing, and vehicular attack near the University of California, Santa Barbara, killing six and injuring fourteen before taking his own life. He left behind a YouTube video and a 107,000-word manifesto blaming women for his "suffering." He exclaimed in his last video: "I don't know why you girls aren't attracted to me, but I will punish you all for it."[63]

To this day, incels canonize the twenty-two-year-old as "Saint Elliot Rodgers," and have done the same for others over the years.

After twenty-five-year-old Alek Minassian, allegedly an incel, plowed through pedestrians in a van on a busy street in Toronto on April 28, 2018, fellow incels wrote, "Prepare the way to incel sainthood for Sir Alek," and "It is a good time to be an incel . . . Thank you St. Rogers, thank you St. Minassian."[64]

The influence of incels and other misogynist communities can be seen throughout this new generation of neo-Nazis. Searches for terms like "stupid bitch" or "femoid" in far-right Telegram channels and chat groups consistently yield hits. Even prominent far-right figures like Daily Stormer founder Andrew Anglin call women "femoids" and stress "that women are purely objects and property . . . All of their functions surround the act of birthing and caring for children."[65]

None of this is to say that Balliet wasn't actually a neo-Nazi, or that his attack was not, first and foremost, an attack motivated by a neo-Nazi agenda. However, this overlap between the far right and incel communities shows that Balliet, whether he knew it or not, was a product of both. He evidently followed Brenton Tarrant and saw himself as another actor in the line of post-Christchurch "Saints." But to view Balliet strictly as a neo-Nazi overlooks the other communities and movements that overlap with the far right, with incels and other "manosphere" constituents being prevalent among them. As cultural critic and academic Angela Nagle writes, "What we now call the alt-right is really this collection of lots of separate tendencies that grew semi-independently but which were joined under the banner of a bursting forth of anti-PC cultural politics through the culture wars of recent years."[66]

In other words, today's young neo-Nazis aren't *just* neo-Nazis. Their origins and entry points into this new far right come from an array of other communities just as much as they do from the pages of *Mein Kampf.*

— ⊗⊗⊗ —

One week after the Halle attack, on October 16, 2019, Congressional Subcommittee on Intelligence and Counterterrorism chair Max Rose published an open letter to the U.S. State Department. Rose's letter, cosigned by thirty-nine other members of the Subcommittee, opens in part by referencing my tweets the day of the attack, in which I stressed that Balliet's attack was part of this "screw your optics" network of "Saints." As I said:

> The similarity between this video and New Zealand attacker's underscores that these are not isolated attacks by people merely holding similar beliefs. [The Halle attack] is another installment from a global terrorist network, linked together via online safe havens much like ISIS.[67]

After this introduction, the subcommittee's letter gets to the gripe at hand—one I too had been calling attention to for the past ten years: the double standards in the way the U.S. government combats terrorism. The letter stated:

> Today, if an American citizen swears allegiance to the Islamic State . . . and spreads their message of terror, there are several resources available to the federal government to counter the threat. However, if that same American citizen swears allegiance to a violent white supremacist extremist group overseas and spreads their message of terror, the Federal government does not have access to the same tools.

It's true. The U.S. government classifies overseas terrorist groups like ISIS as Foreign Terrorist Organizations (FTOs). Thus, any act of supporting or being a member of ISIS is in itself a crime—or, as criminal complaints often word it, "conspiracy to provide material support and resources to a foreign terrorist organization." Authorities have used this legal framework for the past two decades to pursue al-Qaeda and ISIS operatives who weren't themselves planning to carry out violence, but nonetheless facilitated the group's violent agenda.

For example, in October of 2019, the Department of Justice announced the arrest of a thirty-four-year-old man named Ashraf al-Safoo. An Iraqi-born American citizen living in Chicago, Safoo was known as "Abu Al'-Abbas Al-Iraqi" in his work for a prominent ISIS-linked media group called Khattab Media Foundation. The criminal complaint against him read:

> Al-Safoo and [his coconspirators] were working at the direction of and in coordination with ISIS and ISIS' media office, created and disseminated ISIS propaganda, recruited for ISIS, encouraged individuals to carry out attacks on behalf of ISIS, and supported violent jihad on behalf of ISIS and ISIS' media office.

Indeed, Khattab Media was a prominent group which, like others of its stature, proliferated content under the tenants set forth by ISIS. When ISIS announced a new social media campaign, Khattab followed suit with corresponding content: warnings against voting in the 2018 Egyptian presidential election, sectarian threats to Shi'ites in Baghdad, threats that "Russia is [ISIS's] Next TARGET" ahead of it hosting the 2018 FIFA World Cup. Safoo never killed anyone himself, nor did he plan to. His guilt lied in the terrorist organization whose status he was propping up and in the incitements for attacks Khattab Media issued.

Here's where the double standards come in. Standing FTO designations by the U.S. government are pretty comprehensive, spanning jihadi groups like Abu Sayaaf Group in the Philippines, Marxist militant organizations like Revolutionary Armed Forces of Colombia (FARC), Jewish ultra-orthodox nationalist parties like Kahane Chai in Israel, and separatist groups like Liberation Tigers of Tamil Eelam (LTTE) in Sri Lanka. What you won't find, however, are many white supremacist organizations, despite the violence those organizations have produced.

Given the effectiveness that FTO designations grant law enforcement in counterterrorist work, Rose's letter suggested the designation of groups like the Azov Battalion, a Ukrainian neo-Nazi paramilitary group. Azov formed from other paramilitary forces as war broke out between Ukraine and Russian-backed forces in the country's Donbass region. Like the ISIS supporters enamored by the new caliphate declared in Iraq and Syria, white supremacists and neo-Nazis praised Azov as heroic race warriors, with some even openly fundraising for the group.[68]

And, just like ISIS supporters, many were keen to join as foreign fighters in Azov's cause. One Stormfront user asked, "how would a Westerner find his way into say the Azov battalion?. . . could an English speaker make his way into their ranks you think?" Another replied, "I was actually considering this myself . . . if anyone has any information, [private message] me."[69]

Azov was receptive to such prospects. In April 2015, a Stormfront post attributed to Azov's "Foreign Volunteers Coordinator" announced, "For the first time the regiment is opening is [*sic*] doors to U.S citizens," offering modest pay, weapons, and training.[70] White supremacists from around the world flocked to Ukraine to fight with the group in the years following.[71]

All that said, who wouldn't agree with Rose and his Subcommittee in calling for more consistent designations? After all, here are two terrorist movements taking off around the same time: one fighting a holy war in Iraq and Syria, the other fighting for the white race in Eastern Europe; one designated as an FTO, one not. Absurdly, it wasn't even until 2018 that the United States quietly banned the sale of arms to Azov, further demonstrating how long this group stayed out of the view (or care) of the U.S. government.

But if Azov was designated as an FTO in the United States, would that have stopped attacks by Bowers, Earnest, and Crusius? These individuals had never joined or formed connections with Azov or any other foreign militant group. The closest things to international factions these men had were their cliques on Gab and 8chan. The same can be said about Balliet.

Today's terrorist threats are different than they were ten or twenty years ago. Today's terrorists—particularly, the ones carrying out mass-casualty attacks—aren't joining groups. They're joining movements, communities, and reactionary cultural currents that are impossible to designate as terrorist entities: incels, misogyny, or chan board Nazism.

Making the problem even harder to tackle is that these movements and currents exist almost entirely online, which means that their threats have no borders. The effects of an attack in Christchurch cannot be contained to New Zealand; its repercussions ripple outward to every corner of the globe with internet access. There is no such thing as a localized threat from these new types of terrorist movements. An attack on a mosque near Oslo should not be viewed as an isolated matter for Norway to deal with; it should be viewed as an international security matter.

Even if an attacker does belong to a group, such groups are becoming less static every year. The internet allows groups like Moonkrieg Division and Feuerkrieg Division to be created, rebranded, dissolved, and replaced faster than any government agency would ever be able to keep up with. Thus, the threats from the "screw your optics" current and other terrorist groups are becoming increasingly impractical to designate.

The radicalization of today's terrorists—whether jihadist, far-right, or otherwise—is inseparable from cultural and societal changes. They are incels who can't get a hang of the dating scene. Young Muslims who don't see themselves represented in pop culture. Men who feel threatened by growing feminist currents around them. Products of a world where a thirteen-year-old kid can run a multinational terrorist network from his laptop. Reactionaries, contrarians, and misfits seeking answers and senses of belonging.

In the case of far-right extremism, the movement's entire agenda is open-ended: *If you have a gripe, we can find a place for you.* Even in the aftermath of Balliet's attack in late 2019, it was clear that as extremist and toxic internet cultures change around new societal shifts, the far right will change accordingly, building a new bridge for every new fringe movement outside of mainstream culture. As such, communities once barely associated with the far fight were merging into it, soon to add yet more complexity and contradiction.

10

TINFOIL HAT TERRORISM

Mass shootings like Christchurch and El Paso are enormously devastating, but they're one of many problems facing society. Just look at what 2020 brought: over half a million in the United States and millions worldwide dead from COVID-19; democratic societies being devoured from the inside; truth and lies becoming a matter of opinion skewed by political side, whether it be about the safety of a vaccine or who actually won the 2020 U.S. presidential election.

So how much does the "screw your optics" current matter in the grander scheme of things? How much of a concern are some sparse, seemingly inevitable terrorist attacks, when the very foundations of civilization are crumbling beneath us?

A lot, as it turns out. Quite a lot. Because these issues are much more interrelated than they might seem.

———— ∞∞∞ ————

"Screw your optics" is in many ways life-blood infusion into decades-old far-right conspiracy theories. White genocide, Zionist Owned Governments (ZOGs), and other conspiracy theories are foundational premises of these movements. They are what separates the far right from your average bigots and racists. Posts on longstanding forums like

Stormfront have long described a world run by "pedophiles in Congress" and "Jew pedophiles." Prominent figures like William Luther Pierce warned whites of the "New World Order enthusiasts" who embrace ideals like feminism at the white race's peril.[1] These narratives give the far right a sense of urgent purpose and often serve as substitutes for ideology.

But when 8chan came along, it put a new fire to these baseless conspiracy theories, pushing users to act on them with increased urgency. Brenton Tarrant thought Muslim immigrants were out-populating whites in the West.[2] Patrick Crusius believed Hispanic "invaders" were replacing whites in the United States.[3] John Earnest believed the Jews systematically "use mass immigration to displace the European race."[4] Stephan Balliet likewise blamed this "decline of birthrates" in part on feminism, a product of Jews.[5] These were different versions of the same white genocide narrative, thrown into the nuclear reactor that was 8chan. One by one, far-right attackers were launched out of 8chan with the urgent sense that they faced an existential threat.

The "screw your optics" crowd wasn't alone in its conspiracy theories on 8chan. The conspiracy theories that drove them were accompanied by others on the site, which, while branded differently, boiled down to the same tropes and recurring characters: government "pedophile rings," secretive cabals pulling strings, and scapegoat figures like George Soros and the Rothschild family. The common emphasis among all these theories was that everything is on the line, everything stands to be lost. And like those of white supremacists, these conspiracy theories inspired violence.

As seen with the far right's most vile neo-Nazis, 8chan's no-rules ethos made it the dumping ground for conspiracy theorists too extreme for sites like 4chan and Reddit: the racists and bigots, the ones calling to hang their enemies. All such rhetoric was fair game on 8chan.

Niche as the site may have seemed, it was a major force that helped shape the dystopia we live in today. Not just from a domestic terrorism standpoint, but also in a much wider way.

———— ∞∞∞ ————

By the end of 2016, 8chan was becoming more than a den of online trolls and video gamers. It now held grotesque political influence. 8chan's owner Jim Watkins, whose son Ron Watkins helped run the site as an administrator, proudly said as much himself a year after the election, bragging that 8chan "helped get Trump elected."[6]

He wasn't wrong. Along with sites like 4chan and Reddit, 8chan played a critical part in making Trump an internet-culture phenomenon. Trump was a loaded, transgressive statement unto himself: a walking rejection of the political correctness, social justice causes, and political charades these chan board and Redditors hated. Mixing these elements with his cartoonish bravado, Trump became a staple of 8chan meme-makers and trolls: Pepe the frog memes with Trump's wavy hair, pictures of Trump's Republican rivals mocked as "cuckservatives."[7]

8chan's election-related memes went together with its conspiracy theories. The site played no small part in perpetuating conspiracy theories related to Hillary Clinton, long a human embodiment of their perceived "deep state." 8chan was filled with threads with titles like "Clinton Foundation a cover for pedophile ring" and fake news about how the Clinton Foundation was being investigated for "child exploitation" and "sex crimes with minors."[8]

The most popular of these theories, "Pizzagate," emerged when Hillary Clinton campaign manager John Podesta's emails were hacked and leaked shortly before the 2016 presidential election. Users on 8chan and other sites, as well as popular conspiracy theorists like Alex Jones, began picking out "codes" from the emails and baselessly deduced that Democrats were running a child sex trafficking ring.[9]

This outlandish theory had real-world consequences. On December 4, 2016, a twenty-eight-year-old man from North Carolina named Edgar Maddison Welch drove to a Washington, DC pizza restaurant called Comet Ping Pong, where Pizzagate theorists said children were held in the basement. Armed with an AR-15 style rifle, he walked through the entire establishment. Welch quickly realized that there were no children being held captive. He even fired toward a locked door at what he thought would be the basement, but found it was only a computer closet.[10] No one was harmed by the shots.[11]

Welch's failure to uncover confirmation of Pizzagate theories didn't matter. To this day, Comet Ping Pong still faces death threats, attempted arson attacks, and demonstrations by Pizzagate believers outside its doors.[12]

These conspiracy theories exuded out of sites like 8chan and into mainstream conversation, especially by those in Donald Trump's orbit. Henchmen like retired Lieutenant General Michael Flynn, one of Trump's most prominent surrogates, seemed in tune with what people posted on such sites. On November 2, 2016, Flynn tweeted the link to an article and stated, "U decide—NYPD Blows Whistle on New Hillary Emails: Money Laundering, Sex Crimes w Children, etc. . . . MUST READ!"[13]

Both Watkins and 8chan users continued pushing conspiracy theories into the chaotic start of Trump's presidency, creating counternarratives to the scandals Trump faced by mid-2017, which included the Mueller probe into election interference from Russia, staff dysfunction, and Trump's firing of FBI Director James Comey, to name a few.[14]

8chan threads from that time harped on all sorts of conspiracy theories, such as that of Seth Rich, a murdered Democratic National Committee (DNC) staffer who 8chan users—in lockstep with outlets like Fox News—baselessly suggested was assassinated for leaking Clinton campaign emails to WikiLeaks.[15] Users on the site even acknowledged their role in keeping the conspiracy theory alive, with one user writing on May 16, 2017, "Don't let this topic die, it's trending worldwide right now. Fox news is covering it, Assange and Wikileaks retweeting this stuff, and twitter is blowing up, don't let the cucks bury it."[16]

As impactful as these theories were on American political discourse, a much larger, longer-lasting and ominous one was in the works. Hoax artists were riding the wave of recent years' chan board conspiracy theories by pretending to be government officials from the FBI, CIA, and White House with secret information from inside the so-called deep state.[17] In October 2017, a 4chan poster by the alias "Q" (referring to Q-level Department of Energy Top Secret clearance) began making their own posts about a secret cabal of deep-state pedophiles and Satan-worshippers inside the government. Q's messages, which came to be known as "Q drops," were intentionally cryptic, making vague warnings of major plots happening within the government and suggestively asking if intersecting events were only "coincidence."

Q drops came to form a formidable movement known as QAnon. They were essentially a continuation of Seth Rich and Pizzagate conspiracy theories that preceded it, merging them all under its umbrella brand. Q drops were pro-Trump, and anti–Trump's enemies—presented as the work of a renegade hero seeking to "drain the swamp" and fight this supposed evil cabal of Satanists.

Yet at times these theories were nearly identical to ones pushed by the far right. Neo-Nazis often invoke centuries-old "blood libel" narratives of Jews killing Christian children to use their blood in rituals.[18] Today, blood libel narratives seem reincarnated in the QAnon-boosted conspiracy theory called "Frazzledrip," which asserts that Hillary Clinton and other powerful Democrats were murdering young children and drinking their blood to ingest a chemical called adrenochrome.[19] Similarly, the "Cultural Marxist" conspiracy theory espoused by the far right and other right-wing communities is a blatant recreation of an older theory called "Cultural Bolshevism." The former states that elite intellectuals are using popular culture to inject leftist and communist values into Western society.[20] The latter, espoused by Hitler and other German nationalists, asserted the same of progressive intellectuals and artists of the time—same story, same anti-Semitic undertones.[21]

But in late November of 2017, not long after Q drops began picking up steam, the activity relocated to 8chan after the poster behind Q declared that 4chan was "infiltrated."[22] Now, Q drops had a permanent and exclusive home on 8chan. To ensure reliable authentication of Q drops, 8chan admins granted Q their own series of verified trip codes, which are publicly visible user IDs attributed solely to them.[23]

QAnon brought change to 8chan, particularly in terms of demographics. In posts on 8chan's QAnon boards where users analyzed Q's posts, many slipped in commentary about their "aching" backs and the exhaustion of "trying to talk to a 6 [year-old]."[24] They identified as small business owners, Gen-X and Baby Boomer parents. A January 2018 tweet from 8chan's Twitter account even humorously acknowledged their new userbase: "We joked about it for years, but #QAnon is making it a reality: Boomers! On your imageboard."[25]

This new user population brought a shift in tone. Responses to Q drops were noticeably less cynical and irony-drenched than the transgressive, profanity-filled exchanges elsewhere on the site. They used words like "Patriot" without cynicism and expressed love for fellow Q comrades. It wasn't hard to imagine longer-standing 8chan users rolling their eyes as QAnon adherents wrote such earnest posts as, "Love to you all, my magnificent fellow anons."[26]

But with the comradery grew outwardly militant dedication. Discussions among QAnon adherents often devolved into violent incitements against their perceived deep-state enemies. Frustrated that Q drops were not giving enough details, a QAnon adherent wrote in 2018, "give me a sign and i'll fight.. protect. . . . hang those fucks! lynch them. . no secret deals or secret jailtime or whatever. . . . we have the right to know!"[27]

QAnon adherents, as well as Watkins himself, built an entire infrastructure around the movement: archive sites of Q drops, discussion boards on other platforms, pages and accounts on social media and messenger platforms like Facebook, QAnon, and beyond. As the central point of Q drops and discussions, 8chan was at the core of this infrastructure. Even as some platforms turned up their censorship of QAnon activity, the movement proved impervious. In March 2018, Reddit banned its largest QAnon community, which held over 20,000 members at the time, on the basis that it was "encouraging or inciting violence and posting personal and confidential information."[28] But it made no dent against the movement. The only effect was that QAnon became yet more reliant on 8chan.

As QAnon ballooned within the trenches of 8chan, the sense of militancy among its adherents grew to the point of direct action. In May 2018, Q began hyping an upcoming report from the Office of the Inspector General (OIG), which they claimed would prove collusion between the FBI, the Department of Justice, and Democrats to sabotage Trump's presidential campaign. One Q drop told 8channers to brace themselves for the report:

Puzzle coming together?

We have reached our cruising altitude of 40,000 ft. long ago.

As we prepare to land, please fasten your seatbelt and make sure your seat back and folding trays are in their full upright position.

Q[29]

The OIG report, released on June 14 of that year, gave an unflattering assessment of former FBI Director James Comey, but did not provide the bombshell that QAnon adherents wanted.[30] QAnon's conclusion was that there had to be another OIG report—a buried one that would confirm what Q had been preparing them for. The day after the report was released, a man in his early thirties named Matthew Wright blocked a bridge near the Hoover Dam.[31] Armed with a rifle in an armored truck, he held up a sign demanding, "Release the OIG Report." Wright fled after a standoff with authorities and was finally arrested after a chase. In his truck, they found assault rifles, handguns, and a trove of ammo.[32]

QAnon's adherents were spellbindingly locked into the movement. Throughout 2018, individuals began showing up to Trump rallies in Pennsylvania, Florida, Ohio, and elsewhere holding up signs reading "WE ARE Q" and "WWG1WGA" (Where We Go One, We Go All).[33]

With 8chan being the primary place for Q drops, these Trump-supporting conspiracy theorists were being trafficked into the very same place where the far right's "screw your optics" current was about to take off. 8chan's landing page alone was wired for cross-pollination, providing a sampler platter of all of the site's discussions under sections like "Latest Headlines" and "Fast Threads." That meant that an impressionable QAnon supporter going to 8chan for the latest Q drop discussions on a date like October 30, 2018, just a few days after Bowers's Pittsburgh attack, could have also seen threads such as "Trump visits Pittsburgh synagogue. Hmm that was quick" and "Amerikikes BTFO [blown the fuck out]."[34] Or, just a week later on November 7, they would have seen "Niglet Girls Engaged for Marriage at Birth—Feminists and SJWs [social justice warriors] Completely Silent."[35]

Even if a QAnon adherent tried to steer clear of such openly racist or bigoted discussions, it was often easier said than done. After all, how would the October 30 /pol/ thread "CNN gives us a gift" on 8chan's land-ing page not pique the curiosity of QAnon adherents,[36] who saw CNN as an enemy of their beloved President Trump? Should a QAnon adher-ent have clicked on it, they would have arrived on a thread about pun-dits decrying radicalized "white men," to which /pol/ users declared embracingly:

> White men are capable of so much damage and have the intelligence
> and fortitude to back up their claims of ending them. Think about that
> niggers, jews, gooks, etc. We haven't even stepped out our doors yet and
> you keep fucking pushing us. We tried reasonable and this is where it
> got us.[37]

The overlaps between QAnon and the far right weren't limited to the online space shared. The similar foundations of their conspiracy theories—the "globalist" plots, the "string-pulling bankers," the baseless accusations of government and Hollywood "pedophiles"—created bonds between these movements that were stronger than either side would want to admit. As a result, both movements seemed to act with the same sense of frantic urgency, albeit with different targets. On December 19, 2018, for example, police arrested a California man in possession of explosive-making devices. Police stated he was plotting to blow up a satanic temple monument in Illinois to "make Americans aware of 'Pizzagate' and the New World Order."[38] A few months later, on March 16, 2019, twenty-four-year-old Anthony Comello gunned down Gambino crime family leader Francesco Cali. Comello was reportedly obsessed with QAnon conspiracy theories. He believed he had the "protection of President Trump" and that Cali was part of the deep state. In a court appear-ance, Comello was even photographed with the letter "Q" written on his hand.[39]

By the spring of 2019, 8chan helped produce yet another pipeline of terrorists. On March 15, 2019, Brenton Tarrant left his manifesto behind on /pol/ prior to his mass shooting in Christchurch, triggering a wave of copycat attackers to come from the platform. It was only a month later, on April 27, that 8chan dweller John Earnest shot up the synagogue in

Poway, California. Days after Earnest's shooting, the FBI obtained a search warrant of 8chan's hosting location in Reno, Nevada, citing "probable cause to believe that within 8chan . . . will be found evidence of violations of federal law" regarding recent terrorist attacks.[40]

No warrant or news story could yet quell 8chan, though. The site remained active all the way through spring and into the summer. At the same time, the conspiracy theories feeding domestic terrorist attacks had become a foremost concern of law enforcement. An internal FBI document from May 30, 2019, identified radicalized individuals like Robert Bowers and Mathew Wright as part of a larger tide of "anti-government, identity based, and fringe political conspiracy theories."[41] These groups and movements, according to the document, were "very likely to encourage" extremist violence, in no small part because of the internet spaces where their ideas festered:

> The FBI assesses these conspiracy theories very likely will emerge, spread, and evolve in the modern information marketplace, occasionally driving both groups and individual extremists to carry out criminal or violent acts.[42]

If toxic internet communities were indeed the fuel to these dangerous conspiracy theories, it begged the question: Why was 8chan still up? This document was issued just two months after Tarrant's Christchurch attack and one month after Earnest's Poway synagogue attack, both of which were inextricably linked to 8chan. The site was cornering the market on domestic terrorism, yet nothing was done to stop it. If anything, the ideas emanating out of the site were gaining influence not just among terrorists, but among those in the so-called mainstream. By 2019, U.S. congressional candidates out of states including Florida and Minnesota even began openly nodding to Q in their campaigns.[43] It was mind-blowing: the same movement inspiring terrorist attacks was also producing national-level politicians.

It wasn't until Patrick Crusius's deadly El Paso shooting on August 3, 2019, that 8chan finally lost its host.[44] White supremacists and neo-Nazis continued setting up shop on Telegram. Meanwhile, the "drops" that powered QAnon stopped completely. This was peculiar given that Q, a supposed government insider trying to dispatch information to a massive following, could have posted on any other site when 8chan went down. Regardless, 8chan's story was far from over, as were those of the movements it helped grow.

⚬⚬⚬

Despite 8chan's evident role in far-right terrorist attacks up to that point, its removal in August of 2019 was the result of public pressure, not law enforcement or legislative initiative. The public knew well enough what was going on with 8chan, and the information and communications technology (ICT) companies keeping it alive weren't liking the negative spotlight.

The ultimate death blow to 8chan came when Cloudflare, the company that provided 8chan's online security from hackers and service disruptors, parted ways with it. A statement from Cloudflare read, "Even if 8chan may not have violated the letter of the law in refusing to moderate their hate-filled community, they have created an environment that revels in violating its spirit."[45]

But news of 8chan's removal also created curiosity among the public. What kind of person would want to run 8chan? Shouldn't they bear some sort of responsibility for all that had happened? An international spotlight grew on 8chan's owner, Jim Watkins, a U.S. Army veteran in his mid-fifties living in the Philippines. Authorities in the Philippines opened investigations into Watkins and the U.S. Congress summoned him for questioning.[46]

Meanwhile, the media was also intrigued by this character: the parted gray bangs, the sideburns and mustache, his spacey way of speaking. Adding to it all was his business background in online porn content and other off-color ventures, his obsession with fountain pens, and his fraught relationship with 8chan's founder Fredrick Brennan, who had since cut ties with the site.[47] Enamored, the *Washington Post, Business Insider*, and other outlets wrote profile pieces on Watkins, who seemed so fittingly bizarre for a site like 8chan.[48]

This long-overdue scrutiny of 8chan wouldn't last, though. The focus on Watkins and his site gradually shifted toward other issues coming out of the tech world, including Facebook's policies on political ads and a Senate report on how Russia used social media to influence the 2016 elections.[49] The world was too big and too quick-moving to focus on one man and his website. By the time Watkins walked out of his closed-door session with the House Homeland Security Committee that fall, he had already weathered Congress's short attention span.[50] He even pinned a "Q" lapel to his collar that very day, as if it was all a marketing stunt to him, and that he knew he wouldn't get into trouble.[51]

Perhaps there was something about Jim and Ron Watkins that seemed harmless. What damage could this eccentric man and his son do? After all, 8chan was gone now, so why harp on the issue?

But Watkins knew that he had a demonstrably powerful tool in 8chan, and he wasn't going to part with it so easily. As he stated himself in a rebuke of 8chan's elimination, the site had only been "temporarily removed."[52] As promised, on November 2, just three months after the El Paso massacre, 8chan came back from the dead—and with far less vulnerability. This revitalized 8chan, now branded as "8kun," was bolstered by an array of web services far less likely to jump ship as a result of another high-profile terrorist attack linked to the site. The domain was registered under a China-based company called Eranet and received web hosting and protection from a Washington State–based company called VanwaTech.[53] The server protection didn't actually come from Vanwa-Tech itself but from CNServers, a company with offices in the United States and China.[54]

8kun was just one piece of a newly fortified infrastructure built around QAnon. The movement's adherents, as well as Watkins himself, set up archive sites of Q drops, discussion boards on other platforms, and pages and accounts on social media and messenger platforms like Facebook, Twitter, and beyond. Meanwhile, Q drops gave shout-outs to the "patriots" from other countries and incorporated their countries' governments into the QAnon narrative. Chatter on QAnon 8kun threads in the coming years likewise pointed toward an international array of adherents, who their American counterparts welcomed.

"UK Anon here. . . . . WG1WGA world wide 07."[55]

"Cheers from a still enslaved Italy."[56]

"Q is fighting the worldwide ruling class, the global illuminati/masonic Deep State"[57]

"We Love you UK Family!! Great Awakening Worldwide."[58]

New Q drop sites were launched by names such as "OperationQ," "QAlerts," and "QAnonbin," as well as other sites like "BidenEmails."[59] All of these sites used VanwaTech servers and protection.

Watkins furthermore launched a company called "Is It Wet Yet" that September as "an information hub for all the projects we've been working on and a launchpad for future endeavors."[60] Among these endeavors was 8kun, which the site directed users to. And despite Is It Wet Yet's clear connection to 8chan, it was still able to use the services of Cloudflare, the same company that had severed ties with 8chan not long before.[61]

Watkins even revived the original 8chan URL, which redirected users to 8kun.[62] The domain was registered through hosting company Epik, despite its statement from August 6 that the company would "not provide site hosting services to the controversial message board service known as 8Chan" due to "the elevated possibility of violent radicalization on the platform."[63] Essentially, Epik was saying that it wouldn't host 8chan, but in reality it helped keep its domain up to redirect to a carbon copy of the same website hosted on other servers. Talk about chutzpah.

None of this was surprising. Epik was the same company that had saved Gab after it was removed following Robert Bowers's attack in Pittsburgh the year before. To this day, Gab continues to use Epik as a domain registrar. Thus, as it held onto 8ch.net as a registrant, far-right users and conspiracy theorists on Telegram and other sites rejoiced that Epik and its CEO, Rob Monster, had come to save yet another online free-for-all:

OK, everyone. We all owe Rob CEO of @epik another round of appreciation for picking up 8ch.net as their registrar when they were knocked off cloudFlare (cloudunfair). He has again, stood up against DS and MSM just as he did for GAB. So please, extend thanks to another protector of free speech.[64]

Epik and VanwaTech's intersections here weren't coincidental. In 2019, Monster bought a cybersecurity provider called Bitmitigate from VanwaTech's head Nick Lim, and Lim has claimed to be a partial owner of VanwaTech and Epik.[65] Both Lim and Monster claimed to share a common zealotry for free speech—and stomach to do business with some of the worst sites online. Sites hosted by Lim have included the far-right news site the Daily Stormer, which Lim has described as a way to "get [his] service out there."[66]

Whether it was called 8kun or any other name, 8chan was back in business. Q drops resumed, users came back, and Watkins walked away from it all unscathed. He also pulled in some of the same companies that disavowed his site so shortly before. Is It Wet Yet even sold 8kun t-shirts and merchandise. The web copy on the site was enough to make one's head explode: "Make a bold statement with 8kun merch. Those with true grit can get the in-your-face 8kun logo for the ultimate triggering reaction."[67] The site soon expanded this merch to include Q shirts, flags, and other items.

Call me cynical, but it was hard to see all of this as anything but Jim and Ron Watkins winning in the end.

⸎

If congressional grilling, government investigations, and investigative journalism couldn't bring down 8chan, what would? And what would come of the overlap between QAnon and the "screw your optics" far-right? Sure, neo-Nazi types rolled their eyes at the "Qtards" and "MAGAturds" around them, just as QAnon "Patriots" resented accusations that there could be white supremacists among them. Yet circumstances would soon have a way of translating common conspiracy theories into common enemies and, from there, common causes. With 2020 just a few short months away, both movements were soon to adapt to a completely different world.

In September of 2019, authorities announced the arrest of a twenty-four-year-old U.S. Army soldier from Kansas named Jarret William Smith. Smith, a well-connected figure within the "screw your optics" and siege groups scene on Telegram, offered his military advice to prospective terrorists.[68] A couple of weeks before he was arrested, Smith explained to fellow neo-Nazis in a group chat that Trump supporters, while not aligned with them, seemed ripe for radicalization. Trump supporters were becoming ostracized and alienated from the mainstream by the political establishment, just like neo-Nazis always had been. As a result, the key to the acceleration Smith and his brethren sought might exist within the very "MAGApedes" they had always scoffed at:

> The enemy threw fits over hats, signs, kids smiling, and shows of simple patriotism. MAGA supporters got attacked. There is no better way to show people there is no political solution than to let them get repeatedly attacked until they figure out that no one is coming to save them.[69]

I'll admit that Smith's post didn't feel that significant the first time I read it. But months later, it would prove prophetic.

11

FAR RIGHT 2.0

I was on the West Coast on a business trip in early January 2020, not too far from where my eldest son and his wife had moved a couple of years earlier. They frequently came to visit us on the East Coast, but I sorely missed them when they were away. I miss all my children when they're not around.

This was a somewhat more complicated visit, though. Their move to the other side of the country was something my husband and I had ardently objected to, and in a way, seeing them happy where they were required giving them a stamp of approval I was still reluctant to do. After moving to the United States from Israel in the 1990s, we were so excited to *become Americans*, but there was one part of our Middle Eastern upbringings we refused to part with: that family stays close together. In Israel—and even as I could recall of Iraq in my younger years—children of all ages spent weekends with their families. Usually, married couples shared Shabbat dinner on Friday night with one side of the family, and lunch on Saturday with the other. Grandparents were there to help raise the kids and spend time with them every moment they could.

The concept of one's children permanently leaving home when they turn eighteen didn't fit with these traditions. When my kids went to college, they used to come home as often as possible. My eldest was no exception. Whether it was via regular flights as an undergrad, four-hour drives during medical school, or from whichever medical establishment he began practicing at, he always made it home. Our American-born neighbors and friends couldn't believe we were so keen on these visits, but to us, it was a given. I would wake up early on Friday morning to make sure that each of them had their favorite food at Shabbat dinner. Secular as we all were, having Shabbat dinner felt important. So many Jews had died over two and a half millennia simply for *being* Jewish, my father in Iraq being just one of many millions. I always felt that it was our responsibility to keep our heritage, traditions, and history alive, as our ancestors trusted us to do.

And that's exactly what we did—and seemed we always would do—until our son told us he wanted to move to the West Coast. He'd found a great job as a physician, good pay, and wanted to try life on the other side of the United States.

"What do you mean *move*? What's there that isn't here?" my husband and I said. "You have a great job; you have everything you could ever wish for."

Nothing he said persuaded us, but he insisted. "Ima, you and Abba were about my age when you left your families in Israel and moved here. So how is this different?"

We had no good answer, and eventually we gave in. As life continued to change, we learned to accept it. People often resist change because they think the traditions and systems they've lived by are somehow permanent. Other times, they think they can't change *themselves*—that a shifting world or circumstances has left them behind. But as I walked down the beach one day while visiting them in their new home, I started to feel happy for my son and daughter-in-law. Change just pulls you with it sometimes, whether you're ready or not.

Yet it turned out that I, as well as the rest of the world, had much to adapt to that wasn't in anyone's sights.

"Have you and Abba been keeping up with safety measures?" my son asked. "This new coronavirus coming out of China is no joke."

I'd seen some news reports about it over the last week or so, but I wasn't terribly alarmed. But if he was worried about it, there was probably something to it.

"Why would I need to take any special measures?" I asked.

"It's like the SARS virus from 2003, but it's looking like it might be worse. Much worse. You and Abba should probably stop traveling until we figure out how bad this thing is. Face masks and gloves wouldn't hurt either."

He went on and on about how this new coronavirus was different from other strains, and how frighteningly little scientists knew about it. I didn't fully understand everything he was saying, but I nodded along. Could he be overreacting? The SARS outbreak was deadly, but it seemed like it came and it went and was largely forgotten. Maybe he was just jumping to worst-case conclusions from all the scientific data he was reading?

Before I left for my red-eye flight, my son handed me a light blue surgical mask for the flight home and made me promise I'd wear it. When I wished him goodnight before taking off, he asked if I was actually wearing it, so I sent him a selfie. He replied in all caps, "YOU'RE WEARING IT UPSIDE DOWN."

I laughed and repositioned the mask, unaware of how used to this I'd become before the end of winter.

⸰⸰⸰

The first U.S. case of COVID-19 was announced in Washington State on January 20, 2020, less than a week after I arrived back to the East Coast. And just a couple of months later it seemed the entire world was on fire: mandatory business shutdowns, entire school years brought to a halt, citizens ordered to stay in their homes. Medical staff in New York City didn't have enough body bags to dispose of the dead.[1] In Italy, cemeteries were overflowing, forcing dead bodies into improvised morgues and coffin-filled churches.[2]

Everyone was affected in one way or another. Not long after I left for home, my son was nearly exposed to a COVID-19-positive patient whose case was mishandled. Meanwhile, my family members in New York were getting sick with the virus. The stress was inescapable.

As expected, these new circumstances had a major impact on terrorist groups as well. ISIS, al-Qaeda, and their supporters were all over the unraveling crisis, calling it God's punishment against the West.[3] They also called for lone wolf attackers to take advantage of newly overloaded law enforcement forces around the world, which seemed to manifest in ISIS-inspired attacks and plots in Germany, Iraq, the Maldives, the Philippines, and France.[4]

It wasn't enough to simply say that the coronavirus changed the world. It *enveloped* the world, down to every little aspect of our lives. Most significantly, lockdowns made the public more reliant on the internet than ever. Laptops and smartphones were lifelines to information about recommendations from the Centers for Disease Control and Prevention (CDC), statewide closures, reopenings, and other critical matters—not to mention what was left of our social lives. Facebook's website traffic alone surged 27 percent from the time the first U.S. COVID-19 death was reported on February 29.[5]

And it was on social media that rumors, misinformation, and outright lies about the coronavirus were spreading like wildfire: warnings that vaccines that hadn't even been developed yet would contain microchips, fake news about martial law, and other insane statements.[6] Cellular towers in Europe and North America were being set aflame by arsonists who believed the 5G technology was either causing or accelerating the spread of coronavirus.[7] A World Health Organization (WHO) official summed it up accurately that February: "We need a vaccine against misinformation."[8]

It was true, COVID-19 misinformation was itself a virus, and QAnon was systematically spreading it. By the time COVID-19 hit, the QAnon movement was already planted in all corners of the internet and social media. It had influencers on YouTube and Twitter. QAnon-slanted blogs and websites were shared across an array of QAnon groups and pages on Facebook, as well as Telegram and alternative social media platforms. Even if you didn't know exactly what QAnon was, you saw traces of it all over social media: hashtags like "#WWG1WGA," people baselessly calling politicians and celebrities "pedophiles."[9]

As soon as news of the pandemic engulfed the world, QAnon influencers and social media accounts were well positioned to inject themselves into the fray. QAnon YouTubers told people to stave off

COVID-19 by drinking bleach.[10] QAnonners on Twitter warned that the virus was being leveraged for profit by Bill Gates.[11] On Facebook and Telegram, they claimed that people of Asian descent were more vulnerable to the virus.[12] No conspiracy theory was too ridiculous to pull into their movement.

"5G NETWORK IS UP AND RUNNING EVERYWHERE WHERE COVID-19 OUTBREAKS OCCUR," wrote a QAnon Telegram channel on February 27, 2020.[13]

Q drops likewise helped to steer the misinformation, framing the pandemic as a way to "shelter" presidential contender Joe Biden from public appearances and sabotage Trump's economic "gains." Q drops also contextualized COVID-19 within the elections coming up that fall, characterizing the virus as a way to "push" mail-in voting. One Q drop from April read:

> What is the primary benefit to keep public in mass-hysteria re:
> COVID-19?
> Think voting.
> Are you awake yet?
> Q[14]

QAnon supporters echoed these lines. "PANDEMIC of [sic] DEM PANIC???" wrote a user in a QAnon group chat. A QAnon tweet similarly read, "Deep State released the virus to create chaos since nothing stopping Trump."[15]

If there was ever a time for QAnon conspiracy theories to stick, this was it. People didn't have to reconstruct their worldview to believe in something like deep-state cabals anymore. The "proof" was right in front of them, as tangible as anything they'd ever experienced: their businesses shut down, their jobs lost, confined to their homes, their lives as they knew it upended. Virtually anyone could be pulled in.

As a result, QAnon was growing beyond what it had been before. QAnon's Facebook and Telegram presences had showed steady but modest growth until COVID-19 hit. From then, it skyrocketed.[16] QAnon channel and group creation roughly doubled in the full year between

March 2019 and March 2020, right up until the first lockdowns were announced. But in half as long, between March 2020 and September 2020, QAnon channels and groups nearly tripled.[17] Some research suggested increases in QAnon activity of over 70 percent.[18]

What was once mostly an American focused movement was becoming a global one. QAnon accounts, particularly on Telegram, were being created in a growing score of languages: English, German, Spanish, Dutch, Portuguese, Italian, Turkish, French, and more.[19] It seemed any country was suited to link into the movement.

At this point QAnon was growing beyond the Q drops that once informed its direction, and thus away from 8chan owner Jim Watkins, whose site was the primary source of those drops. QAnon was an open-ended, open-sourced conspiracy theory brand. Anything and everything applied.

As for the far right, the pandemic was a dream come true. White supremacists and neo-Nazis had always predicted their "SHTF [shit hit the fan] scenario" when their inevitable race war would be triggered.[20] Some called this coming conflict "RaHoWa" (Racial Holy War) or the "boogaloo," speaking of it like a religious prophecy.[21] And when COVID-19 enveloped the entire planet, virtually the entire far right agreed: this was the time to make it happen. Neo-Nazi accelerationists urged followers to use the coronavirus as a bioweapon, even calling to intentionally cough on people and infect fruit at supermarkets.[22]

But the "screw your optics" gameplan changed during the pandemic; their targets weren't limited to the standard synagogues, mosques, and establishments frequented by minorities anymore. The coronavirus enabled them to apply their conspiracy theories about ZOG and white genocide to the entire world around them. They claimed the Jews used the Chinese to create the virus and that agencies like WHO and pharmaceutical companies were in on the plot.[23] Doctors, hospital workers, and health agencies were all part of the plan to eliminate whites—and thus were targets.

As a result, the far right and QAnon took on a new level of mutual resemblance. It wasn't just the conspiracy theory tropes that they had in common anymore. They were now seeing and describing nearly identical narratives about the wretched world in front of them: the same antagonists, the same plots, and the same secretive agendas between governments and billionaires.

These evolving conspiracy theories quickly manifested into real-world violence, as seen with Timothy Wilson, a thirty-six-year-old U.S. Navy veteran and hardcore neo-Nazi living in Missouri.[24] Wilson was a prominent member of some of the most violent far-right communities on Telegram and a fanatical voice of the "screw your optics" current, often praising attackers like Robert Bowers and criticizing the inaction of others in the movement.[25] Wilson had been considering carrying out attacks on the far right's conventional targets prior to the pandemic, including a mosque, a synagogue, and a school with a large population of Black students.[26] But it was coronavirus conspiracy theories that now consumed his mind. He believed the virus was real, but also that "zog is using [the pandemic as] an excuse to destroy our people."[27]

"They scare people and have society break down . . . Mark my words it's coming I hope people are ready."[28]

When the mayor of Wilson's town announced a lockdown to contain the spread of COVID-19, he decided to act. On March 25, 2020, Wilson set out to detonate a car bomb at the Kansas City area's Belton Regional Medical Center, which he believed to be treating coronavirus patients.[29] He dubbed his plot "operation boogaloo," intended "to create enough chaos to kick start a revolution."[30] Wilson committed suicide during a firefight with FBI agents when they went to arrest him.[31]

The types of coronavirus conspiracy theories that consumed Wilson also drove others to attempt attacks. And they weren't just Nazis. The wave of violent action motivated by QAnon and QAnon-adjacent conspiracies—Edgar Maddison Welch's shooting in Comet Ping Pong in DC, Matthew Wright's confrontation at the Hoover Dam, and so on—gained new life from the coronavirus pandemic. On March 31, 2020, less than a week after Wilson's attempted hospital bombing, a forty-four-year-old train engineer named Eduardo Moreno intentionally derailed a train near a Navy hospital ship in Los Angeles because he believed it was part of a government takeover related to the pandemic.[32]

"The whole world is watching," Moreno told the officer who arrested him. "I had to. People don't know what's going on here. Now they will."[33]

It was also around the same time that nurses, doctors, and hospital personnel started getting death threats and finding their car tires slashed outside the hospitals they worked in.[34] By early April, public health spokesperson and White House advisor Anthony Fauci was forced to increase his personal security.[35]

This violent embrace of conspiracy theories spread outside of the United States. On July 2, 2020, a Canadian Rangers reservist named Corey Hurren crashed a truck through the gates of Prime Minister Justin Trudeau's residence, armed with an assault-style rifle.[36] Hurren, a follower of QAnon, was apprehended by authorities before he could shoot anyone.[37]

"I just wanted to get through to someone what was going on," Hurren later told a psychiatrist in chilling similarity to Moreno's words months before him.[38] "I was afraid for the future of my children and what was going to be."[39]

Shortly before his attack, Hurren made a post to his Instagram about "Event 201," referring to a conspiracy theory that Bill Gates and other wealthy elites had planned the coronavirus pandemic.[40] Other posts further signal his immersion into QAnon conspiracy theories, providing a case study of the movement radicalizing him and others around him. A March 27, 2020, post read:

> Has anyone else been following "Q" and the "White Rabbit" down the rabbit hole and how this all relates to the Corona virus/COVID-19 situation? Lots of coincidences in all these "Q" posts if this turns out to be a "Nothingburger."[41]

Users replied, "When did you wake?????" and "I've seen some posts on fb about Q but didn't dig in. I may just go down the hole today though."[42] Another gave a direct link to a Q drop archive.[43]

These threats and attacks were wake-up calls to social media companies. Hate content, harassment, and incitement for violence were no longer adequate content removal criteria by themselves. Whether from a domestic security standpoint or a public health standpoint, misinformation and conspiracy theories were dangers on their own. Social media companies scrambled to tamper down on the fake cures and conspiracy theories posted on their platforms. That March, Facebook announced it would implement fact checks to such problematic posts and remove others.[44] It also removed several QAnon accounts, groups, and pages posting content in "inauthentic" coordination with each other, marking the first time the platform publicly took action against QAnon.[45] Twitter and Reddit likewise announced similar measures the same month, as did Google and YouTube.[46] Companies like TikTok, Facebook, Amazon, and Google teamed up with WHO to try to provide accurate information on the crisis.[47]

The problem was that QAnon wasn't limited to its signature hashtags and posters with giant Q's slapped on them. QAnon theories were infecting discourse in a much larger sense. They used misleading if not totally wrong interpretations of scientific data. Websites propagating QAnon conspiracy theories about COVID-19 presented themselves as reliable news agencies, while influencers touted their roles as self-styled analysts.[48] The movement also utilized seemingly agreeable hashtags like "#SaveTheChildren," which gained millions of interactions on Facebook and Instagram while advancing baseless claims of sex trafficking rings and pedophilia.[49]

One of QAnon's most significant points of entry into discourse were the anti-lockdown protests popping up in the United States and other countries. The sentiments driving these protests were diverse—perceptions of government overstepping, fear of permanent economic ruin, distrust in public health agencies—but most parties involved seemed compatibly skeptical of how severe the novel coronavirus was. Hearing the chants and reading signs from maskless protesters gathered tightly together, it was often hard to tell where the QAnon narratives ended and others began:

"FAUCI LIED MAINSTREET DIED"

"SUPPORT SMALL BIZ . . . F*CK BILL GATES"[50]

It wasn't just QAnon injecting itself into anti-lockdown rallies. Common characters at anti-lockdown demonstrations came to include militia groups, street-brawling right-wing activists like The Proud Boys, and neo-Nazis holding up anti-Semitic caricatures calling Jews "the real plague."[51] By grasping onto this common cause with the larger masses of anti-lockdown protesters, far-right groups and movements were now able to advance even closer to the mainstream than they had already.

Fueling the fire was President Trump, whose messaging during the pandemic was similarly erratic and recklessly inaccurate. He consistently defended anti-lockdown protesters, as seen in a White House briefing in April of 2020.[52] He reasoned, "They've got cabin fever. They want their lives back . . . I've never seen so many American flags. These people love our country. They want to get back to work."[53]

With Trump's implicit assurances of impunity, these activists became emboldened and increasingly aggressive. Words like "boogaloo" became staples of protesters' vocabularies, and death threats surfaced against governors and legislators. Even Trump's rhetoric played into the mood, with an April 17, 2020 string of tweets calling to "LIBERATE" states enacting coronavirus lockdowns, specifically mentioning Minnesota and Michigan.[54]

The same day as Trump's tweets, more protesters gathered outside of Minnesota governor Tim Walz's residence, adding to anti-lockdown protests that started the day before. One sign read, "If ballots don't free us bullets will."[55] Two weeks later, on May 1, armed protesters poured into the Michigan State Capitol after Governor Gretchen Whitmer extended a stay-at-home mandate.[56]

The actionable differences between these anti-lockdown submovements were diminishing. It wasn't that neo-Nazis, militia members, and QAnon types had bonded into one homogenous, uniform organization. But looking at *what* they were doing, *where* they were coalescing, and the issues and conspiracy theories energizing their respective movements, they were all in lock-step synergy with one another. As such, what many understood as the far right—a collection of white supremacist, ultra-nationalist, and ultra-conservative groups and submovements—was quickly being replaced by a more nebulous, but much larger, Far Right 2.0.

This Far Right 2.0 was pulling in everyone within reach: MAGA supporters, anti-vaxxers, people who felt violated by face-mask mandates. And as if COVID-19 wasn't enough, the most culturally and racially charged events of the twenty-first century were just around the corner, soon to bond all of these parties even more tightly together.

It was just before midnight on August 25, 2020, when seventeen-year-old Kyle Rittenhouse was running with an assault-style rifle through a parking lot in Kenosha, Wisconsin, about a half-hour drive from his home in Illinois.[57] Two days before Rittenhouse arrived to the town, a police officer shot a Black man named Jacob Blake four times in the back, making Kenosha the latest site of protests and generating violent unrest elsewhere across the country.[58]

Three months earlier, on May 25, 2020, a police officer named Derek Chauvin had pinned a forty-six-year-old Black man named George Floyd to the ground with his knee for over eight minutes.[59] Floyd repeatedly told Chauvin "I can't breathe," but the officer never removed his knee.[60] Disturbing cell phone footage of the murder sparked protests, riots, and enduring waves of activism in the United States and the world, with the Black Lives Matter (BLM) movement at the helm.[61]

Several protests turned to riots in cities like Minneapolis, Philadelphia, Miami, Oakland, Chicago, and Los Angeles.[62] As people around the world looked on in fear at news coverage of burning police cars, looting, and entire neighborhoods with boarded-up windows, militia groups and other right-wing activists began organizing brigades of gunwielding volunteers to—as they put it—protect property and residents across the United States.[63] In Kenosha, Rittenhouse was himself the epitome of this absurd new dystopia: a baby-faced high school student patrolling the city streets with other armed individuals, welcomed by police officers as they waited for the arson and broken windows to resurge upon nightfall.[64]

But for many of these right-wing activists, it was about more than protecting windows.

For months, President Trump had been fomenting rage around these protests, attributing the violent parts of these demonstrations to his new favorite boogeyman, antifa. Short for "anti-fascist," antifa is a movement that, as its name states, works against fascism and far-right ideology. Adherents of the movement range from journalistically minded researchers seeking to out neo-Nazis in public office to destructive anarchists throwing Molotov cocktails at protests.[65] But to Trump, antifa was a card to throw back at objectors every time they accused him of feeding into the Far Right 2.0.

More, antifa was a perfectly oversimplified enemy to rally the Far Right 2.0 against. On May 31, he tweeted that the United States would be "designating ANTIFA as a Terrorist Organization."[66] It was a match thrown onto gasoline. Across the Far Right 2.0, this was taken as a message by the president himself that it was open season against racial justice protesters.

"So . . . Theoretically if this passes . . . Are we a Counter-Terrorist organization?" wrote a Proud Boys Telegram channel the day Trump announced he would be "designating" antifa.[67] The same emboldened attitude could be seen from every corner of the far right. A July 18 post by Brien James, leader of the American Guard far-right group, proposed:

> The cops, the government, and even our president dont seem to know what to do about antifa . . . Give the Proud Boys, American Guard, Bikers for Trump, and the militias 48 hours of immunity from prosecution in taking whatever actions needed to put these terrorists down.[68]

James himself was an embodiment of the Far Right 2.0's rapidly overlapping factions, with a history of violence with skinhead groups only to end up preaching "the Constitution and the Bill of Rights" via the American Guard.[69]

Meanwhile, young anti-government extremists began attending counterprotests armed as part of the so-called boogaloo movement. "Boogaloo" is a memetic term taken from a 1984 movie called *Breakin' 2: Electric Boogaloo*, though among far-right groups it refers to a coming civil war (which they refer to as "Civil War 2: Electric Boogaloo").[70]

The details of this civil war vary between hardline libertarian and neo-Nazi contexts: who the targets are, if the war is racial or anti-government in nature, and so on. These increasingly present boogaloo movement types at protests and counterprotests—identifiable by their rifles and Hawaiian-styled shirts under their flak jackets—fit into the former category.[71]

In June, three boogaloo movement individuals from Nevada were arrested for a plot to spark violence at ongoing BLM protests.[72] FBI agents found rags and gasoline on the men, intended for making Molotov cocktails, as well as aerosol cans and weapons in one of their trucks.[73]

Such arrests might have seemed like successful aversions of violence, but they still sent a troubling signal: it wasn't just the neo-Nazis seeking acceleration toward the boogaloo anymore. The Far Right 2.0 believed they were at war, and they saw their enemies under one umbrella. They conflated Trump's antifa boogeyman with all of their perceived enemies: the communists, the cultural Marxists, the anarchists, the Democrats, BLM, big tech companies, and mainstream media. Anyone to the left of them—or, as it seemed, anyone *other* than them.

"Blaming Antifa is not enough," wrote Proud Boys chairman Enrique Tarrio in a May 30 Telegram post. "Antifa and BLM share the same communistic and 'Whites are the devil' bullshit. They're both domestic terrorists and both deserve to get kicked in the mouth."[74]

Almost every possible condition for unity was set in place for this Far Right 2.0: the sense of existential threat from their common enemy in "the left," racially and culturally charged protests across the country, lockdowns, and a president who seemed to have their back in every conceivable way. All they needed now was a story to solidify their warfare narrative.

Around 11:45 p.m. in Kenosha on August 25, a thirty-six-year-old demonstrator named Joseph Rosenbaum chased Rittenhouse into a parking lot when a shot was fired nearby.[75] Immediately after, Rosenbaum was shot by Rittenhouse as he attempted to disarm him. Rosenbaum's wounds were fatal.[76]

Rittenhouse began running down the street as demonstrators chased him. He fell down in the middle of the street, at which point twenty-six-year-old Anthony Huber hit him with a skateboard. Ritten-house shot him too, killing him instantly.[77]

He also shot at twenty-six-year-old Gaige Grosskreutz, a former para-medic who came to the protests to help any injured demonstrators.[78] Grosskreutz, who was also armed with a handgun, moved toward Rit-tenhouse before the teenaged boy shot him in the arm, severely damag-ing his bicep.[79]

This sequence of events was the final catalyst to solidify this still-nascent Far Right 2.0. If Rittenhouse's shootings had happened any other year, neo-Nazis wouldn't have given him the time of day because he was by no means one of their own; he was actually exactly the type of "MAGAtard" conservative that neo-Nazis despised. To them, Trump was "an ignoramus who makes money for the Jews" and pandered to racial minorities for political support.[80] Anyone who supported him was a blind fool.

But the unrest of 2020 changed the far right's equations. Anti-lockdown protests, conspiracy theories, and now racial justice protests gave them new inroads into communities much larger than their own. If someone was to push the United States closer to a race war, it would more likely be a kid like Kyle Rittenhouse than a blatant white supremacist like John Earnest. Who better to stoke the fire of racial and cultural resentments throughout the United States and pull in more people toward their cause? As one far-right Telegram channel put it, Rittenhouse was the poster child of the acceleration they sought:

White Pill: youth are buying guns and traveling to urban war zones hungry for direct action. Huge step forward . . .
   Whatever you think about Kyle Rittenhouse, his militia friends, or even the other side of commies armed with guns or explosives, finally militancy is capturing the spirit of young men. Accelerate[81]

Politics be damned, white supremacists began lauding this teenager as "Saint Rittenhouse." Far-right groups from around the world voiced their solidarity. New Zealand–based group Action Zelandia members photographed themselves with a banner reading "JUSTICE FOR KYLE

RITTENHOUSE."[82] Spanish far-right group Bastion Front likewise made a banner reading, "KYLE LIBERTAD . . . DEFENDER TU VIDA NO ES DELITO" ("FREE KYLE . . . DEFENDING YOUR LIFE IS NOT A CRIME").[83] The Sweden-based Nordic Resistance Movement discussed Rittenhouse in an hour-long podcast, saying he "deserved a medal."[84]

Support for Rittenhouse even came from the most hardline of neo-Nazi and siege groups, the last entities you'd expect to embrace such a relatively mainstream conservative. The National Socialist Order (NSO), a successor group to Atomwaffen Division (AWD), made doctored posters of Rittenhouse holding his assault rifle in front of the neo-Nazi Black Sun symbol with messages reading "MOW DOWN ANTIFA" and "MOW DOWN BLM SCUM," and "MOW DOWN KIKES."[85]

Neo-Nazi and white supremacists' celebration was just one component of a much larger outcry of solidarity with Rittenhouse from the

FIGURE 11.1 Poster by National Socialist Order depicting Kyle Rittenhouse in front of a Neo-Nazi Black Sun symbol and providing an email address (redacted) for prospective recruits.

same movements attending anti-lockdown protests and BLM counter-protests: Proud Boys, QAnon, militia groups, and even some hardliner political pundits in the media. On social media, users posted about Rittenhouse using phrases like "based rittenhouse" and hashtags like "#KenoshaHatTrick."[86] They didn't all hype the racial angle like the white supremacists did, but they nonetheless saw Rittenhouse as a soldier in a culture war—and as it was increasingly seeming, an *actual* war—against the left.

The Far Right 2.0 was becoming more cohesive than ever. The movement was a hive of contradicting actors—anti-government militias seeking to attack protesters at the direction of the federal government, hyper-nationalists partnered with libertarians—all telling the same conspiracy theories, fighting the same enemies.

All the while, social media companies were escalating their initiatives to cool tensions stemming from the swirl of anti-lockdown, coronavirus conspiracy, and other types of content on their platforms. Tech companies didn't have the same First Amendment restrictions that limited the government from intervening in toxic activity online, and they began exercising their immense power more forcefully than ever before. In late May, Facebook carried out sweeping, systematic removals of accounts connected to the Proud Boys and American Guard, claiming they were using the platform to organize violence at protests.[87] In July, Twitter announced it had removed 7,000 QAnon accounts.[88] Earlier, in May, Twitter had even begun fact-checking Trump himself after he tweeted that mail-in ballots would be "substantially fraudulent." Twitter responded by placing a blue exclamation point next to his tweet, calling his claim "unsubstantiated."[89]

"Twitter is completely stifling FREE SPEECH, and I, as President, will not allow it to happen!" Trump wrote in reply.[90]

But as mainstream social media companies worked to kick this toxic energy off their platforms, they were only pushing them into building a more robust online infrastructure.

12

WILL BE WILD

Twitter, Facebook, and Google weren't the only companies trying to tamper down on the Far Right 2.0 in 2020. In late June of that year, Reddit banned one of its most notorious communities, The_Donald. The community was created in June 2015 for Donald Trump, who had just announced his presidential run.[1]

Reddit, which reported over 50 million daily users by the end of 2020, is one of the most influential sources of information and discussion online.[2] Imagine a more sophisticated and mainstream version of 4chan: people sharing and commenting on memes, news, viral videos, and other online content across differently themed communities called "subreddits." The site also exhibited far more moderation than 4chan and 8chan, earning the ire of many users from spaces like /pol/, who scoffed at it as a den of liberalism.

The_Donald was one of Reddit's last major bastions of Trump-meming 4chan types. It was a long road of warnings that led to its removal, including constant outcry from other Reddit communities as well as the subreddit's June 2019 quarantining, which effectively hid The_Donald from users not directly looking for it.[3] This reprimand didn't come from nowhere. The_Donald users doxed anti-Trump activists via the subreddit's corresponding Discord server, justified attacks like the 2019 Christchurch massacre, and promoted events like the 2017 "Unite the Right" white supremacist rally in Charlottesville.[4] It was also an early incubator of conspiracy theories that helped give way to QAnon, Pizzagate, and conspiracy theories about murdered Democratic National Committee staffer Seth Rich.[5] So when Reddit finally announced in June of 2020 that it was banning The_Donald, it was widely seen as an overdue event.[6] The only problem was that the 800,000 members that The_Donald accumulated didn't suddenly disappear from the internet.[7] In fact, they had been preparing for this day for a long time.

In 2019, a team of moderators from The_Donald started working on a website to mirror their subreddit.[8] One of those moderators, a U.S. Army veteran named Jody Williams, registered and hosted the site with Epik, the same company that for years had helped keep sites like Gab, the Daily Stormer, and 8chan alive.[9] TheDonald.win was born.

The site was essentially a copy of The_Donald subreddit, all the way down to its interface and usernames.[10] The difference, though, was that there was no more moderation, no more walking on eggshells.[11] Much like users on 8chan and Telegram, TheDonald.win users displayed far less restraint in expressing hostile and extremist views than they did on Reddit.[12] Like 8chan, brazen anti-Semites and racists were gaining larger voices among your standard MAGA supporters. Upon launching, a sticky post from a moderator titled "Why are we winners?" was placed atop of the landing page.[13] It bragged about how they had survived Reddit's ban, what was in store for the site, and how they could continue to "redpill" the masses from their new home:

> we are literally the biggest meme distribution center on the internet . . . Reddit is fucked, but we make our imprint on Facebook, Twitter, Instagram, and just seeing a meme on your phone and showing it to your buddy in person or a text . . . So long as you're sharing memes from here, we're effective.[14]

And indeed, the content on TheDonald.win was vile. Users talked as if they were anticipating—if not looking forward to—a civil war. One user wrote in December 2019, with a bonus flare of misogyny:

Trump buys time but after him that's it. And it's not just the usa, it's the whole west. Country will balkanize, and we start over after probably a lot of death, hopefully no liberal values, women don't vote (let's be honest women voting and being in politics is what brought us here), etc etc.[15]

This talk of death was a common staple of TheDonald.win in one way or another. "The governor should hang," wrote one user of Michigan Governor Whitmer for her stay-at-home mandate that April.[16] Another wrote, "She needs a fast trial and then hanged."[17]

So, by the time Reddit banned r/The_Donald, the community had little to worry about. It could now fester free from the censorship and moderation rules of Reddit, pulling in new pieces of the growing Far Right 2.0.

But TheDonald.win was just one site among several others reacting to rapidly changing tides in social media censorship. The coalescing array of groups and movements within anti-lockdown protests were creating their own online infrastructure of "alternative" platforms. As social media platforms like Twitter, Reddit, YouTube, and Facebook continued to crack down on QAnon and extremist MAGA accounts, some of these alternative platforms got high-profile boosts.

On June 18, 2020, Trump reelection campaign manager Brad Parscale tweeted, "Hey @twitter your days are numbered," along with a link to an endorsement of a social media platform called Parler.[18] Immediately, top Trump supporters joined Parler. A week later, Senator Ted Cruz posted a video of himself likewise endorsing Parler: "This platform gets what free speech is all about, and I'm excited to be a part of it."[19]

Parler was, as Cruz and others described it, a free speech alternative to mainstream social media platforms. It was founded in 2018 by two University of Denver grads named John Matze Jr. and Jared Thomson, with the backing of prominent Republican donor Rebekah Mercer. Parler's microblogging design is similar to Twitter, with "parleys" (the site's version of tweets) limited to 1,000 characters.[20]

As big tech censorship became a central issue in the age of the coronavirus, the company was quick to capitalize. On June 15, 2020, amid escalating censorship against Trump, Parler issued "A Declaration of Internet Independence," calling for users to "#Twexit to Parler."[21] Its statement echoed Trump and his supporters' anger by questioning Twitter's "so-called 'fact checkers'" and calling the company a "Tech Tyrant."[22]

Much like Gab and other "free speech" social media sites, Parler was already home to blatantly white supremacist content.[23] Parler usership surged, acquiring nearly 2.5 million app downloads around that time.[24] It was an amplification of an already toxic environment. New accounts were drenched in QAnon imagery and hashtags like "#WWG-1WGA" and "#Pizzagate." Other accounts were run by prominent Proud Boys leaders.

The Far Right 2.0's migration to alternative platforms wasn't viewed as a problem by many. Quite the opposite: out of sight, out of mind. On the one hand, the amount of disinformation significantly decreased on major social media platforms. But on the other hand, when the most toxic user communities of any platform coalesce on rules-free alternatives like Parler or TheDonald.win, it's recipe for disaster. And Parler and TheDonald.win were only the beginning.

On Telegram, neo-Nazis and white supremacists were further overlapping with supporters of the Proud Boys, militias, and QAnon adherents. "Proud Boys: Uncensored," a Telegram channel associated with the Proud Boys' more overtly white nationalist members and supporters, went from 4,500 members in June to nearly 8,000 by the end of September.[25] Gab was seeing its own growth. The company reported 3.7 million monthly visitors and 1.2 million cumulative registered accounts as of April 2020, up nearly 300,000 from the year before.[26] WeGo, a social media platform created in 2017 specifically for QAnon, went from 22,643 users and 792,901 posts in early May to 37,560 users and 1,131,532 posts by the end of August.[27]

This was all leading to a specific objective. As is the case with any infrastructure, the Far Right 2.0's online infrastructure was built to accommodate something. In this case, that something was the reelection of Donald Trump. It didn't matter if you were a Trump-hating neo-Nazi or a Trump loving QAnon adherent; if you had any footing in this Far Right 2.0 current in the United States, you knew that the

2020 election was about your survival. Trump, love him or hate him, was the only thing holding back whatever existential threat you believed you faced: antifa-ravaged cities and towns, children forced into "Cultural Marxist" programs at school, a socialist takeover of the U.S. government, Democratic politicians ramping up their sex trafficking rings.

Trump had to win. He was going to win. Any other outcome would be impossible and unacceptable. Stolen. Fraudulent. A coup. A declaration of war.

WARNING: IF DONALD TRUMP DOESN'T WIN THIS ELECTION, THE POLICE WILL BE ABOLISHED AND BLACKS WILL COME TO YOUR HOUSE AND KILL YOU AND YOUR FAMILY. THE MEDIA WILL NOT REPORT IT. IF YOUR FRIENDS POST ABOUT IT ON SOCIAL MEDIA, THEY WILL BE ARRESTED FOR HATE SPEECH. THIS ISN'T ABOUT POLITICS ANYMORE, IT IS ABOUT BASIC SURVIVAL.

> —message set to the banner section of the Daily Stormer
> prior to the 2020 U.S. presidential election[28]

Not that I'm necessarily a Trumper or a Q larper, but Trump refusing to leave office regardless of the election outcome and declaring himself president indefinitely would objectively be the best thing for us.

Not because he's some savior of the white race, rather because it would crank the chaos up to 100 and bait the left into starting a war with us that they have no hope in hell of winning.

Day Of The Rope, in real life.

> —August 9, 2020, post to Neo-Nazi Telegram channel[29]

Highly coordinated [funded] _domestic terrorism.
FEDs involved [US rights [c]_surveillance]
[D] controlled areas.
Media blackout.
ELECTION gaming.
Q

> —September 10, 2020, Q drop

PATRIOTIC AMERICANS UNITED AGAINST:
BIDEN KID SNIFFERS & EPSTEIN PEDOPHILES
ANTIFA TERROR & DEMOCRAT VOTER VIOLENCE
SOCIAL MEDIA CENSORSHIP & CANCEL CULTURE
CHINA VIRUS HYPE GLOBALIST SCUM & THEIR FAKE NEWS
NEO-MARXISM & WOKE CAPITALISM

—from a poster for an October 3, 2020,
demonstration in Ohio, shared by the Proud Boys[30]

Do the DC criminals out to steal president Trump's reelection with fraudulent ballots realize how many heavily armed MAGA patriots with world-class military accessories will show up at the white house if anyone makes a move to illegally remove president Trump? It will beBIBLICAL. Ex Military MAGA patriots will serve at the pleasure of the president as supplemental presidential law enforcement when called into action.CODE RED

—October 4, 2020, post to QAnon Telegram chat group[31]

The election was over. But it was far from over.

Even those most hopeful of Trump's reelection were preparing for this. The entire year leading up to the election had been a movement-wide primer of conspiracy theories about mail-in ballots, deep-state collusion, and "false flag" crises formed against Trump. Thus, before Biden's victory was officially announced on November 7, there was consensus across the Far Right 2.0 that Biden had stolen the election from Trump and that there was no democratic, nonviolent way to fix this.

Militia groups, many of which formed against the perceived tyranny of President Obama and the federal government, were now pledging their lives to wherever Trump might steer them. Stewart Rhodes, leader of the Oath Keepers militia group, wrote:

Know this: millions of American military and law enforcement veterans, and many millions more loyal patriotic American gun owners stand ready to answer your call to arms, and to obey your orders to get this done.[32]

The Proud Boys and their supporters were on the same page. "Guys we are officially in a civil war weather [sic] we like it or not," wrote one user in a Proud Boys–associated Telegram chat group.[33] The day Biden was projected as the winner, a Parler user wrote to Proud Boys chairman Enrique Tarrio, "let us know when the shooting begins[.] I have no patience for anything less."[34]

"War is inevitable," wrote a neo-Nazi Telegram channel.[35] One replied, "Hurry up already I've been preparing for years."[36]

This consensus wasn't limited to particular groups and their supporters. Across far-right online venues, users with no formal affiliation reminded each other that this was what they'd been preparing for, even expressing joy that their "thousands of rounds of ammo . . . won't go to waste now."[37]

There was no question in the Far Right 2.0 anymore. Civil war was here. All they needed was a signal.

And indeed, the signal came. On December 19, 2020, after tweeting more misinformation about the election, Trump ended his tweet by writing: "Big protest in D.C. on January 6th. Be there, will be wild!"[38] The president was referring to a demonstration set for January 6, coinciding with Congress's vote to certify Joe Biden's victory. The event, called the "Save America Rally," was already shaping up for a major turnout, but when Trump himself tweeted of the event, it sent ripples through the incensed Far Right 2.0. To them, the tweet was an order from their leader. And "will be wild" meant that nothing was off the table. Instantly, followers on all platforms mobilized their communities.

QAnon chat groups announced: "Trump is asking all patriots and all those who dont want to take the leap into oppression and slavery to go to Washington D.C. on January 6, 2021 . . . Trump states: Be there it will be wild."[39]

The Proud Boys, militia groups, and others similarly showed Trump's tweet, declaring, "THE PRESIDENT IS CALLING ON US TO COME BACK TO WASHINGTON ON JANUARY 6TH FOR A BIG PROTEST— 'BE THERE, WILL BE WILD.'"[40]

SITE reported on many of these statements and discussions, but the volume was overwhelming. Every reporter, client, and associate I spoke to had the same creeping feeling I did. Something was going to happen, but we didn't know what or how big it would be. Yet as January 6 neared, those planning to attend this "wild" rally made their intentions increasingly clearer. On Parler, Proud Boys chairman Enrique Tarrio detailed his group's preparation for the January 6 event and how its members would skirt attention:

> The ProudBoys will turn out in record numbers on Jan 6th but this time with a twist . . .
>
> We will not be wearing our traditional Black and Yellow. We will be incognito and we will spread across downtown DC in smaller teams.[41]

The Far Right 2.0 seemed to truly believe they had received permission from Trump to arm themselves for political violence and revolution—and they now had the uninterrupted online infrastructure to plot it all. While platforms like Facebook continued escalating their purges of QAnon, boogaloo, militia, and other content throughout the election season, the Far Right 2.0 continued growing on alternative platforms.[42] New users were flocking to Parler, which saw well over three million new downloads of the app in the week after the elections alone.[43] It even became the most downloaded app on both Google and Apple, and claimed its user base doubled by the end of the month to over 10 million accounts.[44]

Similar upticks were seen for MeWe, another alternative social media platform used by the Far Right 2.0, and Newsmax, an outlet that helped perpetuate debunked "Stop the Steal" conspiracy theories.[45] Gab likewise saw immense growth, with CEO Andrew Torba bragging in a November 10 blog post that Gab was "the fastest growing alternative media platform on the internet":

> This week was Gab's best performing week in our four year history. To give you an idea of just how fast we are growing: Gab was visited 7.7 million times in all of October (up 99% from September,) but this past week alone we've seen 7.15 million visits and growing.[46]

Torba's claims seemed to check out when looking at the QAnon group memberships on Gab doubling in just a month's time. The "QAnon and the Great Awakening" group, one of many on Gab, went from 21,000 members in October to 41,000 in November. At the same time, "QAnon Research" went from 13,000 to 25,000 members and "QAnon" went from 11,000 to 27,000.[47]

The same could be seen with General Michael Flynn, whose adoration among QAnon adherents only increased after he posted an oath of office pledge on July 4, 2020, ending with the QAnon saying, "Where we go one, we go all."[48] He posted the video less than two weeks after a Q drop instructed followers to "take the oath" via the same words.[49] Flynn's Parler account, already amassing 118,000 followers that June, nearly tripled to over 430,000 by November 2020.[50]

Among the most concerning venues was TheDonald.win. The platform received over 18 million visits in November, and according to cofounder Jody Williams, saw more than a million visits a day in December.[51] Instantly after Trump tweeted that January 6 would be "wild," TheDonald.win set the tweet as a sticky entry titled, "Daddy says be in DC on January 6."[52] Trump's message was clear as day to users on the site. They wrote, "Well, shit. We've got marching orders, bois" and "LET'S MAKE THIS MARCH BIBLICAL PATRIOTS!"[53]

This thread alone generated close to six thousand responses, marking the start of what was looking more and more like an openly coordinated terrorist plot.

" 'Will Be Wild' is a hidden message for us to be prepared . . . as in armed," one user wrote of Trump's December 19 tweet. Another replied, "That's kind of how I took it."[54]

Others expressed the same: "He can't exactly openly tell you to revolt . . . This is the closest he'll ever get."[55]

"Trumps tweet said 'Wild' implying wild West in my mind," a member of the forum similarly concluded.[56]

"Not telling you what to do but I will be open carrying and so will my friends. We have been waiting for Trump to say the word," read one post. "There is not enough cops in DC to stop what is coming."[57]

It was clear to these users on TheDonald.win that this was more than a protest. This was an operation. Scores of posts throughout December and into early January discussed *Minecraft*, the video game that far-right extremists reference alongside incitements or plotting messages to provide what they believe will be plausible deniability. As one wrote: "You can't bring weapons on a plane in minecraft, gonna be driving."[58]

"Forget the property destruction, you go after the traitors directly," one wrote. "A military strategist also told me it's a good idea to have a list of their family members as well."[59]

Just as the tides shifted against the far right's nonviolent "do nothings" after Robert Bowers's Pittsburgh synagogue shooting, those now leading the charge in the Far Right 2.0 had no patience for anyone calling for moderation. As one user in TheDonald.win wrote:

> Patriots who STILL, AT THIS POINT IN TIME, are too cowardly
> to condone violence, are part of the problem.
>   IT. NEEDS. TO FUCKING. HAPPEN.[60]

Exact plans and operations were detailed. And much of what was posted on TheDonald.win seemed to correspond directly to what ended up unraveling on January 6.[61] Members discussed the plan for how to "barge into the Capitol through multiple entryways" and bring "handcuffs and zip ties to DC" for "citizen's arrests" of politicians.[62] One wrote, "Be prepared to secure the capitol [building]. There will be plenty of ex military To guide you."[63]

Users became gravely specific with their planning, including who they were targeting and how. "Encircle congress. Make sure they can't leave. Primary objective," one post read.[64] Another also targeted congress in much darker terms:

> The objective is Congress. We make it so they can either leave in one
> of two ways:
>   1. dead
>   2. certifying Trump the rightful winner[65]

In a grimly accurate prediction, one user wrote, "I don't see Trump sending any federal resources or military in to help the local corrupt agencies. They'll be on their own."[66]

Users on TheDonald.win also helped with logistical matters, with dozens listing their rideshares or organizing new ones. Others called for "every hotel full of patriots" to "hold a meeting in the hotel lobby" before the rally to "get organized" and "disperse in groups accordingly."[67] They also shared links and directed one another to where they could further coordinate on Discord, Facebook, and other platforms, and even raise funding for those who could not afford to make the trip to DC on their own.[68]

Then January 6 happened.

Everyone knows how the day unfolded: Trump's speech in which he urged "if you don't fight like Hell, you're not going to have a country anymore," swarms of incensed rioters at the Capitol, police officers and rioters killed and injured, and so many other details of that day that will remain etched in the memory of those who witnessed the day's events.[69] It was the ultimate real-life manifestation of the Far Right 2.0's uninterrupted online activity, with each corner of the movement represented in some way or another as they converged in DC. There were shirts, flags, and hats with QAnon mantras like "Trust the Plan" and emblems of militia movements like the Three Percenters and the Oath Keepers. There were Confederate flags and rope nooses. Inside the Capitol building, a man with a shirt reading "CAMP AUSCHWITZ . . . WORK BRINGS FREEDOM" stormed through the halls beside another individual in a TRUMP 2020 hat, helping hold up a broken piece of a nameplate reading, "SPEAKER OF THE HOUSE NANCY PELOSI."[70]

And with the United States still sifting through the rubble of that day, we watched the same maddingly familiar script play out once more.

—————— ∞ ——————

Many unanswered questions about the January 6 Capitol siege remain: Why were the Capitol Police so grossly unprepared? Why was the deployment of the National Guard so delayed?

But one thing is certain: this didn't come out of the blue. All the planning that went into the January 6 riot—the zip ties, the incitements, the movement-wide sense of direction, the coordination—happened in broad daylight on sites like TheDonald.win. As the *Wall Street Journal* reported in the siege's aftermath, "The SITE Intelligence Group, which monitors extremist groups, sent more than two dozen alerts between Dec. 23 and Jan. 7 noting the rising risk of violence related to the coming gathering."[71] Those alerts went to our many law enforcement partners. And that was just from us; other monitors were also raising red flags. The government's lack of preparation was not a failure of intelligence, as some said of 9/11 at the time. This was a blatant failure to act on available intelligence—by far the worst I'd seen in my entire career.

Sure, some coordination happened on apps like Facebook Messenger, but the real mobilization took place on TheDonald.win, Parler, 8kun, and the like. Posts on TheDonald.win indicate that this was where many seemed to have found their way into the private chats to begin with.

It was the same story of an internet-fueled terrorist catastrophe we'd been following in recent years—only on a much larger and more coordinated scale.

On January 8, amid new public scrutiny of Parler's role in the Capitol siege, both Apple and Google delivered ultimatums to the company for "moderation improvement" plans.[72]

Parler CEO John Matze wasn't having any of it.

"We will not cave to pressure from anti-competitive actors!" he wrote on the platform.[73] "We will and always have enforced our rules against violence and illegal activity. But we WONT cave to politically motivated companies and those authoritarians who hate free speech!"[74]

The next day, Apple and Google removed Parler from their app stores, citing an "ongoing and urgent public safety threat" and the company's lack of "adequate measures" to address it.[75] The same day, Amazon Web Services announced it would be cutting off its services to Parler on January 10, claiming that the platform "cannot comply with our terms of service and poses a very real risk to public safety."[76] It marked the first such move against Parler by Amazon, whose two years of providing hosting services to the platform reportedly evolved into a $300,000-a-month source of revenue.[77]

The Far Right 2.0 needed a new home: somewhere with appealing features and a proven track record of little to no moderation. You may have already guessed where I'm going with this.

"Telegram is the only viable alternative at the moment," wrote popular white nationalist activist Nick Fuentes, known for starting the America First Political Action Conference (AFPAC), for which at least one banner was seen during the Capitol siege.[78] Far-right 4chan users likewise wrote the day after Parler's removal, "COME TO TELEGRAM NOW" while listing far-right channels.[79] QAnon users said the same, writing that "patriots need to gather under one banner on Telegram."[80]

So began yet another mass online migration to Telegram by users too extreme for other mainstream social media platforms. In November 2020, a Proud Boys associated chat group had less than 2,000 members. But after branding itself as "Parler Lifeboat" when the platform was removed, the Telegram chat group reached well over 13,000 members by the end of January 2021.[81] Similar surges were seen across all the Far Right 2.0's overlapping submovements after Parler went down. A QAnon chat group on Telegram with 6,524 members in November 2020 similarly shot up to over 23,380 by late January.[82] The overtly white nationalist Proud Boys: Uncensored Telegram channel went from 16,000 subscribers at the beginning of January to nearly 45,000 by the end of the month.[83] With that, this increasingly influential channel directed fellow white nationalists to cater to these new Parler refugees pouring into Telegram:

> Parler being shut down has sent tens of thousands (or more) of people to telegram. All of them are seeking refuge and looking for answers since their Q-bullshit lied to them. Maga people are demoralized.
>
> Now is our opportunity to grab them by the hand and lead them toward ideological truth. Join their normie chats and show them love and unity . . . Introduce videos that will open their eyes (you know which ones).[84]

Neo-Nazis on Telegram also had their eyes on this new wave of recruitment prospects. Many circulated the lengthy "Comprehensive Redpill Guide," detailing how to radicalize those energized by the Capitol siege and providing templates of how to reach out to such prospects without scaring them away with blatant anti-Semitism and racism. The guide concluded, "Big Tech made a serious mistake by banishing conservatives to the one place where we have unfettered access to them, and that's a mistake they'll come to regret!"[85]

These developments didn't seem to factor into many lawmakers' responses to the Capitol siege, though. Congress began calling for hearings and investigations in the months that followed, with many Democrats seeking to scrutinize Parler for its role in the January 6 siege.[86] Republicans, meanwhile, seemed to take more issue with Google, Apple, Amazon, and other companies cutting off Parler.[87] None of it mattered, though, because Parler registered its domain with Epik in January and by February was fully operational again—another save by Epik.[88] It even took the cybersecurity services of the Russia-based DDoSGuard, the same company that protected VanwaTech so that it could help provide servers for 8chan and a dozen QAnon sites.[89]

Meanwhile, founders of TheDonald.win broke away from Williams, who was quickly distancing himself from the site he had cocreated. All that was connected to Williams was the domain registration, so to bring TheDonald.win back up, all the remaining unapologetic admins had to do was change the domain to "Patriots.win." Upon doing so, these new admins boldly declared in a statement on the landing page, "The Donald has evolved to Patriots.win. Don't worry, everything else is the same."[90]

The site's new registrar? You guessed it: Epik.

This is where things go beyond déjà vu. It's Bill Murray in *Groundhog Day*: the same names reappearing in the same exasperatingly familiar story, and nothing done to stop it from repeating itself over and over again.

In this book's latter chapters, I have made little mention of ISIS. That's because by this point in the "screw your optics" current's evolution—paired with the formation of the Far Right 2.0—ISIS no longer applied. Both of these global movements received enormously different treatments. One side was all but smothered to death online, while the other was able to survive long enough to inject itself into other extremist movements. One side was shunned by societies around the globe, while the other infused itself into mainstream political discussion. One side prompted consensus among governments, tech companies, and societies that it was a danger to the world, while the other found refuge with "free speech"–preaching companies that hardly seemed to apply the same rationale toward jihadi extremists.

These double standards seemed more absurd throughout 2020. Far-right terrorism had already surpassed jihadi terrorism in U.S. death tolls in 2019, after Patrick Crusius's attack in El Paso.[91] Amid an epidemic of coronavirus conspiracies, unrest over social justice issues, and events like Kyle Rittenhouse's shooting in Kenosha, did any of it seem on track to get any better? After all, the most significant attack on U.S. democracy hadn't come from a secret ISIS chat group. It came from TheDonald.win, public accounts on Parler, and sites protected by tech giants like Cloudflare (the same company that protected Gab and 8chan for so long, only to then protect 8chan's mother company, IsItWetYet.com). ISIS may have been playing the same internet radicalization game as the far right, but the rules were vastly different. The group's online presence was the world's most glaring example of where free speech ends: terms like "discourse" and "both sides of an argument" had absolutely no application to ISIS's toxic online community and the mass-casualty terrorist acts to which it systemically gave way. Furthermore, recent years of collaboration between tech companies in disrupting ISIS's online recruitment machine, whether sustained or brief, showed that the techniques and technology to eliminate online terrorist communities exist.

To put it another way, ISIS was confirmation that when it comes to combatting far-right terrorist movements online, the only thing that's missing is the will to act. Telegram alone is proof of this. To date,

Telegram constantly deletes ISIS and al-Qaeda accounts, bots, channels, and chat groups with laser-focused efficiency. This makes my job harder at times, but if it means jihadi terrorist groups are that much harder to reach, I wholeheartedly welcome it. But apart from some sporadic removals of high-profile accounts, it seems that every corner of this new Far Right 2.0 remains largely untouched, from accelerationist neo-Nazis to QAnon.[92] Give me sixty seconds on Telegram and I can easily find you anti-vax conspiracy theories, doxed targets of attack incitements, and suggestions for terrorist attacks—maybe even all in the same channel.

Yet as impactful as the actions (or lack thereof) by platforms like Telegram are, they are not the only players on the field. Telegram is just one platform, just like Parler is one platform, or Gab is one platform. These radicalization hubs don't exist by themselves, but rather via much larger infrastructures of web hosting, registrars, cyber protection, and other services. These intertwined knots (or "stacks," as they've been called) of information and communications technology (ICT) companies are often left out of focus when looking to the sources of the internet's most toxic environments.[93] As a result, demands for accountability narrowly target sites like 8chan and Parler, while the hosts, registrars, app stores, and other companies propping them up receive little or no criticism. Such tunnel vision is a core facilitator of the near-identical trajectories of terrorist currents and movements like the "screw your optics" far right and Far Right 2.0, as summarized simply in the steps here:

1. The extremist community is pushed off major social media and streaming platforms.
2. Members of the extremist community, while removed from larger populations, migrate to lesser-known (and often lesser-moderated) platforms, where they become further radicalized.
3. Once established on its new platform(s), violence from this extremist community begins to increase until public pressure forces companies to halt services to the platform(s) where they are housed.
4. Extremists find new platforms to exploit as hubs while their former hubs often resurface with the help of alternative registrars, web hosts, and other companies.

One of my primary aims in writing this book has been to show as vividly as possible the oxygen that keeps modern-day extremist movements like ISIS or the Far Right 2.0 alive and thriving. In 2007, I testified twice before Congress that the government could eliminate all the al-Qaeda leaders and training camps it wanted to, but if they didn't address the online havens of these threats they would continue to grow, just as they had been doing so dramatically after 9/11. As I urged, "If I come with one thing, one theme, after my brief testimony, I hope that it will be that the internet is a crucial battleground in the war on terror that must be contested in a more effective way."[94] Fifteen years later, I find even more relevance and urgency in my assertion.

Some readers might imagine an implied call for legislation or government intervention in what I've laid out here. This is not at all the case. Crafting effective government policy is a messy, time-consuming venture—and in this regard, a guaranteed quagmire of wholly legitimate First and Fourth Amendment concerns. Many Americans often lose sight of how unique these rights to free speech and privacy are, and how quickly they would miss those rights if they were to wane. These features of American life aren't something we should tinker with haphazardly, and if that means that someone down the street from me gets to write articles claiming that Jews like me secretly control the world, so be it.

The United States is already equipped with laws and court rulings clearly stating that the First Amendment does not protect incitements to riot or carry out other "imminent lawless action."[95] Add these American legal realities to the far more aggressive anti-extremist laws in Europe and elsewhere, and you have more than enough legal tools at hand. In other words, many of the types of messages shown throughout this book—which I suspect no rational person would mistake for mere "speech"—were never legal to begin with. The question is when will governments start seeking out and acting upon such legal violations from the far right with the same vigor as they do for jihadists.

Yet as the world's fight against jihadi terrorists' online infrastructures has shown, it was never so much any government making progress as it was the private sector. It took many nudges from government agencies and the general public, but social media and ICT companies eventually came together to build a massive digital wall between ISIS and the people they wish to recruit or intimidate. What the world got from all of this was a wealth of tested and proven strategies that we have sadly not seen fully adapted and implemented against far-right extremism. That the tech sector holds so much power in fighting far-right extremism should at this point be expected, because it speaks to the very nature of such actors. They are products of the environments that tech companies have built, thus making those very companies the best-equipped (and most responsible) to counter them.

I always intended for this book to offer a diagnosis: something to help governments, researchers, the tech sector, and the general public better understand the nature of internet-age terrorism so that they could better fight it. Nonetheless, I will suggest the following as guiding principles for crafting counterterrorism approaches.

For starters, timeliness is of the essence. I don't think it is out of the question to consider that if Cloudflare had immediately removed 8chan after Christchurch the way it did after El Paso, a lot of violence could have been prevented. Instead, the site was able to stay up long enough to foster a movement around Brenton Tarrant, and Robert Bowers before him, allowing it to solidify into something much harder to control come summer 2019. When a terrorist leaves behind a manifesto for brethren on a website, a tech company affiliated with that website shouldn't wait for another attack to begin assessing what is happening there and how their own services might be contributing to it. Cut off the snake's head early, before it can grow into a monster.

Quick action cannot be expected without an informed and incentivized tech sector, though. For as many registrars and web hosts that don't seem to care about facilitating terrorist movements, there are also many that don't seem to know they are doing exactly that. Large companies and small companies alike should stay up to date on what the internet's most toxic sites and platforms are. This is not so different from many of the useful partnerships formed in the fight against ISIS: companies large and small could keep abreast of this information via collectively run information-sharing coalitions and consortia, funded by whichever among them could afford to chip in.

Perhaps most fundamental will be a collective understanding of what responsibilities come with providing any service on the internet. The internet is a real place, just as real as the supermarkets we shop at, the restaurants we eat in, and hotels we stay in. Beyond the laws these places are bound by, they also have their own rules, designed to protect themselves and their customers. If someone causes a disturbance at a movie theater, restaurant, or bar, they will be kicked out—not by any particular law tailored to address this specific behavior, but by the rules of the private venue they're in. Internet-based services must say the same: *this is our establishment; if you don't like our rules, get out.*

Such rules already exist with most ICT and social media services. Even the web-based services used most significantly by terrorists have sufficient terms and conditions to cut them off; the problem is that they don't enforce these rules the way a movie theater enforces its own. When registering on Telegram, which currently serves as the main internet hub for both ISIS and far-right extremists, users must agree to the platform's terms that they will not "promote violence on publicly viewable Telegram channels, bots, etc."[96] Most remaining ISIS channels and chat groups have gone private, but far-right terrorist channels still promote violence publicly with little to no action from Telegram. Even Epik similarly claims the right to "cancel the registration" of any site that encourages "unlawful behavior by others, such as hate crimes [and] terrorism," among other activities.[97] Yet at the same time it has enabled Gab, Parler, TheDonald.win (and its newer version, Patriots.win), and scores of QAnon sites—all despite their demonstrated links to hate crimes and terrorism.

If more tech companies enforce their own rules that *already exist*, the online infrastructures keeping poisonous internet spaces alive will become smaller and smaller. When a far-right–riddled site like 8chan or Parler is running well, it's usually because major web services companies like Amazon or Cloudflare are somewhere in the background keeping it afloat, knowingly or not. The more critical lifelines a poisonous site loses, the more it is forced to rely on less dependable alternatives. It's not for nothing that Parler was at one point paying Amazon Web Services more than $300,000 a month for hosting; shadier hosting companies overseas, while easier for disreputable sites to do business with, don't offer anywhere near the scalability required to handle the web traffic a site like Parler was bringing in at its peak.[98] Without that scalability, these sites become slower and draw fewer and fewer users.

Even if companies like Epik refuse to come on board to address the problem, there are still other Jenga blocks to pull away: hosts, DDoS mitigation services, and so on. The more companies that proactively deny their services to extremist cesspools, the harder it is for a platform like Gab or 8kun to keep up a well-running operation. Because as much as extremist communities love to speak of steadfastness, never underestimate how quickly slow server speeds, download requirements, blacklisting on app stores, and other inconveniences can disperse their online parties.

I don't overlook the fact that the private sector, like the government, has the capacity to undermine one's freedom—in this case, freedom of speech. If enough of the public comes to agree that an ICT company's anti-terrorism and anti-hate policies amount to unfair treatment to one group of people or an undesirable "nanny state" of discourse, they would be right to demand those policies be changed. You would likely find mine among such voices. But tech companies cannot and should not halt action simply out of fear of every fallacious "free speech" tirade to follow. I have yet to be shown any such tech sector action that amounts to the oppressive Orwellian internet that free speech absolutists describe.

Any tech company still shrugging off today's online terrorist cesspools as inevitable byproducts of free speech is negligent at best and copping out at worst. These horrifying phenomena cannot be chalked up to social or political circumstances alone, with the internet being a mere "neutral" reflection of that environment. The internet itself, and all the components within it, is an active part of the problem. The sooner we admit that spaces like /pol/ and TheDonald.win have no productive value in online discourse, the sooner we can start pushing things in the right direction.

The weight of ICT and social media companies' responsibility cannot be overstated. Internet companies, from social media to web hosts, are what allow this new breed of terrorists to exist as they do. How else could a thirteen-year-old boy from Estonia form an international neo-Nazi organization like Feuerkrieg Division?[99] How else could a movement like QAnon turn into a worldwide terrorist threat? An endless sea of internet users around the globe partakes in this movement without even knowing who "Q" is. QAnon exists almost entirely as a cyber entity—no bases, no headquarters, no leadership structure—but its real-world impact on public safety and democracy is no less pressing.

These internet-based movements are proving to be both malleable and enduring. Despite Q drops halting, the movement's apparatus of websites, social media accounts, Telegram channels, and other components has continued to grow. Mounting research from journalists and documentarians make a compelling case that Jim or Ron Watkins (or both) have been posting as Q after hijacking the identity in January 2018, but it doesn't matter.[100] Q could be confirmed as Ron Watkins or a pastry chef in Chicago tomorrow, and QAnon would still press on regardless. For QAnon and other submovements within the Far Right 2.0, every societal development is a new thing to capitalize on, whether it be anti-vax agendas or backlash against "woke" culture.

This new reality is just as empowering as it is daunting. These online spaces are, after all, battlefronts that require no lives lost, no blood spilled—only a collective sense of direction and priority. That's a fight in which tech companies and consumers alike should seek a dutiful part.

As I type this final chapter from my son's home on the West Coast, I can hear my new grandchildren fussing in the other room. Maybe these adorable new faces will be what finally gets this new grandmother to close her laptop and forget, if only for a short moment, about all the evil in the world. As my son had already asked me several times, only half-jokingly: "Is your work more important than your grandchildren?"

Perhaps the two aren't so separate, because I sincerely hope my work may help protect them now and in the future.

Right now, from the other room, I hear the voices of children who will inherit a society built on the decisions we make today. I also see an opportunity to learn from where we've gone wrong: the double standards we apply to masked militants holding Qurans as opposed to those holding copies of the Constitution. How we keep applying the same failed solutions to clamp down on the conditions that breed terrorism, expecting that *this time* it might actually work. And yes, how we let work drown out what little time we have with our loved ones.

We can determine our future, and that of our children and children's children, by *changing* the way we think and act.

Here's to change.

AFTERWORD

What "Change" Looks Like a Year Later

Today is February 25, 2022. It's been roughly a year since I was hunkered into a room at my son and daughter-in-law's house on the West Coast, closing my book with the hopeful line, "Here's to change." Now, I'm back at my laptop nearly 3,000 miles away on the East Coast. My grandchildren are starting to look like toddlers with full heads of hair, sounding out their first words.

Indeed, a lot has changed.

Well over 700 people have been arrested for their role in the January 6 Capitol insurrection, including high-profile members of groups like the Proud Boys and Oath Keepers.[1] In his Inauguration speech in January 2021, President Joe Biden declared, "And now [there is] a rise of political extremism, white supremacy, domestic terrorism that we must confront and we will defeat."[2] That summer, the White House announced a series of measures intended to combat extremism, including the first-ever National Strategy for Countering Domestic Terrorism.[3] The Department of Justice and the FBI have even formed special domestic terrorism units to counter the threat.[4]

Alongside such developments, however, the threat of domestic extremism has evolved as well. The so-called Q persona is still radio silent, but QAnon has seeped even deeper into society via anti-vaccine conspiracy theories and electoral politics. Ron Watkins—the former admin of

8chan, whereon QAnon and the "screw your optics" far right grew—announced he was running for U.S. Congress in Arizona's 1st Congressional District. Watkins remains a celebrity across the Far Right 2.0, with hundreds of thousands of followers on platforms like Telegram and Gab (nearly half a million on the latter alone).[5]

On the ground, some parts of the Far Right 2.0 focus on locally oriented campaigns regarding COVID-19 mitigation measures, the migrant situation at the southern border, critical race theory, elections, and the like. The threat from the Proud Boys, which were one of the most high-profile groups to attend the January 6 riots, has shifted in the last year. Its chapters have aimed their aggressive activism toward grassroots activities, attending school board meetings and local events.[6] It appears the group is still growing, too. Toward the end of 2021, for example, the Proud Boys promoted upcoming chapters in France, Belgium, and Spain to accompany the thirteen other international chapters it claimed to hold across Great Britain, Ireland, Portugal, Germany, the Philippines, Japan, and Australia.[7]

Meanwhile, militia movements recruit in full force for what they believe is an "inevitable civil war" and organize vigilantism in response to the "massive incursion of migrants" or "government tyranny" of COVID-19 mitigation measures.[8] The more measures and mandates, the more anger.

The frequent targets of violent threats are no longer limited to national figures like Nancy Pelosi, Anthony Fauci, and Joe Biden, but also educators, healthcare officials, locally elected officials, police, flight attendants, and corporate executives.[9] Virtually anyone can, by some measure or another, become a target. Indeed, related violence has included everything from a QAnon-adhering woman running her vehicle into a vaccination tent site in Tennessee in May 2021 to a California man who, after stating he had been "enlightened" by QAnon and other conspiracy theories, murdered his two children with a spearfishing gun (a ten-month-old daughter and a two-year-old son).[10] This crisis isn't limited to America. From Israel to Spain, from Brazil to New Zealand, it's everywhere.

Not quite the change I wished for.

The unfortunate truth is that our society is still as vulnerable to these threats as it ever was. And why is that?

As I told the *Washington Post* on the one-year anniversary of the January 6 riot, "The U.S. government can arrest every single rioter who entered the Capitol building last year, but it won't make these dangerous incitements disappear, or prevent another January 6. Because those behind the keyboard, who played vital roles in organizing, coordinating and mobilizing the community for January 6, continue to incite and recruit, and proved to be untouchable."[11]

This book began by describing a new shift in the far right sparked by the 2018 Pittsburgh synagogue shooting. As such, Gab was a critical part of the story: how it served as a safe haven for hate, how it contributed to Bowers's decision to attack, how it survived despite all the public outrage. Now, after all this time, it remains. More, it serves as one of the most telling case studies of how little progress was made in tackling extremism online. Today, it is one of the most prominent venues for far-right communities online. And it's still the same cesspool it was on October 27, 2018, and January 6, 2021. Posts mourn the January 6 Capitol rioters as "political prisoners" while comment threads cascade with N-word-filled racist rants, defense of "Aryan culture," and resentment of "the Jew bankers."[12] A QAnon chat group with over 12,000 members has made over twenty posts and reposts in the last ten hours about everything from pro-Russia memes to videos declaring "The Vaccinated Have AIDS."[13]

Gab is so much more than a fringe platform for discussion, though. It expanded to become a digital mall, a media outlet, and an enterprise. At the time of the Pittsburgh attack, Gab held just under half a million accounts.[14] Not long after the January 6 riot, it appeared to hold at least four million.[15] Gab CEO Andrew Torba has claimed "90 million monthly visitors" to his site in the thirty days leading to February 12, 2022.[16] This count seems exaggerated compared to what is shown by web analytics services, one of which puts Gab at 11.6 million visits for January 2022.[17]

But there is nonetheless a lot happening on Gab that numbers alone don't describe. Gab provides its own "Gab Marketplace" in lieu of Amazon, "Gab TV" instead of YouTube, and a Gab Medical Community with "tens of thousands" of so-called experts providing healthcare advice—not to mention paid advertisements.[18] It is a whole world unto itself. Users can discuss Jewish-led cabals, buy beauty products, browse classifieds, and get questionable medical opinions all on the same browser tab.

The last year should have been a story about how January 6, 2021, served as a wake-up call—and how governments, the private sector, and civil society together chipped away at this toxic online infrastructure piece by piece. Instead, the opposite happened. The infrastructure expanded and mutated like a virus. And Gab is just one of many pieces of this alternative online infrastructure. In the year-long span between February 2021 and February 2022, Parler has been visited well over 70 million times.[19] Bitchute, the far right's alternative to YouTube that houses endless collections of Nazi and conspiracist videos, has been visited over 300 million times.[20] Gettr, a Twitter-like platform used by far-right extremists, has been visited over 43 million times and downloaded on the Google Play store five million times since it was launched roughly half a year ago.[21] That's not even counting the increasingly popular far-right–friendly livestreaming platforms like Odysee and Rumble.[22] There are simply too many to list.

While the information and communications technology (ICT) sector plays the most critical part in keeping these dangerous communities alive, the government must also adapt to this internet age of terrorism. It's hard to be encouraged by arrests and new initiatives of the last year when looking at TheDonald.win (Patriots.win), whereon many of the most brazen voices that incited and helped coordinate the January 6 insurrection have continued pushing for armed struggle. SITE has profiled dozens of Patriots.win users who, after providing tactical advice and instructions to the January 6 mob, applied the same violent energy toward graphic threats in support of January 6 "political prisoners" and healthcare providers implementing COVID-19 mitigation measures, among other focuses.[23]

It cannot be said that these TheDonald.win members aren't known to law enforcement. In recent months I learned how SITE's reports leading into the Capitol insurrection were shared widely across multiple government agencies, thanks to a series of *Politico* articles based on documentation obtained through the Freedom of Information Act. These instances included a November 9, 2020 email from an FBI intelligence analyst to federal and state-level intelligence and law enforcement, warning them to "keep your head on a swivel."[24] This sharing of SITE's alerts persisted all the way up to a flurry of documents circulated among law enforcement officials in the days before January 6.[25]

Almost every relevant agency in the U.S. government received the alerts we were putting out at SITE: the plans to bring zip ties to the Capitol and arrest politicians, the expectation of civil war and executions, the widely held perception that Trump had green-lighted all of it. SITE sent more than two dozen alerts between December 23 and January 7 noting the rising risk of violence related to the coming gathering.[26]

The problem at hand doesn't come from any single website like The-Donald or Gab or Bitchute or Telegram, but rather what they create together: an entire digital existence steeped in misinformation, fear, and hatred. In many ways, it's a crisis much bigger than the Far Right 2.0 or any other movement. It is a crisis of society itself.

Reporters and associates frequently ask me, "Do you think we might see another January 6–level event in the future?" Acknowledging this extremist dystopia of the Internet Age, how could my answer be anything but yes? In 2021 it was Trump's election loss; in the years to follow, virtually any event could serve as the spark: trucker convoys, more vaccine mandates, the 2024 election—it's all gasoline-drenched tinder to the Far Right 2.0.

It's not all hopeless, though. A precedent has been set by toppling ISIS's online infrastructure. Similar measures can be adapted to tackle far-right violent extremists' online sources. In some ways, we are better-equipped: in 2001, authorities refused to acknowledge the problem, which led to a massive intelligence failure; in 2022, policy makers have identified the problem. As the Department of Homeland Security's February 7, 2022 bulletin stated, misinformation could "undermine public trust in government institutions to encourage unrest, which could potentially inspire acts of violence."[27]

And, as the *Politico* articles substantiated, the Capitol insurrection was not the result of an intelligence failure—it was a profound failure to *act* based on glaringly obvious red flags that were well-known across all levels of law enforcement. What is needed now is a holistic, wide-reaching, and collaborative approach between the ICT sector and policy makers. This means moving beyond the individual social media giants to look at the broader infrastructure and networks that support the alternative ecosystems of misinformation-producing content. Every one of these hate- and conspiracist-filled forums relies on web hosting services and a network of infrastructure that is subject to regulation and should be held accountable for its content. Because ultimately, in reality, facts *do* matter.

NOTES

1. FROM JIHAD TO WHITE JIHAD

1. "Obama Election Spurs Race Threats, Crimes," NBC News, November 15, 2008, https://www.nbcnews.com/id/wbna27738018#.XbSdDOhKhPY.

2. "Rightwing Extremism: Current Economic and Political Climate Fueling Resurgence in Radicalization and Recruitment," Extremism and Radicalization Branch, Homeland Environment Threat Analysis Division (Department of Homeland Security, April 7, 2009), https://irp.fas.org/eprint/rightwing.pdf.

3. Mark Preston, "White Supremacists Watched in Lead Up to Obama Administration," CNN, January 16, 2009, https://www.cnn.com/2009/POLITICS/01/16/obama.white.supremacists//

4. Alexandra Minna Stern, *Proud Boys and the White Ethnostate: How the Alt-Right is Warping the American Imagination* (Boston: Free Beacon Press, 2019), 111–112.

5. "Saudi National Charged with Conspiracy to Provide Material Support to Hamas and Other Violent Jihadists," Office of Public Affairs (The Department of Justice, March 4, 2004), https://www.justice.gov/archive/opa/pr/2004/March/04_crm_137.htm.

6. For an in-depth look at Stormfront's character in 2009, see Lorraine Bowman-Grieve, "Exploring 'Stormfront': A Virtual Community of the Radical Right," *Studies in Conflict & Terrorism* 32, no. 11 (October 2009): 989–1007.

7. Neal Caren, Kay Jowers, and Sarah Gaby, "A Social Movement Online Community: Stormfront and the White Nationalist Movement," *Research in Social Movements, Conflicts and Change* 33 (2012): 172–173, https://www.emerald.com/insight/content/doi/10.1108/S0163–786X(2012)0000033010/full/html.

8. Caren, Jowers, and Gaby, "A Social Movement Online Community."

9. Paul Joseph Watson, "Pentagon Front Groups Release Laughable Olympics 'Terror' Video," *Prison Planet*, August 8, 2008, https://www.prisonplanet.com/pentagon-front-groups-release-laughable-olympics-terror-video.html.

10. Joanne M. Miller, Kyle L. Saunders, and Christina E. Farhart, "Conspiracy Endorsement as Motivated Reasoning: The Moderating Roles of Political Knowledge and Trust," *American Journal of Political Science* 60, no. 4 (October 2016): 824–844.

11. Stormfront.org, web archive, May 10, 2008, https://web.archive.org/web/20090626231911/http://www.stormfront.org/forum/project.php?issueid=19.

12. Stormfront.org, web archive, December 29, 2009, https://web.archive.org/web/20100113070850/https://www.stormfront.org/forum/project.php?issueid=19&page=54. Here and throughout, quotes from online postings retain the spelling and punctuation of the originals; [sic] is inserted only when meaning would otherwise not be clear.

13. Stormfront.com, web archive, September 10, 2009, https://web.archive.org/web/20090910074432/https://www.stormfront.org/forum/.

14. Stormfront.org, web archive, December 29, 2009, https://web.archive.org/web/20100113070850/https://www.stormfront.org/forum/project.php?issueid=19&page=54.

15. Stormfront.com, web archive, https://web.archive.org/web/20210929205651/https://www.stormfront.org/forum/project.php?issueid=19&page=2.

16. Nazispace.net, accessed October 2009, http://www.nazispace.net/poll/view/id_81/. For an exploration of this subject see Gabriel Weimann, *www.terror.net: How Modern Terrorism Uses the Internet* (Washington, DC: United States Institute of Peace, 2004).

17. "Radical Muslim Group Warns 'South Park' Creators," CBS, April 21, 2010, https://www.cbsnews.com/news/radical-muslim-group-warns-south-park-creators/.

18. "Virginia Man Pleads Guilty to Providing Material Support to a Foreign Terrorist Organization and Encouraging Violent Jihadists to Kill U.S. Citizens," United States Department of Justice, September 16, 2014, https://www.justice.gov/opa/pr/virginia-man-pleads-guilty-providing-material-support-foreign-terrorist-organization-and.

19. "White Supremacist Incites for Lone Wolf Attacks Against Officials," SITE Intelligence Group, January 26, 2011, https://ent.siteintelgroup.com/Far-Right-/-Far-Left-Threat/white-supremacist-incites-for-lone-wolf-attacks-against-officials.html.

20. Fred Taylor, *Exorcising Hitler: The Occupation and Denazification of Germany* (London: Bloomsbury, 2011).

21. David H. Bennett, *The Party of Fear: The American Far Right from Nativism to the Militia Movement* (New York: Vintage Books, 1995), 273–332.

22. Bennett, *The Party of Fear*.

23. Diane McWhorter, *Carry Me Home* (New York: Simon & Schuster, 2001), 20.

24. For an overview of the bombing campaign, see Donald Q. Cochran, "Ghosts of Alabama: The Prosecution of Bobby Frank Cherry for the Bombing of the Sixteenth Street Baptist Church," *Michigan Journal of Race and Law* 1, no. 1 (2006): 1–31. Cochran was the lead prosecutor in the case against Cherry, the last individual to be prosecuted for his participation in the bombing.

25. Brian Montopoli, "DHS Report Warns of Right Wing Extremists," CBS News, April 14, 2009, https://www.cbsnews.com/news/dhs-report-warns-of-right-wing-extremists/.

26. For an in-depth exploration about the obsession among white nationalists with *The Turner Diaries*, see J. M. Berger, *The Turner Legacy: The Storied Origins and Enduring Impact of White Nationalism's Deadly Bible* (The Hague: International Centre for Counter-Terrorism, 2016).

27. Stern, *Proud Boys and the White Ethnostate*, 17–32.

28. "Introduction to Selected White Supremacist Forums: Far-Right / Far-Left Threat: Articles," SITE Intelligence Group, January 21, 2011, https://ent.siteintelgroup.com /Far-Right-/-Far-Left-Threat/introduction-to-selected-white-supremacist-forums .html.

29. "White Supremacists Encourage Continued Violence Against Officials," SITE Intelligence Group, January 20, 2011, https://ent.siteintelgroup.com/Far-Right-/-Far-Left -Threat/white-supremacists-encourage-continued-violence-against-elected-officals .html.

30. Alexander Tsesis, "Terrorist Communication on Social Media, *Vanderbilt Law Review* 70, no. 2 (2017): 201.

31. William Yardley, "Bomb Is Found in Backpack Before March Honoring King," *New York Times*, January 18, 2011, https://www.nytimes.com/2011/01/19/us/19bomb.html.

32. "MLK Parade Bomber, Horrific Hate Crime Prevented; Case Solved," FBI, January 13, 2012, https://www.fbi.gov/news/stories/mlk-parade-bomber.

33. "MLK Parade Bomber, Horrific Hate Crime Prevented."

34. "Online Profile of MLK Day Bombing Suspect Kevin Harpham," SITE Intelligence Group, March 11, 2011, https://ent.siteintelgroup.com/Far-Right-/-Far-Left-Threat /online-profile-of-mlk-day-bombing-suspect-kevin-harpham.html.

35. Thomas Clouse, "Bomb Suspect May Have Fantasized About Race Wars," *The Spokesman-Review*, March 10, 2011, https://www.spokesman.com/stories/2011/mar/10 /bomb-suspect-may-have-fantasized-about-race-wars/.

36. Year2183, "I'm 29 years living in Sweden," Stormfront, October 2008, https://www .stormfront.org/forum/t434311–118/.

37. ThoughtCriminal14, "Welcome, friend!" Stormfront, October 13, 2008, https://www .stormfront.org/forum/t434311–118.

38. Truck Roy, "Welcome, year2183," Stormfront, October 13, 2008, https://www .stormfront.org/forum/t434311–118.

39. Matthew Taylor, "Breivik Sent 'Manifesto' to 250 UK Contacts Hours Before Norway Killings," *The Guardian*, July 26, 2011, https://www.theguardian.com/world/2011/jul /26/breivik-manifesto-email-uk-contacts.

40. Sara Robinson, "Plagiarized By a Murderer: Norway's Anders Breivik Stole My Words," *New York Magazine*, August 10, 2011, https://nymag.com/intelligencer/2011 /08/plagiarized_by_a_murderer_when.html.

41. Asne Seierstad, *One of US: The Story of a Massacre in Norway—and It's Aftermath* (New York: Farrar, Straus and Giroux, 2014), 276–296.

42. "Survivors in Norway Describe Scenes of Terror," NPR, July 23, 2011, https://www.npr .org/2011/07/23/138634243/norway-rescuers-search-waters-after-island-attack.

43. "Survivors in Norway Describe Scenes of Terror."

44. "Anders Behring Breivik: The Indictment," *The Guardian*, April 16, 2012, https://www
    .theguardian.com/world/2012/apr/16/anders-behring-breivik-indictment.

45. "Anders Behring Breivik: The Indictment."

46. "Anders Behring Breivik: The Indictment."

47. "Skinhead Neo-Nazis React to Attacks in Norway, Call for Murder of Breivik," SITE
    Intelligence Group, July 25, 2011, https://ent.siteintelgroup.com/Far-Right-/-Far-Left
    -Threat/skinhead-neo-nazis-react-to-attacks-in-norway-call-for-murder-of-breivik
    .html.

48. "Forum Members Justify Norway Attacks, Predict Future Attacks," SITE Intelligence
    Group, July 25, 2011, https://ent.siteintelgroup.com/Far-Right-/-Far-Left-Threat/forum
    -members-justify-norway-attacks-predict-future-attacks.html.

49. "White Supremacists React to Norway Attacks," SITE Intelligence Group, July 24,
    2011, https://ent.siteintelgroup.com/Far-Right-/-Far-Left-Threat/white-supremacists
    -react-to-norway-attacks.html.

50. "White Supremacists React to Norway Attacks," SITE Intelligence Group.

51. "Please post ALL items about the 'Oslo killer' in this thread!," Stormfront, accessed
    September 29, 2021, https://web.archive.org/web/20210929154420/https://www
    .stormfront.org/forum/t818918-2/?postcount=12.

52. Ingliist, "What do you think a civil war is??," Stormfront, July 24, 2011, https://www
    .stormfront.org/forum/t818918-13/.

53. Toby Archer, "Breivik's Mindset: The Counterjihad and the New Transatlantic Anti-
    Muslim Right," in *Extreme Right-Wing Political Violence*, ed. Max Taylor, Donald
    Holbrook, and P.M. Currie (New York: Bloomsbury, 2013), 169–177.

54. Anders Breivik, *2083: A European Declaration of Independence,* Open Source Docu-
    ment. https://www.washingtonpost.com/r/2010-2019/WashingtonPost/2011/07/24/Nati
    onal-Politics/Graphics/2083+-+A+European+Declaration+of+Independence.pdf.

55. Breivik, *2083*.

56. Breivik.

57. Alex Linder, "Not true," VNN, July 31, 2011, https://vnnforum.com/showthread.php
    ?t=130582&page=15.

58. "Frazier Glenn Miller," Southern Poverty Law Center, accessed February 9, 2021,
    https://www.splcenter.org/fighting-hate/extremist-files/individual/frazier-glenn
    -miller.

59. Rounder, "Happy Birthday Joe Snuffy!!!," VNN, May 1, 2007, https://vnnforum.com
    /showthread.php?p=531504;"Online Profile of MLK Day Bombing Suspect Kevin
    Harpham," SITE Intelligence Group, March 11, 2011, https://ent.siteintelgroup.com
    /Far-Right-/-Far-Left-Threat/online-profile-of-mlk-day-bombing-suspect-kevin
    -harpham.html.

60. "Breivik Killed Sons and Daughters of Race Traitor Politicians," VNN, July 26, 2011,
    https://vnnforum.com/showthread.php?t=130582.

61. "Breivik Killed Sons and Daughters of Race Traitor Politicians," VNN.

62. John Eligon, "White Supremacist Convicted of Killing 3 at Kansas Jewish Centers,"
    New York Times, August 31, 2015, https://www.nytimes.com/2015/09/01/us/white
    -supremacist-convicted-of-killing-3-at-kansas-jewish-centers.html.

63. Eligon, "White Supremacist Convicted of Killing 3."

64. Judy L. Thomas, "F. Glenn Miller Jr. Talks for the First Time About the Killings at Jewish Centers," *Kansas City Star*, November 15, 2014, https://www.kansascity.com /news/local/crime/article3955528.html.

65. Thomas, "F. Glenn Miller Jr. Talks for the First Time."

66. Erica Goode and Serge F. Kovaleski, "Wisconsin Killer Fed and Was Fueled by Hate-Driven Music," *New York Times*, August 8, 2012, https://www.nytimes.com/2012/08 /07/us/army-veteran-identified-as-suspect-in-wisconsin-shooting.html?page wanted=all.

67. Lindsey Bever, "A White Supremacist Web Site Frequented by Lillers," *Washington Post*, April 18, 2014, https://www.washingtonpost.com/news/morning-mix/wp/2014 /04/18/posters-on-one-white-supremacist-site-have-killed-almost-100-people -watchdog-says/.

68. Elaine Quijano, "Question of Motive Remains in Sikh Temple Shooting," CBS Evening News, August 7, 2012, https://web.archive.org/web/20120808110205/http://www .cbsnews.com/8301–18563_162–57488654/question-of-motive-remains-in-sikh -temple-shooting/.

69. "MLK Parade Bomber," FBI, January 13, 2012, https://www.fbi.gov/news/stories/mlk -parade-bomber.

70. Carrie Johnson, "FBI Says it Sent Bulletin on Texas Assailant Hours Before Attack," NPR, May 7, 2015, https://www.npr.org/sections/thetwo-way/2015/05/07/404986056 /fbi-says-it-sent-bulletin-on-texas-assailant-hours-before-attack.

71. Jessica Taylor, "Trump Calls for 'Total and Complete Shutdown of Muslims Entering' US," NPR, December 7, 2015, https://www.npr.org/2015/12/07/458836388/trump -calls-for-total-and-complete-shutdown-of-muslims-entering-u-s.

72. Arun Frey, "'Cologne Changed Everything'—The Effect of Threatening Events on the Frequency and Distribution of Intergroup Conflict in Germany," *European Sociological Review* 36, no. 5 (October 2020): 684–699.

73. "Neo-Nazis Celebrate Violence Against Refugees in Germany," SITE Intelligence Group, January 12, 2016, https://ent.siteintelgroup.com/Far-Right-/-Far-Left-Threat /neo-nazis-celebrate-violence-against-refugees-in-germany.html.

74. "Swedish Minister Looks Forward to Europe Turning into Africa," Stormfront, July 2, 2014 https://web.archive.org/web/20170820145146/https://www.stormfront.org/forum /t1050146/.

2. SCREW YOUR OPTICS

1. Meg O-Connor and Jessica Lipscomb, "Social Media Posts Show Florida Bomber Cesar Sayoc Held Extremist Views," *Miami New Times*, October 26, 2018, https://www .miaminewtimes.com/news/cesar-sayocs-social-media-posts-show-florida-bomber -cesar-sayoc-held-extremist-views-10859874.

2. Rita Katz (@Rita_Katz), "The threat of #WhiteSupremacists movements," Twitter, October 26, 2022, https://twitter.com/Rita_Katz/status/1055838486786383873.

3. Brian Michael Jenkins, Andrew Liepman, and Henry H. Wallis, *Identify Enemies Among Us: Evolving Terrorist Threats and the Continuing Challenges of Domestic Intelligence Collection and Information Sharing* (Santa Monica, CA: RAND Corporation, 2014), 7–9.

4. Jenkins, Liepman, and Wallis, *Identify Enemies Among Us*.

5. Tarleton Gillepsie, *Custodians of the Internet: Platforms, Content Moderation, and the Hidden Decisions That Shape Social Media* (New Haven, CT: Yale University Press, 2018), 36–40.

6. Avner Barnea, "Challenging the 'Lone Wolf' Phenomenon in an Era of Information Overload," *International Journal of Intelligence and Counterintelligence* 31, no. 2 (2018): 228.

7. Alexander Meleagrou-Hitchens and Seamus Hughes, "The Threat to the United States from the Islamic State's Virtual Entrepreneurs," *CTC Sentinel* 10, no. 3 (2017): 2–6.

8. Mallory Shelbourne, "ISIS Threatens Attacks in US Over Trump's Jerusalem Decision," *The Hill*, December 14, 2017, https://thehill.com/policy/international/terrorism/364841-isis-threatens-attacks-in-us-over-trumps-jerusalem-decision; "Al-Qaeda Leader Calls for Jihad on Eve of US Embassy Moving to Jerusalem," *The Guardian*, May 13, 2018, https://www.theguardian.com/world/2018/may/14/al-qaida-leader-jihad-us-embassy-move-jerusalem.

9. Judah Ari Gross, "Shin Bet Chief: After Trump Declaration, Palestinian Unrest Could Last 6 Months," *Times of Israel*, December 24, 2017, https://www.timesofisrael.com/shin-bet-chief-west-bank-gaza-highly-unstable-after-trump-declaration/.

10. Simon Clark, *How White Supremacy Returned to Mainstream Politics* (Washington, DC: Center for American Progress, July 1, 2020), 4–7, https://www.americanprogress.org/issues/security/reports/2020/07/01/482414/white-supremacy-returned-mainstream-politics/.

11. "White Supremacists Lament ICE Agents Supposedly Releasing Illegals in 'Huge Numbers' in Arizona," SITE Intelligence Group, October 18, 2018, https://ent.siteintelgroup.com/Far-Right-/-Far-Left-Threat/white-supremacists-lament-ice-agents-supposedly-releasing-illegals-in-huge-numbers-in-arizona.html; American-Robin, "ICE Releases Illegals in Huge Numbers in Arizona," Stormfront, October 17, 2021, https://www.stormfront.org/forum/t1260863/?postcount=10#post14624377.

12. Dara Lind, "The Conspiracy Theory That Led to the Pittsburgh Synagogue Shooting, Explained," *Vox*, October 29, 2018, https://www.vox.com/2018/10/29/18037580/pittsburgh-shooter-anti-semitism-racist-jewish-caravan.

13. Emma Grey Ellis, "Gab, the Alt-Right's Very Own Twitter, Is the Ultimate Filter Bubble," *Wired*, September 14, 2016, https://www.wired.com/2016/09/gab-alt-rights-twitter-ultimate-filter-bubble/.

14. Allie Conti, "Stormfront Users Say Site Is Collapsing Because Founder's Wife Stopped Paying for It," *Vice*, April 5, 2018, https://www.vice.com/en/article/d35xw7/white-supremacist-stormfront-collapse-don-black-wife-paying-bills-vgtrn.

15. "Gab.ai Mossad clickbait?," Stormfront, October 11, 2017, https://web.archive.org/web/20180806174245/https://www.stormfront.org/forum/t1227165/.

16. Ellis, "Gab, the Alt-Right's Very Own Twitter."

17. Rich Lord and Ashley Murray, "Bowers' Favorite Social Media Site Reeling, Defiant," *Pittsburgh Post-Gazette*, October 28, 2018, https://www.post-gazette.com/local/city /2018/10/28/Robert-Bowers-favorite-social-media-site-reeling-defiant-Gab-Andrew -Torba/stories/201810280179.

18. Lord and Murray, "Bowers' Favorite Social Media Site Reeling."

19. Robert Bowers (@onedingo), "just want to put this psa out there for all the vile degenerate oven dodgers," Gab, September 28, 2018, https://gab.com/onedingo/posts /36781061.

20. Robert Bowers (@onedingo), "that's ok. the ovens run 24/7," Gab, October 2, 2018, https://gab.com/onedingo/posts/37218894.

21. f r o g w a v e (@___ribbit), "Jews are waging a propaganda war against Western civilization and it is so effective that we are headed towards certain extinction within the next 200 years and we're not even aware of it," Gab, October 21, 2018, https://gab .com/___ribbit/posts/39294896.

22. "History," Who We Are, HIAS, https://www.hias.org/who/history.

23. "History," Who We Are, HIAS.

24. Adam Serwer, "Trump's Caravan Hysteria Led to This," *The Atlantic*, October 28, 2018, https://www.theatlantic.com/ideas/archive/2018/10/caravan-lie-sparked-massacre -american-jews/574213/.

25. Rachel Nusbaum, "Rallying for Refugees," *HIAS Blog*, HIAS, January 26, 2017, https:// www.hias.org/blog/rallying-refugees.

26. Farmer General (@Farmer-General), "How about GTFO jews!," Gab, October 4, 2018, https://gab.com/Farmer-General/posts/37470261.

27. Robert Bowers (@onedingo), "Why hello there HIAS! You like to bring in hostile invaders to dwell among us?," Gab, October 10, 2018, https://gab.com/onedingo/posts/38156461.

28. Robert Bowers (@onedingo), "HIAS likes to bring invaders in that kill our people," Gab, October 27, 2018, https://gab.com/onedingo/posts/40000418.

29. "Worshipers in Hiding, Waiting for Death: How the Pittsburgh Synagogue Massacre Unfolded," *People*, October 30, 2018, https://people.com/crime/worshipers-in -hiding-waiting-for-death-how-the-pittsburgh-synagogue-massacre-unfolded/.

30. "A Rabbi Says He First Thought Gunfire Was the Sound of a Fallen Metal Coat Rack. Then He Saw People Running," CNN, October 29, 2019, https://www.cnn.com/2018 /10/29/us/rabbi-recounts-shooting-pittsburgh-cnntv/index.html.

31. Bill Schackner, "From Calm to Crisis: 911 Center Workers Sprang into Action During Synagogue Massacre," *Pittsburgh Post-Gazette*, November 1, 2018, https://www .post-gazette.com/news/crime-courts/2018/11/01/tree-of-life-synagogue-shooting -allegheny-county-911-dispatcher-pittsburgh/stories/201811010157.

32. Campbell Robertson, Sabrina Tavernise, and Sandra E. Garcia, "Quiet Day at a Pittsburgh Synagogue Became a Battle to Survive," *New York Times*, October 28, 2018, https://www.nytimes.com/2018/10/28/us/pittsburgh-synagogue-shooting.html.

33. Robertson, Tavernise, and Garcia, "Quiet Day at a Pittsburgh Synagogue Became a Battle to Survive."

34. Robertson, Tavernise, and Garcia.

35. Robertson, Tavernise, and Garcia.

36. Michael Wines and Stephanie Saul, "White Supremacists Extend Their Reach Through Websites," *New York Times*, July 6, 2015, https://www.nytimes.com/2015/07/06/us/white-supremacists-extend-their-reach-through-websites.html.

37. "White Supremacists React to Charleston Church Shooter's Death Penalty Sentence," SITE Intelligence Group, January 11, 2017, https://ent.siteintelgroup.com/Far-Right-/-Far-Left-Threat/white-supremacists-react-to-charleston-church-shooter-s-death-penalty-sentence.html.

38. Kathleen Belew, *Bring the War Home: The White Power Movement and Paramilitary America* (Cambridge, MA: Harvard University Press, 2018), 234.

39. Alexandra Minna Stern, *Proud Boys and the White Ethnostate: How the Alt-Right is Warping the American Imagination* (Boston: Beacon Press, 2019), 111–112.

40. Stern, *Proud Boys and the White Ethnostate*.

41. "White Supremacists Debate Whether to Have a Second 'Unite The Right' Rally, Some Suggesting Shedding Nazi Imagery," SITE Intelligence Group, August 18, 2017, https://ent.siteintelgroup.com/Far-Right-/-Far-Left-Threat/white-supremacists-debate-whether-to-have-a-second-unite-the-right-rally-some-suggesting-shedding-nazi-imagery.html; Danger2443, "Unite the Right 2: Washington D.C.," Stormfront, August 17, 2017, https://www.stormfront.org/forum/showthread.php?p=14224158&postcount=4.

42. Martin Rudner, "Al Qaeda's Twenty-Year Strategic Plan: The Current Phase of Global Terror," *Studies in Conflict & Terrorism* 36, no. 12 (2013): 959

43. Bruce Hoffman, "A First Draft of the History of America's Ongoing Wars on Terrorism," *Studies in Conflict & Terrorism* 38, no. 1 (2015): 81.

44. Charles R. Lister, *Al-Qaeda, the Islamic State and the Evolution of An Insurgency* (New York: Oxford University Press, 2015), 235–239.

45. "ISIL Spokesman Denounces General Command of al-Qaeda," SITE Intelligence Group, April 18, 2014, https://ent.siteintelgroup.com/Multimedia/isil-spokesman-denounces-general-command-of-al-qaeda.html.

46. "ISIL Spokesman Denounces General Command of al-Qaeda."

47. Thomas Joscelyn, "AQIM Rejects Islamic State's Caliphate, Reaffirms Allegiance to Zawahiri," *Long War Journal*, FDD, July 14, 2014, https://www.longwarjournal.org/archives/2014/07/aqim_rejects_islamic.php.

48. "AQAP Rebukes Abu Bakr al-Baghdadi, Rejects IS' 'Caliphate,'" SITE Intelligence Group, November 20, 2014, https://ent.siteintelgroup.com/Statements/aqap-rebukes-abu-bakr-al-baghdadi-rejects-is-caliphate.html.

49. Daniel Byman, "Explaining Al Qaeda's Decline," *Journal of Politics* 79, no. 3 (2017): 1113–1115.

50. Anna Kruglova, "'I Will Tell You a Story about Jihad': ISIS's Propaganda and Narrative Advertising," *Studies in Conflict & Terrorism* 44, no. 2 (2020): 115–137.

51. Dylan Roof made this very critique. See Wines and Saul, "White Supremacists Extend Their Reach."

52. Bill Chappell, "Census Finds a More Diverse America, as Whites Lag Growth," NPR, June 22, 2017, https://www.npr.org/sections/thetwo-way/2017/06/22/533926978/census -finds-a-more-diverse-america-as-whites-lag-growth.

53. Daniel Cox, Rachel Lienesch, and Robert P. Jones, "Beyond Economics: Fears of Cultural Displacement Pushed the White Working Class to Trump," PRRI, May 9, 2017, https://www.prri.org/research/white-working-class-attitudes-economy-trade -immigration-election-donald-trump/.

54. George Hawley, "The Demography of the Alt-Right," Institute for Family Studies, August 9, 2018, https://ifstudies.org/blog/the-demography-of-the-alt-right.

55. Richard Wike, Bruce Stokes, and Katie Simmons, "Europeans Fear Wave of Refugees Will Mean More Terrorism, Fewer Jobs: Sharp Ideological Divides Across EU on Views About Minorities, Diversity and National Identity," Pew Research Center, July 11, 2016, https://www.pewresearch.org/global/2016/07/11/europeans-not-convi nced-growing-diversity-is-a-good-thing-divided-on-what-determines-national -identity/.

56. "Amid the Usual Deflections, Some White Supremacists Call Synagogue Shooting a Way to 'Fight Back,'" SITE Intelligence Group, October 27, 2018, https://ent .siteintelgroup.com/Far-Right-/-Far-Left-Threat/amid-the-usual-deflections-some -white-supremacists-call-synagogue-shooting-a-way-to-fight-back.html.

57. "Amid the Usual Deflections, Some White Supremacists Call Synagogue Shooting a Way to 'Fight Back.'"

58. Thomas J. Main, *The Rise of the Alt-Right* (Washington, DC: Brookings Institute Press, 2018), 20–28.

59. "Neo-Nazis Welcome News of Synagogue Shooting as 'Good,' Say that Murdering Jews is 'Righteous,'" SITE Intelligence Group, October 29, 2018, https://ent.siteintel group.com/documents/far-right-far-left/945-site-intelligence-frfl-10-29-2018-neo -nazis-welcome-news-of-synagogue-shooting-as-good-say-that-murdering-jews-is -righteous/file.html; Alex Linder, "[#1 Thread] White Freedom Fighter Robert Bowers Exterminates 11 Loxists in Pittsburgh [October 2018]," VNN Forum, October 29, 2018, https://vnnforum.com/showpost.php?p=2254514&postcount=82.

60. "Neo-Nazis Welcome News of Synagogue Shooting as 'Good,'" SITE Intelligence Group.

61. Rita Katz (@Rita_Katz), "6) The Gab social media platform is a cesspool for extreme rhetoric from white supremacists, who use it as a safe haven. Shows that while major platforms like Twitter and Facebook receive brunt of criticisms, smaller ones like Gab often evade such demands for accountability," Twitter, October 27, 2018, https://twitter .com/Rita_Katz/status/1056251245650984962.

62. Brett Stevens (@alternative_right), "What should the future of Jewish people in the West be?," Gab, October 28, 2018, https://gab.com/alternative_right/posts/40096550.

63. Rita Katz, "Inside the Online Cesspool of Anti-Semitism That Housed Robert Bowers," Politico, October 29, 2018, https://www.politico.com/magazine/story/2018/10/29 /inside-the-online-cesspool-of-anti-semitism-that-housed-robert-bowers-221949/; Alex Linder (@Alex_Linder), "remember, these jews murdered sixty million whites

just like you and me," Gab, October 28, 2018, https://gab.com/Alex_Linder/posts
/40073955.

64. Katz, "Inside the Online Cesspool of Anti-Semitism That Housed Robert Bowers."

65. Hitchens and Hughes, "The Threat to the United States."

66. Hitchens and Hughes.

67. "American Jihadist in Somalia Advises Prospects to Fight in Syria and Iraq," SITE Intelligence Group, November 7, 2014, https://ent.siteintelgroup.com/Western -Jihadists/american-jihadist-in-somalia-advises-prospects-to-fight-in-syria-and -iraq.html.

68. Rita Katz, "The Power of a Tweet: Elton Simpson and the #TexasAttack," *InSITE Blog on Terrorism and Extremism*, May 5, 2015, https://news.siteintelgroup.com/blog /index.php/categories/jihad/entry/382-the-power-of-a-tweet-elton-simpson-and-the -texasattack.

69. Hitchens and Hughes, "The Threat to the United States."

70. Farmer General (@Farmer-General), "Never any truth, just insults," Gab, October 1, 2018, https://gab.com/Farmer-General/posts/37103966.

71. Farmer General (@Farmer-General), (image), Gab, October 4, 2018, https://gab.com /Farmer-General/posts/37470304.

72. Katz, "The Power of a Tweet."

73. "Far-Right Social Network Gab Goes Offline After Domain Host Pulls the Plug," Yahoo, October 29, 2018, https://www.yahoo.com/now/far-social-network-gab-goes -123157772.html.

74. Jon Levine, "Far-Right Social Network Gab Back Online After Finding New Host," *The Wrap*, November 5, 2018, https://www.thewrap.com/far-right-social-network-gab -back-online-after-finding-new-host.

75. "White Supremacists Celebrate Gab Returning Online, Drawing in Some Who Didn't have Accounts Previously," SITE Intelligence Group, November 5, 2018, https://ent .siteintelgroup.com/Far-Right-/-Far-Left-Threat/white-supremacists-celebrate -gab-returning-online-drawing-in-some-who-didn-t-have-accounts-previously .html.

76. SITE Intelligence Group, "White Supremacists Celebrate Gab Returning Online"; Henry Louis Mencken, "BREAKING: Gab Is Back Online," Stormfront, November 4, 2021, https://www.stormfront.org/forum/t1262421/.

77. Farmer General (@Farmer-General), "The Existence of jews anywhere on Earth is a Threat to Every non-jew on this Planet. Especially Aryans and Christians," Gab, November 8, 2018,https://gab.com/Farmer-General/posts/40525282; Farmer General (@Farmer-General), "It's a ((((Coincidence)))) that the holocaust never Happened, but it Should have!," Gab, November 8, 2018, https://gab.com/Farmer-General/posts /40533199.

78. Peter Smith, "Tree of Life Rabbi Jeffrey Myers: A Face of Tragedy, a Voice for Peace," *Pittsburgh Post-Gazette*, November 12, 2018, https://www.post-gazette.com/news /faith-religion/2018/11/12/Rabbi-Hazzan-Jeffrey-Myers-Tree-of-Life-Or-LSimcha -synagogue-mass-shooting-Pittsburgh-profile/stories/201811090143.

3. THE TERROR SYMBIOSIS

1. Timothy Egan, "Computer Student on Trial Over Muslim Web Site Work," *New York Times*, April 27, 2004, https://www.nytimes.com/2004/04/27/us/computer-student-on -trial-over-muslim-web-site-work.html.

2. George Michael, "The Legend and Legacy of Abu Msab al-Zarqawi," *Defence Studies* 7, no. 3 (2007): 341

3. Fawaz A. Gerges, *ISIS: A History* (Princeton, NJ: Princeton University Press, 2016), 52–63.

4. "Jihadists Celebrate Beheadings on Message Boards," SITE Institute, September 22, 2004, https://siteinstitute.org/bin/articles.cgi?ID=publications7904&Category=pub lications&Subcategory=0.

5. "Jihadists Celebrate Beheadings on Message Boards," SITE Institute.

6. "Use of Saw in Beheadings," SITE Intelligence Group, October 1, 2004, https://ent .siteintelgroup.com/Jihadist-News/use-of-saw-in-beheadings.html.

7. Ronald H. Jones, *Terrorist Beheadings: Cultural and Strategic Implications* (Carlisle, PA: Strategic Studies Institute, U.S. Army War College, 2005), 5–8.

8. "A Child's Video Eulogy for Abu Musab al-Zarqawi," SITE Intelligence Group, July 24, 2006, https://ent.siteintelgroup.com/Jihadist-News/7-24-06-a-child-s-video-eulogy -for-abu-musab-al-zarqawi.html.

9. "A Child's Video Eulogy for Abu Musab al-Zarqawi," SITE Intelligence Group.

10. "Al-Zarqawi's Message to the Fighters of Jihad in Iraq on September 11, 2004," MEMRI Special Dispatch Series No. 785, September 15, 2004, https://www.memri.org/reports /al-zarqawis-message-fighters-jihad-iraq-september-11–2004.

11. Gerges, *ISIS*, 72–77.

12. Michael, "The Legend and Legacy," 343–344.

13. Gabriel Weimann, "The Psychology of Mass-Mediated Terrorism," *American Behav- iorial Scientist* 52, no. 1 (2008): 70

14. Walter Laqueur, *Terrorism* (Boston: Little, Brown, and Company: 1977), 49.

15. Beverly Gage, *The Day Wall Street Exploded: A Story of America in Its First Age of Terror* (New York: Oxford University Press, 2009).

16. Johann Most, "Action as Propaganda," Freiheit, July 25, 1885, http://dwardmac.pitzer .edu/Anarchist_Archives/bright/most/actionprop.html.

17. Michael, "The Legend and Legacy," 344.

18. Marwan M. Kraidy, "The Projectilic Image; Islamic State's Digital Visual Warfare and Global Networked Affect," *Media, Culture & Society* 39, no. 8 (2017): 1–2.

19. Georgia Holmer and Adrian Shtuni, *Returning Foreign Fighters and the Reintegra- tion Imperative*, United States Institute of Peace Special Report (Washington, DC: United States Institute of Peace, 2017), https://www.usip.org/sites/default/files/2017– 03/sr402-returning-foreign-fighters-and-the-reintegration-imperative.pdf.

20. "Amaq Identifies Strasbourg Gunman as an IS 'Soldier,'" SITE Intelligence Group, December 13, 2018, https://ent.siteintelgroup.com/Statements/amaq-identifies -strasbourg-gunman-as-an-is-soldier.html; Hannah Beech and Jason Gutierrez, "ISIS

Bombing of Cathedral in Philippines Shows Group's Reach into Asia," *New York Times*, January 28, 2019, https://www.nytimes.com/2019/01/28/world/asia/isis -philippines-church-bombing.html.

21. Barbara Wozjazer, Arnaud Siad, and Sarah Dean, "Three Men Sentenced to Death for Killing Scandinavia Hikers in Morocco," CNN, July 18, 2019, https://www.cnn.com /2019/07/18/europe/morocco-scandinavian-tourist-deaths-intl/index.html.

22. Laqueur, *Terrorism*, 50.

23. "Electronica Neo-Nazi Song Glorifies Synagogue Shooter Robert Bowers," SITE Intel- ligence Group, January 11, 2019, https://ent.siteintelgroup.com/Far-Right-/-Far-Left -Threat/electronic-neo-nazi-artist-glorifies-synagogue-shooter-robert-bowers.html; Terrorschism, "TERRORSCHISM—GOING IN," January 20, 2019, https://www .bitchute.com/video/xyG1FEwGOtkv/.

24. Elian Peltier, "France Repatriates Several Orphan Children Who Were Stranded in Syria," *New York Times*, March 15, 2019, https://www.nytimes.com/2019/03/15/world /europe/france-isis-repatriates-children.html.

25. "Australia Will Not Risk Bringing ISIS Families Back from Syria, Scott Morrison Says," National News, March 14, 2019, https://www.thenationalnews.com/world /oceania/australia-will-not-risk-bringing-isis-families-back-from-syria-scott-morrison -says-1.836871.

26. Major Bummer, "Australian Shitposters," Know Your Meme, July 24, 2016, https:// knowyourmeme.com/memes/australian-shitposters; Patrick Begley, "Alleged Mosque Shooter's Meme Popular with Australian Far-Right Group," *Sydney Morning Herald*, March 15, 2019, https://www.smh.com.au/national/nsw/alleged-mosque-shooter-s -meme-popular-with-australian-far-right-group-20190315-p514ns.html.

27. "Alleged New Zealand Mosque Attacker Calls for the Death of Angela Merkel and Sadiq Khan in Manifesto," SITE Intelligence Group, March 15, 2019, https://ent .siteintelgroup.com/Far-Right-/-Far-Left-Threat/alleged-new-zealand-mosque -attacker-calls-for-the-death-of-angela-merkel-and-recep-tayyip-erdogan-in -manifesto.html.

28. "Alleged New Zealand Mosque Attacker," SITE Intelligence Group.

29. "Well lads, it's time to stop shitposting and time to make a real life effort post," 8chan, March 15, 2019, archived at https://archive.is/ihpnE.

30. Sam Sherwood, "Christchurch Terror Attack: Son Was on the Phone to His Mum When He Was Shot and Killed," Stuff, March 17, 2019, https://www.stuff.co.nz /national/crime/111348557/christchurch-terror-attack-son-was-on-the-phone-to-his -mum-when-he-was-shot-and-killed.

31. New Zealand Royal Commission, *Report of the Royal Commission of Inquiry into the Terrorist Attack on Christchurch Masjidain on March 15, 2019*, vol. 1, https:// christchurchattack.royalcommission.nz/assets/Report-Volumes-and-Parts/Ko-to -tatou-kainga-tenei-Volume-1.pdf, 46.

32. New Zealand Royal Commission, *Report of the Royal Commission of Inquiry*.

33. Nikki Macdonald, "Alleged Shooter Approached Linwood Mosque from Wrong Side, Giving Those Inside Time to Hide, Survivor Says," Stuff, March 18, 2019, https://www

.stuff.co.nz/national/christchurch-shooting/111378767/brenton-tarrant-approached
-linwood-mosque-from-wrong-side-giving-those-inside-time-to-hide-survivor-says.

34. Kurt Bayer and Anna Leask, "Chirstchurch Mosque Terror Attack Sentencing: Gunman Brenton Tarrant Planned to Attack Three Mosques," *New Zealand Herald*,
August 23, 2020, https://www.nzherald.co.nz/nz/christchurch-mosque-terror-attack
-sentencing-gunman-brenton-tarrant-planned-to-attack-three-mosques/Y5ROAI
RQY6TJTU7XI63YHBT7YI/.

35. Sam Sherwood, "Christchurch Terror Attack: Woman 'Brutally' Killed as She Went
to Check on Her Husband," Stuff, March 20, 2019, https://www.stuff.co.nz/national
/christchurch-shooting/111411271/christchurch-terror-attack-woman-brutally-killed
-as-she-went-to-check-on-her-husband.

36. Euan McKirdy, Paula Newton, and Merieme Arif, "6 Dead in Quebec Mosque Shooting," CNN, January 30, 2017, https://edition.cnn.com/2017/01/29/americas/quebec
-mosque-shooting/index.html.

37. Nick O'Malley, "'The 9/11 of Far-Right Terrorism': From Christchurch to El Paso," *Sydney Morning Herald*, August 5, 2019, https://www.smh.com.au/world/north-america
/the-9–11-of-far-right-terrorism-from-christchurch-to-el-paso-20190805-p52dxk
.html.

38. "Alleged New Zealand Mosque Attacker," SITE Intelligence Group.

39. Adam Taylor, "New Zealand Suspect Allegedly Claimed 'Brief Contact' with Norwei-
gian Mass Murderer Anders Breivik," *Washington Post*, March 15, 2019, https://www
.washingtonpost.com/world/2019/03/15/new-zealand-suspect-allegedly-claimed
-brief-contact-with-norwegian-mass-murderer-anders-breivik/.

40. "Alleged New Zealand Mosque Attacker Calls for the Death of Angela Merkel
and Sadiq Khan in Manifesto," SITE Intelligence Group, March 15, 2019, https://
ent.siteintelgroup.com/Far-Right-/-Far-Left-Threat/alleged-new-zealand-mosque
-attacker-calls-for-the-death-of-angela-merkel-and-recep-tayyip-erdogan-in
-manifesto.html.

41. "Alleged New Zealand Mosque Attacker," SITE Intelligence Group.

42. "Alleged New Zealand Mosque Attacker," SITE Intelligence Group.

43. "Alleged New Zealand Mosque Attacker," SITE Intelligence Group.

44. See Fernando Reinares, *Al-Qaeda's Revenge: The 2004 Madrid Train Bombings* (New
York: Columbia University Press, 2017).

45. Reinares, *Al-Qaeda's Revenge*.

46. Souad Mekhennet, "Militant Groups Are Using Christchurch Mosque Shootings to
Spread a Message of Hate," *Washington Post*, March 20, 2019, https://www
.washingtonpost.com/world/national-security/militant-groups-are-using-christ
church-mosque-shootings-to-spread-a-message-of-hate/2019/03/20/ccd930ca-4a6f
-11e9-b79a-961983b7e0cd_story.html.

47. "IS Supporter Calls to Attack Relatives of New Zealand Mosques Shooter, Strike
Churches," SITE Intelligence Group, March 15, 2019, https://ent.siteintelgroup.com
/Chatter/is-supporter-calls-to-attack-relatives-of-new-zealand-mosques-shooter
-strike-churches.html.

48. "Jihadists Incite for Attacks on Churches as Reciprocity for New Zealand Shootings," SITE Intelligence Group, March 16, 2019, https://ent.siteintelgroup.com/Chatter /jihadists-incite-for-attacks-on-churches-as-reciprocity-for-new-zealand-shootings .html.

49. "Jihadists, Both AQ- and IS-Aligned, Enraged by Attack at New Zealand Mosques, Demand and Incite for Revenge," SITE Intelligence Group, March 15, 2019,https://ent .siteintelgroup.com/Chatter/jihadists-both-aq-and-is-aligned-enraged-by-attack-at -new-zealand-mosques-demand-and-incite-for-revenge.html.

50. "IS Spokesman Disputes U.S. Declaration of Victory, Condemns New Zealand Shootings," SITE Intelligence Group, March 18, 2019, https://ent.siteintelgroup .com/Statements/is-spokesman-disputes-u-s-declaration-of-victory-condemns -new-zealand-shootings.html.

51. "Al-Qaeda Calls Muslims to Avenge New Zealand Shootings But Avoid Targeting Places of Worship," SITE Intelligence Group, March 23, 2019, https://ent.siteintelgroup .com/Statements/al-qaeda-calls-muslims-to-avenge-new-zealand-shootings-but -avoid-targeting-places-of-worship.html.

52. "Far-Right User on Social Media Paints Execution Video of Scandinavian Woman as Prelude to 'Race War,'" SITE Intelligence Group, December 21, 2018, https://ent .siteintelgroup.com/Far-Right-/-Far-Left-Threat/far-right-user-on-social-media -paints-execution-video-of-scandinavian-woman-as-prelude-to-race-war.html.

53. Jeremiah Coombs (@jeremiahcoombs), "There is a race war coming, prepare and train now," Gab, December 21, 2018, https://gab.com/groups/133; Douglas gulbrand-sen (@Dougiegpr1), "Yup There Are No good Muslims. Until we ALL understand, that they will continue preparing to overtake the U.S.," Gab, December 21, 2018, https://gab .com/Dougiegpr1/posts/9381852444099529; "Far-Right User on Social Media Paints Execution Video of Scandinavian Woman as Prelude to 'Race War,'" SITE Intelli-gence Group.

54. Roger Eatwell, "Community Cohesion and Cumulative Extremism in Contempo-rary Britain," *Political Quarterly* 77, no. 2 (2006): 204–216; Julia Ebner, *The Rage: The Vicious Circle of Islamist and Far-Right Extremism* (London: I. B.Tau-ris, 2017).

55. Rita Katz, "New Zeland Shooting: White Supremacists and Jihadists Feed Off Each Other," *The Daily Beast*, March 20, 2019, https://www.thedailybeast.com/new-zealand -shooting-white-supremacists-and-jihadists-feed-off-each-other.

56. Tarrant, *Replacement*, 8.

57. "The Lesson of Christchurch," The Roper Report, April 10, 2019, https://web.archive .org/web/20190827071719/http://theroperreport.whitenationalists.net/2019/04/10 /the-lesson-of-christchurch/.

58. "With Turning Tides: Tarrant and Our Acceleration (GTFIH)," 8chan, March 26, 2019, https://8ch.net/pol/res/13030320.html; "Users on Chan Board Continue to Discuss 'Acceleration,' Bombing, and Setting Fire to Mosques," SITE Intelligence Group, March 27, 2019, https://ent.siteintelgroup.com/Far-Right-/-Far-Left-Threat

/users-on-chan-board-continue-to-discuss-acceleration-bombing-and-setting-fire
-to-mosques.html.

59. "Guides on lone wolf activism," 8chan, March 27, 2021, https://8ch.net/pol/res/13034541
.html; "White Supremacist Discussion Address US-Based Mosque, Suggesting Future
Attack," SITE Intelligence Group, March 28, 2019, https://ent.siteintelgroup.com/Far
-Right-/-Far-Left-Threat/white-supremacist-discussion-address-us-based-mosque
-suggesting-future-attack.html.

60. "White Supremacist Discussion," SITE Intelligence Group.

61. "In Incitement-Filled Thread, Far-Right Users Discuss How to Probe Refugee Camp,
Give Implied Incitement for Attack," SITE Intelligence Group, March 27, 2019, https://
ent.siteintelgroup.com/Far-Right-/-Far-Left-Threat/in-incitement-filled-thread-far
-right-users-discuss-ways-to-broadcast-an-attack-on-refugees.html.

62. "Facebook officially bans all white nationalist & separatist posts," 8chan, March 27,
2021 https://8ch.net/pol/res/13033792.html; "In Incitement-Filled Thread, Far-Right
Users Discuss How to Probe Refugee Camp, Give Implied Incitement for Attack,"
SITE Intelligence Group, March 27, 2019, https://ent.siteintelgroup.com/Far-Right-/-Far
-Left-Threat/in-incitement-filled-thread-far-right-users-discuss-ways-to-broadcast-an
-attack-on-refugees.html?auid=17751.

4. THE MAKING OF A TERRORIST

1. "New Details Emerge on California Synagogue Shooting Suspect," CBS News,
April 30, 2019, https://www.cbsnews.com/news/poway-synagogue-shooting-suspect
-john-earnest-was-scholar-athlete-california-state-university-san-marcos-2019
-04-30/.

2. Joel Shannon, Chris Woodyard, Julie Makinen, and Amy Dipierro, "California Synagogue Shooting: Suspect Known as Quiet, Smart While Authorities Question If He
Was Hateful," USA Today, April 28, 2019, https://eu.usatoday.com/story/news/nation
/2019/04/28/california-synagogue-shooting-who-suspect-john-t-earnest/360858
3002/.

3. "San Diego Shooter: From Dean's List Student to White Nationalist Terrorist," Times
of Israel, April 28, 2019, https://www.timesofisrael.com/san-diego-suspect-was-deans
-list-student-apparently-posted-anti-jewish-screed/.

4. John Earnest, Manifesto, Open Source Document, https://bcsh.bard.edu/files/2019/06
/Earnest-Manifesto-042719.pdf.

5. Earnest, Manifesto; "Alleged San Diego Synagogue Shooter Shares Manifesto, Incites
Other White Men to Fight Jews," SITE Intelligence Group, April 27, 2019, https://ent
.siteintelgroup.com/Community-Alert/alleged-synagogue-shooter-shares-manifesto
-incites-other-white-men-to-fight-jews.html.

6. Katie Mettler, "The Chabad Synagogue Shooting Victims: A 'Special' Rabbi, Two
Israelis and a 'Woman of Valor,'" Washington Post, April 29, 2019, https://www

.washingtonpost.com/religion/2019/04/28/chabad-synagogue-shooting-victims
-rabbi-two-israelis-woman-valor/.

7.   Mettler, "The Chabad Synagogue Shooting Victims."

8.   "Poway Synagogue Shooting Captured on Video, Prosecutors Say, as They Describe
     Attack," *Los Angeles Times*, May 2, 2019, https://www.latimes.com/local/lanow/la
     -me-san-diego-synagogue-shooter-camera-explainer-john-earnest-20190502-story
     .html.

9.   "Rabbi Hails Heroes Who Chased Off Poway Synagogue Gunman: 'Terrorism, Evil
     Will Never Prevail,' " *ABC7*, April 29, 2019, https://abc7news.com/rabbi-yisroel
     -goldstein-chabad-of-poway-california-san-diego-synagogue-shooting/5275030/.

10. "California Synagogue Shooting Suspect Makes First Court Appearance," NBC
     San Diego, May 14, 2019, https://www.nbcsandiego.com/news/local/john-earnest
     -california-synagogue-shooting-suspect-to-appear-in-court/160022/.

11. Sara Sidner, "Girl Shot in Synagogue Attack Says 'He Was Aiming at the Kids,' " CNN,
     April 29, 2019, https://www.cnn.com/2019/04/29/us/poway-synagogue-victim-noya
     -dahan/index.html.

12. Sidner, "Girl Shot in Synagogue."

13. Sidner.

14. "Jewish Family's Home Tagged with Swastikas," Fox 5 San Diego, April 8, 2015, https://
     fox5sandiego.com/2015/04/08/jewish-familys-home-tagged-with-spray-painted
     -swastikas/.

15. Sidner, "Girl Shot in Synagogue."

16. Sidner.

17. Earnest, *Manifesto*.

18. Elliot Spagat and Julie Watson, "Suspect in California Synagogue Attack Stuns Fam-
     ily with Radical Turn," CBS 8, April 29, 2019, https://www.cbs8.com/amp/article/news
     /nation-world/suspect-in-california-synagogue-attack-stuns-family-with-radical
     -turn/507-2ca320ef-cd41-4e68-86ce-86755748b8ff.

19. Spagat and Watson, "Suspect in California Synagogue Attack."

20. Doha Madani, " 'Our Great Shame': Poway Shooting Suspect's Family Releases Pub-
     lic Apology," NBC News, April 29, 2019, https://www.nbcnews.com/news/us
     -news/our-great-shame-family-poway-shooting-suspect-releases-public-apology
     -n999731.

21. Alex P. Schmid, "Radicalisation, De-Radicalisation, Counter-Radicalisation: A Con-
     ceptual Discussion and Literature Review," International Centre for Counter-
     Terrorism Research Paper (The Hague, March 2013).

22. Earnest, *Manifesto*.

23. Mohammaed Hafez and Creighton Mullins, "The Radicalization Puzzle: A Theoreti-
     cal Synthesis of Empirical Approaches to Homegrown Extremism," *Studies in Con-
     flict & Terrorism* 38, no. 11 (2015): 958–975.

24. Hafez and Mullins, "The Radicalization Puzzle."

25. Colin P. Clarke, *After the Caliphate: The Islamic State and the Future of the Terrorist
     Diaspora* (Cambridge: Polity Press, 2019), 25–27.

26. "Nusra Front Fighter Offers Narrative of His Radicalization," SITE Intelligence Group, May 8, 2015, https://ent.siteintelgroup.com/Western-Jihadists/nusra-front-fighter-offers-narrative-of-his-radicalization.html.

27. "Alleged New Zealand Mosque Attacker Calls for the Death of Angela Merkel and Sadiq Khan in Manifesto," SITE Intelligence Group, March 15, 2019, https://ent.site intelgroup.com/Far-Right-/-Far-Left-Threat/alleged-new-zealand-mosque-attacker-calls-for-the-death-of-angela-merkel-and-recep-tayyip-erdogan-in-manifesto.html.

28. Rich Lord, "How Robert Bowers Went from Conservative to White Nationalist," *Pittsburgh Post-Gazette*, November, 2018, https://www.post-gazette.com/news/crime-courts/2018/11/10/Robert-Bowers-extremism-Tree-of-Life-massacre-shooting-pittsburgh-Gab-Warroom/stories/201811080165.

29. Elliot Spagle, "Suspect in California Synagogue Attack Stuns Family with Radical Turn," CBS8, April 29, 2019, https://www.cbs8.com/amp/article/news/nation-world/suspect-in-california-synagogue-attack-stuns-family-with-radical-turn/507-2ca320ef-cd41-4e68-86ce-86755748b8ff.

30. Earnest, *Manifesto*.

31. Earnest.

32. Earnest.

33. Earnest.

34. Earnest.

35. Earnest.

36. "Alleged New Zealand Mosque Attacker," SITE Intelligence Group.

37. Earnest, *Manifesto*.

38. Andrew Johnson, "Suspect of Possible Arson Attack at Escondido Mosque Leaves Note Referencing New Zealand Terrorist Attacks," *NBC San Diego*, March 24, 2019, https://www.nbcsandiego.com/news/local/islamic-center-escondido-mosque-epd-efd-sdso-reported-arson-unit/81831/.

39. Johnson, "Suspect of Possible Arson Attack."

40. *United States v. Earnest*, 19-cr-1850-AJB (S.D. Cal. Dec. 10, 2021), available at https://www.justice.gov/opa/press-release/file/1161421/download.

41. Earnest, *Manifesto*.

42. Earnest.

43. "Happening san diego now. Check cuckchan," 8chan, April 27, 2021, https://8ch.net/pol/res/13193323.html; "Far-Right Forum Celebrates San Diego Synagogue Shooter's Manifesto, Mock Attack," SITE Intelligence Group, April 27, 2019, https://ent.siteintelgroup.com/Far-Right-/-Far-Left-Threat/far-right-forum-celebrate-san-diego-synagogue-shooter-s-manifesto-mock-attack.html.

44. "Far-Right Forum Celebrates," SITE Intelligence Group.

45. "Far-Right Forum Celebrates," SITE Intelligence Group.

46. There Is No Political Solution, "HEIL SAINT EARNEST," Telegram (channel), August 8, 2019, https://t.me/TINPS.

47. "Far-Right Forum Celebrates," SITE Intelligence Group.

5. SAINTS AND SOLDIERS

1. Abu Muhammad al-Adnani ash-Shami, "A New Statement by IS Spokesman Abu Muhammad al-'Adnani ash-Shami," Open Source Document, September 22, 2014, https://scholarship.tricolib.brynmawr.edu/bitstream/handle/10066/16495/ADN2014 0922.pdf.

2. Ralph Ellis, "Canadian Police Say Man Who Ran Down, Killed Soldiers Was 'Radicalized,'" CNN, October 22, 2014, https://www.cnn.com/2014/10/21/us/canada -soldiers-killed-officer-attack/index.html.

3. "Ottawa Shooting Suspect Michael Zehaf-Bibeau Had 'Very Developed Criminality,'" CTV News, October 23, 2014, https://www.ctvnews.ca/canada/ottawa-shooting -suspect-michael-zehaf-bibeau-had-very-developed-criminality-1.2067255.

4. Laila Kearney, "NYC Police Say Hatchet Attack by Islam Convert Was Terrorism," Reuters, October 24, 2014, https://www.reuters.com/article/us-usa-newyork -hatchet/nyc-police-say-hatchet-attack-by-islam-convert-was-terrorism-idUSKCN0IC2 RG20141024.

5. "French Police Shoot Dead Knife-Wielding Man in Police Station," Reuters, December 20, 2014, https://www.reuters.com/article/us-france-shooting/french-police-shoot -dead-knife-wielding-man-in-police-station-idUSKBN0JY0KI20141220; "Manhunt on for Suspect in Deadly Denmark Attack," CBS News, February 14, 2015, https://www .cbsnews.com/news/copenhagen-cafe-attack-free-speech-event/.

6. Miron Lakomy, "Cracks in the Online 'Caliphate': How the Islamic State Is Losing Ground in the Battle for Cyberspace," *Perspectives on Terrorism* 11, no. 3 (2011): 39.

7. Lizzie Dearden, "Revered as a Saint By Online Extremists, How Christchurch Shooter Inspired Copycat Terrorists Around the World," *Independent*, August 24, 2019, https:// www.independent.co.uk/news/world/australasia/brenton-tarrant-christchurch -shooter-attack-el-paso-norway-poway-a9076926.html.

8. Dearden, "Revered as a Saint By Online Extremists."

9. There Is No Political Solution (@TINPS), Telegram, October 10, 2019.

10. "pbuh" stands for "Peace be upon him"; /pol/ bot—Day of the Rope edition (@Pol-8chbot), Telegram, October 27, 2019.

11. "Far-Right Forum Argue the Effectiveness of San Diego Synagogue Shooting, Compare to Christchurch," SITE Intelligence Group, April 29, 2019, https://ent .siteintelgroup.com/Far-Right-/-Far-Left-Threat/far-right-forum-argue-the -effectiveness-of-san-diego-synagogue-shooting-compare-to-christchurch.html.

12. "The overall value of shootings," 8chan, May 16, 2019, https://8ch.net/pol3/res/37 .html; "Far-Right Forum Continue Discussing What Targets to Pursue with Violence, Mention New Zealand Prime Minister," SITE Intelligence Group, May 21, 2019, https://ent.siteintelgroup.com/Far-Right-/-Far-Left-Threat/far-right-forum-continue -discussing-what-targets-to-pursue-with-violence-threaten-new-zealand-prime -minister.html.

13. Pure Hate (@PureHatred88), Telegram, July 22, 2019.

14. "ITS TIME," 8chan, August 3, 2021 https://8ch.net/pol/res/13561044.html; "El Paso Shooter Calls Attack Response to 'Hispanic Invasion' in Far-Right Manifesto," SITE

Intelligence Group, August 7, 2019, https://ent.siteintelgroup.com/Far-Right-/-Far-Left-Threat/el-paso-shooter-calls-attack-response-to-hispanic-invasion-in-far-right-manifesto.html.

15. Doug Stanglin, "Report: EL Paso Shooter Bought Weapon from Raomania, Ammo from Russia," *USA Today*, August 29, 2019, https://www.usatoday.com/story/news/nation/2019/08/29/el-paso-shooter-report-says-he-bought-gun-romania/2149413001/.

16. Nate Ryan, "El Paso Walmart Manager Relives Mass Shooting Terror at His Store," KVIA, August 8, 2019, https://web.archive.org/web/20190811123110/https://www.kvia.com/news/el-paso/walmart-store-manager-relives-saturday-s-shooting/1107366007.

17. Ryan, "El Paso Walmart Manager Relives Mass Shooting."

18. "El Paso Mass Shooting Arrest Warrant," *Washington Post*, August 9, 2019, https://www.washingtonpost.com/context/el-paso-mass-shooting-arrest-warrant/1ffd2f8f-a950-402e-93b3-5c2dd922b514/.

19. "El Paso Mass Shooting Arrest Warrant."

20. Molly Smith, " 'I Did Lose My Nephew Right in Front of Me': El Paso Shooting Survivor Faces Loss," *El Paso Times*, August 6, 2019, https://www.elpasotimes.com/story/news/2019/08/06/el-paso-shooting-victim-javier-amir-rodriguez-family/1936875001/.

21. Molly Smith, "Juan de Dios Velasquez Moved to El Paso for Its Safety, But Found Death at Walmart Instead," *El Paso Times*, August 9, 2019, https://www.elpasotimes.com/story/news/crime/2019/08/09/el-paso-walmart-mass-shooting-victim-juan-de-dios-velasquez-buried/1971658001/.

22. Rachel Chason, Annette Nevins, Annie Gowen, and Hailey Fuchs, "As His Environment Changed, Suspect in El Paso Shooting Learned to Hate," *Washington Post*, August 9, 2019, https://www.washingtonpost.com/national/as-his-environment-changed-suspect-in-el-paso-shooting-learned-to-hate/2019/08/09/8ebabf2c-817b-40a3-a79e-e56fbac94cd5_story.html.

23. Emma Parker, "El Paso Shooting Suspect Branded 'Weird' Boy Who 'Would Pick His Nose and Eat Scabs," *Daily Star*, August 5, 2019, https://www.dailystar.co.uk/news/world-news/el-paso-walmart-shooter-suspect-18853003.

24. Chason et al., "As His Environment Changed."

25. Tim Arango, Nicholas Bogel-Burroughs, and Kate Benner, "Minutes Before El Paso Killing, Hate-Filled Manifesto Appears Online," *New York Times*, August 3, 2019, https://www.nytimes.com/2019/08/03/us/patrick-crusius-el-paso-shooter-manifesto.html.

26. Patrick Crusius, *The Inconvenient Truth*, Open Source Document, https://randallpacker.com/wp-content/uploads/2019/08/The-Inconvenient-Truth.pdf.

27. Crusius, *The Inconvenient Truth*.

28. "El Paso Shooter Identified Online as Trump Supporter Who Didn't Like 'Race Mixing,'" NewsOne, August 3, 2019, https://newsone.com/3883517/el-paso-shooter-patrick-crusius/.

29. Crusius, *The Inconvenient Truth*; "El Paso Shooter Calls Attack Response," SITE Intelligence Group.

30. "El Paso Shooter Calls Attack Response," SITE Intelligence Group.

31. "El Paso Shooter Calls Attack Response," SITE Intelligence Group.

32. Terrorwave Refined (@TerrorwaveRefined), Telegram, August 5, 2019; "El Paso Attack Suspect Dubbed a 'Saint' By White Supremacist Groups," SITE Intelligence Group, August 5, 2019, https://ent.siteintelgroup.com/Far-Right-/-Far-Left-Threat/el-paso -attack-suspect-dubbed-a-white-supremacist-saint.html.

33. The Bowlcast (@Bowlcast333), Telegram, August 5, 2019.

34. "Tarrantade À El Paso: Une Vingtaine De Chicanos Au Tapis," Blanche Europe, August 4, 2019, https://blanche-europe.info/2019/08/04/tarrantade-a-el-paso-une- vingtaine-de-chicanos-au-tapis/; "French White Nationalist Blog Labels El Paso Shooter 'Hero,' " Translates Manifesto," SITE Intelligence Group, August 5, 2019, https://ent.siteintelgroup.com/Far-Right-/-Far-Left-Threat/french-white-nationalist -blog-labels-el-paso-shooter-hero-translates-manifesto.html.

35. Lily Hay Newman, "Cloudflare Ditches 8chan. What Happens Now?," Wired, August 5, 2019, https://www.wired.com/story/cloudflare-8chan-support-ddos/.

36. April Glaser, "Where 8channers Went After 8chan," Slate, November 11, 2019, https:// slate.com/technology/2019/11/8chan-8kun-white-supremacists-telegram-discord -facebook.html.

37. Trym Mogen, "Politiet: Kan ikke knyttes til Manshaus," Dagbladet, February 2, 2020, https://www.dagbladet.no/nyheter/politiet-kan-ikke-knyttes-til-manshaus/72091378; Oscar Gonzalez, "8Chan, 8kun, 4chan, Endchan: What you need to know," CNET, November 7, 2019, https://www.cnet.com/news/8chan-8kun-4chan-endchan-what -you-need-to-know-internet-forums/.

38. Tom Cleary, "Philip Manshaus: 5 Fast Facts You Need to Know," Heavy, August 12, 2019, https://heavy.com/news/2019/08/philip-manshaus/.

39. "Norway Mosque Shooting: Man Opens Fire on Al-Noor Islamic Centre," BBC, August 10, 2019, https://www.bbc.com/news/world-europe-49308016.

40. "Norway Mosque Shooting: Man Opens Fire on Al-Noor Islamic Centre."

41. Henrik Pryser Libell, "After Attack on Norway Mosque, Body Found at Home Tied to Assailant," New York Times, August 10, 2019, https://www.nytimes.com/2019/08 /10/world/europe/norway-mosque-shooting.html.

42. Lefteris Karagiannopoulos, "Shooting at Norway Mosque Investigated as 'Possible Act of Terrorism'—Police," Reuters, August 11, 2019, https://www.reuters.com/article/uk -norway-attack-idUKKCN1V1099?edition-redirect=uk.

43. "Norwegian White Nationalist Who Killed Stepsister and Launched Failed Attack on Mosque Sentenced to 21 Years' Jail," ABC News, June 11, 2020 https://www.abc.net.au /news/2020–06–11/norwegian-white-nationalist-philip-manshaus-guilty-sentenced /12346618; "Norway Mosque Shooting Probed as Terror Act," BBC, August 11, 2019, https://www.bbc.com/news/world-europe-49311482.

44. Svein Vestrum Olsson, Maria Knoph Vigsnaes, Runa Victoria Engen, Sverre Holm- Nilsen, Anette Holth Hansen, and Mari Malm, "Terrorsaken: Politiet bekrefter at Johanne (17) ble funnet drept," NRK, August 12, 2019, https://www.nrk.no/osloogviken /terrorsaken_-politiet-bekrefter-at-johanne-_17_-ble-funnet-drept-1.14658028.

45.   Olsson, Knoph Vigsnaes, Engen, Holm-Nilsen, Holth Hansen, and Malm, "Terrorsaken."

46.   Jason Burke, "Norway Mosque Attack Suspect 'Inspired by Christchurch and El Paso Shootings,'" *The Guardian*, August 11, 2019, https://www.theguardian.com/world /2019/aug/11/norway-mosque-attack-suspect-may-have-been-inspired-by -christchurch-and-el-paso-shootings.

47.   Burke, "Norway Mosque Attack Suspect."

48.   Anonymous, "well cobbers it's my time," Endchan, August 10, 2019, https://endchan. xyz/pol/res/73841.html.

49.   "Norway Mosque Attack: Bruised Suspect Manshaus Appears in Court," BBC, August 12, 2019, https://www.bbc.com/news/world-europe-49318001.

50.   Brenton Tarrant's Lads (@Tarrants_Lads), August 11, 2019; "Neo-Nazi Group Praises Norwegian Mosque Shooter Among Other Far-Right Terrorist 'Saints,'" SITE Intelligence Group, August 12, 2019, https://ent.siteintelgroup.com/Far-Right-/-Far-Left -Threat/neo-nazi-group-praises-norwegian-mosque-shooter-among-other-far -right-terrorist-saints.html.

51.   Unititled-redpills, "There was a court hearing," Telegram, September 12, 2019, https://t.me/untitledredpills.

52.   Adam Taylor, "Omar Mateen May Not Have Understood the Difference Between ISIS, al-Qaeda and Hezbollah," *Washington Post*, June 13, 2016, https://www.washingtonpost .com/news/worldviews/wp/2016/06/13/omar-mateen-may-not-have-understood-the -difference-between-isis-al-qaeda-and-hezbollah/.

53.   Taylor, "Omar Mateen."

54.   Taylor.

55.   Taylor.

56.   Andrew Buncombe, "Abdul Razak Ali Artan: Ohio State Attacker May Have Been Self-Radicalised Despite Isis Branding Him a 'Soldier,'" *Independent*, November 29, 2019, https://www.independent.co.uk/news/people/abdul-razak-ali-artan-ohio-state -attacker-self-radicalised-isis-claim-soldier-a7446546.html.

57.   Buncombe, "Abdul Razak Ali Artan."

58.   "FBI Chief Says No Sign California Shooters Were Part of a Larger Group," Reuters, December 4, 2015, https://www.reuters.com/article/us-california-shooting-comey -idUKKBN0TN2K920151204.

59.   Artemis Mosthaghian, "Synagogue Shooting Suspect Booked on One Count of Murder in the First Degree," CNN, April 28, 2019, https://edition.cnn.com/us/live-news /california-synagogue-shooting-live-updates/h_47cc10e03f8f5a97ff3e9f9180a2dc05.

60.   Cleary, "Philip Manshaus."

6. CONTROL THE MEMES, CONTROL THE PLANET

1.   Users on chan boards often refer to each other ironically as "fags," fitting with a larger use of homophobic slurs across the far right.

2. SS Wehrwolf Combat Unit, "#vetting" (server), Discord, accessed May 15, 2019.

3. Golo Mann, *The History of Germany Since 1798* (London: Penguin Books, 1990), 560.

4. Bernhard Forchtner and Christoffer Kolvraa, "Extreme Right Images of Radical Authenticity: Multimodal Aesthetics of History, Nature, and Gender Roles in Social Media," *European Journal of Cultural and Political Sociology* 4, no. 3 (2017): 252–281.

5. SS Wehrwolf Combat Unit, "#squads" (server), Discord, accessed May 15, 2019, https://research.calvin.edu/german-propaganda-archive/story2.htm.

6. Michael Edison Hayden, "Mysterious Neo-Nazi Advocated Terrorism for Six Years Before Disappearance," Southern Poverty Law Center, May 21, 2019, https://www.splcenter.org/hatewatch/2019/05/21/mysterious-neo-nazi-advocated-terrorism-six-years-disappearance.

7. Ernst Hiemer, "The Poisonous Mushroom," from *Der Giftpilz* by Julius Streicher, 1938 (Source: Calvin University German Propaganda Archive), https://research.calvin.edu/german-propaganda-archive/story2.htm.

8. Hiemer, "The Poisonous Mushroom."

9. "Julius Streicher: Biography," Holocaust Encyclopedia, United States Holocaust Memorial Museum, accessed December 13, 2021, https://encyclopedia.ushmm.org/content/en/article/julius-streicher-biography.

10. "Culture in the Third Recih: Disseminating the Nazi Worldview," Holocaust Encyclopedia, United States Holocaust Memorial Museum, accessed December 13, 2021, https://encyclopedia.ushmm.org/content/en/article/culture-in-the-third-reich-disseminating-the-nazi-worldview.

11. Aristotle A. Kallis, *Nazi Propaganda and the Second World War* (New York: Palgrave MacMillan, 2005).

12. "Julius Streicher," Holocaust Encyclopedia.

13. Pierre M. James, *The Murderous Paradise: German Nationalism and the Holocaust* (Westport, CT: Praeger, 2001).

14. James, *The Murderous Paradise.*

15. Melissa Eddy, "Germany Seeks Tunisian Tied to Berlin Christmas Market Attack," *New York Times*, December 21, 2016, https://www.nytimes.com/2016/12/21/world/europe/berlin-christmas-market-attack.html; "IS Amaq Reports Ohio State Attacker a 'Solider of the Islamic State,'" SITE Intelligence Group, November 29, 2016, https://ent.siteintelgroup.com/Statements/is-amaq-reports-ohio-state-attacker-a-soldier-of-the-islamic-state.html; "IS Claims New Year's Eve Nightclub Attack in Istanbul, Turkey," SITE Intelligence Group, January 2, 2017, https://ent.siteintelgroup.com/Statements/is-claims-new-year-s-eve-nightclub-attack-in-istanbul-turkey.html.

16. "2016 Hate Crime Statistics," Criminal Justice Information Services Division, FBI, https://ucr.fbi.gov/hate-crime/2016.

17. Mark Berman, "As More Jewish Facilities Get Threats, All 100 Senators Ask Trump Administration for 'Swift Action,'" *Washington Post*, March 7, 2017, https://www.washingtonpost.com/news/post-nation/wp/2017/03/07/as-more-jewish-facilities-get-threats-senators-ask-trump-administration-for-swift-action/.

18. Eleanor Beardsley, "After Attack, an Uproar Over a Call For French Jews to Quit Wearing Yamulkes," NPR, January 14, 2016, https://www.npr.org/sections/parallels /2016/01/14/463010103/after-attack-an-uproar-over-a-call-for-french-jews-to-quit -wearing-yarmulkes; Cnaan Liphshiz, "Will Europe's Jews Stop Wearing Kippahs? Most Already Have," Jewish Telegraphic Agency, April 25, 2018, https://www.jta.org /2018/04/25/global/will-europes-jews-stop-wearing-kippahs-already.

19. Julia Edwards Ainsley, Dustin Volz, and Kristina Cooke, "Exclusive: Trump to Focus Counter-Extremism Program Solely on Islam—Sources," Reuters, February 3, 2017, https://www.reuters.com/article/us-usa-trump-extremists-program-exclusiv -idUSKBN15G5VO.

20. Real3039, Celtchar, "Trump: White Supremacist Groups No Longer Targeted as Violent Extremists," Stormfront, February 2, 2017 https://www.stormfront.org/forum /t1198089/; "White Supremacists Celebrate Trump's Measure to Remove Them from Counter-Extremism Focus," SITE Intelligence Group, February 2, 2017, https://ent .siteintelgroup.com/Far-Right-/-Far-Left-Threat/white-supremacists-celebrate -trump-s-measure-to-remove-them-from-counter-extremism-focus.html.

21. "White Supremacists Celebrate," SITE Intelligence Group.

22. "White Supremacists Celebrate," SITE Intelligence Group.

23. Ayy lMao, "Moonman-Right wing death squads (music video)," December 14, 2016, https://web.archive.org/web/20170212212401/https://www.youtube.com/watch ?v=AIeA-l7k4wM.

24. Ayy lMao, "Moonman-Right wing death squads (music video)"; "White Supremacists Share and Discuss ' "Parody' " Rap Song About Killing African-Americans and Jews," SITE Intelligence Group, February 21, 2017, https://ent.siteintelgroup.com/Far-Right -/-Far-Left-Threat/white-supremacists-share-and-discuss-parody-rap-song-about -killing-african-americans-and-jews.html.

25. IDreamAboutCheese, "Moonman," Know Your Meme, December 3, 2009, https:// knowyourmeme.com/memes/moon-man.

26. Ayy lMao, "Moonman-Right wing death squads (music video)."

27. "White Supremacists Share and Discuss 'Parody' Rap Song About Killing African-Americans and Jews," SITE Intelligence Group, February 21, 2017, https://ent .siteintelgroup.com/Far-Right-/-Far-Left-Threat/white-supremacists-share-and -discuss-parody-rap-song-about-killing-african-americans-and-jews.html.

28. "White Supremacists Share and Discuss ' "Parody' " Rap Song," SITE Intelligence Group.

29. Don Black, "Welcome to the Stormfront discussion board," Stormfront, October 26, 2001, https://www.stormfront.org/forum/t4359.

30. Anonymous, "IT'S FUCKING STARTED," 4chan, October 30, 2017, archived at https://archive.4plebs.org/pol/thread/147216255.

31. Angela Nagle, Kill All Normies: The Online Culture Wars from Tumblr and 4chan to the Alt-Right and Trump (Washington, DC: Zero Books, 2017).

32. 53rockwell, "Re: 8chan refugees welcome here?," Stormfront, September 14, 2019. https://www.stormfront.org/forum/t1290130.

33. SwissGerman, "8chan refuggees welcome here?," September 14, 2019, https://www
.stormfront.org/forum/t1290130/.

34. Ari Perliger, *American Zealots: Inside Right-Wing Domestic Terrorism* (New York: Columbia University Press, 2020)

35. Vegas Tenold, *Everything You Love Will Burn: Inside the Rebirth of White National-ism in America* (New York: Nation Books, 2008).

36. "Timeline of the Muslim Ban," ACLU, accessed December 28, 2021, https://www.aclu
-wa.org/pages/timeline-muslim-ban.

37. Rita Katz, "ISIS Hunter; Time to Wake Up to the White Nationalist Terror Threat," *The Daily Beast*, April 10, 2017, https://www.thedailybeast.com/isis-hunter-time-to
-wake-up-to-the-white-nationalist-terror-threat?ref=author.

38. Imran Awan, "Cyber-Extremism: Isis and the Power of Social Media," *Social Science and Public Policy* 54 (2017): 138–149.

39. "Years of Achievements in the Country of the Unifiers," audio speech from Abu Omar al-Baghdadi, Emir of the Islamic State of Iraq, April 16, 2007, https://ent.siteintelgroup
.com/Multimedia/site-institute-4–17–07-isoi-furqan-baghdadi-speech-41607.html.

40. Jynette Klausen, "Tweeting the Jihad: Social Media Networks of Western Foreign Fighters in Syria and Iraq," *Studies in Conflict & Terrorism* 38 (2015): 1–22.

41. "ISIS Uses 'Nutella, kittens,' to Lure Women Recruits," *Al Arabiya News*, February 19, 2015, https://english.alarabiya.net/en/variety/2015/02/19/ISIS-uses-Nutella-kittens-to
-lure-women-recruits.

42. Abu Dujana (@dujana99lives), "I don't see why Japan has a problem with #IS," Twitter, January 20, 2015, https://twitter.com/dujana99lives/status/557613871746547712.

43. Annika Fredrikson, "Where Did ISIS Get All Those Toyotas? US Treasury Investi-gates," *Christian Science Monitor*, October 7, 2015, https://www.csmonitor.com/World
/Global-News/2015/1007/Where-did-ISIS-get-all-those-Toyotas-US-Treasury
-investigates.

44. Abu Abdullah Britani (@AbuAbdullah_RT), "Is the State sponsored by Toyota Hilux?," Ask.fm, August 2014, http://ask.fm/AbuAbdullah_RT/answer/116578568523.

45. Abu Khalid Al Oozi (@abukhalidaloozi), "Haters gon hate, potatoes gon potate, and the islamic state gon remain a state (bi ithnillah)," Twitter, July 9, 2015, https://twitter
.com/abukhalidaloozi/status/619320966347390976.

46. "IS Recruiter Slams Supporters Not Donating or Migrating as 'Hypocrites,'" SITE Intelligence Group, February 11, 2016, https://ent.siteintelgroup.com/Western
-Jihadists/is-recruiter-slams-supporters-not-donating-or-migrating-as-hypocrites
.html.

47. "Jihadist Recruiter Stresses Secrecy Prior to Migration, Suggests Ways to Keep a Low Profile," SITE Intelligence Group, December 2, 2014, https://ent.siteintelgroup.com
/Western-Jihadists/jihadist-recruiter-stresses-secrecy-prior-to-migration-suggests
-ways-to-keep-a-low-profile.html.

48. Awan, "Cyber-Extremism."

49. Rita Katz, "From Teenage Colorado Girls to Islamic State Recruits: A Case Study in Radicalization via Social Media," *inSITE Blog on Terrorism and Extremism*,

November 11, 2014, https://news.siteintelgroup.com/blog/index.php/categories
/jihad/entry/309-from-teenage-colorado-girls-to-islamic-state-recruits-a-case
-study-in-radicalization-via-social-media.

50. Katz, "From Teenage Colorado Girls to Islamic State Recruits."
51. Katz.
52. Katz.
53. Rita Katz, "As the Caliphate Crumbles, a Female American ISIS Member Makes a
Pitch for Redemption," Insite Blog on Terrorism & Extremism, SITE Intelligence
Group, February 21, 2019, https://news.siteintelgroup.com/blog/index.php/categories
/jihad/entry/439-as-the-caliphate-crumbles,-an-american-isis-member-makes-a-pi
tch-for-redemption.
54. Katz, "As the Caliphate Crumbles."
55. "IS Supporter Calls for Attacks on U.S. Soldiers, Suggests Methods," SITE Intelligence
Group, October 19, 2015, https://ent.siteintelgroup.com/Chatter/is-supporter-calls-for
-attacks-on-u-s-soldiers-suggests-methods.html.
56. "IS Fighter Advises Lone Wolves to Get Jobs at McDonald's to Poison Food," SITE
Intelligence Group, August 12, 2015, https://ent.siteintelgroup.com/Western-Jihadists
/is-fighter-advises-lone-wolves-to-get-jobs-at-mcdonald-s-to-poison-food.html.
57. "IS Fighter Calls for Attack in U.K., Offers Private Advice for Conducting Attacks,"
SITE Intelligence Group, July 16, 2015, https://ent.siteintelgroup.com/Western
-Jihadists/is-fighter-calls-for-attack-in-u-k-offers-private-advice-for-conducting
-attacks.html.
58. "Man Being Monitored by Terror Investigators Is Fatally Shot by Law Enforcement
in Boston," WBUR News, June 2, 2015, https://www.wbur.org/news/2015/06/02/officer
-involved-shooting-roslindale.
59. "British IS Fighter Claims to Have Advised Boston Attacker Usaamah Rahim," SITE
Intelligence Group, June 12, 2015, https://ent.siteintelgroup.com/Western-Jihadists
/british-is-fighter-claims-to-have-advised-boston-attacker-usaamah-rahim.html.
60. "Alleged New Zealand Mosque Attacker Calls for the Death of Angela Merkel and
Sadiq Khan in Manifesto," SITE Intelligence Group, March 15, 2019, https://ent.site
intelgroup.com/Far-Right-/-Far-Left-Threat/alleged-new-zealand-mosque-attacker
-calls-for-the-death-of-angela-merkel-and-recep-tayyip-erdogan-in-manifesto
.html.
61. "Alleged New Zealand Mosque Attacker," SITE Intelligence Group.
62. "Alleged New Zealand Mosque Attacker," SITE Intelligence Group.
63. "Alleged New Zealand Mosque Attacker," SITE Intelligence Group.
64. "Alleged New Zealand Mosque Attacker," SITE Intelligence Group.
65. Julia R. DeCook, "Memes and Symbolic Violence: #proudboys and the Use of Memes
for Propaganda and the Construction of Collective Identity," *Learning, Media and
Technology* 43, no. 3 (2018): 485–504.
66. More on this in chapter 5.
67. Pink Guy (a.k.a. "Filthy Frank") is an internet personality who makes comedy
material.

68. John Earnest, *Manifesto*, Open Source Document, https://bcsh.bard.edu/files/2019/06 /Earnest-Manifesto-042719.pdf.

69. Earnest, *Manifesto*.

70. "SAN DIEGO SYNAGOGUE SHOOTING," 8chan, April 27, 2019, https://8ch.net/pol /res/13194034.html; "Far-Right Forum Celebrate San Diego Synagogue Shooter's Manifesto, Mock Attack," SITE Intelligence Group, April 27, 2019, https://ent .siteintelgroup.com/Far-Right-/-Far-Left-Threat/far-right-forum-celebrate-san -diego-synagogue-shooter-s-manifesto-mock-attack.html.

7. THE VIRAL CALIPHATE

1. Joby Warrick, "Leak Severed a Link to Al-Qaeda's Secrets," *Washington Post*, October 9, 2007, https://www.washingtonpost.com/wp-dyn/content/article/2007/10/08 /AR2007100801817_2.html.

2. Randall Mikkelsen, "U.S. Says Has Copy of Purported Bin Laden Tape," *Reuters*, September 7, 2007, https://www.reuters.com/article/idINIndia-29400420070907.

3. Warrick, "Leak Severed a Link to Al-Qaeda's Secrets."

4. Randi Kaye, "Osama Bin Laden's Message to Americans; Parents of Madeleine McCann Now Prime Suspects?," September 7, 2007, http://transcripts.cnn.com /TRANSCRIPTS/0709/07/acd.01.html.

5. "Osama Video Pointer to Dangerous World: Bush," *Hindustan Times*, September 9, 2007, https://www.hindustantimes.com/world/osama-video-pointer-to-dangerous -world-bush/story-uEUCkBEPuayKRiPicCmIiP.html.

6. Rita Katz, "Follow ISIS on Twitter: A Special Report on the Use of Social Media by Jihadists," Insight Blog on Terrorism & Extremism, SITE Intelligence Group, June 26, 2014, https://news.siteintelgroup.com/blog/index.php/categories/jihad/entry/192 -follow-isis-on-twitter-a-special-report-on-the-use-of-social-media-by-jihadists.

7. Rita Katz, "The Islamic State Has a New Target: Twitter, and its San Francisco Employees," *Washington Post*, September 18, 2014, https://www.washingtonpost .com/posteverything/wp/2014/09/18/the-islamic-state-has-a-new-target-twitter-and -its-san-francisco-employees/.

8. "Pro-IS Media Groups Warn Twitter of Retribution by Lone Wolves for Account Suspensions," SITE Intelligence Group, March 2, 2015, https://ent.siteintelgroup.com /Jihadist-News/pro-is-media-group-warns-twitter-of-retribution-by-lone-wolves -for-account-suspensions.html.

9. "Islamic State Tries Diaspora and Quitter as Social Media Alternatives," SITE Intelligence Group, July 22, 2014, https://news.siteintelgroup.com/blog/index.php /categories/jihad/entry/213-islamic-state-tries-diaspora-and-quitter-as-social-media -alternatives.

10. Rita Katz, "IS Releases of Haines Beheading Video Marks Full Circle Journey Back to Twitter," INSITE Blog on Terrorism & Extremism, SITE Intelligence Group, September 14, 2014, https://news.siteintelgroup.com/blog/index.php/categories/jihad

/entry/284-is-release-of-haines-beheading-video-marks-full-circle-journey-back-to
-twitter-1.

11. Peter Gelling, "American Journalist Likely Being Held by Syrian Government: James
Foley Was Abducted at Gunpoint in Northern Syria This Past November," Salon,
May 3, 2013, https://www.salon.com/2013/05/03/american_journalist_likely_being_
held_by_syrian_government_partner/.

12. Chelsea J. Carter, "Video Shows ISIS Beheading U.S. Journalist James Foley," CNN,
August 20, 2014, https://www.cnn.com/2014/08/19/world/meast/isis-james-foley
/index.html?hpt=hp_t1.

13. Ishaan Tharoor, "Remembering Steven Sotloff Through His Journalism," *Washington Post*, September 2, 2014, https://www.washingtonpost.com/news/worldviews/wp
/2014/09/02/remembering-steven-sotloff-through-his-journalism/.

14. Carter, "Video Shows."

15. "IS Beheads Captured American James Wright Foley, Threatens to Execute Steven Joel
Sotloff," SITE Intelligence Group, August 19, 2014, https://ent.siteintelgroup.com
/Multimedia/is-beheads-captured-american-james-foley-threatens-to-execute
-another.html.

16. Rita Katz, "The Overlooked Goal of the Islamic State's Beheading Video: Recruitment," inSITE Blog, SITE Intelligence Group, August 23, 2014, https://news
.siteintelgroup.com/blog/index.php/categories/jihad/entry/241-the-overlooked-goal
-of-the-islamic-state%E2%80%99s-beheading-video-recruitment-1.

17. Abu Dujana #IS (@abudujana47), "The brother that executed James Foley should be
the new Batman. #IS," Twitter, August 24, 2014, https://twitter.com/abudujana47
/status/503516989445648384.

18. "IS Beheads Joel Sotloff, Threatens to Execute Briton David Cawthorne Haines," SITE
Intelligence Group, September 2, 2014, https://ent.siteintelgroup.com/Jihadist-News
/is-behead-steven-joel-sotloff-threatens-to-execute-briton-david-cawthorne-haines
.html.

19. At this time, ISIS was on its brief (and failed) stay on the VK social media platform
as a primary point of release, where its followers would further disseminate media
across Twitter and other platforms.

20. "Queen of the FAKE Bin Laden video Rita Ktaz/SITE is the 'source' for the fake ISIS
'beheading' videos . . . as usual," *Big Dan's Big Blog*, September 3, 2014, https://
bigdanblogger.blogspot.com/2014/09/queen-of-fake-bin-laden-videos-rita.html.

21. "Channels: Broadcasting Done Right," Telegram, September 22, 2015, https://telegram
.org/blog/channels.

22. Mike Butcher, "Telegram Says It's Hit 62M MAUs and Messaging Activity Has Doubled," Tech Crunch, May 13, 2015, https://techcrunch.com/2015/05/13/telegram-says-its
-hit-62-maus-and-messaging-activity-has-doubled/.

23. Danny Hakim, "Once Celebrated in Russia, the Programmer Pavel Durov Chooses
Exile," *New York Times*, December 2, 2014, https://www.nytimes.com/2014/12/03
/technology/once-celebrated-in-russia-programmer-pavel-durov-chooses-exile
.html?ref=technology&_r=1.

24. Amar Toor, "Telegram Hits 100 Million Users as CEO Voices Support for Apple Over FBI," *The Verge*, February 23, 2016, https://www.theverge.com/2016/2/23/11098310 /telegram-100-million-users-pavel-durov-apple-fbi.

25. Rita Katz, "Almost Any Messaging App Will Do—If You're ISIS," VICE, July 14, 2016, https://www.vice.com/en/article/kb7n4a/isis-messaging-apps.

26. "Pro-IS Jihadists Launch Telegram Channel for Distributing Group Releases," SITE Intelligence Group, September 27, 2015, https://ent.siteintelgroup.com/Jihadist -News/pro-is-jihadists-launch-telegram-channel-for-distributing-group-releases .html.

27. "Pro-IS Telegram Channel Publishes Video Tutorial for Obtaining Secure Email Addresses, Virtual Phone Numbers," SITE Intelligence Group, November 13, 2015, https://ent.siteintelgroup.com/Multimedia/pro-is-telegram-channel-publishes -video-tutorial-for-obtaining-secure-email-addresses-virtual-phone-numbers .html.

28. Rita Katz, "How Terrorists Slip Beheading Videos Past YouTube's Censors," Mother-board: Tech by Vice, May 26, 2017, https://www.vice.com/en/article/xyepmw/how -terrorists-slip-beheading-videos-past-youtubes-censors; "Message Details Telegram Channels' Connections to IS, Group's Verificatoin Process for Social Media Accounts," SITE Intelligence Group, June 10, 2016, https://ent.siteintelgroup.com/Western -Jihadists/message-details-telegram-channels-connections-to-is-group-s -verification-process-for-social-media-accounts.html.

29. "Pro-IS Telegram Channels: Twitter & Facebook for Recruitment, Telegram from the Converted," SITE Intelligence Group, December 10, 2015, https://ent.siteintelgroup .com/Western-Jihadists/pro-is-telegram-channels-twitter-facebook-for-recruitment -telegram-for-the-converted.html.

30. "2015 Paris Terror Attacks Fast Facts," CNN, November 4, 2020, https://www.cnn.com /2015/12/08/europe/2015-paris-terror-attacks-fast-facts.

31. Patrick J. McDonnell and Alexandra Zavis, "Slain Paris Plotter's Europe Ties Facili-tated Travel from Syria," *Los Angeles Times*, November 19, 2015, https://www.latimes .com/world/europe/la-fg-paris-attacks-mastermind-20151119-story.html.

32. Rita Katz, "Coordinated Celebration by IS Supporters for Paris Attack May Speak to Group's Involvement," *INSITE Blog on Terrorism & Extremism*, SITE Intelligence Group, November 14, 2015, https://news.siteintelgroup.com/blog/index.php/categories /jihad/entry/403-coordinated-celebration-by-is-supporters-for-paris-attack-may -speak-to-group%E2%80%99s-involvement.

33. Shane Harris, "The is ISIS's New Favorite App for Secret Messages," *The Daily Beast*, April 13, 2017, https://www.thedailybeast.com/this-is-isiss-new-favorite-app-for -secret-messages.

34. Natasha Lomas, "After Paris Attacks, Telegram Purges ISIS Public Content," Tech Crunch, November 19, 2015, https://techcrunch.com/2015/11/19/telegram-purges-isis -public-channels/.

35. "EU Internet Referral Unit—EU IRU," Europol, accessed November 1, 2020, https:// www.europol.europa.eu/about-europol/eu-internet-referal-unit-eu-iru.

36. Damian Paletta and Siobhan Hughes, "Paris Attacks Fuel Debate Over Spying," *Wall Street Journal*, November 17, 2015, https://www.wsj.com/articles/paris-attacks-fuel -debate-over-spying-1447807995.

37. Rong-Gong Lin II and Richard Winton, "San Bernadino Suspects 'Sprayed the Room with Bullets,' Police Chief Says," *Los Angeles Times*, December 4, 2015, https://www .reuters.com/article/us-california-shooting-encryption-idUSKCN0VI22A.

38. Dustin Volz and Mark Hosenball, "FBI Director Says Investigators Unable to Unlock San Bernadino Shooter's Phone Content," February 9, 2016, https://www.reuters.com /article/us-california-shooting-encryption-idUSKCN0VI22A.

39. Rita Katz, "Jihadists Are Making Their Plans Public. Why Hasn't the FBI Caught On?," *Washington Post*, December 17, 2015, https://www.washingtonpost.com/news/in -theory/wp/2015/12/17/jihadists-are-making-their-plans-public-why-hasnt-the-fbi -caught-on/.

40. House Homeland Security Committee Majority Staff Report, "Terror Gone Viral: Overview of the 243 ISIS-Linked Incidents Targeting the West," Homeland Security Committee, October 2018, https://www.hsdl.org/?abstract&did=817196; "Nice Attack: What We Know About the Bastille Day Killings," BBC, August 19, 2016, https://www .bbc.com/news/world-europe-36801671.

41. "In New Magazine 'Rumiyah,' IS Calls for Lone-Wolf Attacks in Australia, West," SITE Intelligence Group, September 5, 2016, https://ent.siteintelgroup.com/Statements /in-new-english-magazine-rumiyah-is-calls-for-lone-wolf-attacks-in-australia-west .html.

42. "Automatic Brakes Stopped Berlin Truck During Christmas Market Attack," DW, December 28, 2016, https://www.dw.com/en/automatic-brakes-stopped-berlin-truck -during-christmas-market-attack/a-36936455; "Stockholm Truck Attack: Who Is Rakhmat Akilov," BBC, June 7, 2018, https://www.bbc.com/news/world-europe -39552691; Benjamin Mueller, William K. Rashbaum, and Al Baker, "Terror Attack Kills 8 and Injures 11 in Manhattan," *New York Times*, October 31, 2017, https://www .nytimes.com/2017/10/31/nyregion/police-shooting-lower-manhattan.html.

43. "Brussels Explosions: What We Know About Airport and Metro Attacks," BBC, April 9, 2016, https://www.bbc.com/news/world-europe-35869985; "Manchester Arena Blast: 19 Dead and More Than 50 Hurt," BBC, May 23, 2017, https://www.bbc .com/news/uk-england-manchester-40007886.

44. Daniel Boffey, "Remove Terror Content or Be Fined Millions, EU Tells Social Media Firms," *The Guardian*, September 13, 2018, https://www.theguardian.com/media/2018 /sep/13/social-media-firms-could-face-huge-fines-over-terrorist-content.

45. Katz, "How Terrorists Slip Beheading Videos."

46. Rita Katz, "To Curb Terrorists Propaganda Online, Look to YouTube. No, Really," *Wired*, October 20, 2018, https://www.wired.com/story/to-curb-terrorist-propaganda -online-look-to-youtube-no-really/.

47. Courtney Radsch, "GIFCT: Possibly the Most Important Acronym You've Never Heard Of," Just Security, September 30, https://www.justsecurity.org/72603/gifct -possibly-the-most-important-acronym-youve-never-heard-of/.

48. Radsch, "GIFCT."

49. "Europol and Telegram Take on Terrorist Propaganda Online," Europol, November 25, 2019, https://www.europol.europa.eu/newsroom/news/europol-and-telegram -take-terrorist-propaganda-online.

50. "IS Media Scatters to Alternative Platforms Following Telegram Crackdown," SITE Intelligence Group, December 4, 2019, https://ent.siteintelgroup.com/Dark-Web-and -Cyber-Security/is-media-scatters-to-alternative-platforms-following-telegram -crackdown.html; "Hoop Messenger Gaining Traction Among IS & Supporters as Telegram Crackdown Continues," SITE Intelligence Group, May 14, 2020, https://ent .siteintelgroup.com/Dark-Web-and-Cyber-Security/hoop-messenger-gaining-traction -among-is-supporters-as-telegram-crackdown-continues-2.html; "Pro-IS Group Continue to Establish Presence on Blockchain Messenger," SITE Intelligence Group, January 17, 2020, https://ent.siteintelgroup.com/Dark-Web-and-Cyber-Security /pro-is-groups-continue-to-establish-presence-on-blockchain-messenger.html; "IS Media Activists Use Decentralized Social Network to Spread English Propaganda," SITE Intelligence Group, June 27, 2019, https://ent.siteintelgroup.com/Dark-Web-and -Cyber-Security/is-media-activists-use-decentralized-social-network-to-spread -english-propaganda.html.

51. "Jihadists Vent Frustrations as Telegram Deletion Campaign Continues, Search for Haven," SITE Intelligence Group, November 27, 2019, https://ent.siteintelgroup.com /Articles-and-Analysis/jihadists-vent-frustrations-as-telegram-deletion-campaign -continues-search-for-haven.html.

52. Rita Katz, "Telegram Has Finally Cracked Down on Islamist Terrorism. Will It Do the Same for the Far-Right?," *Washington Post*, December 5, 2019, https://www .washingtonpost.com/opinions/2019/12/05/telegram-has-finally-cracked-down-islamist -terrorism-will-it-do-same-far-right/.

53. "Amaq Reports Melbourne Attacker an IS Fighter," SITE Intelligence Group, November 9, 2018, https://ent.siteintelgroup.com/Statements/amaq-reports-melbourne -attacker-an-is-fighter.html; "IS Identifies Belgium Attacker as 'Bakr al-Beljiki' in Naba 134 'Exclusive,'" SITE Intelligence Group, May 31, 2018, https://ent.siteintelgroup .com/Periodicals/is-identifies-belgium-attacker-as-bakr-al-beljiki-in-naba-134 -exclusive.html?auid=10025; "IS Notes Toronto Attack 'Echoed Widely Among Crusaders' in Naba 141," SITE Intelligence Group, July 27, 2018, https://ent.siteintelgroup .com/Periodicals/is-notes-toronto-attack-echoed-widely-among-crusaders-in-naba -141.html?auid=11316; "IS' 'Amaq Reports Trèbes Attacker a 'Soldier' of the Group," SITE Intelligence Group, March 23, 2018, https://ent.siteintelgroup.com/Statements /is-amaq-reports-trebes-attacker-a-soldier-of-the-group.html; "IS' 'Amaq Posthumously Releases Video of Paris Knife Attacker," SITE Intelligence Group, May 13, 2018, https://ent.siteintelgroup.com/Multimedia/is-amaq-posthumously-releases-video-of -paris-knife-attacker.html?auid=9644; "IS Reiterates Claim for Paris Suburb Knife Attack in Naba 145, Stresses Role of France in 'Crusader Coalition,'" SITE Intelligence Group, August 31, 2018, https://ent.siteintelgroup.com/Periodicals/is-reiterates-claim -for-paris-suburb-knife-attack-in-naba-145-stresses-role-of-france-in-crusader

-coalition.html?auid=12239; "Amaq Identifies Strasbourg Gunman as an IS 'Soldier,'" SITE Intelligence Group, December 13, 2018, https://ent.siteintelgroup.com/Statements /amaq-identifies-strasbourg-gunman-as-an-is-soldier.html?auid=14728.

54. "IS Claims London Bridge Attack, Calls Knifeman an IS 'Fighter,'" SITE Intelligence Group, November 30, 2019, https://ent.siteintelgroup.com/Statements/is-reports -london-bridge-attacker-an-is-fighter.html; "IS Declares South London Knifeman One of Its 'Fighters,'" SITE Intelligence Group, February 3, 2020, https://ent .siteintelgroup.com/Statements/is-declares-south-london-knifeman-one-of-its -soldiers.html; "IS Claims Credit for Vienna Attack," SITE Intelligence Group, November 3, 2020, https://ent.siteintelgroup.com/Statements/is-claims-credit-for -vienna-attack.html.

55. "Is ISIS' Comment on the Manhattan Attack Out of the Ordinary? Not Really," *SITE Blog on Terrorism and Extremism*, November 6, 2017, https://news.siteintelgroup.com /blog/index.php/categories/jihad/entry/432-is-isis%E2%80%99-comment-on-the -manhattan-attack-out-of-the-ordinary-not-really.

8. TERRORGRAM

1. Moonkrieg Division (@MoonKrieg), Telegram, February 11, 2020, https://t.me /MoonKrieg/22; "Neo-Nazi Group Urges Violent Attack on Hate Monitoring Organization," SITE Intelligence Group, February 11, 2020, https://ent.siteintelgroup .com/Far-Right-/-Far-Left-Threat/neo-nazi-group-urges-violent-attack-on-adl -headquarters.html; Moonkrieg Division (@MoonKrieg), Telegram, February 12, 2020, https://t.me/MoonKrieg/40, https://t.me/MoonKrieg/36; "Neo-Nazi Group Targets European Airline in Violent Propaganda," SITE Intelligence Group, Febru- ary 14, 2020, https://ent.siteintelgroup.com/Far-Right-/-Far-Left-Threat/neo-nazi -group-targets-european-airline-in-violent-propaganda.html.

2. "Neo-Nazi Group Claims It Left Racist Flyers Outside Church," AP, October 16, 2019, https://apnews.com/article/596f748679034024a2407f34f5cd508a.

3. Rachel Lerman, "New Zealand Shooter Steeped Attack in Dark Internet Culture," AP, March 15, 2019, https://apnews.com/article/aed6b228bd8c47ef89a2062056afofdb; Drew Harwell and Craig Timberg, "8chan Looks Like a Terrorist Recruiting Site After the New Zealand Shootings. Should the Government Treat It Like One?," *Washington Post*, March 22, 2019, https://www.washingtonpost.com/technology/2019/03/22/chan -looks-like-terrorist-recruiting-site-after-new-zealand-shooting-should-government -treat-it-like-one/.

4. Robert Klemko, "A Small Group of Sleuths Had Been Identifying Right-Wing Extrem- ists Long Before the Attack on the Capitol," *Washington Post*, January 10, 2021, https://www.washingtonpost.com/national-security/antifa-far-right-doxing-identities /2021/01/10/41721de0–4dd7–11eb-bda4–615aaefd0555_story.html.

5. Boards like /pol/ were often invaded by "shills" from other online communities who secretly worked on that community's behalf, often against the values or agenda of

/pol/. 8chan, April 1, 2019, https://8ch.net/pol/res/13059745.html (archived at: http://archive.fo/Vo58p); "8chan Users Urge Migration to Telegram," SITE Intelligence Group, April 2, 2019, https://ent.siteintelgroup.com/Far-Right-/-Far-Left-Threat/8chan-users-urge-migration-to-telegram.html.

6. "Pro-IS Jihadists Launch Telegram Channel for Distributing Group Releases," SITE Intelligence Group, September 27, 2015, https://ent.siteintelgroup.com/Jihadist-News/pro-is-jihadists-launch-telegram-channel-for-distributing-group-releases.html.

7. Richard Blumenthal (@SenBlumenthal), Twitter, March 16, 2019, https://twitter.com/SenBlumenthal/status/1106991693860089856.

8. Brenton Tarrant, Facebook, March 13, 2019, https://www.facebook.com/brenton.tarrant.9/posts/2349224875296871 (archived at https://archive.is/o/9UScB/https://www.facebook.com/brenton.tarrant.9/posts/2349224875296871); Brenton Tarrant, Facebook, March 13, 2019 (archived at https://archive.is/o/9UScB/https://www.facebook.com/brenton.tarrant.9/posts/2349224761963549); Brenton Tarrant, Facebook, March 13, 2019, https://www.facebook.com/brenton.tarrant.9/posts/2349217145297644 (archived at https://archive.is/o/9UScB/https://www.facebook.com/brenton.tarrant.9/posts/2349217145297644).

9. Politico Staff, "We Won't Let That Happen: 'Trump Alleges Social Media Censorship of Conservatives," August 18, 2018, https://www.politico.com/story/2018/08/18/trump-social-media-censorship-conservatives-twitter-facebook-787899.

10. Jacinda Ardern, "A Little More About the Christchurch Call," Facebook, May 12, 2019, https://www.facebook.com/watch/?v=376139916443776.

11. "Supporters," Christchurch Call, accessed March 11, 2021, https://www.christchurchcall.com/supporters.html.

12. "US Says It Will Not Join Christchurch Call Against Online Terror," BBC, May 15, 2019, https://www.bbc.com/news/technology-48288353.

13. "US Says It Will Not Join Christchurch Call Against Online Terror," BBC.

14. Richard Blumenthal (@SenBlumenthal), Twitter, March 16, 2019, https://twitter.com/senblumenthal/status/1106991695424561152.

15. Adi Robertson, "8chan Goes Dark After Hardware Provider Discontinues Service," The Verge, August 5, 2019, https://www.theverge.com/2019/8/5/20754943/8chan-epik-offline-voxility-service-cutoff-hate-speech-ban.

16. Neinchan, accessed August 5, 2019, http://127.0.0.1:43110/1DdPHedr5Tz55EtQWxqvsbEXPdc4uCVi9D/;"Far-Right Online Haven 8chan Resurfaces on Dark Web Following El Paso Shooting," SITE Intelligence Group, August 6, 2019, https://ent.siteintelgroup.com/Dark-Web-and-Cyber-Security/far-right-online-haven-8chan-resurfaces-on-dark-web-following-el-paso-shooting.html.

17. Ben Hoyle, "Neo Nazis Give Kiev a Last Line of Defence in the East," The Sunday Times, September 5, 2014, https://www.thetimes.co.uk/article/neo-nazis-give-kiev-a-last-line-of-defence-in-the-east-ocsqncjv3hd.

18. Awakeningdawn, "How to Join the Volunteer Battalions of Ukraine?," Stormfront, February 10, 2015, https://www.stormfront.org/forum/t1087971/ (archived at https://web.archive.org/web/20170110110929/https://www.stormfront.org/forum/t1087971/);"White Supremacist Looks to Join Ukrainian Battalions," SITE Intelligence Group,

February 15, 2015, https://ent.siteintelgroup.com/Far-Right-/-Far-Left-Threat/white-supremacist-looks-to-join-ukrainian-battalions.html.

19. National Socialist Club (@nscdixie), Telegram, July 14, 2020, https://t.me/nscdixie/154;"Carrying Confederate Flags, Neo-Nazi Groups Attends March in Opposition to Black Lives Matter Protest," SITE Intelligence Group, July 15, 2020, https://ent.siteintelgroup.com/Far-Right-/-Far-Left-Threat/carrying-confederate-flags-neo-nazi-group-attends-march-in-opposition-to-black-lives-matter-protest.html; Rita Katz (@Rita_Katz), "@SITE_FRFL investigation finds father and son behind attempt to blow up Mosque near #Siena #Italy championed the Azov Battalion, a Neo-Nazi Ukrainian paramilitary group with massive support by the global far-right movement," Twitter, November 13, 2019, https://twitter.com/rita_katz/status/1194704229757313024?lang=en.

20. Alexander Reid Ross, Emmi Bevensee, and ZC, "Transnational White Terror: Exposing Atomwaffen and the Iron March Networks," Bellingcat, December 19, 2019, https://www.bellingcat.com/news/2019/12/19/transnational-white-terror-exposing-atomwaffen-and-the-iron-march-networks/.

21. Ross, Bevensee, and ZC, "Transnational White Terror."

22. Ross, Bevensee, and ZC, "Transnational White Terror."

23. Jason Wilson, "Christchurch Shooter's Links to Austrian Far Right 'More Extensive Than Thought,'" The Guardian, May 15, 2019, https://www.theguardian.com/world/2019/may/16/christchurch-shooters-links-to-austrian-far-right-more-extensive-than-thought.

24. Proud Boys (@proudboysusa), Telegram, channel created November 20, 2018, https://t.me/proudboysusa.

25. "Racism Inc.," Telegram Analytics, accessed March 15, 2021, https://tgstat.com/channel/@WhiteIsRight.

26. "Multiculturalism™ Revamped," Telegram Analytics, accessed March 15, 2021, https://tgstat.com/channel/@Multiculturalism.

27. "inSite on Technology and Terrorism: Alt-Right Encrypted—How Far-Right Extremists' Migration to Telegram has Reinforced their Terrorist Threat," SITE Intelligence Group, December 11, 2019, https://ent.siteintelgroup.com/inSITE-Report-on-Technology-and-Terrorism/insite-on-technology-and-terrorism-alt-right-encrypted-how-far-right-extremists-migration-to-telegram-has-reinforced-their-terrorist-threat.html.

28. "inSite on Technology and Terrorism," SITE Intelligence Group.

29. "Alt Skull Revealed: Owner of White Nationalist Telegram Channel Is an English Instructor Living Abroad," Angry White Men, August 11, 2020 https://angrywhitemen.org/2020/08/11/alt-skull-revealed-owner-of-white-nationalist-telegram-channel-is-an-english-instructor-living-abroad/.

30. Alt Skull's Charnel House, Telegram (channel), July 10, 2019, https://t.me/Alt_Skull.

31. Breadpilled, Telegram, May 12, 2019, https://t.me/BreadPilled.

32. Tucker's Accelerationists National Revivalist Alliance, "Time is of the essence people. This channel and every other /terrorgram/ channel won't last forever," Telegram (channel), July 9, 2019, https://t.me/NationalRevivalist.

33. Souad Mekhennet and Craig Timberg, "Nearly 25,000 Email Addresses and Pass-
     words Allegedly from NIH, WHO, Gates Foundation and Others Are Dumped
     Online," *Washington Post*, April 21, 2020, https://www.washingtonpost.com
     /technology/2020/04/21/nearly-25000-email-addresses-passwords-allegedly-nih
     -who-gates-foundation-are-dumped-online/.

34. Terrorwave Refined, "Don't Forget to Pray to Saint Tarrant," Telegram, July 1, 2019
     (forwarded from Random Anon Channel—Best /pol/ Telegram Channel; originally
     posted May 8, 2019), https://t.me/TERRORWAVEREFINED; Terrorwave Refined,
     poster, July 5, 2019, https://t.me/TERRORWAVEREFINED.

35. Terrorwave Refined, "Slovak's SIEGE Shack is your go-to for guides regarding gam-
     ing irl," Telegram (channel), June 25, 2019, https://t.me/TERRORWAVEREVIVED.

36. "Neo-Nazis Suggest Emulating Structure of Islamic Terrorist Groups," SITE Intel-
     ligence Group, January 17, 2020, https://ent.siteintelgroup.com/Far-Right-/-Far
     -Left-Threat/neo-nazis-suggest-emulating-structure-of-islamic-terrorist-groups
     .html.

37. "Neo-Nazis Suggest Emulating Structure of Islamic Terrorist Groups," SITE Intelli-
     gence Group.

38. MoonKriegDivision **OFFICIAL**, "Welcome to our channel," Telegram, Febru-
     ary 8, 2020, https://t.me/MoonKrieg.

39. "James Mason," Southern Poverty Law Center, accessed January 12, 2022, https://www
     .splcenter.org/fighting-hate/extremist-files/individual/james-mason.

40. James Mason, *Siege: The Collected Writings of James Mason* (Storm Books, 1992), avail-
     able at https://archive.org/stream/Siege_836/siege_djvu.txt"" .

41. Lizzie Dearden, "Why Has Britain Banned a Neo-Nazi Terrorist Group That 'No
     Longer Exists'?," *Independent*, July 14, 2020, https://www.independent.co.uk
     /independentpremium/news-analysis/feuerkrieg-division-terrorist-group-ban-neo
     -nazis-uk-a9618221.html.

42. Feuerkrieg Division **OFFICIAL**, (image of poster declaring "SCREW YOUR
     OPTICS" posted to public setting), Telegram, August 5, 2019, https://t.me/FK_Divi
     sionOFFICIAL.

43. Feuerkrieg Division **OFFICIAL**, "If you are from the New Jersey or New York area
     then message us,"" Telegram, July 28, 2019, https://t.me/FK_DivisionOFFICIAL.

44. Kelly Weill, "Satanism Drama Is Tearing Apart the Murderous Neo-Nazi Group
     Atomwaffen," The Daily Beast, March 21, 2018, https://www.thedailybeast.com
     /satanism-drama-is-tearing-apart-the-murderous-neo-nazi-group-atomwaffen;
     "Order of Nine Angles: What Is This obscure Nazi Satanist Group?," BBC, June 23,
     2020, https://www.bbc.com/news/world-53141759.

45. The truth ended up being far stranger: in January 2020, the leader of The Base was
     revealed to be a forty-six-year-old American named Rinaldo Nazzaro, who had been
     running the group out of Russia. Jason Wilson, "Revealed: The True Identity of the
     Leader of an American Neo-Nazi Terror Group," *The Guardian*, January 23, 2020,
     https://www.theguardian.com/world/2020/jan/23/revealed-the-true-identity-of-the
     -leader-of-americas-neo-nazi-terror-group.

46. "Las Vegas Man Pleads Guilty to Possession of Bomb-Making Components," US Department of Justice, February 10, 2020, https://www.justice.gov/usao-nv/pr/las-vegas-man-pleads-guilty-possession-bomb-making-components.

47. Ben Makuch and Mack Lamoureux, "Neo-Nazis Are Glorifying Osama Bin Laden," Vice, September 17, 2019, https://www.vice.com/en/article/bjwv4a/neo-nazis-are-glorifying-osama-bin-laden.

48. Feuerkrieg Division **OFFICIAL**, "When he told us about his idea we even encouraged him and asked if he needed help, he said he didn't," Telegram, August 15, 2019, https://t.me/FK_DivisionOFFICIAL.

49. "Las Vegas Man Pleads Guilty to Possession of Bomb-Making Components," Department of Justice, District of Nevada, February 10, 2020, https://www.justice.gov/usao-nv/pr/las-vegas-man-pleads-guilty-possession-bomb-making-components.

50. "Las Vegas Man Pleads Guilty to Possession of Bomb-Making Components," Department of Justice, District of Nevada.

51. "Las Vegas Man Pleads Guilty to Possession of Bomb-Making Components," Department of Justice, District of Nevada.

52. "Neo-Nazi Group Posts Flyers with Violent Incitements In Netherlands," SITE Intelligence Group, December 30, 2019, https://ent.siteintelgroup.com/Far-Right-/-Far-Left-Threat/neo-nazi-group-posts-flyers-with-violent-incitements-in-netherlands.html; Telegram.

53. "Neo-Nazi Group Announces Meet-Up in The United Kingdom," SITE Intelligence Group, January 8, 2020, https://ent.siteintelgroup.com/Far-Right-/-Far-Left-Threat/neo-nazi-group-announces-meet-up-in-the-united-kingdom.html.

54. "Youngest British Terrorist Sentenced for Neo-Nazi Manuals Stash," UK Crown Prosecution Service, February 8, 2021, https://www.cps.gov.uk/cps/news/youngest-british-terrorist-sentenced-neo-nazi-manuals-stash.

55. "Youngest British Terrorist Sentenced for Neo-Nazi Manuals Stash," UK Crown Prosecution Service.

56. Daniel De Simone, "Rugy Teenager Paul Dunleavy Jailed for Terror Offences," BBC, November 6, 2020, https://www.bbc.com/news/uk-england-coventry-warwickshire-54843050.

57. Mikk Salu, "Kes on Komandör? Kapo tabas vägivaldse natsiorganisatsiooni eestlasest juhi," Eesti Ekspress, April 7, 2020, https://ekspress.delfi.ee/artikkel/89488391/kes-on-komandor-kapo-tabas-vagivaldse-natsiorganisatsiooni-eestlasest-juhi?.

58. Nick Fagge, "Neo Nazi Feuerkrieg Division—Which Counted Britain's Youngest Terrorist Among Its Members—Is Run By a Thirteen-Year-Old Estonian Boy Who Calls for the 'Rape of Christian Nuns in Hitler's Name' "" The Daily Mail, February 1, 2021, ,https://www.dailymail.co.uk/news/article-9211625/Neo-Nazi-Feuerkrieg-Division-run-Estonian-boy-13-calls-rape-Hitlers-name.html.

59. "Prominent Neo-Nazi Group Announces It Has 'Dissolved,' " SITE Intelligence Group, February 10, 2020, https://ent.siteintelgroup.com/Far-Right-/-Far-Left-Threat/prominent-neo-nazi-group-announces-it-has-dissolved.html.

60. Bobby Bowie, "This is so sad," Telegram (Lunar Lounge chat group), February 8, 2020. https://t.me/LunarLounge88.

61. SorestHH, "Yes i talked with him not so long ago and with the other FKD lead members," Telegram (Lunar Lounge chat group), February 8, 2020. https://t.me/LunarLounge88.

62. SorestHH, "Now since FKD is 'dissolved' people should search for new divisions," Telegram (The Wheat Field chat group), March 3, 2022, https://t.me/thewheatfield.

63. SorestHH, "We are very glad to announce the start of our own división," Telegram (Lunar Lounge chat group), February 8, 2020. https://t.me/LunarLounge88.

64. MoonKriegDivision **OFFICIAL**, "BLOW UP YOUR LOCAL SYNAGOGUE" (poster), Telegram, February 8, 2020, https://t.me/MoonKrieg; MoonKriegDivision **OFFICIAL**, "LYNCH YOUR LOCAL GOOK!" (poster), Telegram, February 9, 2020, https://t.me/MoonKrieg.

65. "Neo-Nazi Group Urges Violent Attack on Hate Monitoring Organization," SITE Intelligence Group, February 11, 2020, https://ent.siteintelgroup.com/Community-Alert/neo-nazi-group-urges-violent-attack-on-adl-headquarters-2.html.

66. "Neo-Nazi Groups Targets European Airline in Violent Propaganda," SITE Intelligence Group, February 14, 2020, https://ent.siteintelgroup.com/Far-Right-/-Far-Left-Threat/neo-nazi-group-targets-european-airline-in-violent-propaganda.html; "Neo-Nazi Group Continues Propaganda Campaign, Incites Attacks on Government Buildings," SITE Intelligence Group, February 20, 2020, https://ent.siteintelgroup.com/Far-Right-/-Far-Left-Threat/neo-nazi-group-continues-propaganda-campaign-incites-attacks-on-government-buildings.html; "Neo-Nazi Group Incites Violence Targeting Religious Schools, Places of Worship in Recruitment Flyer," SITE Intelligence Group, February 28, 2020, https://ent.siteintelgroup.com/Far-Right-/-Far-Left-Threat/neo-nazi-group-incites-violence-targeting-religious-schools-places-of-worship-in-recruitment-flyer.html.

67. The Wigger, "When you put up moonkreig propaganda at a synagogue irl," Telegram (Lunar Lounge chat group), February 16, 2020, https://t.me/LunarLounge88.

68. The Wigger, "13," Telegram (Lunar Lounge chat group), August 27, 2019, https://t.me/LunarLounge88.

69. Paddington, "Man, you banned my homie Sorest," Telegram (NRM Supporter Chat), February 11, 2020, https://t.me/NRMchat.

70. SorestHH, "Thank [handle redacted] for that one," Telegram (Lunar Lounge chat group), February 16, 2020, https://t.me/LunarLounge88.

71. Paddington, "But for now I want to finish uni and get a government position so I can be a useful 'insider' as WLP would say," Telegram (Lunar Lounge chat group), December 7, 2019, https://t.me/LunarLounge88.

72. Paddington, "The only true justification comes from the barrel of a gun," Telegram (NRM Supporter Chat), March 12, 2020, https://t.me/NRMchat; Paddington, "Killing at least one Jew," Telegram (Lunar Lounge chat group), December 23, 2019, https://t.me/LunarLounge88.

73. Paddington, "The MKD protonmail is even more insane," Telegram (NRM Supporter Chat), March 5, 2020, https://t.me/NRMchat; Paddington, "If anyone takes that seriously," Telegram (NRM Supporter Chat), February 17, 2020, https://t.me/NRMchat.

74. Paddington, "No worries," Telegram (NRM Supporter Chat), March 5, 2020, https://t.me/NRMchat.

75. Paddington, "Me and him are both bosnians, the only difference being I actually live in Bosnia so the kikes cant knock on my door daily," Telegram (NRM Supporter Chat), March 5, 2020, https://t.me/NRMchat.

76. "Searches Within Case of Public Incitement to Terrorism Carried Out in Sarajevo," The Prosecutor's Office of Bosnia and Herzegovina, June 15, 2020, http://www.tuzilastvobih.gov.ba/?id=4514&jezik=e.

77. Nejra Džaferagić, "Bosnian Defendant Pleads Not Guilty to Inciting Terrorism," Detektor, February 22, 2021, https://detektor.ba/2021/02/22/toni-basic-optuzen-za-terorizam-negirao-krivicu/?lang=en.

78. Rita Katz, "Neo-Nazis Are Running Out of Places to Hide Online," Wired, July 9, 2020, https://www.wired.com/story/neo-nazis-are-running-out-of-places-to-hide-online/.

9. SEX SELLS (TERROR)

1. MoonKriegDivision **OFFICIAL**, Image of "Snufkin" cartoon character, Telegram, February 12, 2020, https://t.me/MoonKrieg.

2. MoonKriegDivision **OFFICIAL**, Image of "Snufkin" cartoon character.

3. See Yotam Feldner, "'72 Black Eyed Virgins': A Muslim Debate on the Rewards of Martyrs," MEMRI, November 1, 2001, https://www.memri.org/reports/72-black-eyed-virgins-muslim-debate-rewards-martyrs.

4. Rita Katz (@Rita_Katz), "Forgot to mention: this pic by NF shows attacker applying perfume 'for the meeting with Women of Paradise.' Really???," Twitter, March 23, 2015, https://twitter.com/Rita_Katz/status/580135221770764288.

5. Sebastian, "Profile: 'First American Suicide Bomber' in Syria," Alarabiya News, June 1, 2014, https://english.alarabiya.net/perspective/profiles/2014/06/01/Who-was-American-bomber-Moner-Mohammad-Abu-Salha-.

6. "Jihadists Release Second Installment of Interview American Suicide Bomber in Syria, Moner Mohammad Abu-Salha," SITE Intelligence Group, November 25, 2014, https://ent.siteintelgroup.com/Jihadist-News/jihadists-release-second-installment-of-interview-with-american-suicide-bomber-in-syria-moner-mohammad-abu-salha.html.

7. Associated Press, "American Moner Mohammad Abu-Salha Behind Syria Suicide Bombing," CBC, May 30, 2014, https://www.cbc.ca/news/world/american-moner-mohammad-abu-salha-behind-syria-suicide-bombing-1.2660113.

8. Anita Persin, "Fatal Attraction: Western Muslimas and ISIS," Perspectives on Terrorism 9, no. 3 (2015): 27–29.

9.   Talib al-Australi (@baaaqiyah), Twitter, https://twitter.com/baaaqiyah/status/44737 8814436638720; Twitter, https://twitter.com/baaaqiyah/status/447378814436638720.

10.   "Escape from Hell: Torture and Sexual Slavery in Islamic State Captivity in Iraq," Amnesty International, December 23, 2014, https://www.amnesty.org/en/documents /mde14/021/2014/en/.

11.   "Issue 13 of IS' Dabiq Magazine Calls to Kill Shi'Ites, Eulogizes '"Jihadi John,'" SITE Intelligence Group, January 19, 2016, https://ent.siteintelgroup.com/Jihadist-News /issue-13-of-is-dabiq-magazine-calls-to-kill-shi-ites-eulogizes-jihadi-john.html.

12.   "IS Fighters Discuss the Taking of Female Slaves," SITE Intelligence Group, May 19, 2015, https://ent.siteintelgroup.com/Western-Jihadists/is-fighters-discuss-the-taking -of-female-slaves.html.

13.   "IS Fighter Describes Fighters' Focus on Taking Sex Slaves," SITE Intelligence Group, September 1, 2015, https://ent.siteintelgroup.com/Western-Jihadists/is-fighter -describes-fighters-focus-on-taking-sex-slaves.html.

14.   Carol Cratty, "Anwar al-Awlaki Visited Prostitutes, FBI Documents Say," CNN, July 4, 2013, https://www.cnn.com/2013/07/03/us/fbi-al-awlaki-prostitution/index.html; Scott Shane, "A Biker, a Blonde, a Jihadist and Piles of C.I.A. Cash," *New York Times*, October 19, 2012, https://www.nytimes.com/2012/10/20/world/middleeast /danes-wild-tale-of-ruse-to-find-anwar-al-awlaki.html.

15.   Mr. Dr. Uncle Dad Esq. (XXV-100), "im not going to defend them but teh bottom line is they probably woudlnt be race mixing if you ruled them with an iron fist," Telegram (Lunar Lounge chat group), February 21, 2020, https://t.me/LunarLounge88.

16.   Mr. Dr. Uncle Dad Esq. (XXV-100), "im not going to defend them."

17.   Mr. Dr. Uncle Dad Esq. (XXV-100), "im not going to defend them."

18.   Many in the far right praise the British musician Morrissey, formerly the singer of The Smiths, for his support for his anti-immigrant political stances.

19.   barbarian 3, "put em in chains boys . . . ," Telegram (Nordic Frontier Chat), July 9, 2019, https://t.me/NordicFrontierChat.

20.   Dominic Alessio and Robert Wallis, "Racist Occultism in the UK: Behind the Order of Nine Angles (o9A)," Open Democracy, July 23, 2020, https://www.opendemocracy .net/en/countering-radical-right/racist-occultism-uk-behind-order-nine-angles -o9a/.

21.   Alessio and Wallis, "Racist Occultism in the UK."

22.   Alessio and Wallis, "Racist Occultism in the UK."

23.   RapeWaffen Division **OFFICIAL**, "Fun fact," Telegram, November 17, 2019, https://t.me/RapeTibbygram.

24.   RapeWaffen Division **OFFICIAL**, "Fun fact."

25.   "U.S. Army Soldier Charged with Terrorism Offenses for Planning Deadly Ambush on Service Members in His Unit," United States Department of Justice, June 22, 2020, https://www.justice.gov/opa/pr/us-army-soldier-charged-terrorism-offenses -planning-deadly-ambush-service-members-his-unit.

26.   "Durham Neo-Nazi Teenager Convicted of Planning Terror Attack," BBC, November 20, 2019, https://www.bbc.com/news/uk-england-tyne-50470957.

27.   "Ryan Fleming: Neo-Nazi Paedophile Jailed for Messaging Children," BBC, February 12, 2021, https://www.bbc.com/news/uk-england-leeds-56044179.

28.   Cynthia Miller-Idriss, *Hate in the Homeland: The New Global Far Right* (Princeton, NJ: Princeton University Press, 2020), 25.

29.   Helen Lewis, "To Learn About the Far Right, Start With the 'Manosphere,'" *The Atlantic*, August 7, 2019, https://www.theatlantic.com/international/archive/2019/08/anti-feminism-gateway-far-right/595642/.

30.   Alexandra Minna Stern, *Proud Boys and the White Ethnostate: How the Alt-Right is Warping the American Imagination* (Boston: Beacon Press, 2019), 93–102; Seyward Darby, *Sisters in Hate: American Women on the Frontlines of White Nationalism* (New York: Little, Brown and Company, 2020).

31.   Anders Breivik, 2083: A European Declaration of Independence, Open Source Document, 2011, https://www.washingtonpost.com/r/2010–2019/WashingtonPost/2011/07/24/National-Politics/Graphics/2083+-+A+European+Declaration+of+Independence.pdf.

32.   "Alleged San Diego Synagogue Shooter Shares Manifesto, Incites Other White Men to Fight Jews," SITE Intelligence Group, April 27, 2019, https://ent.siteintelgroup.com/Far-Right-/-Far-Left-Threat/alleged-synagogue-shooter-shares-manifesto-incites-other-white-men-to-fight-jews.html.

33.   "Trad Girl / Tradwife—The 'Liberated' Feminist vs Tradwife," Know Your Meme, accessed October 4, 2021, https://knowyourmeme.com/photos/1815505-trad-girl-tradwife.

34.   BBC Breaking News (@BBCBreaking), Twitter, October 9, 2019, https://twitter.com/BBCBreaking/status/1181892268028055553?s=20.

35.   "White Supremacist Community Praises Shooter in Apparent Neo-Nazi Attacks in Germany," SITE Intelligence Group, October 9, 2019, https://ent.siteintelgroup.com/Far-Right-/-Far-Left-Threat/white-supremacist-community-praises-shooter-in-apparent-neo-nazi-attacks-in-germany.html.

36.   "White Supremacist Community Praises Shooter," SITE Intelligence Group.

37.   "White Supremacist Community Praises Shooter," SITE Intelligence Group.

38.   "White Supremacist Community Praises Shooter," SITE Intelligence Group.

39.   "First Person Video From Halle, Germany Shooting Uploaded to Popular Livestream Platform," SITE Intelligence Group, October 9, 2019, https://ent.siteintelgroup.com/Far-Right-/-Far-Left-Threat/first-person-video-from-halle-germany-shooting-uploaded-to-popular-livestream-platform.html.

40.   "Shooting in Halle, Germany: What We Know," Anti-Defamation League, October 9, 2019, https://www.adl.org/blog/shooting-in-halle-germany-what-we-know.

41.   "First Person Video," SITE Intelligence Group.

42.   "First Person Video," SITE Intelligence Group.

43.   "First Person Video," SITE Intelligence Group.

44.   "Germany Synagogue Attack: Who Were the Victims in Halle?," Deutsche Welle, October 18, 2019, https://www.dw.com/en/germany-synagogue-attack-who-were-the-victims-in-halle/a-50875421.

45. "Germany Shooting: Gunman Kills Two After Attacking Synagogue," BBC, October 9, 2019, https://www.bbc.com/news/world-europe-49988482.

46. "Germany Shooting," BBC.

47. "First Person Video," SITE Intelligence Group.

48. "First Person Video," SITE Intelligence Group.

49. "Germany Shooting," BBC.

50. "A Music Lover, a Painter: Victims of Halle Shooting Identified," *Times of Israel*, October 11, 2019, https://www.timesofisrael.com/a-music-lover-a-painter-victims-of-halle-shooting-identified/.

51. "First Person Video," SITE Intelligence Group.

52. "First Person Video," SITE Intelligence Group.

53. Lizzie Dearden, "Stephan Balliet: The 'Loser' Neo-Nazi Suspected of Deadly Attack on German Synagogue," *Independent*, October 10, 2019, https://www.independent.co.uk/news/world/europe/german-synagogue-shooting-halle-attack-latest-stephan-balliet-suspect-neo-nazi-a9150451.html.

54. "Alleged Stephen Balliet Manifesto Circulates in Far-Right Spaces," SITE Intelligence Group, October 9, 2019, https://ent.siteintelgroup.com/Far-Right-/-Far-Left-Threat/alleged-stephen-balliet-manifesto-circulates-in-far-right-spaces.html.

55. "Neo-Nazi Groups Dispute 'Saint Status' of Halle Shooter," SITE Intelligence Group, October 14, 2019, https://ent.siteintelgroup.com/Far-Right-/-Far-Left-Threat/neo-nazi-groups-dispute-saint-status-of-halle-shooter.html.

56. "Alleged Stephen Balliet Manifesto Circulates in Far-Right Spaces," SITE Intelligence Group, October 9, 2019, https://ent.siteintelgroup.com/Far-Right-/-Far-Left-Threat/alleged-stephen-balliet-manifesto-circulates-in-far-right-spaces.html.

57. "Alleged Stephen Balliet Manifesto Circulates," SITE Intelligence Group.

58. David Courbet, "German Suspect in Synagogue Attack Isolated Loner, Unknown in Hometown," *Times of Israel*, October 11, 2019, https://www.timesofisrael.com/german-suspect-in-synagogue-attack-isolated-loner-unknown-in-hometown/.

59. Bruce Hoffman, Jacob Ware, and Ezra Shapiro, "Assessing the Threat of Incel Violence," *Studies in Conflict & Terrorism* 43, no. 7 (2020): 565–587.

60. rope2cope, "Jews have helped propel this society into degeneracy," Incels.co, November 12, 2020, https://incels.co/threads/never-forgot-the-real-enemy-the-jew.257802/post-5868820.

61. rope2cope, "Jews have helped propel this society into degeneracy."

62. Bruce Hoffman and Jacob Ware, "Incels: America's Newest Domestic Terrorism Threat," *Lawfare*, January 12, 2020, https://www.lawfareblog.com/incels-americas-newest-domestic-terrorism-threat.

63. Megan Garvey, "Transcript of the Disturbing Video 'Elliot Rodger's Retribution,'" *Los Angeles Times*, May 24, 2014, https://www.latimes.com/local/lanow/la-me-ln-transcript-ucsb-shootings-video-20140524-story.html.

64. Adam Frisk, "So-Called 'Incels' Celebrate Toronto Van Attack, Praise Alleged Driver Alek Minassian," *Global News*, April 25, 2018, https://globalnews.ca/news/4167272

/incels-celebrate-toronto-van-attack-praise-alek-minassian/; Aaron Feis, "Misogynist Internet 'Incels' Praise Deadly Toronto Attack," *New York Post*, April 24, 2018, https:// nypost.com/2018/04/24/misogynist-internet-incels-praise-deadly-toronto-attack/.

65. Eyes on the Right, "Andrew Anglin Says Women Want to be 'Beaten and Raped' in Juvenile Rant," Angry White Men, April 1, 2017, https://angrywhitemen.org/2017/04 /01/andrew-anglin-says-women-want-to-be-beaten-and-raped-in-juvenile-rant/.

66. Angela Nagle, *Kill All Normies: Online Culture Wars from 4chan and Tumblr to Trump and the Alt-Right* (Winchester, UK: Zero Books, 2017), 19.

67. Rita Katz (@Rita_Katz), Twitter, October 9, 2019, https://twitter.com/rita_katz/status /1181984363979902977.

68. "Female White Supremacist Organization Announces Winter Drive," SITE Intelligence Group, November 10, 2014, https://ent.siteintelgroup.com/Far-Right-/-Far-Left -Threat/female-white-supremacist-organization-announces-winter-drive.html.

69. "White Supremacist Looks to Join Ukrainian Battalions," SITE Intelligence Group, February 13, 2015, https://ent.siteintelgroup.com/Far-Right-/-Far-Left-Threat/white -supremacist-looks-to-join-ukrainian-battalions.html.

70. "Azov Battalion Announces Need for Foreign Instructors in Ukraine," SITE Intelli- gence Group, April 7, 2015, https://ent.siteintelgroup.com/Far-Right-/-Far-Left-Threat /azov-battalion-announces-need-for-foreign-instructors-in-ukraine.html.

71. Adam Taylor, "The Foreigners Who Flocked to Join the Fight—in Ukraine," *Wash- ington Post*, August 22, 2014, https://www.washingtonpost.com/news/worldviews/wp /2014/08/22/the-foreigners-who-flocked-to-join-the-fight-in-ukraine/.

10. TINFOIL HAT TERRORISM

1. William Luther Pierce, "Tribal Thinking," transcript, posted November 19, 2017, *American Dissident Voices*, National Alliance, https://nationalvanguard.org/2017/11 /tribal-thinking/.

2. "Alleged New Zealand Mosque Attacker Calls for the Death of Angela Merkel and Sadiq Khan in Manifesto," SITE Intelligence Group, March 15, 2019, https://ent .siteintelgroup.com/Far-Right-/-Far-Left-Threat/alleged-new-zealand-mosque-attacker -calls-for-the-death-of-angela-merkel-and-recep-tayyip-erdogan-in-manifesto .html.

3. "El Paso Shooter Calls Attack Response to 'Hispanic Invasion' in Far-Right Mani- festo," SITE Intelligence Group, August 3, 2019, https://ent.siteintelgroup.com/Far -Right-/-Far-Left-Threat/el-paso-shooter-calls-attack-response-to-hispanic-invasion -in-far-right-manifesto.html.

4. "Alleged San Diego Synagogue Shooter Shares Manifesto, Incites Other White Men to Fight Jews," SITE Intelligence Group, April 27, 2019, https://ent.siteintelgroup.com /Community-Alert/alleged-synagogue-shooter-shares-manifesto-incites-other -white-men-to-fight-jews.html.

5.   "Deadly Attack Exposes Lapses in German Security Apparatus," *Der Spiegel*, October 11, 2019, https://www.spiegel.de/international/germany/far-right-terrorism-in-germany-shooting-exposes-lapses-in-security-apparatus-a-1291075.html.

6.   Craig Silverman and Jane Lytvynenko, "The Owner of 8chan Has Created a News Source for Internet Trolls," BuzzFeed News, February 22, 2017, https://www.buzzfeednews.com/article/craigsilverman/meet-the-online-porn-pioneer-who-created-a-news-site-for-int.

7.   Ben Schreckinger, "World War Meme," Politico, May/April 2017, https://www.politico.com/magazine/story/2017/03/memes-4chan-trump-supporters-trolls-internet-214856/.

8.   Chan, archival capture from November 2, 2016, https://web.archive.org/web/20161102073813/https:/8ch.net/index.html; Tonic, "All FBI Agents Reports to DC Offices; Prep for Raids, Possible Arrets in Clinton Probes," 8Chan, November 4, 2016, https://web.archive.org/web/20161109233539/http:/8ch.net/newsplus/res/38598.html.

9.   David Folkenflik, "Radio Conspiracy Theorist Claims Ear of Trump, Pushes 'Pizzagate' Fictions," NPR, December 6, 2016, https://www.npr.org/2016/12/06/504590375/radio-conspiracy-theorist-claims-ear-of-trump-pushes-pizzagate-fictions.

10.   Amanda Robb, "Anatomy of a Fake News Scandal," *Rolling Stone*, November 16, 2017, https://www.rollingstone.com/feature/anatomy-of-a-fake-news-scandal-125877/.

11.   Michael E. Miller, "Pizzagate's Violent Legacy," *Washington Post*, February 16, 2021, https://www.washingtonpost.com/dc-md-va/2021/02/16/pizzagate-qanon-capitol-attack/.

12.   Michael E. Miller, "The Pizzagate Gunman Is Out of Prison. Conspiracy Theories Are Out of Control," *Seattle Times*, February 16, 2021, https://www.seattletimes.com/nation-world/the-pizzagate-gunman-is-out-of-prison-conspiracy-theories-are-out-of-control/.

13.   Aaron Blake, "Michael Flynn's Tweet Wasn't Actually About #PizzaGate, But His Son Is Now Defending the Baseless Conspiracy Theory," *Washington Post*, December 5, 2016, https://www.washingtonpost.com/news/the-fix/wp/2016/12/05/did-michael-flynn-really-tweet-something-about-pizzagate-not-exactly/.

14.   Silverman and Lytvynenko, "The Owner of 8chan Has Created a News Source."

15.   Luke Darby, "Fox News Was Duped by a Seth Rich Conspiracy Pushed by Russian Intelligence," *GQ*, July 9, 2019, https://www.gq.com/story/fox-news-seth-rich-conspiracy; Jim Rutenberg, "Sean Hannity, a Murder and Why Fake News Endures," *New York Times*, May 24, 2017, https://www.nytimes.com/2017/05/24/business/media/seth-rich-fox-news-sean-hannity.html.

16.   Anonymous, "Breaking: Seth Rich Murdered—Round 3," 8Chan, May 16, 2017, https://web.archive.org/web/20170517010119/https:/8ch.net/pol/res/9926464.html.

17.   Brandy Zadrozny and Ben Collins, "How Three Conspiracy Theorists Took 'Q' and Sparked Qanon," NBC News, August 14, 2018, https://www.nbcnews.com/tech/tech-news/how-three-conspiracy-theorists-took-q-sparked-qanon-n900531.

18.   Magda Teter, *Blood Liberal: On the Trail of an Antisemitic Myth* (Cambridge, MA: Harvard University Press, 2020).

19. Andrew Whalen, "What Is Frazzledrip? Fake Hilary Clinton Video Builds on Pizzagate Conspiracy Theory," *Newsweek*, December 12, 2018, https://www.newsweek.com/what-frazzledrip-hrc-pizzagate-conspiracy-theory-hillary-clinton-video-huma-1256257.

20. Bill Berkowitz, " 'Cultural Marxism' Catchin On," Intelligence Report, Southern Poverty Law Center, August 15, 2003, https://www.splcenter.org/fighting-hate/intelligence-report/2003/cultural-marxism-catching.

21. Frederic Spotts, *Hitler and the Power of Aesthetics* (Woodstock, NY: Overlook Press, 2002).

22. Q, "Define 'Treason,'" 8chQresearch, QPosts, August 28, 2018, https://qposts.online/post/1945.

23. Kevin Roose, "What Is QAnon, the Viral Pro-Trump Conspiracy Theory?," *New York Times*, March 4, 2021, https://www.nytimes.com/article/what-is-qanon.html.

24. Anonymous, "Never mind what I typed," 8chan (Qresearch2gen board), April 4, 2018, https://web.archive.org/web/20180807100946/https://8ch.net/qresearch2gen/res/11446.html#q11713.

25. 8chan (8ch.net) (@infinitechan), Twitter, January 7, 2018, https://twitter.com/infinitechan/status/950118385517408256?s=20.

26. Anonymous, "2nd Generation Q Research General #16—Going Down the Youtubes Ed-ition," Qresearch2gen, 8chan, April 4, 2018, https://web.archive.org/web/20180807100946/https:/8ch.net/qresearch2gen/res/11446.html.

27. "2nd Generation Q Research General #16—Going Down the Youtubes Ed-ition," Qresearch2gen, 8chan.

28. Brandy Zadrozny and Ben Collins, "Reddit Bans Qanon Subreddits After Months of Violent Threats," NBC News, September 12, 2018, https://www.nbcnews.com/tech/tech-news/reddit-bans-qanon-subreddits-after-months-violent-threats-n909061.

29. Q, "What had to happen first," 8chan (later 8kun), May 17, 2018, https://8kun.top/qresearch/res/1444539.html#1445147.

30. "DOJ OIG Release Report on Various Actions by the Federal Bureau of Investigation and Department of Justice in Advance of the 2016 Election," Office of the Inspector General, US Department of Justice, June 14, 2018, https://oig.justice.gov/press/2018/2018-06-14.pdf.

31. William Mansell, "Man Pleads Guilty to Terrorism Charge After Blocking Hoover Dam Bridge with Armored Truck," ABC News, February 13, 2020, https://abcnews.go.com/US/man-pleads-guilty-terrorism-charge-blocking-bridge-armored/story?id=68955385.

32. Mansell, "Man Pleads Guilty to Terrorism Charge."

33. Tom McCarthy, "QAnon: Latest Trump-Linked Conspiracy Theory Gains Steam at President's Rallies," *The Guardian*, August 3, 2018, https://www.theguardian.com/us-news/2018/aug/03/qanon-conspiracy-theory-trump-rallies; Kirby Wilson, "Dozens of Trump Supporters Championed the 'QAnon' Conspiracy at His Tampa Rally. Here's What You Need to Know," *Tampa Bay Times*, August 1, 2018, https://www

.tampabay.com/florida-politics/buzz/2018/08/01/dozens-of-trump-supporters-championed-the-qanon-conspiracy-at-his-tampa-rally-heres-what-you-need-to-know/; Brandy Zadrozny and Ben Collins, "Reddit Bans Qanon Subreddits After Months of Violent Threats," NBC News, September 12, 2018, https://www.nbcnews.com/tech/tech-news/reddit-bans-qanon-subreddits-after-months-violent-threats-n909061.

34. 8chan, web archive, October 30, 2018, https://web.archive.org/web/20181030233529/https:/8ch.net/index.html.

35. 8chan, web archive, November 7, 2018, https://web.archive.org/web/20181107021137/https:/8ch.net/index.html.

36. 8chan, web archive, October 30, 2018, https://web.archive.org/web/20181030233529/https:/8ch.net/index.html.

37. Anonymous, "CNN Gives us a Gift," 8chan, web archive, October 30, 2018, https://web.archive.org/web/20181030231217/https:/8ch.net/pol/res/12343892.html.

38. Jana Winter, "Exclusive: FBI Document Warns Conspiracy Theories Are a New Domestic Terrorism Threat," Yahoo News, August 1, 2019, https://news.yahoo.com/fbi-documents-conspiracy-theories-terrorism-160000507.html.

39. Ali Watkins, "Accused of Killing a Gambino Mob Boss, He's Presenting a Novel Defense," *New York Times*, December 6, 2019, https://www.nytimes.com/2019/12/06/nyregion/gambino-shooting-anthony-comello-qanon.html.

40. Unsealed Document, "Application for a Search Warrant," United States District Court for the Southern District of California, April 28, 2019, https://www.courtlistener.com/recap/gov.uscourts.casd.626722/gov.uscourts.casd.626722.1.0.pdf.

41. E. J. Dickson, "The FBI Declared QAnon a Domestic Terrorism Threat—and Conspiracy Theorists are Psyched," *Rolling Stone*, August 2, 2019, https://www.rollingstone.com/culture/culture-features/qanon-domestic-terrorism-threat-conspiracy-theory-866288/.

42. Dickson, "The FBI Declared QAnon a Domestic Terrorism Threat."

43. Will Sommer, "A QAnon Believer Is Running for Congress and Is Currently Unopposed in His Republican Primary," *The Daily Beast*, April 10, 2019, https://www.thedailybeast.com/matthew-lusk-meet-the-first-qanon-believer-running-for-congress; Jon Swaine, "Pro-Trump Republican Aiming to Unseat Ilhan Omar Charged with Felony Theft," *The Guardian*, July 25, 2019, https://www.theguardian.com/us-news/2019/jul/25/danielle-stella-republican-ilhan-omar-charged-felony-qanon-trump.

44. Jeff Bercovici, "8chan, a Site Favored By Suspected Mass Shooters, Loses Its Network Hosts," *Los Angeles Times*, August 5, 2019, https://www.latimes.com/business/technology/story/2019-08-04/8chan-cloudflare-mass-shootings.

45. Matthew Prince, "Terminating Service for 8Chan," Cloudflare, August 4, 2019, https://blog.cloudflare.com/terminating-service-for-8chan/.

46. Rambo Talabong, "PNP Urges 8chan's Jim Watkins to Pay to Visit Camp Crame," Rappler, August 15, 2019, https://www.rappler.com/nation/pnp-urges-8chan-jim-watkins-visit-camp-crame.

47. Ben Gilbert, "The Bizarre Life of 8chan Owner Jim Watkins, the Middle-Age Veteran Who Decamped to the Philippines and Runs a Pig Farm," *Business Insider*, August 5, 2019, https://www.businessinsider.com/who-owns-8chan-jim-watkins-life-2019–8 #by-2004-as-the-first-bubble-of-internet-companies-was-popping-watkinsmoved -to-the-philippines-with-his-family-he-continues-to-live-there-2.

48. Drew Harwell and Timothy McLaughlin, "From Helicopter Repairman to Leader of the Internet's 'Darkest Reaches': The Life and Times of 8chan Owner Jim Watkins," *Washington Post*, September 12, 2019, https://www.washingtonpost.com/technology /2019/09/12/helicopter-repairman-leader-internets-darkest-reaches-life-times-chan -owner-jim-watkins/; Gilbert, "The Bizarre Life."

49. Emily Stewart, "Facebook's Political Ads Policy Is Predictably Turning Out to Be a Disaster," Recode, October 30, 2019, https://www.vox.com/recode/2019/10/30 /20939830/facebook-false-ads-california-adriel-hampton-elizabeth-warren-aoc; Report of the Select Committee on Intelligence, "Russian Active Measures Campaigns and Interference in the 2016 U.S. Election Volume 2: Russia's Use of Social Media with Additional Views," United States Senate, https://www.intelligence.senate.gov/sites /default/files/documents/Report_Volume2.pdf.

50. Chris Fransescani, "The Men behind Qanon," ABC News, September 22, 2020, https:// abcnews.go.com/Politics/men-qanon/story?id=73046374.

51. Harwell and McLaughlin, "From Helicopter Repairman."

52. Rappler, "8chan owner summoned to testify before U.S. Congress," Youtube, August 7, 2019, https://www.youtube.com/watch?v=Kq_kH_UdEfo.

53. Fergus Ryan, "Why Are Moscow and Beijing Happy to Host the U.S. Far-Right Online?," *Foreign Policy*, January 22, 2021, https://foreignpolicy.com/2021/01/22/russia -beijing-web-host-far-right-parler-daily-stormer/; Anthony Macuk, "8chan Back Online Under the Name 8kun," *The Columbian*, November 7, 2019, https://www .columbian.com/news/2019/nov/07/8chan-back-online-under-the-name-8kun/.

54. Rita Katz, "What's Worse Than Foreign Election Interference? QAnon," *Wired*, October 30, 2020, https://www.wired.com/story/opinion-whats-worse-than-foreign -election-interference-qanon/.

55. Anonymous, "UK Anon here," 8kun, January 23, 2020, https://8kun.top/qresearch /res/7515739.html#7886759.

56. Anonymous, "I know I'm late," 8kun, December 16, 2019, https://8kun.top/qresearch /res/7515739.html#7886759.

57. Anonymous, "Q is fighting," 8kun, January 20, 2020, https://8kun.top/qresearch /res/7515739.html#q7523043.

58. Anonymous, "We Love you UK Family," 8kun, January 23, 2020, https://8kun.top /qresearch/res/7515739.html#q7523043.

59. Whois Record for Operationq.pub, Whois Domain Tools, retrieved September 21, 2020, https://whois.domaintools.com/operationq.pub; Whois Record for QaNonBin .com, Whois Domain Tools, retrieved September 21, 2020, https://whois.domaintools .com/qanonbin.com; Whois Record for BiDenEmails.com, Whois Domain Tools, retrieved September 21, 2020, https://whois.domaintools.com/bidenemails.com.

60. "Is It Wet Yet, Inc. Reveals 8kun on Lokinet," Is It Wet Yet, November 2, 2019, https://
     isitwetyet.com/launch-pressrelease/.

61. Whois Record for IsItWetYet.com, Whois Domain Tools, accessed April 21, 2021,
     https://whois.domaintools.com/isitwetyet.com.

62. Katz, "What's Worse?"

63. Rob Monster, "Epik Draws Line on Acceptable Use," Epik, August 6, 2019, https://
     www.epik.com/blog/epik-draws-line-on-acceptable-use.html.

64. OEnochO (@OEnochO), Telegram, August 6, 2019, retrieved from "RWCS—THE
     OMEGA PILL" Telegram chat group (https://t.me/KingdomZombe).

65. Katz, "What's Worse?"

66. Ken Schwencke, "Spurned by Major Companies, the Daily Stormer Returns to the
     Web With Help from a Startup," ProPublica, August 18, 2017, https://www.propublica
     .org/article/spurned-by-major-companies-the-daily-stormer-returns-to-the-web
     ?utm_campaign=sprout&utm_medium=social&utm_source=twitter&utm_con-
     tent=1503093250.

67. "Go ahead and wear it out," Is It Wet Yet, web archive, January 1, 2020, https://archive
     .is/LYZZh#selection-345.143–345.443.

68. United States of America v. Jarrett William Smith, United States District Court for
     the District of Kansas, Criminal Complaint, https://www.documentcloud.org
     /documents/6427419-Criminal-Complaint-Smith.html.

69. Anti-Kosmik 2182, "That part is irrelevant," Telegram (Vorherrschaft Division Talk
     Room), September 10, 2019, https://t.me/joinchat/JD1aZ1SqGDpr3yPZb5_VIA.

11. FAR RIGHT 2.0

1. Jonathan Blitzer, "The Body Collectors of the Coronavirus Pandemic," New Yorker,
    April 22, 2020, https://www.newyorker.com/news/our-local-correspondents/the
    -body-collectors-of-the-coronavirus-pandemic.

2. Tom Kington, "Italy Sees Wartime-Era Stress at Hospitals—and Cemeteries," Los
    Angeles Times, March 17, 2020, https://www.latimes.com/world-nation/story
    /2020–03–17/medical-staffs-in-italy-dealing-with-coronavirus-know-what-awaits
    -the-u-s.

3. James Gordon Meek, "Terrorist Groups Spin COVID-19 as God's 'Smallest Soldier'
    Attacking West," ABC News, April 2, 2020, https://abcnews.go.com/International
    /terrorist-groups-spin-covid-19-gods-smallest-soldier/story?id=69930563.

4. "Recent Global Jihad Updates on the COVID-19 Pandemic: April 8–14, 2020," SITE
    Intelligence Group, April 15, 2020, https://ent.siteintelgroup.com/Jihadist-News
    /recent-global-jihad-updates-on-the-covid-19-pandemic-april-8–14–2020.html;
    "Weekly inSITE on the Islamic State for April 15–21, 2020," SITE Intelligence Group,
    April 23, 2020, https://ent.siteintelgroup.com/Weekly-inSITE-on-Islamic-State
    /weekly-insite-on-the-islamic-state-for-april-15–21–2020.html; "Recent Global Jihad
    Updates on the COVID-19 Pandemic: April 29–May 5, 2020," SITE Intelligence Group,

May 6, 2020, https://ent.siteintelgroup.com/Jihadist-News/recent-global-jihad -updates-on-the-covid-19-pandemic-april-29-may-5-2020.html.

5. Ella Koeze and Nathaniel Popper, "The Virus Changed the Way We Internet," *New York Times*, April 7, 2020, https://www.nytimes.com/interactive/2020/04/07 /technology/coronavirus-internet-use.html.

6. "In Pandemic, Rumors of Martial Law Fly Despite Reassurances," *U.S. News*, March 25, 2020, https://www.usnews.com/news/health-news/articles/2020–03–25/in -pandemic-rumors-of-martial-law-fly-despite-reassurances.

7. Adam Satariano and Davey Alba, "Burning Cell Towers, Out of Baseless Fear They Spread the Virus," *New York Times*, April 10, 2020, https://www.nytimes.com/2020 /04/10/technology/coronavirus-5g-uk.html.

8. Malaka Gharib, "Fake Facts Are Flying About Coronavirus. Now There's a Plan To Debunk Them," NPR, February 21, 2020, https://www.npr.org/sections/goatsandsoda /2020/02/21/805287609/theres-a-flood-of-fake-news-about-coronavirus-and-a-plan -to-stop-it.

9. "What Is QAnon and How Are Social Media Sites Taking Action On It?," *Reuters*, October 6, 2020, https://www.reuters.com/article/us-socialmedia-qanon-factbox -idUKKBN26203M.

10. E. J. Dickson, "QAnon YouTubers Are Telling People to Drink Bleach to Ward Off Coronavirus," *Rolling Stone*, January 29, 2020, https://www.rollingstone.com/culture /culture-news/qanon-conspiracy-theorists-coronavirus-mms-bleach-youtube -twitter-944878/.

11. Joseph Guzman, "Bill Gates Is Now the Main Target of Coronavirus Conspiracy The-ories: Report," *The Hill*, April 17, 2020, https://thehill.com/changing-america/well -being/longevity/493339-bill-gates-is-favorite-target-of-coronavirus.

12. Marc-Andrew Argentino, "QAnon Conspiracy Theories About the Coronavirus Pan-demic Are a Public Health Threat," The Conversation, April 8, 2020, https:// theconversation.com/qanon-conspiracy-theories-about-the-coronavirus-pandemic -are-a-public-health-threat-135515.

13. COVID-19 UPDATE + NEWS, "5G NETWORK IS UP AND RUNNING EVERY-WHERE WHERE COVID-19 OUTBREAKS OCCUR," February 27, 2020, Telegram (forwarded to Weaponize Conspiracy chat group), https://t.me/WeaponizeConspiracy.

14. Q, "Think voting," 8chan (later 8kun), April 8, 2020, https://8kun.top/qresearch /res/8722796.html#8722933.

15. Ryan Broderick, "QAnon Supporters and Anti-Vaxxers Are Spreading a Hoax That Bill Gates Created the Coronavirus," BuzzFeed News, January 23, 2020, https://www .buzzfeednews.com/article/ryanhatesthis/qanon-supporters-and-anti-vaxxers-are -spreading-a-hoax-that?bfsource=relatedmanual.

16. "Awaiting the Storm: Tracking QAnon's Global Growth and Laser Focus on the 2020 Election," SITE Intelligence Group, October 14, 2020, https://ent.siteintelgroup.com /inSITE-on-Far-Right/Far-Left/awaiting-the-storm-tracking-qanon-s-global-growth -and-laser-focus-on-the-2020-election.html.

17. "Awaiting the Storm," SITE Intelligence Group.

18. Marc-Andrew Argentino (@_MAArgentino), "From when hen the US went on lock-down the second week of March to the third week of May (week before the death of George Floyd) QAnon Twitter Activity increased by ~71%. Since the start of the civil rights protests QAnon content has dropped by ~85% on Twitter," Twitter, June 16, 2020, 3:04 p.m., https://twitter.com/_MAArgentino/status/1272968429113311234.

19. Shayan Sardarizadeh (@Shayan86), "The decimation of QAnon on Facebook and Insta-gram is pushing supporters to Telegram, a mainstream messaging app with channels and group chats. There are QAnon Telegram channels in English, Spanish, Portuguese, Italian, French, German, Dutch, Japanese, Persian and a few more," Twitter, October 28, 2020, 7:59 p.m., https://twitter.com/shayan86/status/1321602524927897601?lang=en.

20. J. M. Berger, *The Turner Legacy: The Storied Origins and Enduring Impact of White Nationalism's Deadly Bible* (The Hague: International Centre for Counter-Terrorism, 2016), https://icct.nl/app/uploads/2016/09/ICCT-Berger-The-Turner-Legacy -September2016–2.pdf.

21. "RAHOWA," Anti-Defamation League, https://www.adl.org/education/references /hate-symbols/rahowa; "The Boogaloo: Extremists' New Slang Term for a Coming Civil War," ADL, November 26, 2019, https://www.adl.org/blog/the-boogaloo -extremists-new-slang-term-for-a-coming-civil-war.

22. Jamie Ross, "Neo-Nazi Groups Tell Virus-Infected Members to Spray Bodily Fluids at Cops and Jews, Says Report," The Daily Beast, March 23, 2020, https://www .thedailybeast.com/neo-nazi-groups-tell-virus-infected-members-to-spray-bodily -fluids-at-cops-and-jews-says-report.

23. Flora Cassen, " 'Jews Control Chinese Labs That Created Coronavirus': White Suprem-acists' Dangerous New Conspiracy Theory," *Haaretz*, May 3, 2020, https://www .haaretz.com/jewish/.premium-the-jews-control-the-chinese-labs-that-created -coronavirus-1.8809635.

24. Mike Levine, "FBI Learned of Coronavirus-Inspired Bomb Plotter Through Radical-ized US Army Soldier," ABC News, March 26, 2020, https://abcnews.go.com/Politics /fbi-learned-coronavirus-inspired-bomb-plotter-radicalized-us/story?id=69818116.

25. Abby Dodge, "Domestic Terror Suspect Killed By FBI Wanted to Bomb Hospital," KCTV5, March 26, 2020, https://www.kctv5.com/news/send_to_wire_local_only /domestic-terror-suspect-killed-by-fbi-wanted-to-bomb-hospital/article_604f313a -6fa7–11ea-9422-d7a4398bddaf.html.

26. Adam Goldman, "Man Suspected of Planning Attack on Missouri Hospital Is Killed, Officials Say," *New York Times*, March 25, 2020, https://www.nytimes.com/2020/03 /25/us/politics/coronavirus-fbi-shooting.html.

27. "Missouri Neo-Nazi Connected to Hospital Bomb Plot Discussed Attacking Infra-structure, Weaponizing Coronavirus In Chat Groups," SITE Intelligence Group, March 26, 2020, https://ent.siteintelgroup.com/Far-Right-/-Far-Left-Threat/timothy -wilson-coronavirus.html.

28. "Missouri Neo-Nazi Connected to Hospital Bomb Plot," SITE Intelligence Group.

29. Evan Perez and Shortell, "Man Under Investigation for Plotting an Attack at a Hos-pital Believed to Be Treating COVID-19 Patients Was Killed During an FBI

Investigation," CNN, March 26, 2020, https://www.cnn.com/2020/03/25/us/missouri
-man-killed-fbi-investigation/index.html.

30. Steve Vockrodt, "FBI Records Detail Cass County Man's Plot to Bomb Hospital, 'Kick
Start a Revolution,'" *Kansas City Star*, April 15, 2020, https://www.kansascity.com
/news/local/crime/article241910061.html.

31. Vockrodt, "FBI Records Detail Cass County Man's Plot to Bomb Hospital."

32. "Train Operator at Port of Los Angeles Charged with Derailing Locomotive Near U.S.
Navy's Hospital Ship Mercy," Department of Justice, April 1, 2020, https://www.justice
.gov/usao-cdca/pr/train-operator-port-los-angeles-charged-derailing-locomotive
-near-us-navy-s-hospital.

33. "Train Operator at Port of Los Angeles Charged," Department of Justice.

34. "'It's Disgusting': Cars Belonging to Doctors, Nurses Found with Slashed Tires Outside Hospital," News 12 Hudson Valley, April 10, 2020, https://hudsonvalley.news12
.com/its-disgusting-cars-belonging-to-doctors-nurses-found-with-slashed-tires
-outside-hospital-41996190.

35. Isaac Stanley-Becker, Yasmeen Abutaleb, and Devlin Barrett, "Anthony Fauci's Security Is Stepped Up as Doctor and Face of U.S. Coronavirus Response Receives Threats,"
Washington Post, April 1, 2020, https://www.washingtonpost.com/politics/anthony
-faucis-security-is-stepped-up-as-doctor-and-face-of-us-coronavirus-response
-receives-threats/2020/04/01/ff861a16–744d-11ea-85cb-8670579b863d_story.html.

36. Catharine Tunney, "Rideau Hall Intruder Wanted to Have Trudeau Arrested: RCMP
Investigation," CBC, January 9, 2021, https://www.cbc.ca/news/politics/hurren-rideau
-hall-arrest-1.5866297.

37. Tunney, "Rideau Hall Intruder Wanted to Have Trudeau Arrested."

38. Adrian Humphreys, "Corey Hurren on Rideau Hall Attack: 'I Figured As Soon As I
Got on the Property, I Would Get Shot Down,'" *National Post*, March 3, 2021, https://
nationalpost.com/news/canada/corey-hurren-on-rideau-hall-attack-i-figured-as
-soon-as-i-got-on-the-property-i-would-get-shot-down.

39. Humphreys, "Corey Hurren on Rideau Hall Attack."

40. Matthew Brown, "Fact Check: A Bill Gates-Backed Pandemic Simulation in October
Did Not Predict COVID-19," *USA Today*, March 26, 2020, https://www.usatoday.com
/story/news/factcheck/2020/03/26/fact-check-bill-gates-backed-pandemic-exercise
-didnt-predict-covid-19/5081854002/.

41. Grindhousefinefoods, "as anyone else been following 'Q,'" Instagram, March 27, 2020,
https://www.instagram.com/p/B-P2E5IFbOf/.

42. Grindhousefinefoods, "as anyone else been following 'Q.'"

43. Grindhousefinefoods, "as anyone else been following 'Q.'"

44. Nick Clegg, "Combating COVID-19 Misinformation Across Our Apps," Facebook,
March 25, 2020, https://about.fb.com/news/2020/03/combating-covid-19-misinfor
mation/.

45. Matt Binder, "Facebook Removes QAnon Pages and Groups for Inauthentic Behavior," Mashable, May 5, 2020, https://mashable.com/article/facebook-removes-qanon
-inauthentic-behavior/; Kevin Collier and Ben Collins, "Facebook Removes Some

QAnon Pages, Citing Inauthentic Behavior," NBC News, May 5, 2020, https://www
.nbcnews.com/tech/tech-news/facebook-removes-some-qanon-pages-citing-inauthentic
-behavior-n1200636.

46. @Vijaya and Matt Derella, "An Update on Our Continuity Strategy During COVID-
19," Twitter, https://blog.twitter.com/en_us/topics/company/2020/An-update-on-our
-continuity-strategy-during-COVID-19.html; Steven Melendez, " 'I Have a Duty to
Do This': Meet the Redditors Fighting 2020's News War," Fast Company, March 2,
2020, https://www.fastcompany.com/90466966/i-have-a-duty-to-do-this-meet-the
-redditors-fighting-2020s-fake-news-war; Casey Newton, "Google Has Been Unusually
Proactive in Fighting COVID-19 Misinformation," The Verge, March 11, 2020, https://
www.theverge.com/interface/2020/3/11/21173135/google-coronavirus-misinformation
-youtube-covid-19-twitter-manipulated-media-biden.

47. Jesse Convertino, "Social Media Companies Partnering with Health Authorities to
Combat Misinformation on Coronavirus," ABC News, March 5, 2020, https://abcnews
.go.com/Technology/social-media-companies-partnering-health-authorities
-combat-misinformation/story?id=69389222.

48. Citizen Media, website, archived August 9, 2020 at https://web.archive.org/web
/20200809082040/https://citizenmedia.news/; Praying Medic, website, archived
May 10, 2020 at https://web.archive.org/web/20200510234420/https://prayingmedic
.com/.

49. Daniel Funke, "QAnon, Pizzagate Conspiracy Theories co-opt #SaveTheChildren,"
Politifact, August 12, 2020, https://www.politifact.com/article/2020/aug/12/qanon
-pizzagate-conspiracy-theories-co-opt-savethe/.

50. Nikki Schwab, " 'I've Never Seen So Many American Flags!' Donald Trump Defends
Protesters Demanding Lockdown Is Lifted As He Says They Just Have "Cabin Fever'
and 'Love Our Country,' " The Daily Mail, April 19, 2020, https://www.dailymail.co
.uk/news/article-8235387/Trump-says-protesters-just-cabin-fever-love-country
.html.

51. Jason Wilson, "The Rightwing Groups Behind Wave of Protests Against COVID-19
Restrictions," The Guardian, April 17, 2020, https://www.theguardian.com/world
/2020/apr/17/far-right-coronavirus-protests-restrictions; "Known Neo-Nazi Takes
Credit for Antisemitic Sign at Pandemic Lockdown Protest," SITE Intelligence Group,
April 21, 2020, https://ent.siteintelgroup.com/Far-Right-/-Far-Left-Threat/known-neo
-nazi-takes-credit-for-antisemitic-sign-at-pandemic-lockdown-protest.html.

52. James Pasley, "Trump Defends People Resisting Coronavirus Lockdowns—Says
They're 'Good People' Suffering from Cabin Fever," Business Insider, April 19, 2020,
https://www.businessinsider.com/trump-death-threats-governors-good-people
-2020-4.

53. Pasley, "Trump Defends People Resisting Coronavirus Lockdowns."

54. Aaron Rupar, "Trump's Dangerous ' "LIBERATE" ' Tweets Represent the Views of a
Small Minority," Vox, April 17, 2020, https://www.vox.com/2020/4/17/21225134/trump
-liberate-tweets-minnesota-virginia-michigan-coronavirus-fox-news.

55. Ben Collins and Brandy Zadrozny, "In Trump's ' "LIBERATE' " Tweets, Extremists See a Call to Arms," *NBC News*, April 17, 2020, https://www.nbcnews.com/tech/security /trump-s-liberate-tweets-extremists-see-call-arms-n1186561.

56. "Coronavirus: Armed Protesters Enter Michigan Statehouse," *BBC News*, May 1, 2020, https://www.bbc.com/news/world-us-canada-52496514.

57. Teo Armus, Mark Berman, and Griff Witte," "Before a Fatal Shooting, Teenage Kenosha Suspect Idolized the Police," *Washington Post*, August 27, 2020, https:// www.washingtonpost.com/nation/2020/08/27/kyle-rittenhouse-kenosha-shooting -protests/.

58. Azi Paybarah and Marie Fazio, "Kenosha Police Shooting of Black Man Is Investigated by Wisconsin Authorities," *New York Times*, August 23, 2018, https://www .nytimes.com/2020/08/23/us/kenosha-police-shooting.html.

59. Jon Collins, "Police Bodycam Video Shows George Floyd's Distress During Fatal Arrest," *NPR*, July 15, 2020, https://www.npr.org/2020/07/15/891516654/police -bodycam-video-provides-fuller-picture-of-george-floyds-fatal-arrest.

60. Collins, "Police Bodycam Video Shows George Floyd's Distress."

61. Larry Buchanan, Quoctrung Bui, and Jugal K. Patel, "Black Lives Matter May Be the Largest Movement in U.S. History," *New York Times*, July 3, 2020, https://www .nytimes.com/interactive/2020/07/03/us/george-floyd-protests-crowd-size.html.

62. "George Floyd Death: US Protests Timeline," *BBC News*, June 4, 2020, https://www .bbc.com/news/world-us-canada-52921418.

63. Shayan Sardarizadeh and Mike Wendling, "George Floyd Protests: Who Are Boggaloo Bois, Antifa and Proud Boys," *BBC News*, June 17, 2020, https://www.bbc.com /news/blogs-trending-53018201.

64. Lia Eustachwewich, "Kenosha Killer Kyle Rittenhouse Bought AR-15 with Stimulus Check: Report," *New York Post*, November 19, 2020, https://nypost.com/2020/11/19 /kyle-rittenhouse-bought-ar-15-with-stimulus-check-report/.

65. Nicholas Bogel-Burroughs and Sandra E. Garcia, "What Is Antifa, the Movement Trump Wants to Declare a Terror Group," *New York Times*, September 28, 2020, https://www.nytimes.com/article/what-antifa-trump.html.

66. Evan Perez and Jason Hoffman, "Trump Tweets Antifa Will Be Labeled a Terrorist Organization But Experts Believe That's Unconstitutional," *CNN*, May 31, 2020, https://www.cnn.com/2020/05/31/politics/trump-antifa-protests/index.html.

67. "Disarray 2020: Inside the Far Right's Apocalyptic Prepping for Post-Election ' "Civil War,' " SITE Intelligence Group, October 22, 2020, https://ent.siteintelgroup.com /inSITE-on-Far-Right/Far-Left/disarray-2020-inside-the-far-right-s-apocalyptic -prepping-for-post-election-civil-war.html.

68. Brien James outlawed news channel, "The cops, the government," Telegram, July 18, 2020, https://t.me/brienjames.

69. Jordan Fischer, "Who Are the American Guard: Patriotic Nationalists, or Skinheads in Disguise," WRTV ABC, May 25, 2017, https://www.wrtv.com/longform/who-are -the-american-guard-patriotic-nationalists-or-skinheads-in-disguise.

70. "Electric Boogaloo," Know Your Meme, accessed April 20, 2021, https://knowyour meme.com/memes/electric-boogaloo.

71. Jacob Gallagher, "Why the Extremist 'Boogaloo Boys' Wear Hawaiian Shirts," *Wall Street Journal*, June 8, 2020, https://www.wsj.com/articles/why-the-extremist -boogaloo-boys-wear-hawaiian-shirts-11591635085.

72. Michelle L. Price, "Report: FBI Found Weapons, Booby Traps After Arrest of 3 Nevada Men with Military Experience," *Army Times*, June 9, 2020, https://www.armytimes .com/news/your-military/2020/06/09/report-fbi-found-weapons-booby-traps-after -arrest-of-3-nevada-men/.

73. Price, "Report: FBI Found Weapons, Booby Traps After Arrest."

74. Enrique's House of Propaganda, "Ashley made a great point right now," Telegram, May 30, 2020, https://t.me/NobleLeader.

75. Robert Klemko and Greg Jaffe, "A Mentally Ill Man, a Heavily Armed Teenager and the Night Kenosha Burned," *Washington Post*, October 3, 2020, https://www .washingtonpost.com/nation/2020/10/03/kenosha-shooting-victims/.

76. Klemko and Jaffe, "A Mentally Ill Man."

77. Klemko and Jaffe.

78. Klemko and Jaffe.

79. "Man Shot During Kenosha Protest Still Remembers Screams," AP, September 11, 2020, https://apnews.com/article/shootings-police-police-brutality-illinois-kenosha -f3728531963341a2e137fdcb4b7cdc11.

80. Rita Katz, "Violent Protests Are a Neo-Nazi Fever Dream Come True," The Daily Beast, September 3, 2020, https://www.thedailybeast.com/violent-protests-are-a-neo -nazi-fever-dream-come-true.

81. Corona Chan News, "White Pill," Telegram, August 27, 2020, https://t.me/Corona ChanNews.

82. "International Far-Right Community Runs Propaganda Campaigns in Support of Kenosha Shooter," SITE Intelligence Group, September 17, 2020, https://ent .siteintelgroup.com/Far-Right-/-Far-Left-Threat/international-far-right-community -runs-propaganda-campaigns-in-support-of-kenosha-shooter.html.

83. "International Far-Right Community Runs Propaganda Campaigns," SITE Intelligence Group.

84. "International Far-Right Community Runs Propaganda Campaigns," SITE Intelligence Group.

85. "Neo-Nazi Militia's Successor Group Publishes Propaganda Glorifying Kenosha Shooter," SITE Intelligence Group, August 28, 2020, https://ent.siteintelgroup.com /Far-Right-/-Far-Left-Threat/neo-nazi-militia-s-successor-group-publishes -propaganda-glorifying-kenosha-shooter.html.

86. Hampton Stall, David Foran and Hari Prasad, "What's In a Meme? The Rise of ' "Saint Kyle,' " Global Network on Extremism & Technology, October 29, 2020, https://gnet -research.org/2020/10/29/whats-in-a-meme-the-rise-of-saint-kyle/.

87. Matthew Mosk and Mark Osborne, "Facebook Takes Down Proud Boys, American Guard Accounts Connected to Protests," ABC News, June 16, 2020, https://abcnews

.go.com/US/facebook-takes-proud-boys-american-guard-accounts-connected
/story?id=71286604.

88. Rishi Iyengar, "Twitter Takes Down 7,000 Accounts Linked to QAnon," CNN, July 22, 2020, https://www.cnn.com/2020/07/21/tech/twitter-qanon-crackdown/index.html.

89. Katie Paul and Elizabeth Culliford, "Twitter Fact-Checks Trump Tweet for the First Time," Reuters, May 26, 2020, https://www.reuters.com/article/us-twitter-trump/twitter-fact-checks-trump-tweet-for-the-first-time-idUSKBN232389.

90. Paul and Culliford, "Twitter Fact-Checks Trump Tweet."

12. WILL BE WILD

1. Bobby Allyn, "Reddit Bans The_Donald, Forum of Nearly 800,000 Trump Fans, Over Abusive Posts," NPR, June 29, 2020, https://www.npr.org/2020/06/29/884819923/reddit-bans-the_donald-forum-of-nearly-800–000-trump-fans-over-abusive-posts.

2. Jacob Kastrenakes, "Reddit Reveals Daily Active User Count for the First Time: 52 Million," *The Verge*, December 1, 2020, https://www.theverge.com/2020/12/1/21754984/reddit-dau-daily-users-revealed.

3. Caroline Haskins, "Reddit Quarantined r/The_Donald for 'Threats of Violence,'" Vice, June 26, 2019, https://www.vice.com/en/article/a3x88a/reddit-quarantined-r-the_donald-for-threats-of-violence.

4. Ryan Broderick, "Trump Supporters Have Built a Document With the Addresses and Phone Numbers of Thousands of Anti-Trump Activists," BuzzFeed News, May 22, 2017, https://www.buzzfeednews.com/article/ryanhatesthis/trump-supporters-have-built-a-document-with-the-addresses; Ali Breland, "Anti-Muslim Hate Has Been Rampant on Reddit Since the New Zealand Shooting," Mother Jones, March 21, 2019, https://www.motherjones.com/politics/2019/03/reddit-new-zealand-shooting-islamophobia/; Aja Romano, "Reddit Just Banned One of Its Most Toxic Forums. But It Won't Touch The_Donald," *Vox*, November 13, 2017, https://www.vox.com/culture/2017/11/13/16624688/reddit-bans-incels-the-donald-controversy.

5. Abby Ohlheiser, "Fearing Yet Another Witch Hunt, Reddit Bans 'Pizzagate,'" *Washington Post*, November 24, 2016, https://www.washingtonpost.com/news/the-intersect/wp/2016/11/23/fearing-yet-another-witch-hunt-reddit-bans-pizzagate/; David Gilmour, "Reddit and 4chan Trump Supporters Set Out to Prove Seth Rich Murder Conspiracy," Daily Dot, January 27, 2021, https://www.dailydot.com/debug/reddit-the-donald-4chan-seth-rich-murder/.

6. u/spez, "Update to Our Content Policy," Reddit, June 29, 2020, https://www.reddit.com/r/announcements/comments/hi3oht/update_to_our_content_policy/.

7. Sarah Emerson, "Months Before Reddit Purge, The_Donald Users Created a New Home," OneZero, July 2, 2020, https://onezero.medium.com/months-before-reddit-purge-the-donald-users-created-a-new-home-a732f79e4f04.

8. Sara Fischer, "The Next Pro-Trump Social Media Network," *Axios*, November 26, 2019, https://www.axios.com/donald-trump-social-network-reddit-censorship-eo f38e5c-f911–4a24–9552–3afb0f56e4e4.html.

9. Craig Timberg and Drew Harwell, "TheDonald's Owner Speaks Out on Why He Finally Pulled Plug on Hate-Filled Site," *Washington Post*, February 5, 2021, https:// www.washingtonpost.com/technology/2021/02/05/why-thedonald-moderator-left/.

10. Siddharth Venkataramakrishnan, "Far-Right Finds New Online Home in TheDonald.win," *Financial Times*, August 10, 2020, https://www.ft.com/content/23f4d7fe -a478–410d-9d03-d5526b6753d1.

11. Ibid.

12. Manoel Horta Ribeiro, Shagun Jhaver, Savvas Zannettou, Jeremy Blackburn, Emiliano De Cristofaro, Gianluca Stringhini, and Robert West, "Do Platform Migrations Compromise Content Moderation? Evidence from r/The_Donald and r/Incels," Computers and Society, October 21, 2020, https://arxiv.org/abs/2010.10397.

13. Shadowman3001, "Why are we .winners?," (archive) TheDonald.win, November 22, 2019, https://web.archive.org/web/20191203044935/https:/thedonald.win/p/yPrpE /why-are-we-winners/.

14. Ibid.

15. NavyGuy, "Don't get comfy . . . get prepared. This fight is far from over and it's going to get a lot nastier," (archive) TheDonald.win, December 2, 2019, https://web.archive .org/web/20191203044930/https:/thedonald.win/p/3ilXcta/dont-get-comfy-get -prepared-this/c/.

16. EpicTrump, "Michigan residents push back. 233,000 signed an online recall petition against the Democratic governor, four residents sued in federal court in a bid to unravel parts of their stay-at-home executive order as unconstitutional overreaches, Mich GOP house wants easing of the order, protest today," (archive)TheDonald.win, April 15, 2020, https://web.archive.org/web/20200416062116/https:/thedonald.win/p /FMcKYlT4/michigan-residents-push-back—23/c/.

17. Ibid.

18. Brad Parscale (@parscale), Twitter, June 18, 2020, https://twitter.com/parscale /status/1273816418782523394.

19. Cristiano Lima, "Cruz Joins Alternative Social Media Site Parler in Swipe at Big Tech Platforms," Politico, June 25, 2020, https://www.politico.com/news/2020/06/25/ted -cruz-joins-parler-339811.

20. Evie Fordham, "Who Is Parler CEO John Matze?," Fox Business, July 2, 2020, https:// www.foxbusiness.com/technology/john-matze-parler-ceo-founder-twitter; Ivan de Luce, "Meet the People Behind Right-Wing Social Media Site Parler," The Business of Business, November 17, 2020, https://www.businessofbusiness.com/articles/parler -social-media-founders-rebekah-mercer-john-matze/.

21. "A Declaration of Internet Independence," Parler, June 15, 2020, https://web.archive .org/web/20200712154537/https:/news.parler.com/email-letters/declaration-of -internet-independence.

22. "A Declaration of Internet Independence," Parler.

23. Isaac Saul, "This Twitter Alternative Was Supposed to Be Nicer, But Bigots Love It Already," *Forward*, July 18, 2019, https://forward.com/news/427705/parler-news -white-supremacist-islamophobia-laura-loomer/.

24. Jason Murdock, "Parler Surges on App Store as Founder Claims Victory Over 'Tech Tyrants,'" *Newsweek*, June 26, 2020, https://www.newsweek.com/parler-app-store -downloads-appannie-social-media-apple-android-john-matze-1513670; Joshua Brustein, "Social Media App Parler, a GOP Darling, Isn't Catching On," Bloomberg, July 15, 2020, https://www.bloomberg.com/news/newsletters/2020–07–15/social -media-app-parler-a-gop-darling-isn-t-catching-on.

25. Proud Boys: Uncensored, Telegram, channel created May 5, 2019, https://t.me /TheWesternChauvinist.

26. Gab AI inc., *Annual Report*, May 27, 2020, https://sec.report/Document/0001104659– 20–067852/annual_report.pdf?__cf_chl_jschl_tk__=96774488cefab3fb0ac80160cf2b d15809e5f3a0–1617298466–0-AWgdK9yAbudFbHkoiUsgglKmSyFoNriGeN-ht6L6bk-DPT7JLKSPykQMeVXTvTbUPvREMaqeb5LyDmUpPnINpmouZznv15Jyy43Aocroifa oYYVBOqnXDYOrqjoXTheAs75Ym6xgSNlu14XtdTMrrjHHTj_uofNzCGzqunaav-VWyaw2vk_IHMWmDlG6Fu8ckInO66KpoQpCGcIORdDhrrYdmDY5N4aKwG2tB ajNLnX-U86zfWPqEhEoOesDNJQz7_kPLRDWgzgvXJzpdF_UmUJ51r4LQauev4-rrCnjHsa_r1keYXvrAImn9KuY8Qw96b2_54vb6ebzBSS_wyzhwZ30BO975ZFLBka_ BI826-DOXCQl6NU8BiS46RrV4zXRUmyEz7F4GYQ_GlXqioN5fEw6b_sW7VEc-GO1kLNXcQIHCvGD8OFJ_pq_UbRTBV-J8_drgEwmVlGDodPx1_4R-dLyvZk9of NqMpxYZWLTN8c5xOzcnSxi4IDYm4jXYoVMEEhw.

27. WeGo, May 1, 2020, https://web.archive.org/web/20200501134425/https:/wego.social /; WeGo, August 30, 2020, https://web.archive.org/web/20200830165338/https:/wego .social/.

28. "Disarray 2020: Inside the Far Right's Apocalyptic Prepping for Post-Election 'Civil War,'" SITE Intelligence Group, October 22, 2020, https://ent.siteintelgroup.com /Special-Reports/disarray-2020-inside-the-far-right-s-apocalyptic-prepping-for -post-election-civil-war.html.

29. "Neo-Nazi Hopes Possible Electoral Crisis Would Spark Civil War," SITE Intelligence Group, August 10, 2020, https://ent.siteintelgroup.com/Far-Right-/-Far-Left-Threat /neo-nazi-hopes-possible-electoral-crisis-would-spark-civil-war.html.

30. "Far-Right Hate Group Announces '"March For Trump'" In Columbus, Ohio," SITE Intelligence Group, September 2, 2020, https://ent.siteintelgroup.com/Far-Right-/-Far -Left-Threat/far-right-hate-group-announces-march-for-trump-in-columbus-ohio .html.

31. "'It's Go Time in November': User in QAnon Chat Group Shares Statement Claiming 'Heavily Armed MAGA Patriots' Ready to 'Protect Trump,'" SITE Intelligence Group, October 6, 2020, https://ent.siteintelgroup.com/Far-Right-/-Far-Left-Threat/it-s-go -time-in-november-user-in-qanon-channel-shares-statement-on-preparedness-of -american-patriots-in-upcoming-presidential-election.html.

32. "Prominent Militia Group Publishes Open Letter to President Trump, Calling for Invocation of Insurrection Act," SITE Intelligence Group, December 22, 2020,

https://ent.siteintelgroup.com/Far-Right-/-Far-Left-Threat/prominent-militia-group
-publishes-open-letter-to-president-trump-calling-for-invocation-of-insurrection-act
.html.

33. "Far-Right Communities Exclaim '"Civil War is Upon Us'" as Swing State Counts
Tighten," SITE Intelligence Group, November 4, 2020, https://ent.siteintelgroup.com
/Far-Right-/-Far-Left-Threat/far-right-communities-exclaim-civil-war-is-upon-us
-as-swing-state-counts-tighten.html.

34. "'We're Rolling Out': Proud Boys Chairman Mobilizes Members In Response to Projected Trump Defeat," SITE Intelligence Group, November 7, 2020, https://ent
.siteintelgroup.com/Far-Right-/-Far-Left-Threat/we-re-rolling-out-proud-boys
-chairman-mobilizes-members-in-response-to-projected-trump-defeat.html.

35. "Prominent Neo-Nazi Prepper Channel Encourages Followers to 'Strap In' For War
Following Contested U.S. Election," SITE Intelligence Group, November 9, 2020,
https://ent.siteintelgroup.com/Far-Right-/-Far-Left-Threat/prominent-neo-nazi
-prepper-channel-encourages-followers-to-strap-in-for-war-following-contested
-election.html.

36. Ibid.

37. "'Trump or War': 4Chan Users Prepare to Take Violent Action Over Democratic Party's 'Stolen' Victory," SITE Intelligence Group, November 10, 2020, https://ent
.siteintelgroup.com/Far-Right-/-Far-Left-Threat/trump-or-war-4chan-users
-prepare-to-take-violent-action-over-democratic-party-s-stolen-victory.html.

38. Sophia Ankel, "Trump Promises 'Wild' Protests in Washington, DC, on the Day Congress Is Set to Finalize Election Results," *Business Insider*, December 20, 2020,
https://www.businessinsider.com/trump-wild-protests-planned-day-of-electoral
-college-vote-count-2020-12.

39. The Great Awakening—Research, "Trump is asking all patriots," December 19, 2020,
Telegram, https://t.me/q_anons.

40. "'Armed and Ready, Mr. President': Demonstrators Urged to Bring Guns, Prepare for
Violence at January 6 'Stop the Steal' Protest in DC," SITE Intelligence Group, December 25, 2020, https://ent.siteintelgroup.com/Far-Right-/-Far-Left-Threat/armed-and
-ready-mr-president-demonstrators-urged-to-bring-guns-prepare-for-violence-at
-january-6-stop-the-steal-protest-in-dc.html.

41. "Proud Boys Plan Break from Typical Tactics for Upcoming D.C. Demonstration,"
SITE Intelligence Group, December 30, 2020, https://ent.siteintelgroup.com/Far-Right
-/-Far-Left-Threat/proud-boys-plan-break-from-typical-tactics-for-upcoming-d-c
-demonstration.html.

42. Alex Willhelm and Taylor Hatmaker, "Facebook Says It Will Ban QAnon Across Its
Platforms," Tech Crunch, October 6, 2020, https://techcrunch.com/2020/10/06
/facebook-qanon-ban/; Taylor Hatmaker, "Militia Tied to Plot to Kidnap Gov. Whitmer Was Removed from Facebook in Boogaloo Purge," Tech Crunch, October 8, 2020,
https://techcrunch.com/2020/10/08/gretchen-whitmer-kidnapping-plot-facebook
-groups-militias-fbi/.

43. Nicolas Rivero, "Americans Flock to Social Media Platforms Where Misinformation Goes Unchecked," Quartz, November 13, 2020, https://qz.com/1933347/parler-downloads-spike-as-twitter-steps-up-content-moderation/.

44. Taylor Hatmaker, "'Free Speech' Social Network Parler Tops App Store Rankings Following Biden's Election Win," Tech Crunch, November 9, 2020, https://techcrunch.com/2020/11/09/parler-app-store-facebook/; Drew Harwell and Rachel Lerman, "Conservatives Grumbling About Censorship Say They're Flocking to Parler. They Told Us So on Twitter," Washington Post, November 23, 2020, https://www.washingtonpost.com/technology/2020/11/23/parler-conservatives-still-on-twitter/.

45. Hatmaker, "'Free Speech' Social Network"; Lois Beckett and Julia Carrie Wong, "The Misinformation Media Machine Amplifying Trump's Election Lies," The Guardian, November 10, 2020, https://www.theguardian.com/us-news/2020/nov/10/donald-trump-us-election-misinformation-media.

46. Andrew Torba, "Gab.com, the Home of Free Speech Online, Sees Record Growth After Big Tech Election Interference," Gab, November 10, 2020, https://news.gab.com/2020/11/10/gab-com-the-home-of-free-speech-online-sees-record-growth-after-big-tech-election-interference/.

47. Rita Katz (@Rita_Katz), "As mis/disinformation infects #Election2020, citizens are right to examine what is happening on social media platforms like @Facebook, @Twitter, and @YouTube. But as they ban conspiracy theorists & others, these users are increasingly resorting to "alternative" platforms," Twitter, November 12, 2020, https://twitter.com/rita_katz/status/1326932011987169281.

48. "Following Public References to QAnon, U.S. Army General Lionized by Movement," SITE Intelligence Group, September 9, 2020, https://ent.siteintelgroup.com/Far-Right-/-Far-Left-Threat/following-public-references-to-qanon-u-s-army-general-lionized-by-movement.html.

49. Q, "Take the oath," 8kun, June 24, 2020, https://8kun.top/qresearch/res/9730851.html#9731054.

50. Rita Katz (@Rita_Katz), "Same type of growth indicators can be seen on Parler, which has gained popularity as high-profile Trump allies have embraced it this past year. Here's the account of General Flynn, who has become a prophet-like figure within #QAnon, nearly quadrupling in followers," Twitter, November 12, 2020, https://twitter.com/Rita_Katz/status/1326932018190573582.

51. Craig Timberg and Drew Harwell, "Pro-Trump Forums Erupt with Violent Threats Ahead of Wednesday's Rally Against the 2020 Election," Washington Post, January 5, 2021, https://www.washingtonpost.com/technology/2021/01/05/parler-telegram-violence-dc-protests/; Timberg and Harwell, "TheDonald's Owner Speaks."

52. "How a Trump Tweet Sparked Plots, Strategizing to 'Storm and Occupy' Capitol with 'Handcuffs and Zip Ties,'" SITE Intelligence Group, January 9, 2021, https://ent.siteintelgroup.com/inSITE-on-Far-Right/Far-Left/how-a-trump-tweet-sparked-plots-strategizing-to-storm-and-occupy-capitol-with-handcuffs-and-zip-ties-2.html.

53.   "How a Trump Tweet Sparked Plots," SITE Intelligence Group.
54.   "How a Trump Tweet Sparked Plots," SITE Intelligence Group.
55.   "How a Trump Tweet Sparked Plots," SITE Intelligence Group.
56.   "How a Trump Tweet Sparked Plots," SITE Intelligence Group.
57.   "How a Trump Tweet Sparked Plots," SITE Intelligence Group.
58.   "How a Trump Tweet Sparked Plots," SITE Intelligence Group.
59.   "How a Trump Tweet Sparked Plots," SITE Intelligence Group.
60.   "How a Trump Tweet Sparked Plots," SITE Intelligence Group.
61.   "How a Trump Tweet Sparked Plots," SITE Intelligence Group.
62.   "How a Trump Tweet Sparked Plots," SITE Intelligence Group.
63.   "How a Trump Tweet Sparked Plots," SITE Intelligence Group.
64.   "How a Trump Tweet Sparked Plots," SITE Intelligence Group.
65.   "How a Trump Tweet Sparked Plots," SITE Intelligence Group.
66.   "How a Trump Tweet Sparked Plots," SITE Intelligence Group.
67.   "How a Trump Tweet Sparked Plots," SITE Intelligence Group.
68.   "How a Trump Tweet Sparked Plots," SITE Intelligence Group.
69.   Brian Naylor, "Read Trump's Jan. 6 Speech, a Key Part of Impeachment Trial," NPR, February 10, 2021, https://www.npr.org/2021/02/10/966396848/read-trumps-jan-6-speech-a-key-part-of-impeachment-trial.
70.   Liselotte Mas, "Auschwitz, QAnon, Viking Tattoos: The White Supremacist Symbols Sported By Rioters Who Strormed the Capitol," France 24, January 7, 2021, https://observers.france24.com/en/americas/20210108-white-supremacist-symbols-us-capitol; Michael Beschloss (@BeschlossDC), "Note the piece of Speaker Pelosi's wooden nameplate that the invaders have broken off of the wall," Twitter, January 6, 2021, https://twitter.com/beschlossdc/status/1346973532643753984.
71.   Georgia Wells, Ian Talley, and Jeff Horwitz, "'Trump or War': How the Capitol Mob Mobilized on Social Media," Wall Street Journal, January 7, 2021, https://www.wsj.com/articles/trump-or-war-how-the-capitol-mob-mobilized-on-social-media-11610069778.
72.   Ryan Mac and John Paczkowski, "Apple Has Threatened to Ban Parler From the App Store," BuzzFeed News, January 8, 2021, https://www.buzzfeednews.com/article/ryanmac/apple-threatens-ban-parler.
73.   Ryan Mac and John Paczkowski, "Apple Has Threatened to Ban Parler from the App Store," BuzzFeed News, January 8, 2021, https://www.buzzfeednews.com/article/ryanmac/apple-threatens-ban-parler.
74.   Ibid.
75.   Adolfo Flores and John Paczkowski, "Apple Has Banned Parler, the Pro-Trump Social Network, From Its App Store," BuzzFeed News, January 9, 2021, https://www.buzzfeednews.com/article/adolfoflores/apple-parler-ban-app-store.
76.   Jack Nicas and Davey Alba, "Amazon, Apple and Google Cut Off Parler, an App That Drew Trump Supporters," New York Times, January 9, 2021, https://www.nytimes.com/2021/01/09/technology/apple-google-parler.html.

77. John Paczkowski and Ryan Mac, "Amazon Will Suspend Hosting for Pro-Trump Social Network Parler," BuzzFeed News, January 9, 2021, https://www.buzzfeednews .com/article/johnpaczkowski/amazon-parler-aws.

78. "'The Purge Begins': Following Trump's Twitter Ban & Removal of Parler from Popular App Stores, Far-Right Community Contemplates Platform Migrations," SITE Intelligence Group, January 8, 2021, https://ent.siteintelgroup.com/Far-Right -/-Far-Left-Threat/the-purge-begins-following-trump-s-twitter-ban-removal-of -parler-from-popular-app-stores-far-right-community-contemplates-platform -migrations.html; Will Steakin, "How the Far-Right Group Behind AFPAC Is Using Twitter to Grow Its Movement," ABC News, March 12, 2021, https://abcnews .go.com/US/group-afpac-twitter-grow-movement/story?id=76418773; Malachi Bar- rett, "Far-Right Activist Who Encouraged U.S. Capitol Occupation Also Orga- nized 'Stop the Steal' Rally in Michigan," Michigan Live, January 7, 2021, https:// www.mlive.com/politics/2021/01/far-right-activist-who-encouraged-us-capitol -occupation-also-organized-stop-the-steal-rally-in-michigan.html.

79. "'The Purge Begins,'" SITE Intelligence Group.

80. "'The Purge Begins,'" SITE Intelligence Group.

81. Parler Lifeboat (AKA The Great Kingdom Of Zombe), Telegram (chat group), accessed January 26, 2021, https://t.me/KingdomZombe.

82. We Are News Now (AKA We the Pepe), Telegram (chat group), created April 10, 2020, https://t.me/WeAreNewsNow.

83. Proud Boys: Uncensored, Telegram.

84. "Proud Boys-Affiliated Venue Calls on Far-Right Extremist Community to Indoctri- nate Pro-Trump Users as They Migrate to Telegram," SITE Intelligence Group, Janu- ary 11, 2021, https://ent.siteintelgroup.com/Far-Right-/-Far-Left-Threat/proud-boys -affiliated-venue-calls-on-far-right-extremist-community-to-indoctrinate-pro -trump-users-as-they-migrate-to-telegram.html.

85. "'Fan the Flames': Neo-Nazi Community Initiates Campaign to Attract Trump Sup- porters to Violent White Supremacist Movement During Platform Migration," SITE Intelligence Group, January 12, 2021, https://ent.siteintelgroup.com/Far-Right-/-Far -Left-Threat/fan-the-flames-neo-nazi-community-initiates-campaign-to-attract -trump-supporters-to-accelerationist-movement.html.

86. Kevin Collier, "House Oversight Head Asks FBI to Investigate Parler," NBC News, January 21, 2021, https://www.nbcnews.com/tech/tech-news/house-oversight-head -asks-fbi-investigate-parler-n1255170.

87. Critiano Lima, "GOP Lawmakers Grill Google, Apple and Amazon Over Parler Shut- downs," Politico, March 31, 2021, https://www.politico.com/news/2021/03/31/gop -google-apple-amazon-parler-478782.

88. Adi Robertson, "Parler Is Back Online After a Month of Downtime," The Verge, Feb- ruary 15, 2021, https://www.theverge.com/2021/2/15/22284036/parler-social-network -relaunch-new-hosting.

89. Jospeh Menn, Kenneth Li, and Elizabeth Culliford, "Parler Partially Reappears with Support from Russian technology Firm," Reuters, January 18, 2021, https://www

.reuters.com/article/us-usa-trump-parler-russia/parler-partially-reappears-with -support-from-russian-technology-firm-idUSKBN29N23N.

90. Claire Goforth, "Notorious Pro-Trump Forum Rebrands as 'Patriots'" After Post-Capitol Riot Infighting," Daily Dot, January 21, 2021, https://www.dailydot.com /debug/pro-trump-site-renamed-internal-conflict/.

91. Daniel Byman, "Right-Wingers Are America's Deadliest Terrorists," Slate, August 5, 2019, https://slate.com/news-and-politics/2019/08/right-wing-terrorist -killings-government-focus-jihadis-islamic-radicalism.html.

92. Rita Katz, "Neo-Nazis Are Running Out of Places to Hide Online," Wired, July 9, 2020, https://www.wired.com/story/neo-nazis-are-running-out-of-places-to-hide -online.

93. Geoffrey A. Fowler and Chris Alcantara, "Gatekeepers: These Tech Firms Control What's Allowed Online," Washington Post, March 24, 2021, https://www .washingtonpost.com/technology/2021/03/24/online-moderation-tech-stack/.

94. U.S. Congress, Committee on Armed Services, Terrorism, Unconventional Threats and Capabilities Subcommittee, Challenges for the Special Operations Command (SOCOM) Posted by the Global Terrorist Threat, February 14, 2007, https://www .govinfo.gov/content/pkg/CHRG-110hhrg37980/html/CHRG-110hhrg37980.htm.

95. James Wagstaffe, "Incitement to Violence Ain't Free Speech," Just Security, January 15, 2021, https://www.justsecurity.org/74217/incitement-to-violence-aint-free -speech/; Michael S. Rosenwald, "The Landmark Klan Free-Speech Case Behind Trump's Impeachment Defense," Washington Post, February 12, 2021, https://www .washingtonpost.com/history/2021/02/10/brandenburg-trump-supreme-court-klan -free-speech/.

96. "Terms of Service," Telegram, accessed April 16, 2021, https://telegram.org/tos.

97. "Legal," Epik, accessed April 16, 20201, https://www.epik.com/registration.php.

98. Paczkowski and Mac, "Amazon Will Suspend Hosting."

99. Nick Fagge, "Neo Nazi Feuerkrieg Division—Which Counted Britain's Youngest Terrorist Among Its Members—Is Run By a 13-Year-Old Estonian Boy Who Calls for the 'Rape of Christian Nuns in Hitler's Name,'" Daily Mail, February 1, 2021, https:// www.dailymail.co.uk/news/article-9211625/Neo-Nazi-Feuerkrieg-Division-run -Estonian-boy-13-calls-rape-Hitlers-name.html.

100. Dale Beran and Mike Rothschild, "Country of Liars," Reply All, Podcast Audio, September 18, 2020, https://gimletmedia.com/shows/reply-all/llhe5nm; Q: Into the Storm, created by Cullen Hoback, 2021, HBO, https://www.hbo.com/q-into-the-storm.

AFTERWORD: WHAT "CHANGE" LOOKS LIKE A YEAR LATER

1. Alan Feuer, "Stewart Rhodes, Oath Keepers Leader, Is Denied Bail on Sedition Charge," New York Times, January 26, 2022, https://www.nytimes.com/2022/01/26/us /stewart-rhodes-oath-keepers.html.

2. "'We Will Defeat' White Supremacy and Extremism, Biden Says in Inaugural Address," *Associated Press* (republished on KTLA news website), January 20, 2021, https://ktla.com/news/nationworld/we-will-defeat-white-supremacy-and-extremism-biden-says-in-inaugural-address/.

3. "National Strategy for Countering Domestic Terrorism," National Security Council, Executive Office of the President, June 2021, https://www.whitehouse.gov/wp-content/uploads/2021/06/National-Strategy-for-Countering-Domestic-Terrorism.pdf.

4. Matt Zapotosky and Devlin Barrett, "Justice Dept. Forms New Domestic Terrorism Unit to Address Growing Threat," *Washington Post*, January 11, 2022, https://www.washingtonpost.com/national-security/domestic-terrorism-justice-threat/2022/01/11/dfd8d82c-72eb-11ec-8b0a-bcfab800c430_story.html.

5. Ron Watkins [CodeMonkeyZ], Telegram, accessed February 25, 2022, https://t.me/CodeMonkeyZ; (@codemonkey), Gab, accessed February 25, 2022, https://gab.com/codemonkey.

6. "Breakaway Proud Boys Factions Call for Autonomous Chapters Following National Leader's Release from Jail," SITE Intelligence Group, February 3, 2022, https://ent.siteintelgroup.com/Far-Right-/-Far-Left-Threat/breakaway-proud-boys-factions-call-for-autonomous-chapters-following-national-leader-s-release-from-jail.html; Sheera Frenkel, "Proud Boys Regroup, Focusing on School Boards and Town Councils," *New York Times*, December 14, 2021, https://www.nytimes.com/2021/12/14/us/proud-boys-local-issues.html.

7. "Proud Boys Advertise International Recruitment Effort," SITE Intelligence Group, January 4, 2022 https://ent.siteintelgroup.com/Far-Right-/-Far-Left-Threat/proud-boys-advertise-international-recruitment-effort.html.

8. "inSITE Bulletin on Far-Right Extremists: After the Capitol—The Domestic Extremist Landscape One Year Since the January 6 Siege," SITE Intelligence Group, January 5, 2022, https://ent.siteintelgroup.com/inSITE-on-Far-Right/Far-Left/insite-bulletin-on-far-right-extremists-after-the-capitol-the-domestic-extremist-landscape-one-year-since-the-january-6-siege.html.

9. "inSITE Bulletin on Far-Right Extremists," SITE Intelligence Group.

10. "inSITE Bulletin on Far-Right Extremists," SITE Intelligence Group; Elisha Fieldstadt and Andrew Blankstein, "California QAnon Believer Indicted on Charges of Killing His 2 Children with a Spearfishing Gun," *NBC News*, September 9, 2021, https://www.nbcnews.com/news/us-news/california-qanon-believer-indicted-charges-killing-his-2-children-spear-n1278802.

11. Ellie Silverman, Justin Wm. Moyer, and Emily Davies, "Rival Jan. 6 Vigils Reflect Deep Divides Over Insurrection," *Washington Post*, January 6, 2022, https://www.washingtonpost.com/dc-md-va/2022/01/06/dc-vigils-january-6-capitol/.

12. Roaming Centipede (@twoHollowFangs), "Someone tell that to the political prisoners rotting in a DC gulag right now," Gab, February 25, 2022, https://gab.com/twoHollowFangs/posts/107857363582733402; Apolitical (@Apolitical), "Blacks are allowed to peacefully burn down and loot our cities," Gab, February 24, 2022, https://gab.com/Apolitical/posts/107858754729594610.

13. EA Malias Nalvat (@EAMaliasNalvat), "#RussianBear too hard to fuck off," Gab, February 25, 2022, https://gab.com/EAMaliasNalvat/posts/107857874520383478; lightner05 (@jblightner58), "Dr. Zelenko: 'Yes, The Vaccinated Have AIDS,'" Gab, February 25, 2022, https://gab.com/jblightner58/posts/107858121974070602.

14. Rita Katz, "Inside the Online Cesspool of Anti-Semitism That Housed Robert Bowers," Politico, October 29, 2018, https://www.politico.com/magazine/story/2018/10/29 /inside-the-online-cesspool-of-anti-semitism-that-housed-robert-bowers-221949/.

15. It's hard to tell how many of these accounts are active, which is why web traffic is sometimes a more useful metric; Micah Lee, "Inside Gab, the Online Safe Space for Far-Right Extremists," The Intercept, March 15, 2021, https://theintercept.com/2021 /03/15/gab-hack-donald-trump-parler-extremists.

16. Andrew Torba, "How the Gab Medical Community Helped Me Fight Covid," Gab, November 16, 2021, https://news.gab.com/2021/11/16/how-the-gab-medical-community -helped-me-fight-covid/.

17. Semrush, Gab.com analysis, accessed February 25, 2022, https://www.semrush.com /analytics/overview/?q=gab.com&searchType=domain.

18. Andrew Torba, "2022: The Year the Parallel Economy Rises," Gab, January 1, 2022, https://news.gab.com/2022/01/01/2022-the-year-the-parallel-economy-rises/; Andrew Torba, "Investing in the Gab Community," Gab, February 21, 2022, https://news.gab .com/2022/02/21/investing-in-the-gab-community; Andrew Torba, "How The Gab Medical Community Helped Me Fight Covid."

19. Semrush, Parler.com traffic analysis, February 2021–January 2022, accessed February 25, 2022, https://www.semrush.com/analytics/traffic/overview/parler.com?displ ayDate=&dateFrom=2021-02-01.

20. Semrush, Bitchute traffic analysis, February 2021–January 2022, accessed February 25, 2022, https://www.semrush.com/analytics/traffic/overview/bitchute.com?displayDa te=&dateFrom=2021-02-01.

21. Semrush, Gettr.com traffic analysis, February 2021–January 2022, accessed February 25, 2022, https://www.semrush.com/analytics/traffic/overview/gettr.com ?displayDate=&dateFrom=2021-07-01&searchType=domain; Google Play (mobile), Gettr, accessed February 25, 2022, https://play.google.com/store/apps/details ?id=com.gettr.gettr.

22. "German Conspiracist Hosts 'Mock Trial' for Alleged Engineers of COVID-19 'Plandemic,'" SITE Intelligence Group, February 17, 2022, https://ent.siteintelgroup.com /Bioterrorism-and-Public-Health/german-conspiracist-hosts-mock-trial-for-alleged -engineers-of-covid-19-plandemic.html; "'Kill Them All': Kaiser Permanente Threatened After Unvaccinated Nurse Is Escorted Out of Facility," SITE Intelligence Group, November 2, 2021, https://ent.siteintelgroup.com/Bioterrorism-and-Public-Health /kaiser-permanente-threatened-by-conspiracy-theorists-after-unvaccinated-nurse-is -escorted-out-of-facility.html.

23. "Far-Right Groups Advertise Rallies on Anniversary of January 6 Capitol Riot," SITE Intelligence Group, January 4, 2022, https://ent.siteintelgroup.com/Far-Right-/-Far -Left-Threat/far-right-groups-advertise-rallies-on-anniversary-of-january-6

-capitol-riot.html; Yellowandrose, "surround the state capitols," Patriots.win, September 13, 2021 (accessed September 13, 2021), https://patriots.win/p/12kFwdd1Mb/look-ahead-america-announced-thi/c/; Yellowandrose, "the best response is to shoot them in the face," Patriots.win, August 24, 2021 (accessed September 13, 2021), https://patriots.win/p/12jwVdahs7/3-jabs-please-/c/.

24.   Betsy Woodruff Swan, "'Keep Your Head on a Swivel': FBI Analyst Circulated a Prescient Warning of Jan. 6 Violence," *Politico*, September 7, 2021, https://www.politico.com/news/2021/09/07/fbi-warning-jan-6–510020.

25.   Betsy Woodruff Swan, "'The Intelligence Was There': Law Enforcement Warnings Abounded in the Runup to Jan. 6," *Politico*, October 7, 2021, https://www.politico.com/news/2021/10/07/law-enforcement-warnings-january-6–515531.

26.   Georgia Wells, Ian Talley, and Jeff Horwitz, "'Trump or War': How the Capitol Mob Mobilized on Social Media," *Wall Street Journal*, January 7, 2021, https://www.wsj.com/articles/trump-or-war-how-the-capitol-mob-mobilized-on-social-media-1161006 9778.

27.   "Summary of Terrorism Threat to the U.S. Homeland," US Department of Homeland Security, National Terrorism Advisory System, February 7, 2022, https://www.dhs.gov/ntas/advisory/national-terrorism-advisory-system-bulletin-february-07–2022.

INDEX

COLUMBIA STUDIES IN TERRORISM AND IRREGULAR WARFARE

Bruce Hoffman, Series Editor

Ami Pedahzur, *The Israeli Secret Services and the Struggle Against Terrorism*

Ami Pedahzur and Arie Perliger, *Jewish Terrorism in Israel*

Lorenzo Vidino, *The New Muslim Brotherhood in the West*

Erica Chenoweth and Maria J. Stephan, *Why Civil Resistance Works: The Strategic Logic of Nonviolent Conflict*

William C. Banks, editor, *New Battlefields/Old Laws: Critical Debates on Asymmetric Warfare*

Blake W. Mobley, *Terrorism and Counterintelligence: How Terrorist Groups Elude Detection*

Jennifer Morrison Taw, *Mission Revolution: The U.S. Military and Stability Operations*

Guido W. Steinberg, *German Jihad: On the Internationalization of Islamist Terrorism*

Michael W. S. Ryan, *Decoding Al-Qaeda's Strategy: The Deep Battle Against America*

David H. Ucko and Robert Egnell, *Counterinsurgency in Crisis: Britain and the Challenges of Modern Warfare*

Bruce Hoffman and Fernando Reinares, editors, *The Evolution of the Global Terrorist Threat: From 9/11 to Osama bin Laden's Death*

Boaz Ganor, *Global Alert: The Rationality of Modern Islamist Terrorism and the Challenge to the Liberal Democratic World*

M. L. R. Smith and David Martin Jones, *The Political Impossibility of Modern Counterinsurgency: Strategic Problems, Puzzles, and Paradoxes*

Elizabeth Grimm Arsenault, *How the Gloves Came Off: Lawyers, Policy Makers, and Norms in the Debate on Torture*

Assaf Moghadam, *Nexus of Global Jihad: Understanding Cooperation Among Terrorist Actors*

Bruce Hoffman, *Inside Terrorism*, 3rd edition

Stephen Tankel, *With Us and Against Us: How America's Partners Help and Hinder the War on Terror*

Wendy Pearlman and Boaz Atzili, *Triadic Coercion: Israel's Targeting of States That Host Nonstate Actors*

Bryan C. Price, *Targeting Top Terrorists: Understanding Leadership Removal in Counterterrorism Strategy*

Mariya Y. Omelicheva and Lawrence P. Markowitz, *Webs of Corruption: Trafficking and Terrorism in Central Asia*

Aaron Y. Zelin, *Your Sons Are at Your Service: Tunisia's Missionaries of Jihad*